TRANSITI

To the children of Moreland School, who showed what was possible.

Some of the children's names have been changed,
to protect them from fame.

Published by
Rigby,
Melbourne Australia and Chicago Illinois,
and
Heinemann Educational Books, Inc.
70 Court Street, Portsmouth, NH 03801
Offices and agents throughout the world.

Library of Congress Cataloging-in-Publication Data
Routman, Regie.
    Transitions: from literature to literacy/Regie Routman:
foreword by Andrea Butler.
    352 pp
    Bibliography: 70 pp
    Includes index.
    1. Children — Books and reading.
2. Reading (Elementary) — Language experience approach.
3. Teaching — Process method. 4. Whole Language.
I. Title.
LB1573.33.R68 1988
372.4'1—dc19
ISBN 0 7312 0998 2 (Australia)
ISBN 0-435-08467-4 (USA)

Printed in the United States of America

TRANSITIONS

From Literature to Literacy

Regie Routman

Heinemann
Portsmouth, New Hampshire

Melbourne

Contents

Foreword

I first heard of Regie Routman at I.R.A. at Anaheim in 1987. She had approached my colleagues and told them how much she had enjoyed *Towards a Reading-Writing Classroom*, the book I co-authored with Jan Turbill. As Regie explained, our book was great, but it was about children and teachers in Australian schools. What she planned to write was a first-hand account of the experiences of an American teacher who had taken the plunge and joined the growing movement towards a literary and meaning-centered literacy program.

My colleagues and I applauded Regie's initiative and encouraged her to begin writing. She had previously been a little hesitant in approaching a publisher because she intended her book to focus on practice rather than theory. Our own experience, however, told us that teachers in both the U.S. and Australia were crying out for more practical assistance. If I have had some influence on this book, it has been in persuading Regie to include more, rather than fewer, of her personal experiences.

On first reading the manuscript of this book, I was so overwhelmed by the honesty and integrity of Regie's account of her struggle to change her approach to teaching that I read well into the night. The pain was evident. The doubts still showed through. The successes were shared and celebrated. I was reminded of the first book that Jan Turbill edited, entitled *No Better Way to Teach Writing*, in which she documented — warts and all — how some courageous teachers in Australia had changed from a traditional approach to teaching writing to a process approach. But Regie's manuscript was even more powerful — the struggle had been much harder.

So here it is. A book written by a practicing teacher for other interested colleagues. It is rich in ideas and inspiration. It rings true because of its honesty. It is unique. No other book presently available spans the range of issues that Regie's does. She's just as comfortable talking about theory as she is about writing a letter home to parents, or describing a workable borrowing system for library books.

The book I co-authored with Jan Turbill is often complimented because it bridges theory and practice. Regie's book goes far beyond ours. And what's more, it addresses many highly emotive and important political issues currently affecting the education scene.

Regie's book is a celebration of dedication and determination. It's a must for all teachers, consultants and administrators who are serious about meeting the challenge of producing a nation of readers and writers.

Andrea Butler, March 1988

Acknowledgements

This book and the story behind it would not have been possible without the help of many people. Above all, I am grateful to Delores Groves, my principal for seven years at Moreland School and my continuing mentor, colleague, and friend. I remain deeply appreciative of the opportunity she gave me that ultimately made this story possible.

To Mark Freeman, then director of curriculum and currently superintendent, I am indebted for his ability to recognize a possibility and lend his full support and trust. To Ellen Stepanian, director of library media, I am grateful for her expertise and coordination of library and literature services across our district.

I shall always be grateful to Karen Shiba for graciously sharing her first grade classroom and students with me and other teachers that first year — and all the years that have followed — and for continuing to be a first-rate teacher and good friend. To Joan Di Dio, I am indebted for her boundless enthusiasm and creativity, both in her classroom and in contributing to the writing of this book. To Linda Cooper, who continues generously to share her knowledge with other teachers and from whom I have learned so much, I am particularly appreciative. To Joan Servis, who was a major agent of change in our building, I am thankful.

I am grateful to the following educators who thoughtfully read and responded to one or more chapter drafts and offered valuable suggestions: Andrea Butler, Linda Cooper, Joan Di Dio, Vicki Griminger, Tony Manna, Lois Markt, Joyce Pope, Karen Shiba, Jeanette Throne, Sue Walker, Carl Walley, Kate Walley, and Elaine Weiner. Many of their perceptive comments went into the revisions of this book.

For the help of some of our parents, I am much indebted. Debbie Jones helped organize titles and authors in our collection. Marianne Sopko spent hours at the library checking current publishers and dates of book titles, graciously took care of lots of "odds and ends" that needed to be done, and continued to give generously of her time and knowledge in so many ways. Karan Shelley typed letters to permissions editors, typed various parts of the Appendixes, and checked on me regularly to offer her support and friendship.

There are, in addition, many teachers, parents, librarians, and administrators who have contributed to and supported literature-based reading and writing in our school district. In my desire to acknowledge all of them, without omitting any of them, I offer my thanks for their contributions in making the transition — literature to literacy — possible.

To Andrea Butler, I am especially thankful for her tremendous knowledge, her valuable suggestions, and her friendship. She kindly went through the entire manuscript with great care and sensitivity and made excellent suggestions regarding organization, format, and content. The discussions we had together were among the high points in writing this book.

Sue Donovan, my publisher and editor, has been most kind and respectful in supporting and encouraging the personal voice of a teacher. For her vision in seeing that this book was timely and needed, I shall always be grateful. For her careful, personal attention to the manuscript, I am indebted and most appreciative.

To my family, I thank them for their constant, much-needed encouragement, help, and love: Peter, for carefully reading and responding to drafts and patiently teaching a "slow learner" the ins and outs of word processing; Elizabeth, for being proud of my accomplishments and helping me refine some of the writing; and Frank for lending his support and understanding — especially on those days when it seemed so difficult to write.

(opposite) Principal Delores Groves with second-grader Rachel Hill, an avid reader.

1 My Turning Point
Catalysts for Change

One early October, I ended a remedial reading class for five second-graders by reading a favorite book aloud, *The Hungry Thing* (Slepian and Seidler, 1972). The book, a delightful story with equally fine illustrations and done mostly in rhyme, enchanted the children.

"Oh, let *us* read it," they pleaded. "Please."

"No," I said, as their wise teacher. "You can't read this book. It's too hard for you." I still cringe when I remember myself saying those fateful words. But after all, the book had a third-grade readability level, and these children were reading at about a 1.7 reading level according to their standardized test scores. There was no way they could read that book — or so I reasoned.

The children, as children do, persisted, and finally, reluctantly, I agreed to let them "try" it. To my great amazement, with practice and guidance, they could read it. Their motivation was so great and their interest in the story so high that they were able to read in context what the tests indicated they could not.

Imagine their pride several weeks later when these "slow" readers read the book aloud to their class without a mistake and hardly a hesitation. We left our well-used copies of the books in the classroom, and the classroom teacher reported that many of her other students were eagerly reading them.

That incident was the start in giving me confidence to change the way I was teaching reading. I began to examine the vital role of the motivation of a good book in reading success, and to rethink my phonics, sight words, and skills approach. I began to trust myself and to rely on what children could really accomplish. I started combing local bookstores and buying multiple copies of appealing children's books. These books I used to teach reading.

The results with low-ability first-graders were impressive. For three years in a row, typically, two of the five children would test out in June (on a standardized test) as high-ability readers, two would be at the average level, and one would remain as a low-ability reader. The results also included students filled with high self-esteem, pride in their accomplishments, and the joy of being competent readers.

Looking back, I can see that October morning about ten years ago as the beginning of a major transition in my own teaching, learning, and thinking. That group of low-achieving second grade children forced me to examine my beliefs about learning, reading, and what children could really accomplish. Since that time, I have continued to look closely at my own teaching, and to work with many teachers and children in moving away from basal textbooks and worksheets and into exciting children's books and children's own writing as a way of teaching young children to read and write. The empowering of teachers and children has had remarkable results. Teachers, with the support of a wide body of research, have finally had the courage and freedom to trust their intuition about what makes suitable and quality reading material and what young children can really accomplish. Children, predicted to have difficulties learning to read and write, have become competent literacy learners. Parents have become a vital and welcome part of the learning process. The school environment is once again an exciting and rewarding place where children and teachers are thriving.

This book is designed to help *you* make the same transition from the basal into the wonderful world of children's literature. I hope that by sharing the story of what happened and how my philosophy, methods, goals, and expectations have evolved and still continue to change, other teachers and administrators will make their own transition towards more child-centered, literature-based reading and writing.

A Proposal for a Literature Program

As a reading specialist who saw small groups of low-achieving children daily on a "pull-out" basis, I had long been supplementing my skills program with children's books. My training had taught me that if a child is having difficulty with main idea, sequencing, or phonics, you can teach these areas with specially designed materials to improve that skill area. My shelves overflowed with materials to promote skill development. But my intuition told me that these skills and drills were boring, isolated, and unrelated to reading as a whole process, so I "sneaked in" books whenever I could. Each instructional period was only 30 minutes long, and I remember feeling very guilty if the principal walked in and we were "just reading". If there wasn't a completed worksheet, were the children really learning?

Because my principal, Delores Groves, and I were aware that many children were learning to read children's books much more easily and successfully than the basal text, she and the district curriculum director were highly supportive of my written proposal to teach the entire first grade to read using only children's books. We had, truly, nothing to lose. Out of nine elementary schools in our "inner ring suburb" district, our standardized reading test scores were consistently the lowest. Despite our math/computer magnet program to attract voluntary busing of white students, our building remained a majority black student population with about one-third of the first grade students qualifying for Chapter 1 reading support each fall. Typically, by the fall of second grade, up to 50% of the students would be receiving supportive reading services. It was not only their reading abilities that were deficient. In failing to learn to read successfully, their self-esteem and pride in success were also sorely lacking.

The proposal, submitted in the spring of 1983, was titled *First Grade Book Flood*. (See Appendix A for description.) Briefly stated, the proposal aimed to use children's literature to teach reading and promote a love of reading to first-graders who would otherwise be taught through the basal text. The students involved were mostly minority children with limited prereading home experiences. The proposal went on, in some detail, to cite the research that supported the stated objectives. Procedures for implementation and evaluation were also fully stated. These topics will be fully discussed in later chapters.

In the fall of 1983, the proposed program to teach beginning reading was implemented in the first grade class of twenty students. Karen Shiba, the classroom teacher who volunteered to work with me, was an experienced traditional teacher with no background in teaching with literature. She had read the proposal and was excited and enthusiastic about the possibilities. Gradually, as we worked together, her philosophy and methods changed. She embraced the literature approach, adding her own unique teaching style and ideas to it. That first year, we put in countless hours over the summer and after school preparing materials, organizing the program and time schedule, and planning parent involvement and education. I was indeed fortunate to be paired with a highly competent educator who welcomed new ideas and who was willing to share her classroom and students with another teacher.

The realization of a literature-based reading program evolved from direct teaching experience, observations of what children could do, faith in myself and children, strong administrative support, and willingness to take risks. This program was developed by a teacher! While the word "program" is used throughout this book as a convenient description of the various components in teaching with literature, it is imperative to recognize that it is always the children we are teaching and not the program.

In the process of designing the literature program, I spent many hours reading extensively, both out of curiosity and to develop a rationale to support my teaching and findings. I did not, however, take a university course in children's literature. (There was none available locally.) Certainly, such a course would have been helpful, but without it, it has still been possible to move in exciting new directions. I state this emphatically to give fellow teachers the courage to trust themselves, develop and try out new ideas, and add literature to their reading program. The commercial publishers have had such a stronghold on dictating to teachers what and how reading should be taught that we have lost faith in our own good judgments and capabilities.

Looking back, it is interesting to note that the original proposal contained no specific writing component. Truthfully, I hadn't given much thought to the teaching of writing. The exciting new research in writing was just beginning to gain national attention. I did know intuitively that we couldn't use worksheets with exciting children's books. Having just read books and articles by Donald Graves, Lucy Calkins, and Vera Milz, it made sense to add writing as an integral part of our language arts program. The remarkable thing was that we were highly successful — despite the fact that we had no previous training as teachers of writing!

Probably the greatest influence in the organization of our program was the work of Don Holdaway in New Zealand. His *Foundations of Literacy* gave us a wealth of ideas and tremendous support. We embraced his Shared Book Experience and whole class reading of books and poems as a wonderful way to begin our morning. Big Books, which he helped develop, were just becoming commercially available in the United States, and we took full advantage of them. In addition to whole group and individualized reading, we added daily reading groups with the emphasis on reading familiar books for pleasure.

The results and ramifications of what children accomplished that first year exceeded our expectations. The children progressed even farther in reading than we'd anticipated, which presented us with the delightful problem of having to order more difficult books by the spring. The writing and publishing done by the students was truly amazing, and will be described in depth in another chapter. The first grade teacher and I felt victorious, exhilarated, and exhausted. We had never worked so hard nor had a more exciting year teaching!

Standardized test results that May of 1984 indicated that *all* children were at the average to above-average range in word reading, word study skills, comprehension and vocabulary — in spite of the fact that many of the children had depressed scores on the environment subtest (which relates to general information). Subtest scores were somewhat lower when local norms were applied but still represented a substantially increased mean percentile rank in all four reading areas, as compared to previous years. These results have remained consistent over four years and suggest that students taught to read with literature do at least as well as, or better than, children taught with the basal text. Perhaps the most significant factors are the ones the tests don't measure: the positive self-concept and love of books that come from being a successful reader early on.

In the fall of 1984, a total literature-based reading and writing program was implemented in both first grades in our school as well as in the second grade. Also, as a direct result of our students' success, all kindergarten teachers added shared book experience to their language arts program. The third grade incorporated a literature approach in the fall of 1985. In the fourth to sixth grades, teachers have gradually added literature to their basal program, and some have moved to a total literature-based program. A strong support group of teachers has sprung up in our building. We meet regularly, at school and at each other's homes, to share and discuss current research, ideas that have worked well, and problems that have come up. We try to coordinate efforts and expectations across grade levels. We are continually modifying and evaluating our teaching and learning together.

In the beginning, our literature-based reading program was a means of preventing reading failure and achieving early success for at-risk readers. However, the program quickly became a highly desired alternative for all students. Visitors to the classroom commented repeatedly on how fluently the children read and how excited they were about reading and writing. Parents, fully involved in their children's learning, talked about their children reading constantly. Teachers, administrators, and parents from around the district and neighboring school systems came regularly to observe and participate in our classroom.

A first grade classroom where children — mostly minority children — are reading and writing fluently and with obvious pride and pleasure is apparently not a common occurrence. Observing a group of six-year-olds in mid-December reading, chuckling, and making predictions about *Freckle Juice* by Judy Blume is quite a different experience from observing the word-by-word reading of the skills-oriented basal text. Once you have seen and captured the excitement of reading real books, it is hard not to want to be part of it.

While my story begins in first grade, the kindergarten experience is not meant to be minimized in any way. As up to 50% of our entering first-graders are new to our school each year, we are particularly appreciative of those students who have had the rich and meaningful kindergarten experience our district provides. The importance of oral language development, play, and cooperative learning is evident in our kindergartens: activity areas abound with books, writing materials, art media, sand tables, building materials, and home-school-city corners for dress up and role playing. At this time, kindergarten teachers are incorporating shared reading and writing experiences along with some journal writing, activities that will be discussed in this book. Most kindergarten teachers have moved away from a workbook phonics program and teach a "sound of the week" where they immerse children in art, cooking, and multimedia experiences to reinforce letter-sound relationships.

Over the past several years, I have had the privilege of working with many teachers and supporting them in supplementing their basal book program with storybooks or in moving into a total literature-based reading and writing program. I have yet to meet a teacher or administrator who loved the basal. Mostly, they are resigned to it for lack of suitable and workable alternatives. Many, even those with traditional backgrounds, have slowly moved towards integrating children's books and process writing into their language arts program once they have been shown the possibilities.

This book is an attempt to support teachers in making change, and to answer their questions as they move away from the skill-oriented basal text and accompanying worksheets toward pleasure-oriented children's books and self-selected writing. Through describing an existing program that has worked well for teachers and children — and through some discussion of learning theory and philosophy as well as the reading-writing process — my aim is to stimulate thinking and give confidence. The ideas and suggestions presented are intended to show teachers, especially those who are not fully satisfied with their present reading-writing programs, that change *is* possible. But my suggestions are not prescriptions. Ultimately, it is up to the teacher to decide what can be implemented, and how it can be utilized and modified to fit a personal teaching style and philosophy.

Teaching with literature at the beginning levels is difficult and demanding, yet the extra efforts are rewarding. The joy returns to teaching and learning as teachers and children begin to empower and trust themselves and each other.

(opposite) Choosing to read.

2 Why Change?
A Need for "Active Literacy"

The number of Americans who cannot read and write sufficiently, according to PLUS (Project Literacy US, 1987), is more than twenty-three million; the drop-out rate at some urban high schools is above 50%, contributing to our problem of growing illiteracy; and one-third of *all* adult Americans lack the communication skills they need to function productively. Our schools are turning out functional literates, children who can read and write *in school*, but who do not necessarily read and write in other contexts. These students may do reasonably well at word calling, but they have no real understanding of what meaning the words convey. It is time for a change.

Genuine literacy implies using reading, writing, thinking, and speaking daily in the real world, with options, appreciation, and meaningful purposes in various settings and with other people. An actively literate person is constantly thinking, learning, and reflecting, and is assuming the responsibility for continued growth in personal literacy. This broader definition of "active literacy" is defined by the Australian educator Garth Boomer. He defines it as . . .

> the ability to inject one's own thoughts and intentions into messages received and sent; the ability to transform and to *act* upon aspects of the world via the written word.
>
> To function in this way, learners must go much deeper than the coding and encoding of written symbols. Beneath the surface iceberg

of this ability is the ability to revise, to arrange, and to deploy personal experiences and thoughts as well as the ability to imagine other people doing the same thing.
Fair Dinkum Teaching and Learning: Reflections on Literacy and Power, 1985, p. 191

I like Boomer's definition because it goes beyond the definition of literacy as the ability to read and write functionally to the broader context of one who *does* read and write thoughtfully and who does so for meaningful and self-chosen purposes in the real world. For children to become "actively" literate, the school curriculum must move beyond the management of passive, "correct" responding to the facilitation of active, involved, and evaluative thinking. The way we teach reading and writing is critical to the development of "active literacy". Achieving "average" scores on a standardized reading test means one may be proficient in mostly literal level subskills. It does not mean that one is a reader or writer in any meaningful, active, relevant manner.

The truth is that most students learn to read regardless of the approach if the teacher is sincere, cares about kids, and believes in the method and materials being used. The larger issue, however, is that the student may well learn *how* to read without ever acquiring the *desire* to read or a real understanding of what is read. A reader, after all, is a person who *chooses* to read for pleasure and information and who can assimilate that knowledge thoughtfully, not just someone who can pass standardized tests and complete school assignments. A literate person, in the broadest sense of the word, is one who is continually reading, writing, thinking, listening, and evaluating for real purposes in real-life situations.

Why Change the Way We Teach?

Spoken Language as a Developmental Model for Literacy

Most children learn spoken language quite naturally. A child learning to speak uses language in meaningful ways to communicate for real needs. The child is encouraged, indeed rewarded, for attempts and approximations at speaking. If the baby says, "Daddy go side", the adult says in an encouraging, positive manner, "That's right. Daddy is going outside." The caring parent does not say, "That's not right. This is how you say it correctly." The adult recognizes that learning to speak is an ongoing process, that the child will learn to speak correctly in time, that the child needs encouragement and freedom to speak the best way he is able for the stage he is at at that moment. The spoken model is not to be taken lightly. The ability to process language in certain meaningful ways is one of the best predictors of how a five-year-old will do in school.

Young children acquire language, and social and academic skills, developmentally. In a supportive home environment,

1. **they observe 'demonstrations'.**
2. **they are encouraged to participate actively.**
3. **they try out or practice independently.**
4. **they gradually become competent and confident.**

(Holdaway, in *The Pursuit of Literacy: Early Reading and Writing* by Michael Sampson (ed.), 1986, pp. 58-60)

Along the way they are encouraged and admired for their efforts. Many children who have been exposed to reading and writing in the above manner enter school as beginning readers and writers.

In the late 1960s, Don Holdaway, a New Zealand educator, theorized that the ways in which children learn oral language could be used as a developmental model for how children learn to read and write. Working with teachers in New Zealand, he took those principles (listed above) and applied them to the classroom. Using memorable poems, songs, and stories in a shared book experience, he utilized enlarged print and enlarged illustrations to make Big Books so that the child in a classroom could interact with meaningful text much the same way the preschooler interacted with text at his mother's knee in the "bedtime story" environment. With the teacher pointing distinctly to the words as she read the text, the child was encouraged to join in. Later on, little books would be available in the classroom for the children to practice on. Holdaway noted that the complex task of learning to read was accomplished by the learner in a self-monitoring and self-correcting manner, with many approximations leading up to competency. (For a full description of shared book experience, see *The Foundations of Literacy*, Holdaway, 1979.)

Applying the Research on Natural Literacy Learners

By the early to mid 1970s, researchers in different parts of the world, notably Marie Clay in New Zealand, Delores Durkin in the United States, and Margaret Clark in Scotland, had reported on the way very young children learned to read and write before coming to school. Certain environmental factors emerged as common to almost all early readers:

1. **Reading to children,** often the same book repeatedly. (This is the factor mentioned most often in the research literature.)
2. **Seeing a reading model** such as a parent, teacher, or sibling reading.
3. **Availability and utilization of a wide variety of reading**

materials, especially storybooks.
4. **Involvement with writing** such as scribbling, copying, printing, and writing with paper and pencil.
5. **Positive, quality interactive responses with the child** in the reading-writing process.

Research studies of these natural literacy learners give valuable insight into what constitutes a positive reading environment. By taking those factors that most contributed to early reading success and duplicating them in the classroom, one can theorize that, in spite of a home environment where prereading experiences are lacking, reading success will occur. A literature-based approach to teaching beginning reading and writing then becomes a program of prevention rather than remediation. Even our low-ability readers benefit from and understand good literature.

Literature-based reading and writing emerges as a natural way to tie theory and research into children's continued learning of all the language processes — listening, speaking, reading, and writing. Unfortunately, the theory and research on how young children learn to read and write has been largely ignored by the basal book publishers and many educators. One can only speculate on why this is so. Standardized testing, which is the predominant means of measuring reading achievement in the United States, is geared to the basal text and, therefore, promotes it. Many university teacher education programs still teach the basal as the main reading approach, and many educators have not kept abreast of current research.

Sadly, what goes on in the schools often does not complement the way children are learning language so easily and naturally at home. Learning is often compartmentalized, put into skills packets, and based on fragmented materials unrelated to the child's reality; there is very little involvement of real language. The child is rewarded only for the right answer, and usually there is one short right answer which is already in the teacher's head or the teacher's manual. The school reading and writing experience needs to continue to build on the oral and written language experiences all children enter school with. Children need to use language purposefully, meaningfully, and naturally — in whole units, not in small pieces or for teaching skills in a hierarchy.

Why Literature?

Literature has proved to be an excellent vehicle for developing, enhancing, and enriching lifelong, active literacy. Compared to the basal text, it works better. The use of literature for teaching literacy is tried and tested, grounded in research, and based on natural learning theory. New Zealand, the country with the highest literacy rate in the world, has been teaching with literature for over twenty years. Australia has followed suit, refining its methodology for the last fifteen years and continually improving its literacy levels at the same time. Canada and England, in the last ten years or more, have been working towards active literacy using children's literature as a base. Several states in our country are beginning to respect and utilize these powerful models by pushing real books and making changes at the state levels. In Vermont, a state that is known to be "wired" for whole language, a whole language background is a requirement for employment of new teachers. With the implementation of the California Reading Initiative, the state of California foresees no basals being used in classrooms within the next seven to eight years; funds have been allocated and utilized for purchase of selected, notable titles in multiple, paperback copies as an alternative to the basal text. New York state has taken a giant step in 1987 by mandating that every teacher must attend one of five seminars being offered on whole language concepts. New Mexico and Arizona have large, active pockets of whole language/literature-based teaching. Based on my own experience, described in this book, I know that literature works more effectively; that children and teachers enjoy reading and writing more; and that the children become more actively literate.

What is Literature?

Literature includes picture books for younger and older readers, traditional tales such as folk tales, fables, and myths, fantasy (which includes old and new fairy tales), science fiction, poetry, contemporary realistic fiction, historical fiction, nonfiction informational books, and biographies. But the definition of literature incudes a much broader scope than just the categories of books.

Charlotte Huck, who has probably promoted the use of quality literature in the reading program longer and more vigorously than any other American educator, defines literature in this way:

> Literature is the imaginative shaping of life and thought into the forms and structures of language. The province of literature is the human condition; life with all its feelings, thoughts, and insights. The experience of literature is always two dimensional, for it involves both the book and the reader. *Children's Literature in the Elementary School (Fourth Edition)*, 1987, p. 4.

Aidan Chambers, an English educator and writer says: "Literature offers us images to think with." *Booktalk: Occasional Writing on Literature and Children*, 1985, p. 3. In the same book Chambers further states:

> ... I believe literature belongs to all the people all the time, that it

ought to be cheaply and easily available, that it ought to be fun to read as well as challenging, subversive, refreshing, comforting, and all the other qualities we claim for it. Finally, I hold that in literature we find the best expression of the human imagination, and the most useful means by which we come to grips with our ideas about ourselves and what we are. (p. 16)

Language is a condition of being human; literature is a birthright. Entering into this birthright requires that every child be born into an environment that makes its birthright available, accessible, a gift to be desired. (p. 10)

Literature connects us with past and present humanity. Literary reading promotes the language development and thinking that is necessary for an educated, cultural society. It is our job as educators to put all children in touch with excellent literature, especially those books which have the power to change us in some way. "Books that transform me as I read, books that go on working in me afterwards when they have become part of me, often refresh and reinvigorate the language." (Chambers, p. 18).

Advantages of Literature

There are many valid reasons for using literature as the mainstay of a beginning reading and writing program. All these serve to motivate and promote life-long interest in reading. I find the first four reasons particularly significant.

1. **Literature allows meaning to dominate.**
   The beginning reader reads immediately for meaning and views reading as a thinking process. Readable books are predictable in words and outcomes. A story that makes sense is easy to talk about and remember.

2. **Literature use concentrates on the development of readers rather than the development of skills.**
   Students spend most of their time reading continuous text, which allows beginning readers to see themselves as readers right from the start. Research has shown that this has not been the norm for poor readers who spend most of their instruction time on skills and decoding.

3. **Literature promotes positive self-concepts in beginning readers.**
   Because students see themselves as readers of books from the first day of school, they develop positive attitudes about reading and themselves. Regardless of background, apparent deficiencies, and varying development levels, we have never had a child fail to begin to learn to read with the best of children's books. That early success and confidence flows into other academic and social

areas. By contrast, students who fail to learn to read in first grade can carry lifelong scars.

4. **Literature promotes language development.**

   Exposure to the variety of complex syntactical patterns, creative and figurative language, and imagery found in good literature seems to aid comprehension of language in general and to enhance vocabularly development. Since this literary language is not generally found in primary basal readers, popular television programs, or general conversation, it is important that children — particularly lower-achieving children who may not otherwise be exposed to the language of literature — be saturated with good books in the school environment. It has been my experience that vocabulary and multiple meanings of words are best learned and applied through the context of books.

5. **Literature promotes fluent reading.**

   It has been interesting to observe beginning readers reading with fluency from the start. Since the children hear a predictable story as a whole first, and possibly more than once, they come to know phrasing, and they imitate it. Where predicting and sampling are encouraged, they are accustomed to filling in words that make sense. They do not read word for word even when presented with new material. The transference of reading ability to other books is a highly important factor which gives the child confidence and the ability to read independently.

6. **Literature deals with human emotions.**

   Students relate easily to stories that deal with anger, sadness, jealousy, etc., and they have an opportunity to get in touch with their own emotions in a natural, nonthreatening manner. Readers meet characters who have traits like themselves, which makes them feel like an accepted part of the human race. Folk tales and fairy tales teach much about individual longings, conflicts, and failings and can stimulate thoughtful discussion.

7. **Literature exposes students to a variety of story structures, themes, and authors' styles.**

   Children begin to internalize how stories work and come to understand setting, characterization, and plot. Students who hear and read a variety of fiction and nonfiction literature have no difficulty in modeling authors' styles, and love writing and illustrating their own stories.

8. **Literature puts children in contact with illustration at its best.**

   Beautiful illustrations that stand on their own as art are often a component of favorite books. Wordless books tell their stories totally through the depth and detail of the illustrations and can be used creatively with prereaders as well as older children.

Imaginative illustrations inspire children to create their own original pictures.
9. **Literature makes reading fun.**
Why shouldn't school be fun? It is certainly one of the primary reasons teachers move from the basal into literature with such relief. It's hard to love a basal. Daniel Fader, in *The New Hooked on Books,* makes a strong point: "If teachers would see themselves first as purveyors of pleasure rather than instructors in skill, they may find that skill will flourish where pleasure has been cultivated."

Why Literature Is Better for Developing Readers

Comparing the Real Book with an Adapted Text

Years ago, when I first started looking for quality literature, I assumed the stories in the basal credited to well-known authors were presented in their original form. I was surprised to find out that many stories were revised and abridged, and that this was the case over and over again. While there has been a recent attempt to introduce well-known authors and stories into the beginning basal texts, very often the stories are altered and shortened so that the natural language flow, emotional quality, interesting story and spontaneity are lost.

The Story *Too Much Noise* by Ann McGovern appears in an abridged version in a first grade basal text. Interestingly enough, students have no difficulty with the trade book version even though it is more difficult in terms of actual vocabulary. The text of the first two pages of the story appears below, with the original version shown first.

A long time ago there was an old man.
His name was Peter, and he lived in an old, old house.
The bed creaked.
The floor squeaked.
Outside, the wind blew the leaves through the trees.
The leaves fell on the roof. Swish. Swish.
The tea kettle whistled. Hiss. Hiss.
"Too noisy," said Peter.

.   .   .

Peter was an old man
Who lived in an old, old house.
There was too much noise in Peter's house.
The bed made noise.
The door made noise.

And the window made noise.
Peter didn't like all that noise.
Holt, Rinehart and Winston, 1986, in *A Place For Me.*

Beginning readers love reading the original version and read it easily and eagerly. The six lines beginning with "The bed creaked... The floor squeaked..." appear nine times in this short, delightful story. The magic of the language, the rhyme and rhythm, the repetition of the above passage and others throughout the book, and the noisy words themselves ("Swish. Swish." and "Hiss. Hiss.") make it fun to read and actually easier than the basal version.

The original version deals with non-concrete imagery of the sounds of the wind blowing leaves through the trees, leaves falling on the roof, and a whistling tea kettle — rich language which leads children to form mental images of the sounds. By contrast, the story language in the basal reflects only concrete objects and then only to make "noise". The poetic language is gone. The simplified language of the basal assumes that first-graders cannot handle longer sentences, harder words, or imagery. The child has been deprived of exposure to literary language, so necessary for the development of imaginative writing and a love of literature.

Following a workshop presentation where I discussed the differences in the two texts, a first grade teacher came up to me and said, "I've never liked this story and the children find it boring, but I never knew why till now." Another teacher told me that the comparison of the texts of *Too Much Noise* was what ultimately convinced her to use genuine literature in teaching reading.

Concerns about the Basal Text

Unfortunately, an examination of current basal textbooks for beginning readers does not show much improvement in recent times. A look at several series at the 1987 International Reading Association annual convention in Anaheim, California, indicates the prominence of basal text books driven by skills and phonics. There is window dressing, older versions being relatively unchanged but updated with new copyright dates. There is enthusiastic talk by salesmen of "predictable text", "meaningful story", and "real literature", but close scrutiny reveals dull stories, bland illustrations, and text produced with strict readability and skill formulas. There is, in addition, what can be called a "basalizing" of materials. One prominent example is the proliferation of Big Books, some of which are nothing more than oversized texts with stereotyped, colorless pictures and phonetically driven text. Another example is the large number of worksheets that go along with each chapter of every book in a so-called "literature program." There is no way the child can enjoy and appreciate the literature when he is expected to complete extensive paperwork, including writing the definition for many vocabulary words and answering many detailed questions. Buyer beware is a necessary caution indeed.

A look at the philosophies of several current reading series shows phonics and decoding as the first priority in teaching beginning reading, with comprehension defined in terms of teaching skills. Accompanying all the basal texts are detailed teacher manuals telling teachers exactly what and how to teach. The level of these manuals and the hundreds of worksheets that accompany them — to be completed to exact specifications — are demeaning to teachers and to children. They discourage independent thought and imply that teachers and students are not to be trusted.

The intent here is not to single out any one commercial publisher but to indicate that the heart of these basal programs is "skills" first and foremost, with phonics as the primary objective in teaching beginning reading. The belief is that only an intensive grounding in phonics will lead to reading competency. In fact, I have worked with many capable readers who never really "got the hang of" phonics but who are successful readers because they read for meaning in high-quality books that make sense. Conversely, I have worked with students who can only do phonics. They are word-bound, hesitant readers who read for sounds instead of meaning. Good readers, taught to read phonetically, fill in and integrate meaning cues automatically in order to make sense of print. In all likelihood, they ignore much of the phonics they have been taught and rely heavily on meaning. The poor readers never move beyond phonics and looking at words in isolation. They may learn what they are taught, but it is not enough to help them read successfully. The over-emphasis on phonics actually prevents them from using more natural, meaningful strategies. Perhaps most importantly, the pleasurable aspect of reading is lost to the student over-focused on skills and decontextualized text. Controlled vocabulary and phonics do not produce good stories.

The teacher, who may be told by the school district to use the basal, needs at least to be aware that claims that a basal contains "classic literature" are not always valid. Thinking this might be true only at the beginning levels, I analyzed a 1987 sixth grade basal text and was surprised and dismayed to find that 40% of the selections of literature had been altered in some way, "adapted", "condensed", "abridged and adapted", or "edited". The publishers, in their zeal to keep selections to ten to twelve pages, often omit setting, characterization, and descriptive detail and leave a "bare bones" plot while adding stylized illustrations. Many students and teachers are unaware that they are reading an adapted version. The "Acknowledgements" section of the basal which gives this information is always in very fine print and is easily overlooked unless one knows where to look for it or even to look for it at all.

A fourth grade teacher in our district who has since moved into literature-based reading became visibly upset when we compared the basal and original versions of *James and the Giant Peach* by Roald Dahl. What amounted to over thirty pages of original text had been omitted in a short basal selection. The following year she obtained library copies of the original version for her students to read.

As teachers, we need to look carefully at the material we are giving students to read. If we are using an adapted version, we need to know it. We then need to accept responsibility for giving students stories without insight into what characters are thinking, stories without genuine conflict and emotions, writing that has no author's voice, and stories that may turn students off to reading. Often, however, we do have a choice. Why not give the students the best there is, the actual book in all its glory, as the author intended it? If we are using the basal, then let us at least give the students the worthwhile stories and skip the ones we have always found boring.

The Need for a Personal Philosophy

As teachers, we all have a philosophy of education whether we want to have it or not: what we say to children, what we expect from them, and how we teach and conduct ourselves, reflect our beliefs. If we are able to articulate our philosophy and beliefs, then we have the capacity to examine, reflect, refine, and change, and we can listen to new ideas with some frame of reference to evaluate them. If our philosophy is in agreement both with our beliefs and with current educational theory and research, we can be intelligent and consistent in our decision making. Our own growing professional knowledge and philosophy elevate us to being teachers in the highest sense of the word.

A personal educational philosophy evolves from many factors — observing children, demonstration teaching, trying things out, talking with colleagues, keeping up with the research — and will be different for each of us. The important thing is to continue questioning how and why we are doing what we are doing. Does the way we work with children reflect how children learn? Do we have a theory of learning that we can apply to our teaching? Are the children in our classrooms joyful and confident about their learning? A philosophy which is our own gives us empowerment.

Those professionals engaged in promoting "active literacy" are

... those who are determined to try out ideas for themselves, to think deeply and to be convinced slowly; those who are prepared to read more widely when in doubt; and those who wish to influence outcomes from an informed

conviction which they have tested in their own experience... Ideally, the adventure should be undertaken in a slow, open-minded, questioning manner allowing the opportunity for working with the ideas in real situations, or at least for personalizing the ideas by rigorous comparison and reflection.
The Foundations of Literacy by Don Holdaway, p. 11

Whole Language and Process Teaching

Whole language is a philosophy which refers to meaningful, real, and relevant teaching and learning. Whole language respects the idea that all the language processes (listening, speaking, reading, and writing — including spelling and handwriting) are learned naturally and in meaningful context as a whole, not in little parts. Learning activities are open-ended and involve student choice, discussion, and sharing in a social, literate environment. Risk taking and making errors are encouraged as being necessary for optimal language development. Ken Goodman, in his very readable, informative book *What's Whole in Whole Language?* (see *Resources for Teachers* section) discusses whole language learning and theory and how it can be applied to teaching.

At this point in time, I am comfortable integrating the four language modes — listening, speaking, reading, and writing. While much of what I will be writing about encompasses whole langauge concepts and while many would say I am a whole language teacher, I am personally uncomfortable with the pureness that the term "whole language" implies for me. I cannot say at this time that I always have a whole language classroom. I don't always use thematic units; I occasionally teach from part to whole; I am still struggling hard to integrate more areas of curriculum with the language arts — an ideal that is very difficult to attain. I anticipate that this struggle will go on for years. I am also concerned about the possible misuse of the term "whole language" as a new catch phrase that opportunists will exploit to their advantage.

I prefer to use the term "process teaching" — which values the process as well as the product — to denote whole language concepts and developmental learning. Whereas I see whole language as the highest end of the continuum of teaching and learning, with skills teaching at the very lowest end, process teaching allows me to struggle comfortably (or uncomfortably) somewhere in the middle. While I may not be where I want to be, at least I'm moving in the right direction. Process teaching implies that I am in process too. My theories about learning and teaching are continually developing and changing.

It is necessary for all of us as teachers to have an educational philosophy that is backed up by current research and theory. We need this philosophy to be credible to students, parents, administrators, and to ourselves. We need to have a sound rationale for what we are doing. Each of our philosophies will be different, based on our own prior knowledge and experiences, what we understand about how children learn, and our individual personalities. The way each of us works with children will, therefore, be unique.

When I am involved in workshops with teachers, I always start off with and give considerable time and discussion to theory and research. (See *Resources for Teachers* section for recommended books and journal articles.) Many teachers are initially very impatient; they want to be told *how* to use literature and writing. They are frustrated that the familiar packets of ready-made activities aren't available. They want immediate answers, and there are none. It is frightening at first to realize and accept the responsibility for one's own learning and teaching. It becomes empowering and expanding once we take the risk and get our own thinking and decision-making processes going.

My own personal philosophy has developed gradually and evolves from some theoretical concerns about issues that are of vital importance to me:

- Teaching students vs. teaching programs
- Teacher as facilitator vs. teacher as manager
- Process orientation vs. product orientation
- Development of a set of strategies vs. mastery of a series of skills
- Celebrating approximation and risk taking vs. celebrating perfection
- Promoting and respecting individual growth and differences vs. fostering competition
- Capitalizing on a student's strengths vs. emphasizing remediating weaknesses
- Promoting independence in learning vs. dependence on the teacher

These concerns are applied to my beliefs and goals and reflected in my personal philosophy.

My Beliefs	**My Goals**
• All children can learn.	• Have high expectations for all children.
• Children learn to read by reading.	• Surround children with good books.
• Children need to read and write for their own purposes.	• Encourage daily, self-selected reading and writing.
• Spelling develops through writing for real purposes.	• Accept invented spellings and teach spelling strategies.

- Children need many varied language experiences.

- Provide opportunities for children to interact meaningfully with text and each other.

- Children develop self-confidence through early school success.

- Make learning to read and write easy, desirable, and pleasurable.

- Children learn through trial and error.

- Encourage and congratulate children for approximations and risk taking.

- Teachers need ongoing support.

- Encourage in-service and provide teachers with opportunities for professional growth and interaction.

- Young children are capable of high-level comprehension.

- Encourage, model, and give opportunities to practice brainstorming, predicting, and inferential questioning.

- Independent work must be meaningful and relevant.

- Develop literature extension activities including the creative arts.

- Reading must be approached through strategies that focus primarily on meaning.

- Help children develop strategies that utilize semantics and syntax before phonics.

- Vocabulary is learned best in context.

- Teach vocabulary during and after reading.

- Parents have the right and need to be involved in their children's education.

- Communicate regularly and clearly with parents and invite them to be part of the process.

In the process of thinking about and writing this book, I have refined, adjusted, and added to my beliefs and goals, and I expect that I will continue to do so. Process teaching implies movement and adjustments. Where I am philosophically is based on the professional reading and reflecting I am doing, thoughtful discussions with my colleagues, direct observations of children learning, demonstration teaching I have observed, in-service workshops I have attended, and lessons I have attempted and then assessed. All these activities are time-consuming when added to the daily teaching demands. But they are what keep me current, professional, and proud of what I do. All this needs to go on continually for me to keep growing professionally and personally.

Creating Supportive Learning Environments

Perhaps the most critical factor in developing a personal philosophy is the way the teacher views and treats children. Trust, respect, support, and high expectations must be generously and genuinely present for all children. The emotional climate and tone the teacher creates in the classroom may well be the most significant factor in the success of a reading-writing classroom.

One of the most important changes I had to make was to set up a learning environment that encouraged risk taking. Both the children and I genuinely had to feel that it was all right, in fact, even encouraged, to venture a reasoned guess, make a mistake and try again, and give an original response. This was clearly brought home to me during the first months of our program. While I was feeling enormous pressure for our children to succeed (the principal had stated early on, "Those test scores had better be good!"), we were nonetheless given a lot of freedom to make mistakes and refinements and even to fail. The children also had to be given that same freedom.

While our principal came into the classroom almost daily in the beginning, she made very few comments and suggestions. We were busy trying out procedures, schedules, methods, and books, and making many adjustments. We were grateful for her silence and trust. Often, I wondered what she was thinking, but I didn't ask, and she didn't say. She trusted us enough to let us make our own mistakes and changes. When it was clear a lesson went well, she was supportive and encouraging. When a lesson went badly, she said very little, offering a suggestion here and there but basically letting us know it was our job to work out the kinks, and that she would offer support if we needed it.

We must do at least as much for children. They must be given time and encouragement to try out, to refine, to make changes, to take risks in their reading and writing procedures. They must feel safe, valued, and supported for maximum and pleasurable learning to take place.

Most children enter school believing they will learn to read, and the classroom must foster this belief. Each year, on the first or second day of school in our first grade, after *The Bus Ride* (Wagner, 1976) has been heard and read several times as a Big Book, every hand in the room goes up when the teacher asks, "How many of you can read this book?" Believing they can read is the first step towards children's reading success.

Giving up control. I often think that what process teaching is really about is giving up total control. I have no doubt that part of the reason I went into teaching was because I could run things in the classroom. The students could talk only when I gave permission, write only about topics I initiated, and read only the selections that I assigned. My principal once called me "bossy", and I was insulted. It took me months to own up to the fact that it was true. I like things done my way.

In the process of working with teachers and children and growing professionally, I have come to understand how important choice is for all of us. We must all be free to make decisions about what we read and write, when we can speak, what activities we want to participate in. It is this ownership and free choice that makes the experience our own. At the same time, it also makes us more accountable. If a child has difficulty with the basal, the publisher who packaged it can be blamed. But with literature-based reading and writing, the teacher feels more responsible because she is involved in deciding how reading and writing is being taught. While this initially creates some anxiety, ultimately teachers rejoice. One teacher said: "I have more self-esteem now because I have a choice of what literature I use and how I use it. I'm no longer controlled by the basal." Once we as teachers have options, it follows naturally that we foster self-selection and independent thinking in our students.

The role of motivation and engagement. Effective motivation means children are engaged in the task, and engagement — total immersion and involvement — is necessary for learning to take place. "I use the term engagement to characterize the way a learner and a demonstration come together on those occasions when learning takes place." (*Writing and the Writer* by Frank Smith, p. 176). As long as the task is relevant to kids, and they can see a real purpose, there is no need for external motivation. It does not always follow that a teacher-initiated, "motivating" activity will engage children.

I began thinking seriously about motivation when my remedial second grade readers transcended their supposed instructional level. How is it possible that a student can read a book that "should" be too hard for him? Reading tests, from which the instructional level is derived, often reflect only skill mastery and do not reflect enthusiasm and interest.

Every year we have a student who surprises us and makes a breakthrough, reading a book we would have assumed to be too difficult. Several years in a row this happened with Mike Thaler's humorous *A Hippopotamus Ate the Teacher*. The student would love the book and be determined to read it for himself. He would take it home, practice it over and over again, and come back to school triumphant.

It has been my experience that motivation and engagement are particularly important for the disadvantaged or reluctant reader. The smart, obedient students learn to read in spite of the method and materials. The lower-achieving students *need* the motivation and total engagement that a good book provides. These are the students who struggle with phonics. They need the meaning cues and memorableness that a predictable book provides to make sense of print.

Joyce Pope, a seasoned first grade teacher in our district, talked to me about the unnatural motivation a teacher has to create with a basal. She said:

> For years I spent hours making phonics and comprehension games and running off worksheets. But no matter how clever I was, the excitement didn't last long. The basal stories were boring, and I couldn't generate genuine enthusiasm in the group. But story time was always magical. The thrill for me now is to be free to let the literature itself motivate the students. I feel authentic because I've moved from an instructional to an invitational style of teaching. (Best of all, no purple fingernails!)

I, too, was guilty of "artificial motivation" for many years. I spent lots of money on stickers. For every fifty pages students read, they could put a "smelly" sticker on a chart. I was desperate to get those turned-off kids into reading real books. When the literature-based reading program began in the first grade, I was determined that the motivation to read would be intrinsic. The reward would be in the joy and satisfaction of reading a good book. It has worked out exactly that way. There are no stickers. There is no need for them.

The importance of the approach to beginning reading on a child's motivation and attitude toward reading cannot be overestimated, and the best of children's literature engages their interest far more than stories in a basal. Even though it may not be possible to give up the basal entirely at this time, it is possible to begin adding genuine literature to the reading-writing program.

The importance of respect. I was very fortunate to have Andrea Butler, an Australian educator and language consultant, read the manuscript of this book and make some valuable suggestions to me. I was very taken with the fact that she refused to write on the Xeroxed copies of the chapters even though I insisted she do so. She would not "mark" on *my* writing. Instead, she wrote her comments on removable "post-its" which she cut to size and placed at strategic places to make her points. After I removed the "post-its" and made my revisions on the word processor, I would have a "clean" manuscript. What struck me was the respect she had for me as the writer; she would not physically impose her thoughts on my ideas.

We had many discussions about all aspects of teaching, and one conversation in particular left quite an impression on me. We were talking about what makes a whole language teacher different from other teachers, and she said she had concluded that it was "respect" for children. I have thought about that a lot and decided she is right. Respect allows and promotes choice, trust, and independence. Respect accepts children where they are and encourages and congratulates them for their attempts. Respect values children as unique individuals. The language the teacher uses in talking to children carries the tone of her teaching and lets children know if they are respected. If they feel respected, they will feel secure and be able to take risks. So it is with us as adults too. Respect is necessary for optimal learning.

(above) A first-grader selecting a book for independent reading.
(opposite) Karen Shiba with her first grade class, sharing a Halloween poem.

3 The Reading Program
Teaching Reading with Children's Books

Overview

Walking into the first grade classroom, one is immediately struck by the excitement and involvement of the children. There is a "buzz" of activity; everyone is engaged in reading, writing, listening, and speaking activities. Before school and during free-choice activities, children are reading together — Big Books, poems, and favorite stories — writing to each other, composing stories, journal writing, and extending the literature in meaningful ways. During shared experiences and reading groups, there is a feeling of "I can read", "I can write", "I can succeed", as children are supported and guided by the teacher and each other in their learning community.

This chapter will discuss significant aspects of the reading process applicable to the elementary grades and describe an existing literature-based reading program as it functions daily in two first grade classrooms. For the purpose of organization, the writing program and process will be discussed in separate chapters. In reality, reading and writing are taught as an integrated whole, as much as possible. Interestingly enough, by Grade 3 (see Chapter 8), I was unable to separate the processes when writing about them.

Certainly, there are many ways to teach reading and writing with literature. By demonstrating one way reading and writing can be taught with literature, it is hoped that teachers will generate ideas, gain insights, and assume the professional risk of integrating more children's books and process writing into their existing programs. The program described indicates where we are at this point, after four years of refinement, observing children, and reexamining our own philosophies and methods. We started slowly, with one first grade class. The second year, there were two first grade classes and one second grade class. The third year, there was an additional second grade class and one third grade class. The fourth year, there were two classes in each of the Grades 1, 2, and 3 immersed in literature-based reading and writing.

Components of our first grade Literature Program
    Shared Experiences
        Shared book experience
        Reading aloud to children
        Development of strategies, including word attack skills
        Children sharing their own published books/projects
        Collaborative writing
    Journal Writing and Book Publishing
    Reading Groups
    Literature Extension Activities
    Independent Reading

Included in these components are:
- Hearing good literature, an average of six to eight books as well as three to five poems daily. Higher-level questioning techniques are utilized.
- Reading one or more predictable books with teacher guidance. (Predictable books are easy to read because of rhyme, repetition, natural language flow, meaningful story, and quality illustrations.) This is done whole group and in reading groups.
- Development of reading strategies, including word attack skills instruction. As much as possible, word attack skills instruction is integrated into the total reading process.
- An opportunity for students to share completed literature extension projects, published books, and read to the class.
- Independent reading of self-selected books with a nightly "sign-out" program and check-in the next day.
- Writing journals, daily writing of personal experiences and stories using invented spelling.
- Literature extension activities — book publishing, illustrating individual books and poems, story writing, letter writing, collaborative writing, individual activities evolving from thematic units, involvement with the creative arts. (There are no "dittoes".)

Daily Schedule

With the cooperation of our principal, we have a daily two hour block of time for language arts. (See Figure 1a for our original schedule, and Figure 1b for an updated version. These schedules are presented only as a rough guide to what can actually be a very flexible time. Diagram 1 shows how the classroom is organized. See, also, sample lesson plans in Appendix B.) Math, science, social studies and special activities (music, art, library, computer, physical education), take place outside of that time frame, and where possible, literature is integrated into those other subject areas. (See Appendix C for a weekly schedule.) Having sustained time with the whole class gives us quality, uninterrupted time as well as some flexibility. It allows for integration of language arts activities, relaxed time to get to know the children well, and a chance to share ideas.

Shared Experiences

The majority of the shared experiences time, about two-thirds of the hour, is spent reading to and with children. We read to the children all day long — short predictable books, longer stories, requested favorite books, Big Books, poems, children's published books, books from the classroom and school library collection. We are very conscious of the fact that many of our students have not heard many storybooks before coming to school, and we want to saturate them with storybook language and the joy of books. While any reading program can teach most children to read, most programs do not teach children to *love* to read. Because the pleasure factor in reading is emphasized, and because they are surrounded by wonderful books, children pick up the desire to read, and they read constantly.

Daily exposure to quality literature causes the children's reading habit to develop quite naturally and enthusiastically. We see this in the classroom daily, and parents confirm this. Rachel's mom would have to look for her when dinner was ready. "Where's Rachel?" she would ask her other children when Rachel could not be found anywhere. Rachel was always alone in some nook upstairs, contentedly reading a book.

The children also have opportunities to read to and with the whole class. Students eagerly await their turn to read their carefully illustrated published books and completed book projects. They enjoy acting as teacher and asking the other children questions about what they have read. Dramatization and other literature-inspired activities may also take place during this time.

FIGURE 1   DAILY READING AND WRITING SCHEDULES

1a   SEPTEMBER 1983 – JUNE 1987   10AM – 12 NOON

(Schedule fluctuates according to student needs, length and difficulty level of material, number of competent volunteers present.)

10:00–11:00 WHOLE GROUP SHARED EXPERIENCES
10:00–10:15   Big Book(s). chart poems.
10:15–10:30   Teacher reads aloud 1-3 books. Discussion. Inferential questioning.
10:30–10:40   Phonics.
10:40–10:50   Teacher reads aloud 1-2 books. Discussion. Inferential questioning.
10:50–11:00   Students share completed published book or project. This time could also be used to introduce new projects, comment on ongoing work, specific needs in writing, interest centers, etc.
STUDENTS RETURN TO THEIR SEATS
(Reading specialist is available in first grades from 11:00–12:00)
11:00–11:20 JOURNAL WRITING
(Teachers/volunteers circulate and do one-to-one conferencing.)
11:20–12:00   Reading Groups and independent work time. (Students not in reading group are engaged in independent work, which is discussed in Chapter 5.)

1b   SEPTEMBER 1987 – JUNE 1988   9:15 AM – 11:40 AM

9:15–10:15   WHOLE GROUP SHARED EXPERIENCES
Reading and rereading of several Big Books.
Teacher reading and rereading of children's literature (5-6 books, including library books, classroom books and children's published books.) Discussion.
Higher-level questioning.
Reading and rereading of poems in enlarged print (4 new poems each week.) Development of reading strategies, including phonics in context during reading of Big Books.
'Quick phonics' (about 4 minutes.)
Collaborative writing (innovations on text and language experience stories.)
10:15–10:45   JOURNAL WRITING with teacher guidance.
10:45–11:40   READING GROUPS (3) 15-20 minutes for each group. Students not in reading groups are involved in reading, writing and listening activities of their choice.

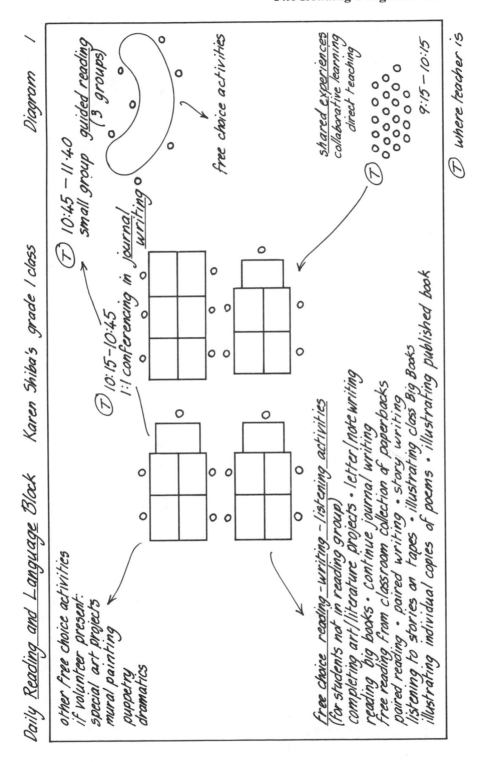

Daily Reading and Language Block   Karen Shiba's grade 1 class   Diagram 1

Ⓣ 10:45 – 11:40
small group guided reading
(3 groups)

free choice activities

shared experiences
collaborative learning
direct teaching

Ⓣ where teacher is

9:15 – 10:15

Ⓣ 10:15 – 10:45
1:1 conferencing in journal writing

other free choice activities
if volunteer present:
special art projects
mural painting
puppetry
dramatics

free choice reading – writing – listening activities
(for students not in reading group)
completing art/literature projects • letter/note writing
reading big books • continue journal writing
free reading from classroom collection of paperbacks
paired reading • paired writing • story writing
listening to stories on tapes • illustrating class Big Books
illustrating individual copies of poems • illustrating published book

Shared Book Experience

Much of the reading that takes place daily occurs during Shared Book Experience. (See *Resources for Teachers* section, especially Don Holdaway, for a thorough description of how a book is introduced, read, reinforced, and enjoyed. See also Andrea Butler, *Shared Book Experience, an Introduction*).

During this time, the students and teacher gather informally in the "reading center" — a specially designated place in the classroom where children sit comfortably on the floor with an unobstructed view of the Big Book easel, the chart stand, and the teacher. During this time, the children read Big Books, with print large enough to be seen by each child. Children are encouraged to predict the story through the illustrations and to listen to confirm their predictions. The teacher then reads the text and points to each word as it is spoken. Children are encouraged to join in when they are ready, and they do so enthusiastically. The one-to-one correspondence between the spoken word and the written word aids fluency, left to right progression, sight vocabulary, and successful reading. Quite naturally, with teacher guidance, children become aware of the concept of a word, spaces between words, and the conventions of print (punctuation, use of capital letters, quotation marks, paragraphs). Poems in enlarged print on chart paper are also shared with the students in much the same way as the Big Book stories. Students are encouraged to react to and interpret the poems on a personal basis. Shared book time is a high energy time for the teacher and students with emphasis on the mutual enjoyment of literature. Through rereading lots of easy, familiar books and thoroughly introducing new books, the reading process gets going quite naturally.

In introducing new books, necessary background knowledge for understanding the story is developed after examining what the students already know. Purposes are set for reading, questions are asked, and predictions will later be adjusted or confirmed. Book discussion might include the title and illustrations, a character's intentions, information about the author, comparison to other stories, and the mood or setting. Vocabulary, as needed for the comprehension of the story, is discussed in context. Literal questions are minimized in favor of higher level questioning ("What do you think...?", "Why do you think...?") which encourages thinking and respects individual and varied responses.

In addition to Big Books, the teacher reads many predictable stories, including old favorites, to and with the children. She invites their participation through listening, choral reading, predicting story outcomes, open-ended questioning, predicting words and phrases, and reacting to story events. Later on in the school year, a full length chapter book such as *Charlotte's Web* by E. B. White or *Winnie the Pooh* by A. A. Milne will also be read daily and discussed. The children are constantly immersed in the rich language of storybooks.

One of the most positive aspects of shared book time is the community spirit that develops. Each child feels the support from the predictable text and whole group experience, and the mood is relaxed, happy, and nonthreatening. Even the child who is not participating orally is following along visually and auditorily. For the children in our community, parents have commented on how well shared book time reinforces values of their culture. Children are encouraged to socialize in a community of friends as opposed to being seated at desks by themselves. Singing and group chanting is encouraged. Group movement and motions, as appropriate to particular books, songs, and poems, take place with high spirits. Children sit with their arms around their friends or holding hands with a buddy. It's an exciting, joyous time.

Questioning Techniques

During question/discussion time, literal questions are minimized and inferential questions are emphasized (predicting, analyzing, applying, evaluating). Getting children to focus ahead through questions about their predictions helps set a purpose for reading, keeps children focused on the story, and seems to aid overall comprehension. The goal is to have students actively participate in using available evidence to come up with thoughtful responses — not correct answers. All students are encouraged to offer predictions and interpretations based on background information, prior knowledge, illustrations, and the storyline.

W. Dorsey Hammond (Oakland University, Rochester, Michigan) suggests some guidelines for promoting comprehension and the reading-thinking process:

1. Ask questions about what children are about to read. This promotes higher level thinking. ("What do you think this story might be about?")

2. Ask important questions that drive the flow of the story. ("What is the major problem that ... has?", "Why is ... in trouble?")

3. Ask questions that encourage students to use knowledge they already have. ("Based on what you've read, what do you think will happen next? Why do you think so?")

4. Encourage students to listen to each other by encouraging student comments without restating what a student has said. ("Do you agree with ... response? Why or why not?") Paraphrasing discourages independent student thinking and puts the teacher, rather than the students, at the center of the discussion.

5. Avoid "diversionary questions" which take time and interest away from the focus of the story. ("Did this ever happen to you?")

Implicit in this type of questioning is a need to allow adequate wait time and encouraging risk taking so all students will participate. For those students reluctant to participate, ask questions that make it easy for them to respond. ("I know you don't know, but take a good guess.") Through the teacher's modeling of inferential questioning techniques, and guided practice, students eventually learn to ask themselves these kinds of questions before, during, and after reading.

Moving Beyond Skills Toward Strategies

Reading instruction in the United States has long been overfocused on skills. The basal text, accompanying worksheets, and mandatory standardized testing have contributed to the emphasis on skills mastery as an end in itself. No one would deny the importance of skills, but their usage needs to be strategic. Children's literature — with all its open-ended possibilities, meaningful text, and rich language — creates natural opportunities for moving beyond skills to developing reading strategies and for affirming reading as a process of getting meaning from print.

Traditionally, when educators have talked about "strategies", the term has been confused with "word attack skills", and word attack skills have generally referred to phonics. Strategies are the thoughtful plans or operations readers use while involved in the reading process; these plans are activated, adjusted, and modified for each new reading situation. Skills are the learned procedures the student has been repeatedly drilled on, and they are automatic, passive, and similar for each reading situation. Strategies imply high-level thinking, integration, and self-direction; skills imply low-level thinking, isolation, and accurate, rapid responses based on previous training. Understanding these differences is critical to understanding reading as a developmental process that the child self-directs and self-regulates. Don Holdaway (*The Foundations of Literacy*, 1979) p. 136, explains the differences:

The major difference between a 'skill' and a 'strategy' is the co-ordinating control of a human mind operating in purposeful, predictive, and self-corrective ways. The major difference, then, between 'skills teaching' and 'strategy teaching' concerns the presence or absence of self-direction on the part of the learner. In skills teaching the teacher tells the learner what to do and then 'corrects' or 'marks' the response. In strategy teaching the teacher induces the learner to behave in an appropriate way and encourages the learner to confirm or correct his own responses — *the teacher does not usurp the control which is crucial in mastering a strategy.*

The good reader, in developing personal strategies, coordinates and utilizes three major cues interactively and efficiently to make sense of print.

semantic cues — what is happening, meaning through text and illustrations

syntactic cues — using knowledge of language patterns, grammatical structure

graphophonic cues — letter-sound relationships, visual knowledge

The reading process, seen as an interaction of these cueing systems, can be viewed diagrammatically as follows:

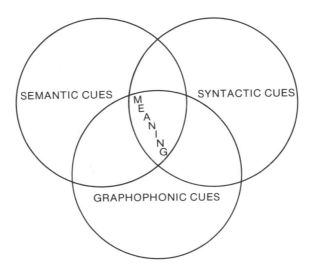

Any one area cannot exist in isolation from the others.

- The interaction of the three cueing systems within the reading process may occur so quickly as to appear simultaneous.

- Effective readers use these cue systems interdependently.

- Ineffective readers tend to rely too heavily upon graphophonic cues.

- The objective of the teacher should be to encourage all children to use the three cueing systems appropriately.

In teaching a skill, it is our job as teachers to help students make it a conscious strategy, not just an automatic response. The good reader who encounters an unknown word samples and predicts, then confirms and self-corrects. We need always to keep in mind that reading for meaning should underlie all encounters with print.

Helping Children Develop Strategies

Most beginning readers — reading meaningful, familiar books — do a number of things quite naturally. They use memory for text and meaning to make sense of print. They go back to the beginning of the sentence and reread when they become stuck. They use picture cues efficiently. They will attempt the unknown word based on the beginning letter-sound. Using the context, a child reading for meaning automatically begins to put in the correct word or a meaningful substitution.

Some examples of students reading for meaning follow:

Nancy read, "This friends like to go places", then made an immediate self-correction based on the structure of the sentence to, "These friends like to go places".

Freddy was reading from *Freckle Juice* by Judy Blume. He read "Ellen was small and cut", then immediately self-corrected to "cute".   "How did you know it was cute?" I asked.
"Cut wouldn't make sense," he responded.

In reading *Snow White and the Seven Dwarfs* (Littledale, 1980), when coming to the phrase "loaves of bread", Victor hesitated on "loaves", read ahead and then got it right. In the same book, he read, "Snow White was a little house", then immediately self-corrected and read, "Snow White saw a little house."

When readers get stuck, the teacher needs to help them to help themselves by providing prompts. Always the message to the child is, "How can you help yourself?" The child soon learns that he is responsible for doing the reading work and that the teacher will help him when necessary.

* Remind the child to start the sentence again. ("Try it again.")
* Ask the child if what he just said made sense. ("Does that make sense?" [semantics] "Does that sound right?" [structure])
* Tell him to skip the word and read on to the end of the sentence. ("Now, what is the word?")
* Encourage him to take an educated guess. ("What do you think it could be?")
* Remind him to take a careful look at the word. ("Could it be. . .?" "What would you expect to see at the beginning of. . .?" "What would you expect to see at the end of. . .?" "What do you see here?")
* Ask him if he can find that word on a previous page. ("Where else did you see that word?")

Sometimes, I use actual gestures and intonations to get the child moving. I might start the word out by saying the beginning sound, or if the word can be acted out in any way I would give a clue. If the word is "yelled", and the child has read "said", I might open my mouth wide as if I were about to yell. The child quickly takes over.

Because the goal is independence, moving beyond self-correcting into self-regulating behavior, it is the teacher's job to help make the student aware of strategies he is using. By saying, "How did you know it was...?", and "How can you tell?", you are making the child conscious of the operations he is using so that he will eventually do this on his own. We can never really know what's going on in the reader's mind in this complex task, but we can facilitate his growing fluency and confidence by positively attending to strategies he is beginning to use and by modeling strategies he needs to be using. The teacher needs to continue to praise and encourage the child for his attempts and approximations. "I like the way you went back to the beginning of the sentence." "I like the way you tried to help yourself by looking for that word on another page." "That was a good guess. Good for you!" By placing emphasis on specific strategies the child is attending to, the child is given the message that what he is doing is important and necessary to the reading process.

Encouraging Prediction

Care needs to be taken not to make error-free reading a goal. Overemphasizing word accuracy may focus attention away from other important high-level strategies and actually inhibit maximum reading achievement — especially at the beginning stages. Once a child is a fluent reader concentrating on meaning, more attention can be given to accuracy. Being able to read every word is not a prerequisite for comprehension. Good predicting means being able to use all available information — from the print, from the story, and from experience — to make a carefully reasoned judgment, as follows.

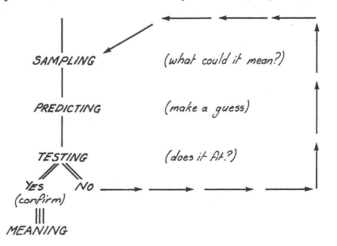

Meaningful substitutions are to be congratulated and encouraged. Encouraging prediction allows the child to test a hypothesis, to make an inference, and to confirm a decision. These are high-level strategies that good readers possess. Negative criticism is avoided by focusing on what the child can do. Confidence in the learner is implied by encouraging him to do the reading work and the monitoring of his own reading, using all of the operations that make up the reading process.

Putting Meaning Before Phonics

Phonics has become a loaded issue. One of the first questions teachers ask when they come to visit our first grades is, "Do you teach phonics?" When we say, "Yes", the sigh of relief is almost audible. It is as if acknowledging some attention to phonics gives credibility to what we are doing. The truth is many educators don't really believe children can learn to read without a heavy phonics base. We believe this because that's what we've been trained to believe. And our belief in the priority of phonics was validated by *Becoming a Nation of Readers: the Report of the Commission on Reading* (Anderson and others, 1985). Among other things, the report indicated that phonics knowledge is primary in facilitating word identification for beginning readers. However, the report also noted beginning readers need more meaningful material than current basals provide and urged publishers to include more memorable stories. Herein lies the contradiction; you can't write good stories if you're worrying about controlled vocabulary and phonic regularity. (See *Becoming a Nation of Readers* . . . for the panel's complete recommendations to teachers, parents, and publishers.)

I believe the reason it has taken me so long to understand the proper perspective of phonics is that decoding was the main emphasis in teaching reading in my undergraduate and graduate courses. I became a phonics expert, learning and applying all the rules and exceptions. Then too, the basal text was pretty much the only option. If there was a choice, it wasn't in which approach, only in which basal. Through years of careful observation of how children respond to reading, my priorities have gradually shifted. I have come to see that meaning must come before phonics in the most optimal reading instruction.

It has become crystal clear to me — and it has taken about ten years to come to this understanding — that children learn phonics best *after* they can already read. I am convinced that the reason our good readers are good at phonics is that in their being able to read they can intuitively make sense of phonics. When phonics is isolated as the main method of teaching, students are prevented from utilizing natural meaningful processes. Reading is then viewed as a word-by-word process which is quite inefficient, nonsensical, and frustrating.

The Transition

Although I have known intellectually that meaning comes before phonics, it did not hit my deep gut level until this past year when I worked part of the time as a Reading Recovery teacher. Reading Recovery is an early intervention program for severely at-risk first-graders who are identified early in the fall of first grade. Students receive fifteen to twenty weeks of thirty minutes a day intensive, one-to-one instruction that combines reading lots of "little books" and writing. The goal is to accelerate the student to the average level of his classroom peers and to make him an independent reader with a self-improving system. The program was developed, researched, and tested by psychologist and educator Marie Clay, in New Zealand, where it is a nationally instituted and funded program.

Up to this time, all my work as a reading specialist had been with groups of children. I had never really observed the reading process with total attention to one student. What I witnessed was that these students relied primarily on meaning — especially picture cues —and memory for text, at the very beginning levels. They became competent readers without ever having mastered short vowels and other phonics generalizations: that understanding would come later. When in difficulty, the last resort was to try phonics — but even then, never in isolation but in the context of the sentence or story.

So with all that, I am still uneasy talking about teaching phonics. I feel guilty because I have taught phonics out of context for many years. I feel apologetic for being unenlightened for so long. During shared experiences, our phonics teaching has followed the book reading and has been taught in isolation in an explicit, sequential manner.

Following the sequence of a program called *Recipe for Reading* by Nina Traub with Frances Bloom (Cambridge: Educators Publishing Service, Inc., 1975), individual sounds have been introduced and the blending of these sounds has been practiced using prescribed words. As much as possible, multisensory activities have been used to present new letter sounds. For example, when the "ch" sound is introduced the children eat *ch*ocolate *ch*ips in addition to reading such words as "chop", "chip", "chap", "chat" and putting in appropriate dramatic movements. Using 9" x 12" cards in enlarged print, one new letter-sound — with its six to ten related words — is introduced each day, and some previous sounds and words are reviewed. As the cards are flashed to the whole group, children join in as they do for shared book experience. There is no pressure, and students learn at their own rate. The children enjoy the fast-paced daily phonics, and visitors to the classroom comment on the children's enthusiasm in chanting the words together. When the children return to their seats, before journal writing begins, students write three to four words from the morning's lesson. This is done collaboratively, with the teacher quickly circulating about the room to offer guidance.

While I no longer believe that this kind of teaching is necessary, I am still somewhat comfortable with the positive effect the phonics knowledge has on the writing. There's no question that children use the letter-sound correspondence in their daily writing where that knowledge is a tool for easier expression.

For teachers used to daily phonics worksheets, it takes time to become convinced that there are workable alternatives. It takes careful observation of young readers, an understanding of the reading process, an open mind, and willingness to risk taking that giant step of meaningfully integrating phonics into the total reading program. For teachers in process, Don Holdaway's *Independence in Reading*, Appendix D, "Sequential Development of Reading Skills', (pp. 157-162) includes a suggested sequence of teaching letter-sound associations according to reading-age levels.

What We Are Moving Toward

Some of us have begun teaching and applying phonics and other word attack skills during shared book experience, in the meaningful context of the story and group situation. This is a big step, one that has evolved gradually as our understanding of the reading process has deepened. We have begun modeling ways of figuring out unknown words in context. For example, using the Big Book we use "post-its" (small, removable, adhesive papers) or a sliding mask (a cardboard window) to cover word parts or whole words in a cloze procedure. Students are asked to predict possibilities and alternatives, and we confirm or revise predictions based on the visual evidence and prior knowledge. (See *Foundations of Literacy*, by Don Holdaway, pp. 75-76 for instructions on masking.)

Karen Shiba, a first grade teacher who taught phonics in isolation for four years, now relates most of her teaching of word attack skills to the rereading of the shared books. She is teaching more and more of the phonics and strategies in the context of the Big Books where she encourages students to make discoveries and see patterns in words. She now spends about four minutes a day on whole group phonics in isolation, but she no longer has the students write the individual words. She states, "I still do a few minutes of whole group phonics because the kids love it, and after the intensity and high energy of shared book time, I find this a calming transition time before students begin journal writing and reading groups."

The Big Book *When Goldilocks Went to the House of the Bears* (Green, Pollock and Scarffe) works well as a book to begin to develop strategies and print awareness with beginning first-graders. The text of this highly predictable book begins:

> *When Goldilocks went*
> *to the house of the bears,*
> *Oh, what did her blue eyes see?*　　p. 3
>
> *A bowl that was BIG*
> *A bowl that was small,*
> *A bowl that was tiny,*
> *And that was all.*　　　　　　　p. 4
>
> *She ate from them, 1. 2. 3.*　　p. 5

The book continues in the same pattern with Goldilocks encountering a chair, a bed, and then a bear.

On the first reading, I read the book in its entirety, and while I might pause and ask the children to predict the next action, the emphasis is on enjoying the book together. On subsequent readings, we begin to examine the text. "Why do you think 'BIG' is in upper case letters?" "What does the '?' mean at the end of the sentence?" "Can someone find the word 'bowl' three times? The word begins with the 'b' sound and ends with the 'l' sound." (I would give the sounds, not the letters, as cues.) "How do you know that is 'bowl'?" (Get them to verbalize so the strategy becomes conscious.) "Can someone find the lower case letter that is the same as 'B'?" (Point to 'B') "What are the two rhyming words on page 4?" "What other words can you think of that also rhyme with 'all' and 'small'?" ('ball', 'tall', 'call', etc.) "How would I write those? What would 'ball' begin with?" (Write it on the board or chart.) "Who can find the word 'was?' It begins like 'when' and 'what'. What letter does it begin with? Who can find another 'was'?"

With very beginning readers developing letter-sound association, I use the context of the story and focus on beginning and ending consonants first, move to digraphs and then consonant blends, and lastly to short vowels and vowel combinations. In reading for meaning, the vowel knowledge is least important. Especially for the struggling reader, short vowels are initially difficult to grasp and are better addressed after the child is already reading. To read the difficult and high-frequency words such as "what", "when", "this", "that", etc., it is the knowledge of consonants and digraphs in meaningful context that will best help the young reader. Always, the reader checks himself by what makes sense. With the lowest-ability readers, these kinds of strategies will need to be reinforced and retaught during reading group. I keep a small blackboard and chalk at the reading table to highlight important words and help make generalizations as we are reading.

While the teacher is guiding and facilitating the lesson, the children are able to figure out most of the responses with help from each other and what they already know about print. As much as possible, it is important not to "tell" the answer but to continue probing until they figure it out. This gives the message that the reader needs to do the thinking and careful examination. Knowledge about letters, punctuation, basic sight vocabulary, and word families are easily learned in the context of a familiar story. Features and words pointed out in the text can be reinforced with enlarged-print word cards, sentence strips which may be cut apart and reassembled, and charts of word-family patterns as they are developed through the context of the story being read.

One activity that works very well in first and second grades is to reinforce the teaching of digraphs (ch, sh, th, wh), consonant blends, and vowel combinations through teacher and student-made wall strips. Using colored mural paper that has been cut in half lengthwise into long strips, I write the phonics combination that has been focused on at the top of the strip and the words from our reading that fit the generalization below it. Students have great fun adding in additional words that fit the pattern as they come across them in their reading and writing. Teachers who have tried this activity report that students who have had difficulty with "traditional" phonics can relate to it in this manner. (Idea adapted from *Towards a Reading-Writing Classroom* by Andrea Butler and Jan Turbill, p. 32.)

The important difference in teaching now is that phonics and word attack skills are taught in a meaningful way, *as the need arises* in the context of the literature, as opposed to a sequential, predetermined hierarchy unrelated to the actual reading of text or to specific students. In my experience, the learning carryover is much greater when the child has a real purpose for learning the skill. By guiding and encouraging children to make thoughtful links and connections, skills become strategies that the student transfers to other reading situations.

Developing a Sight Vocabulary

Just as I have become convinced that phonics is best taught in the context of meaning, the same holds true for sight vocabulary. While we spent the first three years teaching sight vocabulary in isolation through traditional flash card drill of high frequency words, our own observations in the classroom — as well as a wider body of research — confirmed that children were learning these words naturally through repeated readings of favorite books and through their own daily writing.

An analysis of a favorite book, *The Magic Fish* (Littledale, 1969) gives a clear demonstration of how sight words can be mastered naturally and easily in context. (See Figure 2.) Almost 40% of the total list of basic sight vocabulary (Edward Dolch, 1949) is included in this short and easily readable book. Many words occur repeatedly. "Said" occurs 36 times; "want" occurs 21 times; "went" occurs 9 times; "was" occurs 21 times. Reversal problems are uncommon when words which might be confusing are encountered frequently in meaningful context. More importantly, children get continuous practice of sight vocabulary without boring drill, and they easily gain control of words repeated often in the story.

A list of high frequency "Bookwords" that comes from literature for young children, as opposed to basal textbooks, is reproduced as Appendix D. (The number next to each word reflects frequency in occurrence based on four hundred storybooks.) It is recommended that teachers focus on these words as they appear in the context of classroom reading and writing, not in isolation. Nowhere apart from school are reading and writing treated in a decontextualized manner. Another important factor to keep in mind is that dealing with words in isolation seems to be particularly difficult for disadvantaged and low-achieving students who need the added cues the context provides. The most sensible way to help beginning readers acquire a needed sight vocabulary is through meaningful context where the words occur naturally over and over again.

Reading Groups

Developing Fluent Reading

Beginning readers read with oral fluency when they have had repeated exposure to a book through hearing the story, through repeated readings, and through modeling the teacher's reading. Such fluency enables them to assume the role of a reader — reading with inflection, emotion, and enjoyment — and to concentrate on meaning instead of decoding. Much of this practice takes place during reading group.

Once students have understood the concept of a word, left to right directionality, conventions of how a book works, and can do one-to-one matching, they are on their way to reading. At the start of the school year, almost all books have rhyme, rhythm and/or repetition which makes reading for the beginner predictable and easy. Fluency and confidence gradually grow as the students have continuous practice. As children read words more easily, they are better able to concentrate on meaning. In addition, because children are already familiar with the story, having heard it in shared experiences, they read with expression in phrases that flow with the language instead of word-by-word. We might read a story as many as six or more times in

*Figure 2   An Analysis of words in **The Magic Fish** — retold by Freya Littledale*

Dolch Basic Sight Words and number of times occurring
(83 words — comprise 38% of total list of 220)

Word	n	Word	n	Word	n	Word	n
a	27	in	9	they	1	he	8
at	1	it	1	to	34	has	2
and	20	I	20	that	2	here	3
any	1	is	1	then	3	him	10
ask(ed)	7	just	1	tell	9	his	20
are	3	live(d)	2	the	95	put	2
be	14	let	1	this	4	said	36
big	1	make	1	there	4	see	3
but	3	made	3	three	1	shall	3
by	1	me	5	two	1	she	20
call(ed)	4	much	1	too	3	so	10
came	2	must	2	today	1	well	3
can	1	my	4	up	1	will	4
come	3	never	4	upon	1	wish	6
catch	2	no	1	very	1	you	5
day	3	now	7	want	2	your	3
did	2	of	15	what	21	don't	4
does	3	old	4	why	4		
every	1	on	2	with	10		
for	4	once	1	went	1		
from	4	pull(ed)	2	was	9		
go	21	pretty	7	we	6		

Other Words (51) and number of times occurring

Word	n	Word	n	Word	n
wife	25	week(s)	3	throne	1
fish	28	back	15	sitting	1
didn't	2	more	3	time	1
fisherman	18	than	3	silly	1
sea	9	castle	9	beautiful	1
oh	4	mind	4	poor	1
magic	6	woman	2	something	1
house	7	begs	4	felt	1
man	20	prince	3	end	1
home	7	really	2	line	1
gone	3	water	2	nice	1
stars	4	Queen	11	inside	1
moon	4	gold	3	angry	1
sun	4	listen	4	last	1
happy	12	cannot	12	thing	1
hut	4	dress	4	fine	1
gone	3	wore	3	crown	1

reading group at the beginning of the school year. The students do not become bored because each successive reading brings greater success as they become skilled at anticipating which word(s) comes next.

It is clear from their smooth phrasing and intonation that they are understanding the story, as well as enjoying it. Visitors to our classrooms frequently comment on how fluently the children read. It is not something we particularly notice because it is a natural, daily occurrence. When children read meaningful, predictable text they do not read word-by-word and are not word-dependent.

The following steps to develop fluent reading have proven to be successful with beginning readers with whom I have worked:

1. Oral reading of a predictable book to a small group of students. (Most often, the book will have already been introduced through shared book experience.)
2. Rereading of the book with students following visually in their personal copy of the book (the child hears the language and sees the language as he points to each word).
3. Repetition of the story including pauses at predictable words (students supplying words in a modified cloze procedure).
4. Modeling by students of teacher's oral reading, one page at a time.
5. Students alternating reading pages from beginning to end of the book with teacher offering practical guidance as needed.
6. Students practicing reading a book to a parent or sibling.
7. Students reading a book independently.
8. When returning a book, students orally reading one page for fluency check, and orally retelling the story for comprehension check.

As reading proficiency develops, steps 2-4 can gradually be eliminated.

What Happens in Reading Group

The purposes of reading group are to read a familiar book for pleasure in a supportive setting, to develop reading strategies, and to build confidence in students as readers. Through modeling, guided practice, and feedback the student gradually moves toward independence. The teacher selects a book that she feels the students can succeed with and which they will be able to read with minimal teacher guidance. (See *Resources for Teachers, Recommended Literature.*) The book has already been heard and discussed by the whole class, probably on repeated occasions, so children are confident and eager to begin. Emphasis is on developing oral fluency in reading and encouraging students to make sense of print through strategies they are developing. The value of oral reading is in being able to guide the child in helping himself in the predicting, confirming, self-correcting process. By hearing him read and by questioning him, the teacher can model ways for the child to monitor his own reading.

In our two first grade classes, approximately 45 students are divided into six reading groups. Initially, they are grouped homogeneously according to standardized test scores and teacher judgment based on personal observation and input from parents and former kindergarten teachers. While this grouping facilitates effective small group guided instruction, it is important to keep in mind that this grouping is but one part of the reading program. The majority of time devoted to reading takes place with the whole class through shared book experience — where all students are exposed to the same literature and high-level questioning — and through daily self-selected, individualized reading.

Throughout the year, much movement takes place among the groups and is based on student progress, group dynamics, and teacher evaluation. There are no "Redbirds" or "Bluebirds" but rather *The Little Bear* group, the *Freckle Juice* group or simply Brian's group or Anna's group. One of the benefits of teaching reading with literature is that children are definitely less aware of high and low groups. While low-ability students may be reading *Little Bear* books in reading group, high-ability students may be choosing to sign out these books to read independently. Students rarely ask what group they are in, and as all books in the classroom are available to all students to sign out to read independently, there seems to be little competition.

Reading groups convene for approximately fifteen to twenty minutes each. As the reading specialist, I go into the classroom or work in a small room adjacent to the classroom. So, with three teachers (the two first grade teachers and myself), the entire time devoted to six reading groups is about 40 minutes as each of us meets with two groups consecutively. Independent work time is about 20 minutes for each student and includes the time a student is not in reading group. Direct instruction time is maximized in this manner. (Refer to Figure 1b and Diagram 1 in this chapter for current schedule/grouping in a first grade classroom where one teacher has the responsibility for teaching all reading groups.)

The entire reading group time is spent reading a predictable book with continuous, meaningful text, and this is true even for the lowest-ability readers. This is in direct contrast to what usually happens to poor readers who spend most of their reading time on introduction of vocabulary, isolated skills, and decoding with little actual time spent on reading. To develop confidence in the students, many books are read at the same level. This pays dividends later on. When students find the material easy to handle, they can develop and strengthen strategies along with their confidence and fluency. Later on, they will take leaps toward reading more challenging material.

Students take turns reading pages in their personal copies of the book. Sometimes a page will only be read once. Other times, everyone might read the page. Students are expected to follow along visually with their reading fingers to maintain one-to-one matching and attention. Later they follow with their eyes and voice, and with more print on a page, many students use a book marker that they move to reveal one line at a time. Most students give up finger pointing naturally. With a few, where it seems to be slowing down the reading, they may need to be encouraged to read with their eyes only.

Students do not say, "I haven't had that word yet", when they come upon an unfamiliar word. Since they are reading for meaning, they generally make some attempt to fill in what makes sense if the teacher gives enough wait time (up to 10 seconds) and encouragement. One rule that we are very firm on is that another member of the group is not allowed to tell a student a word. The students understand that it is the reader's job to do the work, and the reader needs quiet thinking time to do this. If a student is unable to go on, I might say, "Go back to the beginning of the sentence and try it again" or "Skip that word and read to the end of the sentence. Now what do you think it might be?" Sometimes I use oral cloze and say, "I am going to read up to the difficult word. Listen and follow along. Can you try it now?" If he is still unable to go on, I then ask if someone can help, and the word is supplied. Often the word is just supplied so that the student does not get bogged down by one word in his otherwise fluent reading. It is always the role of the teacher to guide the student in figuring out what options he has and what he already knows that he can apply. If students are helped to see connections and develop strategies, they begin to assume responsibility for their reading and move gradually towards independence.

Each person gets at least one turn to read and usually several opportunities. In the beginning stages, the teacher — or another student — models the pages to be read. At later stages, when the student is reading more confidently, he has the choice of having the page read first by the teacher or trying it himself. While books in levels 1-5 might be read three to five times, books in higher levels may need to be read only once or twice. Students know that this is a fun time. Sometimes, we read pages together, as in *Tikki Tikki Tembo* (Mosel, 1968), where they delight in the sound of the language. They all want to read and volunteer to do so. There is no pressure or competition fostered. There is a spirit of friends sitting down together to read a much-loved story and to help each other doing so. Children can't wait to come to reading group. After a book is completed in group, it goes home to be read, practiced, and enjoyed with the family.

Students not in reading group are working on book projects. While literature extension projects (see Chapter 5 for discussion and examples) are the first priority during independent work time, students may also continue journal writing, illustrating a published book, reading a book, or working in one of the many interest centers throughout the room.

Moving into Silent Reading

Eventually the child moves from oral reading into silent reading, and this occurs in the spring of first grade for many of the children. Although they are initially subvocalizing, they now have the confidence and strategies to read new material independently.

Nathan, a bright child who had struggled with the reading process, needed to be pushed into silent reading. We were reading *The Terrible Mr. Twitmeyer* (Lillian Moore, 1952) in reading group. While we still did some oral reading because the children enjoyed it, now we were spending most of the time predicting ahead and discussing what had happened in a chapter that had been assigned silently. Nathan was visibly uncomfortable with the silent reading. Typically, he would go back to his seat, and every time he couldn't read a word go up to the teacher for help. We kept telling him to skip the word, put in what made sense and go on, explaining that's what good readers do. He finally took the risk, plodded through on his own and realized he could understand the story without being able to read every word. From that point on, there was no stopping him. He read everything in sight.

Independent Reading

One of the most important parts of the literature program is the wide reading students are encouraged to do. Our own observations, together with a wide body of research evidence, clearly affirm that the *amount* of reading children do greatly affects their growth in reading. (Clark, 1976; Fader, 1982; Koeller, 1981) The number of books read positively affects reading comprehension and attitude. Therefore, the classroom as well as the school library must provide access to large numbers of quality books, and each child must be encouraged to read a substantial amount of material in and out of school.

Once a book has been read and discussed in shared experiences, multiple copies are placed in the reading center. Later on in the school year, as students become fluent readers, unfamiliar titles are also available, but the majority of titles and stories — there are about 400 by the end of the year — are familiar to the students. The student, recognizing a favorite title and being familiar with the story, picks up the book by himself or with a friend, and engages in reading-like behavior — going through the pictures and retelling the story in his own words. Through desire and practice, eventually the student reads the book. Because children have experienced the joy of reading, they want to read. When *Pierre* by Maurice Sendak was introduced, read, sung, and seen visually on film, groups of children gathered before school for days and read and sang *Pierre* together. Everyone wanted to be part of the community of readers.

Daily Book Sign Out

Beginning the first month of school, children self-select books and sign them out daily, a great advantage to those students whose homes are not filled with books, who are not regular library users, and who may not have benefited from regular prereading home experiences before first grade. Students may choose to sign out one to two books from the classroom library of commercial and student-authored books. We call the books students sign out for independent reading in all the grades, their WEB books, a term borrowed from the Ohio State University, "The Web" (See *Resources for Teachers* section) to indicate "**W**onderfully **E**xciting **B**ooks.") A letter is sent home to parents the first day of book sign-out. (See Appendix E.) For the first few months, parents need to be actively involved on a daily basis, but gradually this involvement diminishes as children's reading efficiency grows.

It has been interesting to note that some parents who have been reluctant to get involved in their children's education are inadvertently brought into the school community through their children's enthusiasm. Kelly, picked up each day at an after school program, tried to read in the dark as soon as she got into the car. Once in the house, with her coat still on, she said, "Mommy, you must listen to me *now!*" Mom was busy getting dinner together, and Kelly would corner her brother or sister and insist they listen to the book she had signed out from the classroom.

After routines are set up, the children become quite responsible about remembering to bring their books back and forth to school. The student brings the book back from home when he can read it fluently and with understanding (usually one-two days). The classroom teacher, upper grade student volunteers, and I do book check before school and/or at the end of the day. Either the child, student volunteer, or teacher selects a page to be read, and the child is expected to "read it like a book". Since the book has already been discussed in shared experiences, this is mainly a fluency check. In the spring, when the child may be choosing unfamiliar books, it is mainly a comprehension check, and the student may be asked to retell a part of the story. If the student reads smoothly (practically error free and at a good pace) and can tell about the story, the book title and date are entered in the student's reading record. (See Appendix F.) If the book check indicates that the book needs more practice or rereading, the child is encouraged to take it home again, but the final decision is left with the child. Students always have the option of returning or exchanging books they do not like or find too difficult.

The children are quite proficient at choosing books that are at their level. In fact, what they choose often tells us something we have failed to pick up. Sasha, who was reading with the highest-ability readers, was selecting very easy books and thoroughly enjoying them. After observing her more closely in reading group, I could sense a pressure she felt to keep up. We moved her to another group where she began to relax and gain more confidence. While the children have the option to choose any book in the room, they usually know what they can handle, and choose accordingly.

Some Personal Thoughts on Reading

Almost all the reading I do as an adult is free-choice reading. The newspapers, magazines, journals, and books that I read are personally selected. Many of the books are recommended by friends or reviewers; there is fiction and non-fiction, challenging and non-challenging material. Some books I read just to relax, some to gain information. Some favorites I reread for pleasure and new insights. The point is, nobody is telling me what I should read. If they were, I would feel put off reading. Self-selected reading is *essential* if the reading habit is going to develop.

I did not become a reader until I was in high school. I learned the mechanics of reading at school and have memories of completing lots of worksheets, but I did little additional reading outside of the requirements. My mother, who finished several books a week and who was off by herself reading when the rest of the family watched television, kept giving me books, talking about them enthusiastically, and gently coaxing me to give them a try. In that way, I read such books as *The Good Earth* by Pearl S. Buck, *Gone With the Wind* by Margaret Mitchell, *Atlas Shrugged* by Ayn Rand, *Of Human Bondage* by Somerset Maugham, *Madame Bovary* by Gustave Flaubert, and *Anna Karenina* by Leo Tolstoy, and became a reader myself. It was seeing her as a reading model and receiving her encouragement that brought me into the reading community.

I think one of the reasons sustained silent reading is so powerful in the school environment is that students see their teacher engaged in a similar activity. For students who do not have reading models at home, this is critical. In addition, because of the overwhelming amount of television watching children do, the school must assume the responsibilty for developing readers.

4 Using Predictable Books
What You Need to Know

For teachers desiring to try another reading approach, one of the major problems has been that meaningful and readable books for the emergent reader have been difficult to find. Nonetheless, enough quality books *do* exist to make a literature approach feasible and desirable at the very beginning levels. Books that our first-graders have enjoyed and completed successfully within the first several months of school are included in the *Resources for Teachers* section at the end of this book. These are predictable books that are easily readable because of the following qualities:

> **rhyme or rhythmic quality**
> **repetition or cumulative structure**
> **natural language flow**
> **a meaningful story**
> **quality illustrations that match with text**

These are the qualities that make it possible for the very beginning reader to meet immediate success, and these are the books we begin with in shared book experience. Predictable books diminish the need for text with limited vocabulary and phonetic regularity.

The predictable books included in our first grade classroom collection are in paperback editions; they are used in shared book experience, self-selected reading before and during school, reading groups, and at home for independent practice and enjoyment. Some of these titles are available as Big Books — commercial and teacher-made — and there is no doubt that the highlight of each day is the reading together of these Big Books. Along with other stories, children delight in hearing and reading these books over and over again.

We utilize the resources of the school and community libraries to supplement our paperback collection. With the assistance of the librarians, we bring in a wide variety of additional fiction and non-fiction to go along with theme units we introduce in the curriculum.

In addition to storybooks, poetry is a favorite daily part of our shared reading experience. Using poetry anthologies, favorite poems from our childhood, nursery rhymes, and songs and chants, we select what appeals to us personally. The poems relate to the seasons, holidays, months of the year, family, humor, and any topic that interests us and the children. The poems, clearly visible in enlarged print, are read aloud with much expression. The children develop a natural love of poetry, and some begin to write their own poems. Multiple copies of poetry books, such as *Hailstones and Halibut Bones* (Mary O'Neill, 1961), are also part of our classroom collection.

While this chapter will focus on commercial predictable books for beginning readers, "predictable books" also applies to books using children's own language as well as books for older readers. For emergent readers, their own oral language patterns, as well as the common and familiar language experiences they share with others, constitute the most highly predictable reading. For older readers, predictable books use natural language; a meaningful, well-developed story including strong characterization and setting; a clear organizational pattern; repetition of ideas; and quality illustrations that match with the text. Books with these qualities will be referred to in the chapters on Grade 2 and Grade 3.

Rationale for Paperback Books

Initially it was budget considerations that made us buy paperback editions of books. We wanted multiple copies so students could read along in personal copies and four paperback copies could be purchased for the price of one hard-cover book. Surprisingly, with careful attention to book handling and ongoing repair by students and volunteer parents, the books have held up remarkably well. After four years of hard use in our first grades, most of our original copies are still in use.

Besides the acceptable durability, the psychological appeal and intrigue of paperbacks quickly became apparent. Their strikingly colorful covers, their lightness and small size, and their easy transportability, seem to promote a sense of informality. Teachers and librarians report that given a choice, a child will choose a paperback over a hardbound book with the same title. Children *do* judge a book by its cover! This seems to be particularly relevant and motivating for older students who have been turned off to reading and who view the paperback as less threatening. Anyone who doubts the positive effect of a massive dose of paperbacks in a school need only read Daniel Fader's account of the increase in reading interest by boys who had not previously acquired the reading habit. (*The New Hooked on Books*, 1976, pp. 79-96.)

Determining Readability Levels

I stopped using formal measures of readability after my group of second-graders transcended their standardized-test-given reading level. We found that the conventional readability formulae, based on word length (number of syllables) and sentence length, were not helpful in determining reading level for real literature. In fact, it is the short words such as "now", "what", and "then" which create difficulty, while longer words, such as "hippopotamus", "rhinoceros", and "grandfather", are actually easier to read. In a familiar, meaningful story with good picture and context cues, the initial consonant is often enough of a cue for a student to be able to read the word successfully. The interesting length and configuration of the word, plus the visual picture it conjures up, also aid the reader.

Yet, reading level is of great importance in developing a literature program. To facilitate the use of predictable books in our literature program, Karen Shiba, the first grade teacher, and I leveled many of the books in our program from easiest to hardest. In determining readability we used the following factors: size of print, amount and layout of print on a page, consistency of print throughout the book, page format, complexity and layout of sentences, use of punctuation, how well the illustrations aid the text, concept load, organization of the story, clarity and predictability of the text, amount of rhyme and repetition, student interest and reactions, and any other factors that seemed relevant to the particular book.

In this way, a new teacher or substitute coming into the literature program has some rough guidelines on book difficulty. It has also helped us with the organization of such a large number of books. We have designated twelve levels with the most difficult being about mid second grade level. At that point, the child is a fluent, capable reader, and the teacher will find suitable books for the student quite easily. To avoid fostering any competition, we have been careful to code the books with small different-colored shapes for each level (as opposed to numbers). We place these on one corner of the book, and as far as we know, these level markers have gone mostly unnoticed by the students.

The book levels and corresponding books are listed in the *Resources for Teachers* section. Levels listed are approximations at best and are meant only as a guide. Children in another setting might react to the books differently from our children. We "kid tested" the books over a two-year period and made adjustments according to children's reactions. If a group of students seemed to find a book harder than we had originally thought it was, we moved it up a level and tried it there. If they found it easier than we thought, we moved it down a level and tried it with other students. If the book seemed to work consistently well at a particular level, we moved it into that level.

Encouragingly, this approach has support from the International Reading Association and the National Council of Teachers of English. In a joint statement in 1984, these organizations recognized the serious problems that occur when publishers rely solely on readability formulae to determine readability levels. Teacher evaluation and teacher observation of students using texts were amongst the recommended alternative ways of measuring text difficulty.

Examples of Predictable Books

Our first grade classrooms overflow with hundreds of best-loved children's books. These books, which were written and illustrated to bring pleasure to children, serve as the mainstay of our reading program. For easy reference, I have divided them into four categories: rhyme, rhythm and repetition; rhyme; repetition; predictability and high interest. (See *Resources for Teachers* section for detailed listing.) The best books in our list have *all* these elements.

We are always on the lookout for new, quality titles and as budget considerations allow, we incorporate the best of the new books into our program. For example, some exceptional Big Books are now available in science. The unusually clear and beautiful photographs, along with the meaningful content, make these valuable additions. (Rigby Education, 1987.)

Rhyme, Rhythm and Repetition

Some books, like *Who's in the Shed?* (Parkes, 1986) and *I Was Walking Down the Road* (Barchas, 1975), combine rhyme, rhythm, and repetition, making these especially predictable and easy to read. The opening pages from these books follow.

> Down at the farm
> one Saturday night,
> the animals woke
> with a **terrible** fright.

There was *howling*
    and *growling*
    and *roaring*
    and *clawing*

as something was led
    from a truck
      to the shed.

"Who's in the shed?"
everyone said.
"Who's in the shed?"

"Let me have a peep,"
baaed the big white sheep.
"Let me have a peep."

So the sheep had a peep
through a hole in the shed.
What did she see?

The story continues in the format of the last two stanzas with a cow, a mare, a hen, a pig, and finally an indignant circus bear unmasked. *Who's in the Shed?* is a much-loved story. The children enjoy it first as a Big Book in shared book experience, and then in personal, small copies. The books are beautifully and vibrantly illustrated and have additional visual appeal with peepholes cut out of most of the pages. Looking through the peephole reveals an animal part such as an eye or claw, and the children have great fun speculating, along with the animal characters in the book, what the creature could be. Where there is conversation and "speech marks", as they sometimes call quotation marks in New Zealand, boldface type is used. Boldface type, or type in a different color to highlight conversation, is a natural way to encourage children to take notice of this convention.

I was walking down the road.
    Then I saw a little toad.
    I caught it.
    I picked it up.
    I put it in a cage.

I was looking at the sky.
    Then I saw a butterfly.
    I caught it.
    I picked it up.
    I put it in a cage.

I Was Walking Down the Road is a wonderful example of a predictable book that has all the qualities that make it fun and easy to read. The rhyming words are predictable because the picture cues and the rhyme are so reliable. Once they have heard the story once, and even before the first reading is finished, children are chiming in. They know what is coming next. During the first reading I sometimes use a procedure called oral cloze, where I pause and wait for the group to supply the predictable rhyming word at the end of the sentence. I begin:

> "I was working with a rake.
> Then I saw a little . . . . . .

Based on the picture cues and what makes sense and the knowledge that it is a rhyming story, the children predict the word quite easily, even when it is a two-syllable word.

> *"I was reading something funny.*
> *Then I saw a little . . . . . ."*

It is appropriate to ask, "How did you know that word was bunny?" And the child responds, "Because it starts with a "b". For very beginning readers, often the recognition of the initial consonant of a word in meaningful context is enough of a cue to read the word. If the child had said "rabbit", I would probe, "Could that be rabbit?" "Why do you think it's rabbit?" "What letter would you expect to see at the beginning of rabbit?" "What letter would you expect to see at the end of rabbit?" Keeping in mind that we are building an atmosphere of trust and risk taking, you want to explore the child's thinking without saying, "No, that's wrong." You want the child to do the work and the thinking and to realize that he can figure it out for himself, and, in the process of figuring out, that it's all right to make errors.

The three lines *"I caught it.*
I picked it up.
I put it in a cage."

are repeated *eleven* times in this short book. Even low-ability readers pick up the vocabulary with so many repetitions. While "caught" is not a word you would expect to find in a first reader, it becomes easily recognizable once the child is familiar with the story. The child only needs to see the beginning c, look at the picture cues, and use his memory of the story to read the refrain.

Teachers often ask if the child would be able to read "caught" out of context. Probably not at this very early stage, but since all the reading the child is doing is in context, it is not significant at this time. Later in the year, as the child's sight vocabulary grows through doing extensive reading, the answer would be "yes".

An important advantage of a book like this is that difficult words like "was" and "saw" are learned easily. When I was working with learning-disability students, I had whole kits whose primary function was to remediate reversals. With predictable literature, we have no reversals. It is no longer a problem.

> *"I was pushing a wheelbarrow.*
> *Then I saw a little sparrow."*

The child never says, "I *saw* pushing a wheelbarrow" because it doesn't make sense. The child does not say, "Then I *was* a little sparrow" because that does not go with the picture cue or his memory of the story.

On the next to last page, the girl who has now collected nine pets says:

> *"I was looking at my pets.*
> *Then I saw them look at me.*
>
> *I sat a while.*
> *I thought a while.*
> *And then . . ."*

At this point, the children will read the last page without ever seeing it. The book is so predictable that they know the last page says, "I set them free." Children learn that text is predictable and reliable as well as fun and easy to read.

With a book like this, it is easy to get children to make up their own rhyming couplets and write their own versions. Some examples of a collaborative effort between teacher and students might include:

> *"I was watering my plant.*
> *Then I saw a little ant."*
>
> *"I was opening a box.*
> *Then I saw a little fox."*
>
> *"I was eating toast with jam.*
> *Then I saw a little lamb."*

The teacher might supply the first line, if students are having difficulty on their own. The student version can be written as enlarged text on chart paper, made into a Big Book illustrated by the class, or run off as little books for the students to illustrate and read together.

Rhyme

A rhymed story is unforgettable. Rhyming words are fun to join in on and easy to remember. Part of the charm of *The Hungry Thing* (Slepian and Seidler, 1972), a story about a monster with an insatiable appetite, is the delightful rhyme. An excerpt follows:

"He's underfed.
Have some bread."
Said a lady
Dressed in red.
> *"It seems to me*
> *He'd like some tea,"*
> *Said a fellow*
> *Up a tree.*

"A bit of rice
Might be nice,"
Said a baby,
Sucking ice.

The Hungry Thing refuses these offerings and others, but finally, with much help from a little boy, the townspeople figure out how to satisfy the Hungry Thing's desire for food.

"Just look!"
Said the cook.
> *"Let's all try!"*
> *Was the cry.*
So they all got busy.

"Have some smello."
They gave him some Jello.
> *"Have some thread."*
> *They gave him some bread.*
"Have a fanana."
They gave him a banana.

Children love reading this book. Having heard the story at least once before attempting to read it, they are assured of reading at least some words correctly. The rhyme makes anticipating the words easy and fun, and children enjoy creating their own rhyming couplets to offer the Hungry Thing.

Another book that children delight in is *Red Riding Hood* (de Regniers, 1972). The humor, together with wonderful rhyme and a great story, make this book a favorite every year. Even on the first reading I sometimes use oral cloze. Because many of the children are already familiar with this popular fairy tale, and because they have had practice with rhyming words in other stories, they chime in appropriately and feel successful doing so. An excerpt from the book follows:

Soon the wolf fell asleep.
He snored loud and long
A hunter was passing.
He thought, 'Something's wrong.'

> *I never have heard*
> *The old lady snore*
> *That loud and that long.*
> *I'll just look in the door.'*

At some point in the year other versions of *Red Riding Hood* will be introduced and compared, dramatized and drawn about. We use multiple copies of *Little Red Riding Hood: A Story by the Brothers Grimm* (Pincus, 1968) and *Little Red Riding Hood* (Hyman, 1986).

Repetition

The more repetitions there are, and the more predictable the story is, the easier it will be to read. Repeated phrases and repetitive sentence patterns help to aid recall.

Cumulative stories, where one or more previous episodes are repeated and another episode is added, are also much enjoyed. Some children's favorite cumulative stories include: *The Gingerbread Man* (Arno, 1970), *I Know an Old Lady* (Bonne, 1961), *One Monday Morning* (Schulevitz, 1967), *The Runaway Bunny* (Brown, 1977), *The Great Big Enormous Turnip* (Tolstoy, 1968), and *Stone Soup* (McGovern, 1971).

Predictability and High Interest

Janie and the Giant (Barchas, 1977) is an example of a predictable book without rhyme and with very little repetition. The story is so good that the children's interest is held to the very end where they confirm or revise their prediction. The story tells of Janie who meets a conceited giant. The giant threatens to eat her up until Janie cleverly tells him, "If I can do something better than you, will you go away?" The giant agrees and proceeds to show off his talents to Janie. Before going on with the story, I ask the children, "What is it that Janie could possibly do better than a giant?" They respond with such answers as "bake a cake", "sing in a high voice", "draw a picture", "dig a tiny hole". What's important here is to get the children thinking about possibilities and to accept all responses without value judgments. With an "off the wall" response, it is good to say, "Why do you think so?" or "What made you think of that?" or "How would she be able to do that?" Kids need to feel safe in order to take risks, and they feel safe if they know their responses are accepted.

When I use this book in a workshop with teachers, and ask, "What could Janie possibly do better than the giant?", there is usually silence. I try to coax teachers into venturing a guess. I reassure them that I'm not looking for the "right answer". Even so, I always get more elaborate and varied responses from the children. They are more trusting and adventurous. We have been conditioned for too many years to play it safe, get it right, and not to take a risk. We have to become risk takers ourselves before we can expect the children to do so.

The children's attention is now focused ahead to see if their predictions will be accurate. Good listening and recall is assured. They can hardly wait for the end of the story where Janie finally outsmarts the giant by hiding. Because the children's attention is focused ahead, the literal level takes care of itself. Even with very beginning readers, it is important to ask questions like, "Why do you think . . . ?", "How could she . . . ?", "What else could she . . . ?" By modeling higher-level questions, students eventually learn to ask these kinds of questions for themselves.

The Need for Repeated Readings

Typically, a book is introduced during shared book experience and is reread by the teacher at that sitting or at later sittings. Multiple copies are then available for independent reading, and students take the opportunity to try the book alone or with a friend. We read and sing the poems, Big Books, and stories over and over again. Repeated readings of a book — especially if the book has rhyme, rhythm, and repetition — make it easy for the beginning reader to join in. Fluency and comprehension improve if the students are given continuous practice. Language which may not be understood on the first reading may acquire meaning for the child if it is read again and again. As the child reads words more easily, he is better able to concentrate on meaning. In addition, because the child is familiar with the story, he is able to read it with expression in phrases that flow with the language instead of word-by-word. The student's ability to read the story smoothly contributes to the enjoyment of the book. The student also develops an ear for book language, which is so important and influential for good, interesting writing.

It is clear that children actually have a *need* to hear stories repeated. After the first reading of a good book, the children typically applaud and shout out, "Read it again, read it again!" When we take that story into a reading group, we read it as many times as the children like. They let us know, usually quite accurately, when they have had enough practice. Students read confidently because the material is both meaningful and familiar to them. Having the books freely accessible to students also contributes to their desire to read. Once the student is reading predictable books easily, it is not difficult to find good-quality literature at more challenging levels.

(opposite) Readers' Theater in the classroom.

5 Literature Extension Activities
Meaningful Independent Work

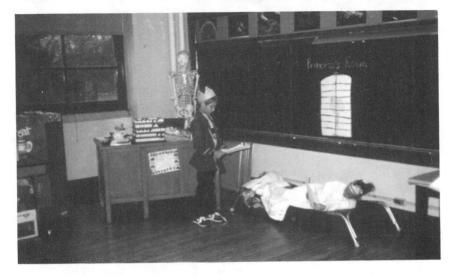

An important part of our language arts program are the activities that extend and complement the literature, as well as those that examine the literature more closely. In place of workbooks and worksheets, we give students pleasurable, challenging opportunities to interact with books and each other. There is no fill-in-the-blank "busy work" to keep students quiet. Instead, we encourage them to be actively involved in their own learning and to use their own strategies to find solutions to open-ended problems.

We see a literature extension activity as any *meaningful* extension of a favorite book, especially if it requires the child to reexamine the text and the illustrations. These activities may include rereading for different purposes, retellings of stories, innovations on stories, collaborations on stories, comparison charts of different versions of a tale, categorizing stories with similar themes, illustrating favorite scenes and characters, acting out a story, rewriting a story into a play, listing alternative solutions for a problem in a story, writing stories for wordless picture books, making a mural, creating simple puppets for a dramatization of a predictable text, analyzing all the books by one author, reading with a partner or partners, charting the sequence of story events, using listening posts with tapes of favorite stories, etc. An extension may be as simple as a discussion of the book or as involved as a class play complete with scenery and costumes. While some of these activities may take place during shared experiences, many will be part of free-choice classroom activity centers during independent work time. As well, many children create their own stories, booklets, and projects at home and proudly bring them to school to share.

Some of the most exciting activities have been collaborative innovations on favorite stories. Karen Shiba's first grade class took a much-loved wordless book and wrote an original text for it. They used *The Bear and the Fly* by Paula Winter (Crown Publishers, Inc. 1976), a story about the havoc that results when a fly comes in the window while a bear family is having dinner. There was great excitement and animated participation in this activity, and the teacher was thrilled at the quality of descriptive language. The children were delighted at seeing the original pictures enlarged and enjoyed coloring them. They loved reading their entire enlarged text, written out by the teacher, as a wall story. Karen noted that the story was particularly easy for the children to read since they had all contributed to the writing in words of their own choosing. Later, the individual pages of the story were bound into a class Big Book that the children enjoyed all year.

The same first grade class read *The Bus Ride* (Wagner 1976) the first week of school and then *The Trolley Ride* (Rigby Education, 1986). They were very taken with the fact that this innovation, written by Australian grade 1 children, had actually been commercially published. They were motivated to write their own version, *The Limousine Ride,* which became a favorite class Big Book, first posted in sequence around the room as a wall story and later bound into a Big Book.

Once children and teachers recognize the potential of using predictable books as springboards for patterned writing and collaborative writing, the possibilities are endless. In early fall, Karen Shiba took the book *Brave Daniel* by Lenore Klein, the story of a boy who pretends to be brave by accomplishing feats that *sound* courageous, and asked her first graders for other ways Daniel could have been brave. These are some of their imaginative responses:

> *Did you know Brave Daniel could pick up a train?*
> *It was a play train.*

> *Once Brave Daniel picked up a house.*
> *It was a block house!*

> *Have you ever wrestled a gorilla?*
> *Brave Daniel did.*
> *It was a stuffed gorilla.*

> *Brave Daniel picked up a tarantula.*
> *It was a plastic tarantula.*

Again, a Big Book, first seen as a wall story, was made for all to enjoy. Innovations on text by children are highly motivating and engaging ways to get children seeing and using the reading-writing connection right from the beginning of school.

One popular classroom activity center is a writing table with book-making supplies. Choosing from various kinds and shapes of paper, students can decide the format, size, and length of their own idea books and assemble them to their own specifications. Another center is a listening post area. Teacher-made and commercial tapes and earphones are set up to go along with books in the classroom and other quality literature. There is also a painting area with easels, a computer, a primary typewriter, a puzzle area, building blocks, games, and a puppetry stage. There are also cozy corners with bean bag chairs for free-choice reading.

As much as possible, we have tried to integrate and extend reading into music and art. We have put some songs on chart paper for the music teacher so she can reinforce concepts of print when introducing a new song. In addition, with the music teacher, we have taken some simple rhythmic books such as *The Bus Ride* (Wagner, 1976), *Each Peach Pear Plum* (Ahlberg, 1983), and *Oh, No!* (Rigby, 1987) and put them to music, making it even easier for children to remember the words. Often, hand motions and dramatic movement are added, contributing to the overall enjoyment of the book/song. At our suggestion, the art teacher took the book *Over in the Meadow* (Langstaff, 1973) and had students make their own slides. These were shown in an all school assembly program while the children sang the song. Under the art teacher's direction, and after a full discussion about what one finds in a meadow, students also collaborated on large sheets to give their own visual interpretations to specified pages in the book. The teacher printed the words, and a beautiful Big Book was put together for class use.

We have also collaborated with the librarian, along with the art and music teachers, in developing units on specific topics such as friendship, folk tales, Halloween, and Valentine's Day. In a unit on bears, students read and sang many songs and stories about bears, made bears out of clay, wrote fiction and nonfiction group and individual bear stories, illustrated different kinds of bears, and brought in their favorite teddy bears and told stories about them.

In Place of Worksheets

In our classroom we make great use of book projects which are developed to reinforce reading, writing, and thinking skills. They take the place of the traditional "seat work". Typical book projects will involve recognizing and reproducing a rhythmic pattern, retelling a familiar story, understanding cause and effect, matching illustrations with text, drawing conclusions, recalling a sequence of events, making comparisons, writing in complete sentences, and using descriptive words. Students have unlimited options to integrate skills in a meaningful context and have fun while doing so. This is in stark contrast to filling in a workbook sheet where a single skill is isolated from anything that is relevant.

Creativity is encouraged and fostered, and children are successful at their own levels. Invented spellings are encouraged; the child writes whatever sounds he hears in a word. While we may pencil in words difficult to read, above the students' writing, there are no red pencil marks. These activities are not graded or corrected. Students are expected and encouraged to complete the activity to the best of their ability. This independent work occupies less than 20% of the total reading instruction time. This is in favorable contrast to the skill and drill seat work that takes up as much as 70% of reading instruction time in a typical American classroom. (Anderson and others, 1985, *Becoming a Nation of Readers*, p. 74.)

When a new project is introduced, an example, done by the teacher or a former student, is shown to students. This visual example serves as a model and helps children better understand the teacher's expectations and directions. At the same time, a group discussion brainstorming possible ideas helps those students who might have difficulty getting started on their own. We have found that the better job we do modeling, especially in the beginning months, the better are the children's results in terms of effort and quality. Later on in the school year, with more involved projects, we may add a written sheet that specifically lists requirements, guidelines, and expectations.

The teacher sets up the format for the project, and usually, a parent volunteer assembles the booklets created by the children. Using a long arm stapler and assorted colored mimeograph paper, we create shape books, small square books, rectangular books, accordion folded paper books, flip books of all different sizes as well as books formed by folding standard size paper in half. The title page always includes "Based on the book by . . .", and students understand that you don't use an author's ideas without giving credit. Parents are so pleased to see original stories in unique book format coming home that we do not have difficulty getting volunteers to do this work for us. Children take pride in completing and illustrating their very own books and projects which they then share with their classmates and take home to read to their families. The children are very excited about book projects. When one is coming to a close, they often ask enthusiastically, "What is our next book project going to be?", and we discuss possibilities.

In the beginning months, students create predictable books based on a familiar pattern of words, which provides structure and ensures success. Careful monitoring is necessary to be sure students have understood directions and expectations. For example, students may be told not to go on to another page until it has been checked by the teacher. It is important that students know their best work is always expected. Later on, as students' reading and writing skills are growing, projects are much more open-ended, and students move along at their own rates.

The first year, we gave all students the same projects to complete. We found, however, that this did not meet individual needs satisfactorily. For our six reading groups in the first two grades, we now have three separate projects going at one time. The two highest ability groups will be doing one project; the two middle groups will be doing a second project; and the two lowest ability groups will be doing a separate project. The project assigned to the high-ability readers in the fall may be done by the low-ability readers in the spring. Projects take one to four weeks to complete depending on the length, complexity, and expectations. The teacher keeps track of students' progress through a check list, dating where the student is daily, or by having students bring projects to reading group where they are quickly checked at the beginning. Students are eager to share what they have written.

In addition to using book projects for independent work, illustrating poems is a weekly activity. The teacher types, wordprocesses, or prints the four to five poems introduced that week. At the end of the week, students illustrate their personal copies to go along with the title and content of the poems. They confer with each other and read together to match the language of the poems with their illustrations. Poems are three-hole punched and kept in a three-ring notebook at home or school. By the end of the school year, each student has a personal poetry anthology of over 150 poems. Parents report their children reading, rereading, and reciting favorite poems over the phone to relatives, to siblings, and to themselves. Their love of poetry is evident at home and school.

Basic concepts can be naturally taught and reinforced through literature without the use of any worksheets. Book projects develop from basic concepts discussed through books, poetry, and everyday happenings. In early fall, the children write and illustrate their own color booklets ("Red is . . .; Yellow is . . .) after hearing many poems related to color. They also read and reread Bill Martin's *Brown Bear, Brown Bear, What Do You See?* which beautifully illustrates all the basic colors through rhythmic rhyme and illustrations, and discuss colors in the room environment. Children write their own booklets on

"Spring" after hearing and discussing many poems, taking observational walks outside, and talking about changes taking place in nature. Having children express their complete thoughts in writing gives a far more accurate picture of the child's understanding of a concept than filling in a worksheet.

Spring IS fun
becas fluors gruo
in the grtin

Over the years, we have developed a file of favorite projects. I do not consider myself a creative person, but the literature we read daily is so memorable that ideas suggest themselves quite naturally. In fact, many of the ideas for the projects that have proved most successful have come directly from the children. The rest of this chapter will be devoted to sharing literature extensions children have enjoyed. Five of these will be presented in specific detail. (See end of chapter for extensions of *Chicken Soup With Rice* by Maurice Sendak, *The Gingerbread Man* by Ed Arno, *The Hungry Thing* by Jan Slepian and Ann Seidler, *I Know an Old Lady* by Rose Bonne, and *The Very Hungry Caterpillar* by Eric Carle.) Others will be discussed in more general terms. The purpose in sharing these ideas is to give teachers confidence to start developing their own. It has been my experience that the most successful projects and extensions are the ones where the teacher has given input and feels ownership. Teachers will also find many useful ideas for literature extension in materials and guides provided by the companies that produce Big Books, as well as other sources. (See *Resources for Teachers.*)

Ideas for Book Projects

Seven Little Monsters by Maurice Sendak

This is a good project to do in the beginning months of school. Take the text of this short, simple, predictable book and reproduce it in the book's original size (4½″ x 9″) with open frames for the pictures. Students will have to talk, read, and problem solve with each other to be sure their illustrations match with the text.

Seven Monsters in a row, see the Seven Monsters go!

Alexander and the Terrible Horrible No Good, Very Bad Day by **Judith Viorst**

This is a favorite both for me and the children. We took the format of the original story about Alexander's awful day and altered it so that the students used their own names in the title and supplied their own episodes.

At breakfast. . . . .
I could tell it was going to be a terrible, horrible, no good, very bad day.
On the way to school. . . . .
I could tell it was going to be a terrible, horrible, no good, very bad day.
At reading time . . . .
I could tell it was going to be a terrible, horrible, no good, very bad day.
At recess. . . . .
I could tell it was going to be a terrible, horrible, no good, very bad day.
At home . . . .
It was a terrible, horrible, no good, very bad day.
My mom says some days are like that.

I could tell it was going to be a terrible, horrible, no good, very bad day.

At recess I fell down and Hert my nee. And everbody Calld Me a crybaby. I got up and told the techer. She Siad They will haf to aPolaJis.

A similar booklet could also be put together with a title such as *The Fantastic, Unbelievable, Terrific, Very Good Day.*

In order to complete this successfully, the child has to understand cause and effect; an action causes or leads to a result or consequence. (For example, Nikole wrote, "On the way to school the bus broke down, and I had to walk"). Through having heard and discussed the original story many times, the children come to understand cause and effect and can apply it without using the terminology. This is in direct contrast to workbook pages that set out to teach cause and effect by definition and in isolation. I have observed a teacher spend 20 minutes just trying to get children to understand the directions on a "cause and effect" page.

Freckle Juice by Judy Blume

This is the humorous story of Nicky Lane who wants freckles and Sharon, who sells him a secret, phony recipe to get them. With this booklet, we used green paper with a Xerox copy of the original cover. Students were asked to retell their favorite part, create their own secret recipe for freckle juice, change one part of the story to suit their own purposes, and tell about some physical attribute they wish they had including why they want it. Original illustrations go along with their text.

Frog and Toad books by Arnold Lobel

In late fall, after a group of first grade students had successfully read and discussed these books, I decided to see if they could understand a story map (see Appendix G) and apply it to writing original stories. We spent much time enjoying the stories and noticing the story elements. After much oral brainstorming and modeling, I gave them the following guide sheet:

Frog and Toad stories
For each story that you write you must have
1. Characters — Frog and Toad
2. Setting — where the story takes place
3. Problem — something is wrong
4. Events — what happens
5. Ending — problem is solved
   Use conversation and speech marks. Look at a Frog and Toad book to see how that is done.
   Make your story sound like it was written by Arnold Lobel. Include friendship and humor.

The children were very successful. Some examples are given in Chapter 6.

The Littles by John Peterson
(See guide sheet in Appendix H)

The Littles are a series of full length, beginning chapter books that detail the adventures of miniature creatures who are just like people except for their size and their tails. Children enjoy adding on to the original stories and creating new episodes.

Mr. Men and *Little Miss* books by Roger Hargreaves
(See guide sheet in Appendix H)

These books, humorously emphasizing particular traits such as "Mr. Bossy", "Mr. Strong", and "Little Miss Tiny", are tremendously popular every year. We construct books of the same size and format, 5″ x 5¼″ with the text on the left side and the illustrations opposite the text on the right side.

Some other books that lend themselves very easily to extension activities through whole group or individual innovations on text include:

Baum, Arlene and Joseph. *one bright Monday morning*.
Cairns, Scharlaine. *Oh, No!*
Cameron, Polly. *I Can't Said the Ant*.
Cowley, Joy. *The Jigaree*.
Cowley, Joy. *Mrs. Wishy-Washy*.
Elting, Mary and Michael Folsom. *Q is for Duck*.
Handy, Libby. *Boss for a Week*.
Hoberman, Mary Ann. *A House is a House for Me*.
Hutchins, Pat. *Rosie's Walk*.
Kellogg, Steven. *Can I Keep Him?*
Krauss, Ruth. *The Carrot Seed*.
Martin, Bill, Jr. *Fire! Fire! Said Mrs. McGuire*.
Mayer, Mercer. *If I Had*.
Melser, June and Joy Cowley. *In a Dark Dark Wood*.
Most, Bernard. *If the Dinosaurs Came Back*.
Parkes, Brenda and Judith Smith. *The Enormous Watermelon*.
Preston, Edna. *The Temper Tantrum Book*.
Viorst, Judith. *I'll Fix Anthony*.
Waber, Bernard. *Ira Sleeps Over*.
Wagner, Justin. *The Bus Ride*.
Zolotow, Charlotte. *The Hating Book*.

Innovating on predictable text and creating extensions from favorite books is a natural way to connect reading with writing and to teach many high level skills. All one needs is an eager group of children, a dash of imagination, some parent volunteers, willingness to take a risk, and trust in what children can accomplish.

While in the first four years of our literature program, independent work time was primarily assigned book projects, generated and structured from the literature; most recently that structure has given way to more freedom. In 1987-1988, Karen Shiba had children use the independent work time for self-selecting reading, writing, and listening activities. (Refer to Figure 1 and Diagram 1 in Chapter 3.) Of this new transition, she says,

> I decided to take a risk, to not supply work, but to let children choose their activities and work individually or with peers while I worked with reading groups. After spending considerable time setting up the routines and making expectations clear, students know they are expected to make their own decisions and monitor their own behavior. Why didn't I try this sooner? It works! My teaching style and strategies continue to change. I'm so pleased with my latest endeavor.

Chicken Soup With Rice by Maurice Sendak

Maurice Sendak has created simple, humorous illustrations and ten-line rhyming poems of about twenty-five to thirty words for each month of the year. Each poem ends with "...chicken soup with rice." The January poem follows:

> *"In January*
> *it's so nice*
> *while slipping*
> *on the sliding ice*
> *to sip hot chicken soup*
> *with rice.*
> *Sipping once*
> *sipping twice*
> *sipping chicken soup*
> *with rice."*

Reading the Book

This book can easily be read out of order according to the particular month of the year. Gather the children around in a comfortable, informal setting such as a Reading Corner. Introduce the month poem as a chart poem that has been handwritten in enlarged print. Hang the poem on a chart stand so that it is clearly visible to all students. Point to each word with a pointer as you read the poem so the child gets the one-to-one correspondence between the spoken and written word as well as left to right sequencing. Read the poem several times a day during the week that it is introduced. Encourage children to join in saying any part or all of the poem as soon as they feel they can.

New poems can continue to be introduced as chart poems in enlarged print on the first school day of each month. Introduce the September poem during the first week of school. Beginning readers will easily memorize it and see themselves as readers. Children eagerly anticipate the start of a new month knowing that a delightful "... chicken soup with rice" poem will begin the month.

Beginning readers love the rhythm, beat, and repetition in *Chicken Soup With Rice*. They delight in calling out the last four lines of each poem that include "... once", "... twice", and "... chicken soup with rice." *Chicken Soup With Rice* is humor and fun at its best, and children love to read this book.

Literature Extension Activities

- Make individual *Chicken Soup With Rice* books shaped like bowls of chicken soup. (See Figure 1 for directions and format.) Illustrations that children make to go along with each month could be fanciful or realistic. Elicit responses from the group for possible pictures. For example, January pictures could include scenes of cold weather, building a snowman, wearing hat and mittens, beginning of the New Year, etc. Students love having their very own *Chicken Soup With Rice* books to read.

- Make individual calendars for each month or one specific month. Give out blank calendar charts. Child copies name of the month at the top and writes in the numbers 1-31 in sequence as organized by the teacher. Understanding of months in sequence, days of the week, and reading a calendar is reinforced.

  Discuss what takes place in a particular month. For example, in October: leaves falling, Halloween, school Open House, students' birthdays, class happenings, field trips, etc. Events can be written and/or illustrated on corresponding calendar days.

- Make a class Big Book. The teacher writes out each month poem in enlarged print on a piece of tagboard 18″ by 24″. Children can draw, color, and cut out pictures or scenes representative of the month and/or poem. Paste pictures on page opposite poem for a collage effect. Laminate each page. Assemble pages in order and bind book together. While simple binding with metal rings works well, plastic comb binding or spiral binding is attractive and durable and can be done inexpensively at a printer's shop.

- Show the 16mm movie "Chicken Soup With Rice" which is directed by Maurice Sendak. Each poem is set to upbeat music composed and performed by Carole King. Children love learning and singing the spirited tunes, especially the last four lines that include "... once", "twice", and "... chicken soup with rice." The movie's clever and whimsical cartoon animation can be used as a springboard for children's own visual creations. This color and sound film is available by itself or as part of the original film, "Really Rosie" (Weston Woods Release, 1976).

For a specific month, tape or secure the large chart poem so it is clearly visible to all students at their desks. Using careful handwriting, each student copies the poem and illustrates it.

- Cook chicken soup with rice as a special culminating activity. Print individual recipes for each child to follow and read. If soup is made at school, students could later write their own words to tell what sequential steps were taken to make the soup. For example, "Step 1. Take a large pot. Fill it half way with water and put it on the stove." This might also be done as a whole class language experience activity and written out in enlarged print on chart paper.

Figure 1   Literature Extension Activity: Chicken Soup with Rice
CHICKEN SOUP WITH RICE BOOK

Materials needed:
tagboard
colored construction paper
brads or metal rings

Directions:
- Cut out a chicken soup bowl template out of tagboard.
  For each student book, trace and cut out enough bowls for the 12 months plus a top cover.
  Cut out bowls in 4 colors to denote and emphasize the seasons and changes in weather. For example, use blue for Dec., Jan., and Feb.; use yellow for Mar., Apr., and May; use green for June, July and Aug.; use brown for Sept., Oct., and Nov.
- Type the 12 month poems, and run off enough copies for each student.
  Students cut around each month poem and paste it on the correct color bowl.
  Each page is illustrated to go along with the month.
- Fasten all 12 completed month bowl-pages plus a bowl cover together with a brad or metal ring.

sample page

The Gingerbread Man by Ed Arno

A freshly baked gingerbread man escapes from the oven and challenges those who try to catch him: a little boy, an old man, an old woman, three farmers, a bear, and finally, a fox who gobbles him up. Six times in the story the gingerbread man says:

> *"I have run away from*
> *a little boy*
> *and an old man*
> *and an old woman*
> *and ...*
> *And I can run away from you too."*

Once children have heard this cumulative tale, they easily and correctly predict words and happenings.

Reading the Book

Before reading the book, ask children what they think the story is about. Continue to have the children predict what will happen as you read through the book.

For example, when the old woman says, 'And when you can smell the gingerbread, call me. But do NOT open the oven door', ask, "What will the little boy do?" When the little boy opens the oven door, ask, "What will happen now?"

By avoiding literal recall and focusing on prediction, higher-level thinking is encouraged and children's attention remains focused as they are listening to find out what will happen next in the story. Accept all responses that are thoughtful.

Much of the book is highly repetitive, as in:

> *"Run, run*
> *As fast as you can.*
> *You can't catch me.*
> *I'm the gingerbread man."*

Encourage children to join in when they are ready.

Excellent children's literature, which includes highly motivating and predictable books such as *The Gingerbread Man* can be used successfully as the core component in a beginning reading program. Good readers develop naturally when they have had repeated exposure to a predictable book through hearing the story, through repeated readings, and through modeling the teacher's reading.

Many basic sight words occur repeatedly and are easily learned in context without boring drill. As examples, note the number of times the following words appear in *The Gingerbread Man*: "catch" — 4 times, "little" — 16 times, "old" — 20 times, "said" — 15 times, "woman" — 12 times, "down" — 5 times, "away" — 12 times.

Literature Extension Activities

- With teacher guidance, children can rewrite *The Gingerbread Man* into a script for a play. Discuss the role of the narrator or storyteller; list all characters from the story; model how narrative can be changed to dialogue.

     The beginning of a possible script follows:

The Gingerbread Man

Cast		
	Storyteller	First Farmer
	Little Boy	Second Farmer
	Old Man	Third Farmer
	Old Woman	Bear
	Gingerbread Man	Fox

Act 1

Setting: In the country kitchen of the old man, old woman, and little boy.

Storyteller: Once upon a time, there was an old man, an old woman, and a little boy. One day the old woman decided to do some baking for the little boy.

Old woman: I will bake you a gingerbread man.

After the play is written, multiple copies of the script can be distributed. The play can be read by the children, acted out in costume, or performed with simple finger or stick puppets. (See Figure 2.) Parts can be interchanged, and scripts can be saved for future use with other students.

- Dramatizations can also be done as spontaneous retellings for an enjoyable comprehension check. Students act out the story using their own original conversation and body movements to tell what happened.
- Compare and contrast different versions of *The Gingerbread Man*. Ask your school librarian to locate other versions of this folktale.
- Encourage children to write their own version or to retell this version in their own writing. The main character could be changed to *The Chocolate Chip Man*, *The Peanut Butter Man*, etc., and the other characters and final outcome could be changed as well. A delightful format that children will love for writing *The Gingerbread Man* in sequence or creating their own version is to make gingerbread men cut-out books much the same way one makes paper doll cut-out books. (See Figure 2.)

Figure 2   Literature Extension Activities: The Gingerbread Man

FINGER PUPPETS

Children or teachers draw a simple representation for each character out of paper or tagboard, allowing a strip to fit over the finger. Examples are shown.

STICK PUPPETS

Make characters on tagboard with crayons, markers, colored paper cut-outs, paint, pipe cleaners, cotton, etc. Cut out the characters. Attach or glue each to a tongue depressor or any suitable stick. Child holds the stick behind a puppet stage, stable, etc. and speaks the part and moves the puppet.

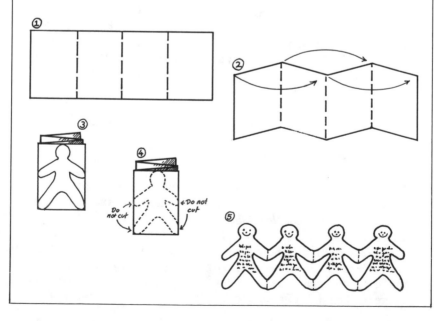

CUT OUT BOOKS

1. Fold a long strip of paper into equal sections.
2. Refold the paper like accordion pleats.
3. Draw a simple gingerbread man on the top sheet.
4. Cut out the design, being careful not to cut through the side edges.
5. Illustrate and write the story onto the pages on both sides.

I Know an Old Lady by **Rose Bonne**

I Know an Old Lady is highly predictable and easy to read because of the rhyme, repetition, and song. It quickly becomes a children's favorite, and, as such, serves as fine reading material in a beginning reading program.

This book and song of utter nonsense delights adults and children with its absurdity and rhythm. An old lady swallows a variety of insects and animals in this cumulative tale that never says "... why she swallowed the fly." An excerpt follows:

> *I know an old lady who swallowed a cat.*
> *Now fancy that, to swallow a cat!*
>
> *She swallowed the cat to catch the bird.*
> *She swallowed the bird to catch the spider*
> *That wriggled and wriggled and tickled inside her.*
> *She swallowed the spider to catch the fly,*
> *But I don't know why she swallowed the fly!*
> *I guess she'll die!*

Reading the Book

Sing *I Know an Old Lady* several times through, and show the pictures as you are singing. Encourage children to join in when they are ready. To encourage good listening, tell the students that on the next time around, they will have to fill in the last word in each line.

Even though children easily memorize this story, by pointing to the words in the book as they read or sing it, they will reinforce basic sight vocabulary. The first line, which begins, "I know an old lady who..." appears eight times at the beginning of each refrain as the old lady swallows a fly, spider, bird, cat, dog, goat, cow, and finally, a horse.

Literature Extension Activities

Students love creating their own *I Know an Old Lady* projects.

- For a comprehension check and for sheer fun, have the class recall everything the old lady swallowed. Place the old lady in the center of a circle that rotates. (See Figure 3.) Students write each animal and, if they can, the rhyming line that goes with it — or you may choose just to have them illustrate the animal. Students then enjoy reading their own "books" to each other by turning the old lady's head to the right.
- Another format for having children enjoy recalling everything the old lady swallowed is to use a large sheet of paper and divide it into eight equal compartments. (See Figure 3.)

Figure 3   Literature Extension Activities: I Know an Old Lady

STORY CIRCLE

Materials needed:
tagboard and/or mimeograph paper
magic markers and/or crayons
brads

Directions:
- Cut out a circle 8″ to 10″ in diameter.
- Divide circle into 8 equal sections.
- Draw and cut out a head about 3″ in diameter. Accentuate the nose as a pointer.
- Push a brad into the center of the head and attach to center of circle.
- Write or type "I know an old lady who swallowed a . . ." on the old lady's head.

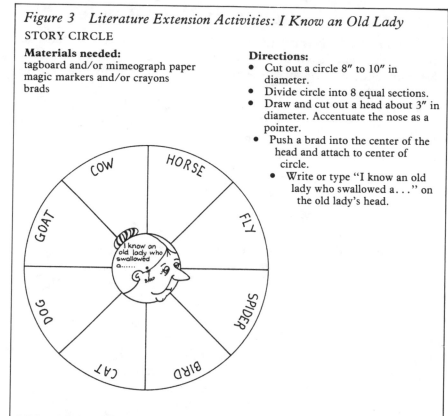

RECALLING AND ILLUSTRATING

- Fold newsprint that is 18″ x 24″ into 8 equal compartments allowing fold at top for title and first line.
- Write the title and first line at the top.
- Have students work individually or in pairs to write in and illustrate what the old lady swallowed.

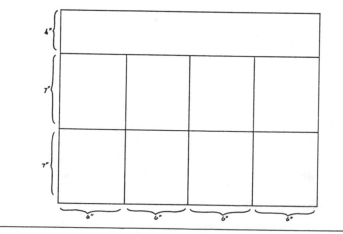

- Have children write their own two or three line verses by choosing another animal the old lady might have swallowed. Some examples, using the same rhythm of *I Know an Old Lady*, follow:

> *I know an old lady who swallowed a flea.*
> *Oh woe is me, to swallow a flea!*
>
> *I know an old lady who swallowed a snake.*
> *Oh what a mistake to swallow a snake.*
>
> *I know an old lady who swallowed an eel.*
> *Oh what a feel to swallow an eel.*
>
> *I know an old lady who swallowed some bees.*
> *Got down on her knees and swallowed some bees.*
> *I think she'll sneeze!*
>
> *I know an old lady who swallowed a lion.*
> *Without hardly tryin' she swallowed a lion.*
> *She might be dyin'.*

- As a variation, keep the same tune and beat but change the main character. For example:

> *I know a poor farmer who planted some wheat.*
> *In mid summer heat, he planted some wheat.*
>
> *I know a poor farmer who planted some beans.*
> *He put on his jeans and planted some beans.*
>
> *I know a poor farmer who planted some corn.*
> *He was so forlorn, he planted some corn*
> *Early one morn.*

The same format, as shown in Figure 3, or your own original format, can be used when children create their own verses.

- Have students draw a large picture of the old lady that shows in her stomach the animals she swallowed.

- Write a story about the old lady. Tell why you think she swallowed the fly. Did she like eating flies? Was it an accident?

- Choose another animal the old lady might have swallowed. In addition to an original rhyme, draw a picture. Put students' original rhymes and illustrations into a class book.

- Make a mobile of the things the old lady swallowed.

The Hungry Thing
by Jan Slepian and Ann Seidler

The Hungry Thing, a friendly monster, comes to town with a sign around its neck that says "Feed Me". In response to, "What would you like to eat?", the Hungry Thing responds with a nonsense word that rhymes with a real food, such as "shmancakes" (for pancakes), "tickles" (for pickles) and "gollipops" (for lollipops). While at first the townspeople and the wise man have difficulty deciding what to feed the Hungry Thing, a little boy offers the solution.

"I think," said the boy, "you all ought to hear
Gollipops... sound like
Dollipops... sound like
Lollipops to me."

The townspeople eventually join in in trying to satisfy the enormous appetite of the Hungry Thing.

Delightful rhyme is sprinkled throughout this fanciful story. Whimsical illustrations hold the reader's attention. Despite some difficult words, beginning readers will push to read this book because of its charm. Much of the book is highly predictable because of the rhyme which also makes sections of it easy to recall. An excerpt follows:

> *"He's underfed.*
> *Have some bread,"*
> *Said a lady*
> *Dressed in red.*

> *"It seems to me*
> *He'd like some tea,"*
> *Said a fellow*
> *Up a tree.*

Hold up the colorful cover of the book, give the title, and ask students to predict what the book might be about. Ask questions to get students thinking. "Could this be a true story?" "What makes you think so?" "Does it take place now or in the past?" "Why do you think so?" "What do you think the creature has around its neck?" "Is it a friendly creature?" "What do you think the title has to do with the story?" Try to accept all answers with statements such as, "That's a possibility," and "I can tell that you're really thinking." By encouraging students to think and predict, students will listen attentively to the story to confirm their predictions.

To set a framework for successful individual reading, read the book orally several times in its entirety in separate sittings. Even on the first reading, students should be encouraged to try to figure out the rhyming pattern. Pause in your reading, and have students complete the rhyme.

In children's learning to read, interest and motivation play a more important role than readability as determined by a formula. A high-quality book, such as *The Hungry Thing*, can be successfully used as part of a literature-based reading program even though the story uses multisyllable words. Words such as "townspeople", "answered", and "gathered" are read easily by beginning readers once they are familiar with the story. Observing the beginning sound in the context of a meaningful sentence is often enough of a cue to read the word correctly.

Literature Extension Activities

- Have students create their own original rhyming couplets for *The Hungry Thing* by modeling the pattern in the book. Be sure to do some oral examples together first.

  "Have some snapple."
  They gave him some apple.
  "Have some lopcorn."
  They gave him some popcorn.

  Tell students to think of an actual food first, and then change the beginning sound to create a nonsense rhyming word. Rhyming couplets can be assembled and illustrated in individual "flip" books. (See Figure 4.)
- Create a Hungry Thing shape book. (See Figure 4.) Use the shape book to have children write the story of *The Hungry Thing* in their own words with their own illustrations. The shape book could also be used to have children write "All About The Hungry Thing." Students could be asked to include where he comes from, why he is so hungry, what his favorite foods are, all about his family, etc.
- Make a Hungry Thing bulletin board or mural. Have children draw pictures of actual foods but label them as the Hungry Thing would. Draw or paint a big Hungry Thing in the center.
- Collect and cut out food photographs from magazines and newspapers, or bring in labels from supermarket items. Paste each label or picture on a page in a blank book of pages that have been stapled together. The student writes the real word and the rhyming nonsense word below it.
- Or students can write Breakfast, Lunch, or Dinner Books:

  On Monday I ate _____ (Tell one item).
  On Tuesday I ate _____ , _____ (Tell two items), etc.

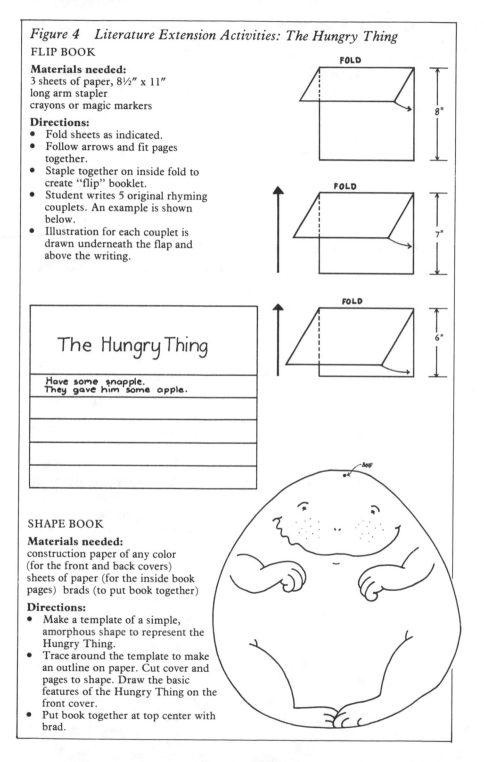

Figure 4   Literature Extension Activities: The Hungry Thing

FLIP BOOK

Materials needed:
3 sheets of paper, 8½" x 11"
long arm stapler
crayons or magic markers

Directions:
- Fold sheets as indicated.
- Follow arrows and fit pages together.
- Staple together on inside fold to create "flip" booklet.
- Student writes 5 original rhyming couplets. An example is shown below.
- Illustration for each couplet is drawn underneath the flap and above the writing.

FOLD
8"

FOLD
7"

FOLD
6"

The Hungry Thing

Have some snapple.
They gave him some apple.

SHAPE BOOK

Materials needed:
construction paper of any color
(for the front and back covers)
sheets of paper (for the inside book pages) brads (to put book together)

Directions:
- Make a template of a simple, amorphous shape to represent the Hungry Thing.
- Trace around the template to make an outline on paper. Cut cover and pages to shape. Draw the basic features of the Hungry Thing on the front cover.
- Put book together at top center with brad.

The Very Hungry Caterpillar
by Eric Carle

A tiny and very hungry caterpillar pops out of an egg and begins to look for food. The author-illustrator Eric Carle beautifully and colorfully takes the reader from Monday to Sunday on an adventure in eating. Pages of the book are cleverly punched to indicate how much and where the caterpillar has eaten.

Finally, after a week of heavy eating, the now big and fat caterpillar builds a cocoon around itself and begins to undergo the change from caterpillar to butterfly. After several weeks, it emerges as a beautiful butterfly.

This book is highly predictable and easy for beginning readers to read because of the repetition and because of the clear way the pictures match up with the text.

Reading the Book

Hold up the book so the children can see it. Point to the words in the title as you say them, and ask the class, group, or student what the book might be about. Encourage students to predict to set a purpose for reading. Students will listen carefully to verify their predictions.

After students have heard the pattern, "... but he was still hungry" several times, encourage them to join in by pausing in your reading. Do this also for the days of the week, "On Wednesday..." "On Thursday...", etc. An excerpt follows:

> *On Monday he ate through one apple, but he was still hungry.*
> *On Tuesday he ate through two pears, but he was still hungry.*
> *On Wednesday he ate through three plums, but he was still hungry.*

Literature Extension Activities

- Have students create their own predictable books based on modeling the pattern of words and pages from "On Monday..." through "On Friday..." but changing the name of the animal and the foods eaten. (See Figure 5 for format.) The book could be *The Very Hungry Animal, The Very Hungry Boy,* etc., or children could choose their own animal or insect — real or imaginary — to fill in. Illustrations are done to match with text.
- Use the same folding, punching, stapling directions to write individual books about the students' lives:

  On Monday I _____ (Tell one thing).
  On Tuesday I _____ and _____ (Tell two things).
  On Wednesday I _____ , _____ , and _____
  (Tell 3 things),

or make the booklets less structured by starting each page with the day of the week.

- Read this book to children in the fall when caterpillars are making their cocoons. Encourage children to look for caterpillars and bring them to school. If the caterpillars are put in suitable containers, the children will witness the metamorphosis from caterpillar to cocoon to butterfly by the spring.

- Get some meal worms in a pet or bait shop. Each child can be given one tiny worm in a small glass jar or margarine cup. With some raw bran and a piece of apple in the container, students can observe first hand the color, body segments, and complete life cycle from larvae to pupa to beetle to egg again.

- Days of the week and number concepts 1-5 are easily reinforced through the story and pictures. Tie in ordinal numbers with days of the week. Monday is the first day of the school week; Tuesday is the second day of the school week; etc.

- Show a film or filmstrip on butterflies or insects with life cycles.

- Read the nonfiction *Caterpillar Diary* (Rigby Education Big Book, 1987) and point out how it is different from a storybook.

- Ask the children to paint a picture of their own beautiful butterfly. Ask them to tell an original story about their butterfly.

- Do a bulletin board called, "Let's Feed the Very Hungry Caterpillar." Give each child a colored paper segment. Break up the segment colors to fit the four basic food groups: 1. dairy, milk, and eggs; 2. poultry, meat, and fish; 3. grains and cereals, pasta, rice, breads; 4. fruit and vegetables. Discuss good nutrition and daily food requirements. Each child contributes a segment with a picture of a food from the color-matched food group. Children could also bring in a food they chose for other children to see and taste.

Figure 5 *Literature Extension Activities: The Very Hungry*
Caterpillar

MAKING A PREDICTABLE BOOK

Materials needed:
3 sheets of paper, 8½″ x 11″
paper punch, stapler

Directions:
- Fold sheets as indicated.
- Follow arrows, and fit pages together.
- Punch one hole in top center of each of five sections.

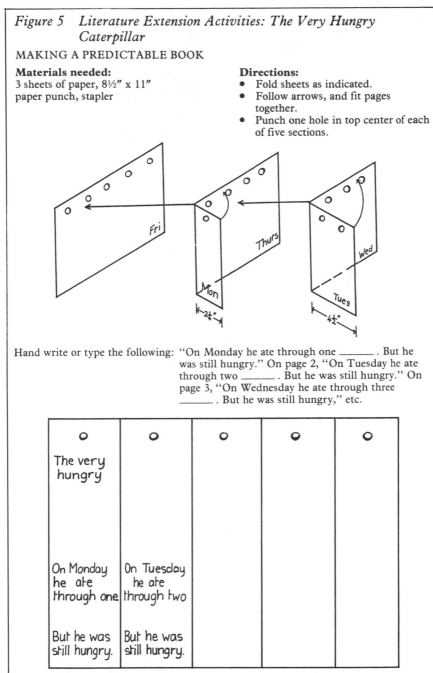

Hand write or type the following: "On Monday he ate through one _____ . But he was still hungry." On page 2, "On Tuesday he ate through two _____ . But he was still hungry." On page 3, "On Wednesday he ate through three _____ . But he was still hungry," etc.

○	○	○	○	○
The very hungry				
On Monday he ate through one	On Tuesday he ate through two			
But he was still hungry.	But he was still hungry.			

- Use ditto masters or Xerox sheets on both sides to make multiple copies.
- Then assemble and staple into individual books.
- The number of holes in the paper matches up with the numbers 1-5, and guides children in drawing the correct number of items.

(above) A literature extension project from a wordless book.
(opposite) A first-grader reading his own published book with the class.

6 The Writing Program
How To Begin It and Keep It Going

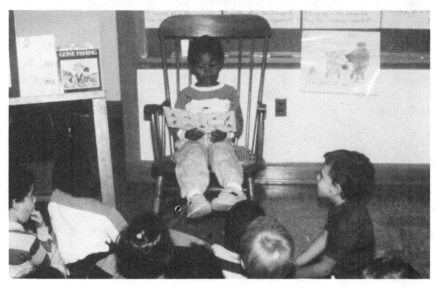

The writing program is an integral and favorite part of our langauge arts program. The students have a reason and an audience for writing. Besides daily journal writing and book publishing, both of which will be discussed in this chapter, they quickly learn to use writing to communicate for varied purposes. They write notes to each other and to teachers through the classroom mailboxes. They write invitations to parents for open houses, plays, and conferences. They write thank you notes to speakers and visitors. Special thank you notes go to classes who have written books for our classroom and students. Cards for special occasions, holidays, and get well wishes are composed and created. Signs and posters promoting books and causes are written.

The range of children's writing varies tremendously, but the acceptance and encouragement of each child at his developmental writing level promotes immediate success and enthusiasm. In the beginning weeks of school, almost everyone draws pictures and uses the details of their pictures to help tell the story. Most of the students begin with some knowledge of consonants and will write the beginning sounds for some words. Others write random streams of letters without spacing. As students become aware of conventions of print — words, spaces between words, punctuation, capitals — they experiment with them daily. For the students lacking letter knowledge to get started, we write for them under their pictures and practice reading with them. We would say to them, "Tell me about your story," and treat them as writers. Each student has a story to tell, and each is successful at his own level. All writing, from a simple drawing to a complete story, is accepted and valued. (See *Resources for Teachers*, especially *Coping With Chaos* by Brian Cambourne and Jan Turbill, for patterns of children's writing behavior.)

In a supportive, literate environment writing improves through daily use, practice, and guidance. Handwriting and fine motor control develop rapidly through daily writing. The formation of letters is formally taught but not overemphasized during self-selected writing and collaborative writing. Conventions of print, spelling, and language patterns develop through repeated practice. Confidence and skills grow as student writing is celebrated and shared.

The Power of Literature as a Model for Writing

There is no question that the way children use language in their daily writing is greatly influenced by the many stories and poems they hear and read daily. Research has confirmed that the kind of reading material children are exposed to directly affects the kind of writing they do.

The language of literature, with its imagery and phrasing, serves as a wonderful model and springboard. Beginning writers internalize the storyline and reuse it to suit their own purposes. They try out speech marks when they need conversation; they experiment with periods and exclamation marks to make the meaning clearer; and most begin to use capital letters and periods with some accuracy. They write chapter stories, include dedication and author pages, table of contents, and incorporate all manner of illustrations in various media.

In late fall, a group of students had read and discussed all the *Frog and Toad* books by Arnold Lobel. After discussion of story elements and much oral brainstorming, the children wrote their own *Frog and Toad* stories. Erica began her story and immediately stated the problem. She used speech marks (quotation marks) quite well.

ONE DAY Toad went to the cracis and he got a job. "Frog" Seaud Toad "I'm secked.

"I don't want to be 3000 feet High" That is to High. "I want to Quit."

"you cant do that." Frog Seaud.

Nathan began with an interesting storyline, and was able to inject humor.

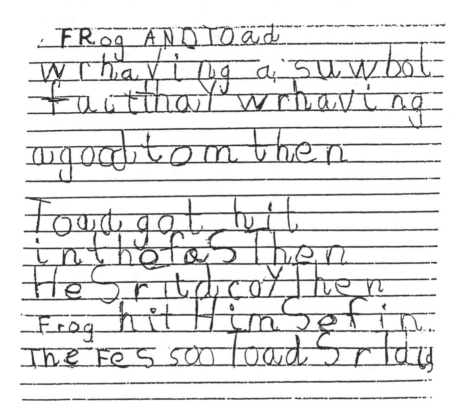

Frog and Toad were having a snowball fight. They were having a good time. Then Toad got hit in the face. Then he started crying. Then Frog hit himself in the face so Toad started laughing.

All of the children were successful in composing several stories based on the model Lobel provided. Most of their stories were several full-length pages each, and their attention and enjoyment in writing and illustrating were sustained over several weeks.

Our children have also written their own versions of *If I Had . . .* by Mercer Mayer, *Clifford* books by Norman Bridwell, *Alexander and the Terrible, Horrible, No Good, Very Bad Day* by Judith Viorst, *Harriet* books by Nancy Carlson, *Freckle Juice* by Judy Blume, ''Mr.

Men'' books by Roger Hargreaves and many others. They are not aware that this is a lot of writing for beginning writers because they are used to writing every day and have ownership over the process and product. They are congratulated for their invented spellings, and at the same time, more conventional spelling is appearing. Expectations for what children can accomplish are high. There are no grades or stickers given. The reward is in the doing, learning, and sharing.

By contrast, when a student enters after the beginning of school and has come from a basal reading program, the writing capabilities are very different. Stuart came in mid November, and the first week he wrote:

> *I like school.*
> *I like to play.*
> *I like to run.*
> *I like to jump.*

He would not put down any word he could not spell correctly. The basal text model he had been provided with limited his written language patterns. It was to be many months before he began to be comfortable with invented spelling, risk taking, and writing for himself.

A Look at One Child: Martin

Since it is always easy to show what the more able students can do, it is often more relevant to use a less able student as an example of how very powerful the literature model is. Martin had not had much exposure to the language of books. Prior to kindergarten, he had been in a Headstart program, and in the fall of first grade, standardized testing indicated that he qualified for Chapter 1 reading.

In his very first journal entry, he shows some letter-sound knowledge.

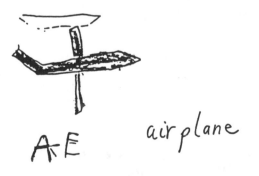

A E

airplane

A R

By the end of October, he has attempted retelling a favorite part of *Too Much Noise* by Ann McGovern. Sound-symbol spelling is limited, but the rhyme and rhythm as well as the repetition of the passage nine times in the story enabled him to be successful.

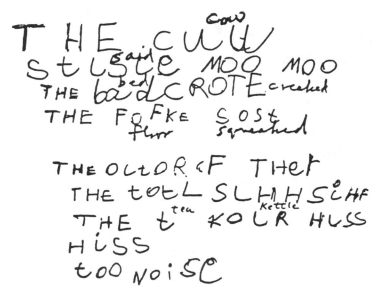

The cow said, "Moo. Moo"
The bed creaked.
The floor squeaked.
The leaves fell on the roof. Swish. Swish.
The tea kettle whistled. Hiss. Hiss.

In December, over a two-day period, he is able to retell an even longer portion of a book, *Fire! Fire! Said Mrs. McGuire* by Bill Martin Jnr. Even though he is still having difficulty with fine motor coordination, he takes control of his writing and accurately recalls twelve of the seventeen lines of the book. He uses dashes freely for unknown medial vowels, and he has taken note of the teacher's spelling of "said" (penciled in) and chosen to use it correctly. It is likely he reread what he had written previously before completing the story the next day.

12 — 19

f-r Fire f-r Fire Fire   shes
mRS   McGuire G-1   Wr where?
W.r when?   sh.es said
mRS   bear said   Dan Down
Dqu Town   she; said   mRS
ba d shc Brown said   w-r a
P.e   sh.es said   mrs
  kite   Wr   wr   Said
12-20 mRS   Vr
  Git   out of my   Wa
Said   mRS   t-y
  ba   door   the   door
Said   ⸺ mrs   or
Wll   I...d   c-r   Said
mrs   w-e   sos   us
and Sa   us   said
mrs Dus   and Sne,
  H   dr   the   se wit
  u   Sa   of boo

"Fire! Fire!" said Mrs. McGuire.
"Where? Where?" said Mrs. Bear.
"Downtown!" said Mrs. Brown.
"What a pity!" said Mrs. Kitty.
"Water! Water!" said Mrs. Votter.
"Get out of my way!" said Mrs. Lei.
"Break down the door!" said Mrs Orr.
"Well, I declare!" said Mrs. Wear.
"Oh, help us and save us!"
    said Mrs. Davis
as she fell down the stairs
    with a sack of potatoes.

In January, his handwriting shows much improvement; he begins his story with a title; some high frequency words are spelled correctly.

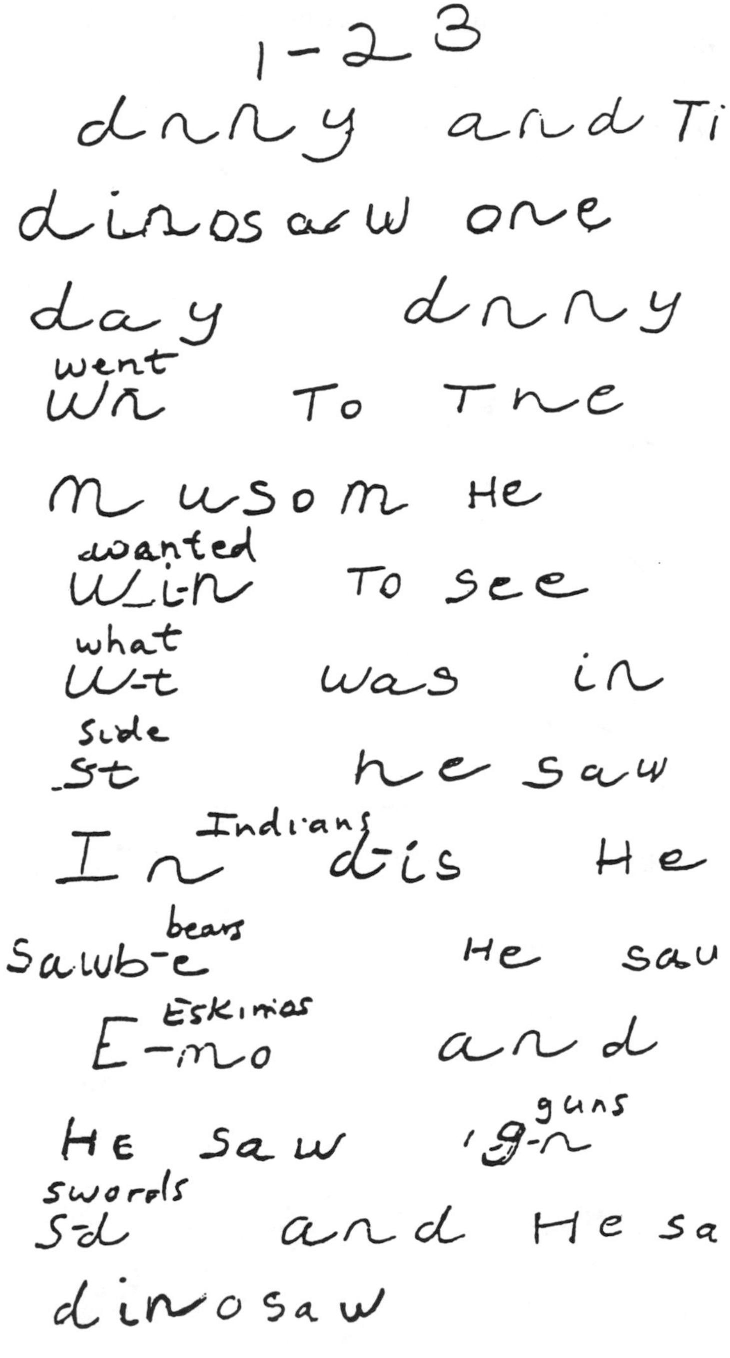

1-23

dnny and Ti

dinosaw one

day   dnny

went
Wn   To Tne

n usom He

wanted
Ulin   To see

what
Wt   was   in

side
St   he saw

In Indians
In dis   He

bears
Sawb-e   He sau

Eskimos
E-no   and

guns
HE saw ig-n

swords
Sd   and He sa

dinosaw

In February, Martin begins a retelling of the African folk tale, *Akimba and the Magic Cow* by Anne Rose. He stays with this story for six consecutive days without referring back to the book. His use of the sentence, "So Akimba set out", has a literary quality not typical for six-year-olds, but it is familiar through hearing and reading the story many times.

The book version says:

> Soon he came to a deep forest.
> He saw an old man chopping firewood.
> Akimba helped him stack the logs.

Martin writes:

> Soon he came to an old man and he helped to stack the wood.

AKa (Akimba) 2-6 and
The mit̄e (Magic)
Cow. AKa (Akimba)
was The Pit (poorest)
man in his
Vis (village) I met (must)
te (took) The Vit (village)
he tg (thought) So
aka set out
Soon he come
To in (an) old
Man and he
h-d (helped) To st (stack) The
Wd (wood)

The strong relationship and interaction that exists between comprehension and meaningful writing is much in evidence here. Martin is actively involved in high-level thinking. A child that is able to retell a story has to understand the language, recall happenings, sequence events, organize information, retrieve details, substitute words of similar meaning, and have a good sense of story. The fact the first-graders learn to do this easily is directly related to the many stories they hear — many of them over and over again.

2-11

GeorGe and
Martha
Vn (Valentines) Tme day
GeorGe md (made)
Martha a
S-l (special) Vn Tme
Martha was
su pd (surprised) and
Then Martha
md a nice
Vn (valentine) Tm for
GeorGe hie was
ve (very) su pd (surprised)
wat (wat) Martha

In late January, Martin has delighted in retelling *George and Martha* stories by James Marshall for six days. Parts of the stories are from the actual books, but he now changes some details and adds new action. He embellishes the original stories with new information. He adds original conversation to go along with Marshall's stories.

In February, Martin writes — for the first time — a completely original story, *George and Martha   Valentine's Day*. (He uses the same rhythm for the title as *George and Martha   One Fine Day*.) He writes two complete pages in one sitting and includes a chapter heading; his storyline and sentence structure show much accomplishment. His growth in literacy in less than six months has been remarkable!

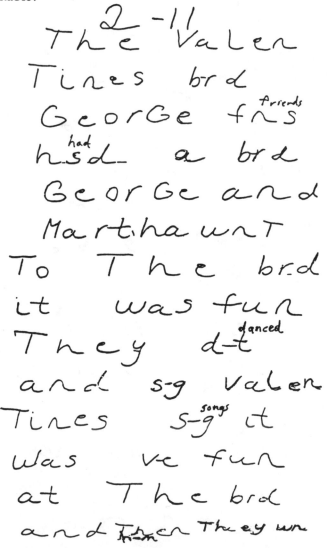

Each year we have children like Martin, without wide exposure to literary language, who rely on literature to find meaning in their writing. I have observed that these children consistently go through the same stages in their writing development:

1   **Exact retelling** — almost word for word,
2   **Partial retelling** with some added details and changes,
3   Same title and characters with some original elements added to the author's structure to make **a mostly new story**, or a complete retelling in child's own language.
4   Same characters but **a totally new story** using similar story elements (such as friendship, humor, conversation.)

Eventually, they write completely original, well-organized and thought-out narratives. Sentence structure, character development, and a fine sense of story have developed naturally.

The Interrelationship between Reading and Writing

Often the first reading children do is of their own language. For many students, their own writing provides the foundation for success in learning to read.

The interrelationship between reading and writing has seemed particularly significant for those students who have been called learning disabled. Franklin was a student who was repeating first grade after "failing" at another school. He believed he could not read or write, and his self-esteem was badly damaged. It was through the writing process that his reading skills developed. Because his own language was meaningful and memorable to him, with practice and support, he could read it. He loved the stories he heard all day and adapted many into his writing. He began to see himself as a reader and writer who could make many choices. As he gained control of his learning, his confidence grew. He was dismissed from the learning disability program at the end of the school year, not a typical occurrence. This is not to say that his problems disappeared. He still had a difficult time with letter-sound relationships, but now that he was focusing on meaning he could compensate well enough to succeed. He was reading at a third grade level by the end of the school year.

Sharon was a student having some difficulty with the beginning reading process. She had written in detail about all four members of her family. This was the last page of her piece about her brother, written in October. A compare and contrast book the second month of school! She was able to read it with great expression.

> People say we look alike, but we do not have the same personality, and we do not have the same fingerprints. He is a boy, and I am a girl. He is silly, and I am serious.

It was Sharon's growing fluency in writing that led to her fluency in reading.

The interrelationship between reading and writing is also very evident during shared book time. Often, shared reading leads into shared writing where teachers and students collaborate on a text. Students, excited about a book, decide to alter it to suit their own purposes. The teacher composes with the children, guiding the pattern and organization of the story while encouraging responses from every child. As the teacher writes in enlarged print, saying and spelling the words aloud as she is writing, the child hears and sees the transcribing process in the relaxed group situation. As in shared reading, observation and participation lead to independent practice and mastery. Through this reading and writing together, each language process is fostered.

After hearing *The Great Big Enormous Turnip* (Tolstoy and Oxenbury, 1983) and reading together the Big Book *The Enormous Watermelon* (Parkes and Smith, 1986), the class wrote their own versions, "The Great Big Enormous Pumpkin". Following the group experience, students wrote similar cumulative stories in their journals such as "The Giant Radish" and "The Humungous Carrot."

In another school in our district, a group of Chapter 1 students working with reading specialist Marilyn Brooks read many *Clifford* books by Norman Bridwell. After writing a group "Clifford" story, the children wrote their own original stories. Marilyn immediately put the stories on the word processor (using conventional spelling, paragraphing, and punctuation), printed them out, and they became highly engaging, predictable text. The children took much pride and joy in being able to read their own stories, and they were able to read their own language far more easily than any commercially prepared reading material.

Students enjoy seeing that a collaborative story can actually become a commercial publication. A whole series of books, *When Lana Was Absent, The Trolley Ride, Munching Mark, The Greedy Gray Octopus, Excuses, Excuses* and others, were written by first grade children in Australia and are now available as Big Books and small books. (Rigby Education, 1986). These books can be used as enjoyable, easy reading books as well as motivational samples of other children's writing.

Shared writing also occurs as a language experience activity. With the guidance of the teacher, the class orally composes a chart story or book about a meaningful, shared experience (a museum trip, a science experiment, a nature walk, a class party, a school event) and the teacher records it with the children looking on. Children's own natural language becomes predictable text that they want to read and can read. (See *Resources for Teachers*, especially Mary Anne Hall and

Lorraine Wilson, for information on the language experience approach as an individualized, group, or class activity.)

Mailboxes

The reading-writing connection is also supported by daily note writing. We introduce "mailboxes" early on in the school year and start by placing a short, personal note in each student's box. (The idea for the mailboxes is adapted from first grade teacher Vera Milz. See *Resources for Teachers*.) Any type of mailbox in the classroom will do as long as each child has a personal space. We use cardboard, shoe organizer boxes from a discount store, and we also have boxes for other teachers and our principal. This is a very easy activity to begin and keep going. Once the teacher has done the initial set-up and given explanations, examples, and purposes of the mailboxes, there is little to do except keep a supply of paper on hand and respond promptly to the students' notes to the teacher. We have paper available on top of the mailboxes, and often this is scrap paper which we have received at no charge from a printing company. For special occasions, like Valentine's Day, we may have pink paper in the shape of hearts. Some students also bring in their own special, personal stationery that they use daily.

The children are thrilled to get mail and ask us and each other what the notes say. In the beginning, the notes are brief and may only have a student's or teacher's name on it with the writer's signature, but messages become increasingly long and specific with time and practice. Children write notes to each other all day long — before school, during free time, at indoor recess — and, as they are writing and receiving notes, they are also reinforcing and improving their reading skills.

Journal Writing

Daily writing on topics selected by students is an integral part of the reading-writing process. Students invent their own spellings using whatever visual and letter-sound knowledge they have, and they write about anything they choose from personal happenings and family, to stories and poems. Journal writing, and the conferencing that goes along with it, helps us to get to know the children and find out what is significant to them.

Procedures

Journal writing takes place daily and begins the first day of school. Each student is given a 8½" by 11" spiral notebook with the student's name and Writing Journal on the cover. Because we have found that it is difficult for first-graders to keep papers organized in a writing folder (we do not use the writing folder until second grade), we purchase notebooks in bulk at a discount store over the summer. The spiral notebook serves as an organized writing record of the student's progress, and each daily entry is dated. Most students complete two spirals in a year, or one oversized spiral notebook. Since we do not give attention to the lines, students generally ignore the lines on the pages until they are ready to use them.

The first day or two, I model a journal entry on the blackboard or overhead projector. I might write my own personal entry and ask them to suggest spellings for me, or we might do a collaborative effort. In either case, discussion follows; I accept their spellings; students learn that there is no "right answer" and that what they think matters and is accepted. We talk about possible topics such as pets, school, family, friends, and each child knows he may choose his own topic. I go around the room and ask students what they are going to write about. In that way, students having difficulty thinking up a topic will be able to piggyback off someone else's idea. It also gives students confidence that a simple topic such as "My Mom" or "Riding My Bike" is just fine. A delightful reading series, *City Kids* (Rigby Education, 1988), which incudes 60 titles such as "Having a Haircut", "Eating Lunch at School", "The Day I Split My Pants", "Cooking Spaghetti", "First Day Back at School" — also serves as a springboard for writing about everyday occurrences. To help students keep the writing going, I suggest "If you don't know what comes in the middle or end of a word, put in a dash (—) and go on." About 25% of the group will pick up on this, and for some students, it seems to help them from getting bogged down on a word, and feeling stuck.

After routines are established, we seldom have to help students think of topics. We talk to students and parents about discussing topics at home and explain that a topic can be anything that is significant to the child. Children come to school expecting to write each day and they are usually prepared to begin. The beauty of journal writing is that everyone can participate meaningfully and successfully. By spring, when we can read most of the student's writing, teachers write at the same time. Students need to observe that writing is a craft that the teacher values, practices, and shares with students.

Conferencing

Because an immediate audience is so important to young writers, we have found it useful to have parent volunteers present during journal writing time so we can respond to each child's piece. This is particularly important in the beginning of the school year when writing is not always readable to us. We walk around, moving a small chair from student to student and spending no more than a minute or two at eye level with each student. We conference informally by asking students to tell about what they're writing, by asking questions to clarify and extend the writing, by giving lots of encouragement and approval, and by demonstrating conventions that the child seems ready to use. With first-graders, very little actual revising, other than adding on, takes place. They are usually quite content to leave their story exactly as they have written it.

As the child reads aloud what is written on paper, the teacher or volunteer lighty pencils in words difficult to decipher. This serves two purposes. First, there is no later frustration going back to a piece when the child can no longer remember and read what has been written. Second, in rereading the writing, the child may choose to use the conventional spelling of a particular word in a new piece. And this happens often. The children are not at all bothered by the adult's additions (they are never corrections). On the contrary, they seem to enjoy the attention being paid to their writing.

Some educators feel that even writing on the child's work should be avoided as it may be perceived by the child or other readers as corrections. They prefer to list words at the side of the page or at the bottom, so the child can understand that this is done for the teacher's purposes. However, we have not found minimal writing on the page to be a problem; we are aware that extreme caution needs to be taken to maintain the child's feeling of ownership for his writing. Always, respect for the child must be primary.

We do not spell for the children. If they ask how a word is spelled, we say, "How do you think it is spelled?" "What sounds do you hear?" "Do the best you can." The children stop asking for spellings once they know that it is their responsibility and that their best efforts will be accepted. On the other hand, we have come to recognize that spelling does not always improve without some teacher guidance. A child who is repeatedly inventing high frequency words may be ready to spell them conventionally. I do not tell the child his spelling is wrong. I say something like, "I notice you have been using the word "when" a lot in your writing." As we call attention to it by neatly penciling in the conventional spelling I say, "This is how it looks in books." While some children move from "wuz" to "was" and "hav" to "have" on their own, others need to be pushed to do so by having it pointed out specifically.

We sometimes use the last few pages of the journal as a personal dictionary for some of the child's high frequency words. Quick, easy access prevents continuous misspellings of a word used often. I might say something like, "You are using the word "brother" a lot in your writing. I am going to put it here for you so you can find it when you need it."

In addition, direct teaching takes place both individually and with the whole class as the teacher recognizes that students are ready for it or need it. For example, our young writers tend to overuse "good", "fun", "nice" and "said". We brainstorm other ways to say these words, as well as asking, "How did you feel when that happened?" "What were you thinking when that happened?" Such discussions can help students move from boring writing to more expressive and definitive language.

Students help each other daily. They sit together in groups of three, four, or five, and discuss their writing. It took us a long time to adjust to the noise level, but we know that language is noisy and does not occur for young children in a silent space. They talk to each other for ideas, subvocalize when they are thinking, ask each other about spelling words, and read each other their writing. They improvise on each other's topics. When Nathan wrote a story, "Cream of Blob Soup", Michael was impressed and followed with a version he called "Mikey Ate the Soup." One year, we had a whole series of sports stories after one boy wrote an in-depth story about baseball star, Pete Rose.

Journal writing — with access to teacher/parent guidance — lasts for about twenty minutes. However, many students choose to continue writing during independent work time, free time, or before school. It is not unusual for a first-grader to continue journal writing for up to an hour. As with any activity or skill one works toward mastering, progress is developmental, and practice makes a significant difference. The sheer act of writing continuously every day positively affects handwriting, length, content, spelling, and mastery of writing conventions. Children view themselves as writers and feel triumphant.

On looking back at the first year we attempted it, journal writing was relatively easy to implement despite our initial fears, traditional writing background, and lack of direct training. However, during those first days and weeks, we felt extremely anxious. We had no idea what children could accomplish or even how much to expect from them. Because we had worried so much about journal writing before we had attempted it, I asked Karen Shiba to reflect back to our first year and share her reactions.

> What would our students ever write that would fill seventy pages of this notebook? It would be an experiment. We were willing and anxious to see what would happen. Little did we know that almost every child in the room would write enough to fill two notebooks or more during that school year.
>
> Expectations were open-ended but conservative during our first year of journal writing. After all, traditional methods had led me to wonder about what could really be expected from a first-grader. What do they possibly know enough about to write a detailed, informational, lengthy story?
>
> We soon found out just how talented six-year-olds are when given

the opportunity to communicate by using invented spellings and the freedom of self-selecting their topics each day. Topics ranged from how to clean a house to a detailed tour of Disney World. Allowing freedom of choice certainly gave us a running start in sustaining student interest in the journals. The use of invented spelling allowed an early emphasis on comprehension and positive attitude.

I preferred, and still prefer, to have a parent help me during journal writing time each day. With parental help, I know I can meet with each child even if it is only for a half a minute. Sometimes, one student will need me for five or more minutes depending on what skill I am introducing or what guidance may be needed for the story presently being written.

During my first year with journal writing, it was difficult for me to keep track of the stories and skills mastered by each child. I was overwhelmed and constantly fighting feelings of inadequacy. Now I know that with time and practice, it becomes easier to remember individual needs and accomplishments just as we do in other subject areas. Somehow what I wanted to try and believe in became a natural and overwhelmingly satisfying part of the education of my students. It took a long while for "everything" to come together. An effective writing program was worth the wait.

As we observed and gently probed to see what children could do, our expectations and confidence grew. Using self-selected topics and invented spellings, it was extremely rare for a child to say, "I can't write" or "I don't want to write." By doing lots of reading and reflecting, and by trusting what children could accomplish, we were successful. (See Calkins, Graves, Milz and others in *Resources for Teachers*.) Parents celebrated their children's accomplishments with us as we communicated our writing goals and objectives and explained invented spelling the first month of school. (See Appendix I).

We have seen a big improvement in the writing skills of our first-graders since journal writing has been taking place one or more days weekly in the kindergarten classes. While many students now enter first grade with some familiarity of the writing process and are able to write most beginning consonants and many final consonants in writing words, there are always several new students at the representational picture stage — without knowledge of letters and sounds. For these children, or for the occasional child who may say, "I can't write", we need to scribe for them, encourage them in bringing forth their personal stories, and guide them in learning enough beginning consonants to enable them to write for themselves. Here is where the trained volunteer is of great assistance. Such students need to have one-to-one guidance and instruction during journal writing so they can move confidently into writing on their own. The volunteer, or teacher, needs to practice formation of letters with the child, write down the story in the child's own language, practice reading it with the child, and point out conventions of print.

Book Publishing

For many children, book publishing is the most exciting part of the literature program. Frequently the first reading some children do is their own published story, so being an author makes as much of an impact on the child as being a reader. Teachers and trained parent volunteers take stories from the writing journals and transcribe them into books. In the beginning, it is important to accept whatever the child has written; later on, only one in every several pieces or more may reach the publication stage, and students understand and accept this. It often seems a magical process for student and volunteer alike, and the procedures and emotional impact are well described here by Karan Shelley, a parent volunteer.

My son was enrolled last fall in second grade at Moreland. I volunteered at school, motivated by such private and ordinary considerations as easing my child's adjustment and learning who was who and who did what. What happened in fact was quite extraordinary and vastly exceeded my small, bored expectations.

What I did was to work about two hours a week with first-graders who were engaged in the literature approach to reading and writing. My job was to serve as an editor/publisher to children who had written stories in their writing journals. By this means I learned about the literature approach to literacy, a powerful and exciting project, my acquaintance with which had signficant effects beyond the academic. My experience with publishing children's books has transformed the way I regard volunteer work, adult-child projects, and student-teacher relations.

The mechanics of publishing were simple. The classroom teacher, with input from the students, decided who was ready to publish. Generally a story was ready to publish when the child had sustained a narrative or story line over several days or weeks in his journal, at a level of proficiency and quality appropriate to his experiences, purposes, and ability. (The standards for publication in May were much higher than in September.) The publishing began with the student reading his story to me. This step was important as a way of reinforcing the reading process and the student's sense of ownership; it was also sometimes essential because of idiosyncratic spelling and handwriting. After hearing the story, I responded to it, sometimes with mild suggestions for organization and cohesiveness. Revisions made usually involved rearranging for clarity and were only done with the child's approval and input. Next I transcribed the story in more or less standard English with standard spelling and punctuation. Sometimes children were very insistent on their own idiom — one author repeatedly requested that I "put excitement in" (exclamation marks); another was determined to begin every sentence with "and" because it was her favorite word. Such choices were always their prerogative.

The transcriptions went into small books made of paper stapled in covers fashioned from wallpaper samples. The text occupied roughly the bottom quarter of each page, the top being reserved for illustration. Each book had a dedication, the date and place of publication, an author page, and pages at the end for comments from adults and comments from children. Records of the titles and dates of the students were kept on charts and at the end of their journals.

The children took considerable pride in publishing books, and the experience had a gentle pleasure about it for them and for me. It was a quiet time usually and casual — sometimes we sat on the floor in the hall. The kind of anxiety that often accompanies adults' efforts to work with children individually was blessedly lacking. Occasionally children *seemed* uninterested in the actual transcription, especially when the books had become long; yet almost never would a child elect to return to class during publication. The children even skipped recess, movies and other "special" activities in favor of publishing.

The power of the literature approach is amply demonstrated in its effectiveness — kids learn to read and write. What is even more important is that this approach permits *all* children, even those who would be considered limited by conventional standards, to bring themselves forth as whole and able. Publication is a joint venture; the child owns the product and retains rights to it. The adult's role is to serve the child by supplying technical competence that the child lacks. Although neatness, legibility and correctness, by whatever wide or narrow measure, are important in confirming the child's pride in the published book, regard for the child and respect for his writing are far more important traits in the adult publisher than any technical virtuosity. The process is dazzling in its simplicity and workability.

The reward, and perhaps the paradox, was that empowering the child made my participation as a volunteer substantive instead of trivial. Rather than attempting to do something for the child (fix him) — which never really works — I provided an opportunity for him to express what was meaningful to him. I was touched by the children's enthusiasm for our task and their affection. Because we shared seriously and equally a project which centered on what the children could do (rather than on their shortcomings), the children appeared quite wonderful to me. I appreciated them. That recognition had special significance for me because I am a white person, and I was working mostly with black children. While this result may seem to be an accidental product of the context and not the process, I claim otherwise. It proves the integrity of the process: when children are respected and provided with an opportunity to demonstrate their abilities, both child and adult are rewarded in unpredictable ways.

We have been extremely fortunate in having a dedicated parent volunteer, Marianne Sopko, take charge of the entire publishing process for us for two years. Not only did she come in daily during our two hour language arts time to publish books with children; she also took the time to do extensive professional reading, engage us in discussion, and attend workshops to further her understanding of the writing process. Because she worked with students one-to-one, she often let us know when a student needed extra support or a mini-lesson in a particular skill. She helped us keep weekly track of who published what, and she kept a daily descriptive log of her publishing conferences which gave us insight into the child's personality and writing skills. She also worked individually with students who were having some difficulty with the writing process. For example, for a student who entered first grade with no letter-sound knowledge, she used his language experience to collaborate on a simple story and practice reading it with him. At the end of the school year, she wrote a brief summary of each child's published works with some personal insights on the child's writing. Her observations have been invaluable to we teachers who do not always have the time to focus in depth on each child's writing. Marianne has gone on in our district to coach other parents and teachers in the publishing process.

Of her own son, whom she observed daily in the first grade, she commented:

> I have learned so much about the writing process from Mike's work. He illustrates how much a child has to say if he is given a way to do it even when his control of mechanics is shaky. He has shown me how the teaching role fits in to help a child gain mastery. I saw how he began to grow stale in a form he felt safe with — the "all-about" book — and how you gave him the confidence to move on. Mike's writing shows fine observations of people and his environment and an unusual ability to focus on others in their own right. He is a great success story, and it has been one of the joys of my life to watch it happen.

Mike had started off with a good sense of story and some knowledge of consonants. He strung letters together without spacing for the first month and needed direct conferencing in order to move to spacing between words. His letter-sound knowledge, particularly for digraphs, vowels, blends, and certain consonants was weak. Nonetheless, he felt confident to write detailed descriptions of people and events and to communicate his vast store of information. With practice and pride, he read his elaborate books to the class; the reading level in his own books was far more difficult than what he could read in our classroom library. It wasn't until May that he wrote his first fiction story, "Two Good Friends" (based on *Two Good Friends* by Judy Delton, 1974), and used conventions of conversation, action, a problem, a beginning, middle, and ending, and some fine descriptive language. For Mike, the transition from writing lots of information about what he knew — his family, his pets, baseball players, movie stars, Greek myths — did not happen automatically. He needed to be guided to take the risk into a new form. Besides daily conferencing which encouraged him, he attended a local young authors' conference where Lillian Hoban spoke about how ideas for her characters came from members of her family. This seemed to give him the impetus to try a new form which he stayed with until the end of school.

Using Children's Published Books as Literature

After the child's story has been transcribed into a book, the student carefully does the illustrations in colored pencil, crayons, or magic marker. The child who does not feel like drawing has the option of "hiring" an illustrator, usually another student or sibling. Then the child practices reading the book for fluency before he reads it to the class and asks questions about it. The book then becomes part of the young author section of the classroom library and may be signed out by students. The children-as-authors' books are as much in demand as the commercial paperbacks and are favorites to be signed out overnight and reread in the classroom. It is interesting to note that while a normal share of commercial paperbacks has been lost over the years, a child's published book has never been lost. Treating the children's works as literature increases the value placed on their writing and allows them to feel validated and rewarded for their efforts.

Initially, it took us some time to treat the children's published books like the literature in our classroom library. In the beginning, when students would read their books to the class, we didn't allow time for discussion and questioning in the way we did with commercial books. It was after reading Donald Graves, *Writing: Teachers and Children at Work* that I was struck by the omission, and we rectified it. Similarly, a page allowing children to comment on each other's books was added to their published book, and the children love this opportunity to comment on their peers' books. Originally, we had only a page for adult comments; my traditional "neatness" background had me too concerned about not wanting the book to look messy. Now the books truly belong to the children.

When Don Holdaway recently visited our district and classroom, he commented that our book publishing completed the circle between home and school. He was particularly struck by the parent comments at the back of each child's book indicating the parents' involvement, concern, and participation in the total literacy process.

In going through all the books published one recent school year, I found the parent comments to be very relevant to the content of the book. Also, extended family members would often comment on the book, and it was clear that the pride felt reached into the community. (See Figure 1 for typical comments.) I also noted that our children wrote only the most kind and supportive remarks, affirming their understanding and appreciation of the efforts involved. (See Figure 2.)

Each school year, we have published over 200 books in our two first grades. About one-third of these are based directly on the literature the children have read, and this factor has remained consistent. The majority of the literature stories are written in the late winter and spring after students have spent months internalizing story structure and story language. About one-third of the books relate to people in the family, including aunts, uncles, cousins, and grandparents. The remaining third includes individual interests, school, friends, trips, pets, special events, holidays, and fantasy stories. Because children have written on topics that are important to them, the writing is memorable. (See Figure 3 for a record of books published by a first-grader.)

Figure 1   Parents' Comments on Students' Published Work

This' book was very good. The story was interesting and exciting. Did you catch any fish? I would like to read your next story.

Love,
GRANDMA

Great Book — Big Daddy
First of many — Grand mother.
Very good — Mrs Little
Very good — Bonnie Daniel
You have potential! — Pastor James

This book helped me to understand how much NATHAN enjoys our family THANKSGIVING. I was pleased that he wrote about so many warm and pleasant things. Keep up the good works

Love
Mom

Figure 2   Children's Comments on Published Work

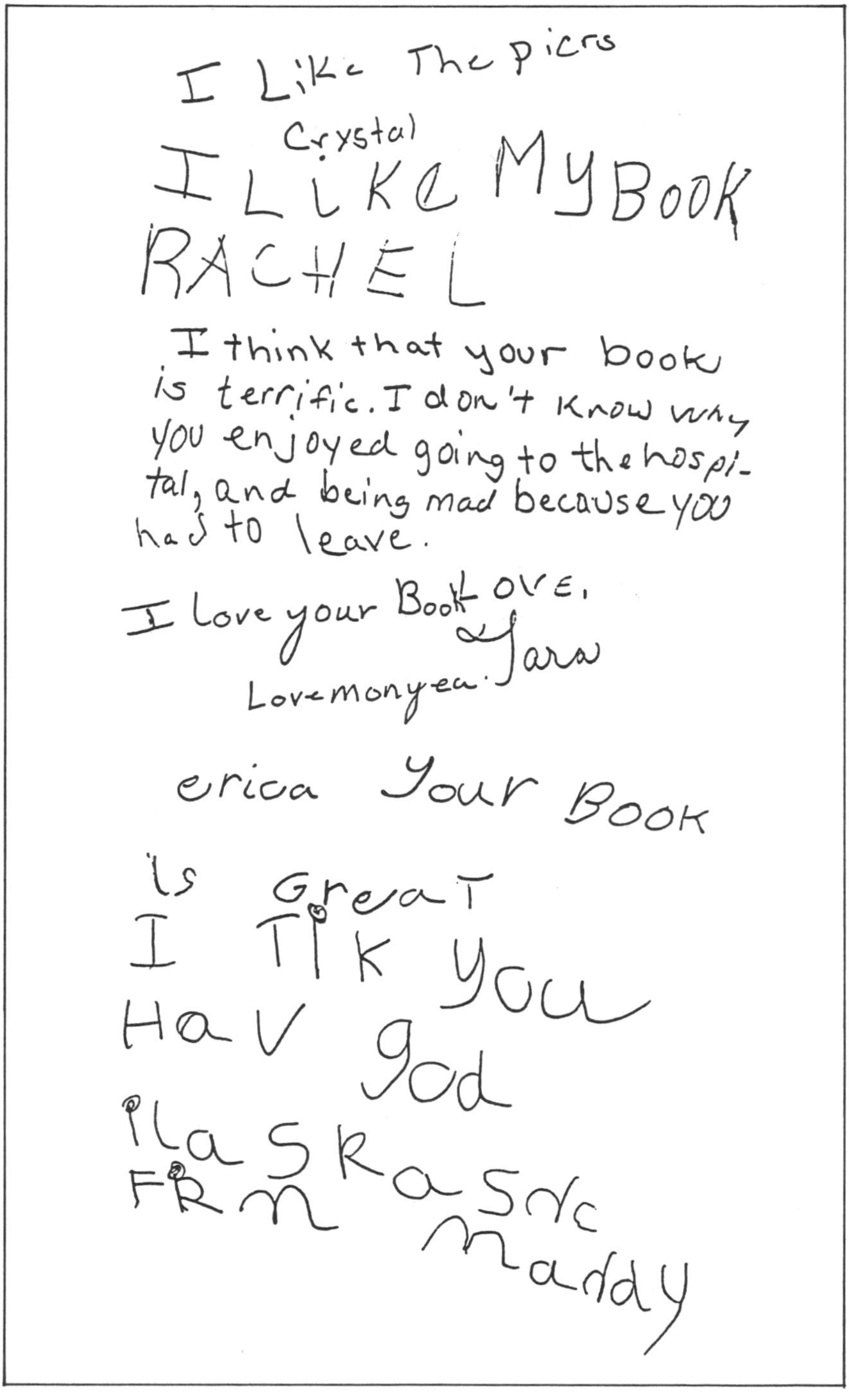

I Like The picrs

Crystal

I LiKe MYBOOK

RACHEL

I think that your book
is terrific. I don't know why
you enjoyed going to the hospital, and being mad because you
had to leave.

I love your Book ove,
Love monyea. Tara

erica Your Book

is great
I Tik you
Hav god
PlaSkaSrc
FRn Maddy

Figure 3　A Student's Publishing Record

Books Published by Nikole

1. Last week, October 1983
2. This week, November 1983
3. Things I Do At School Dec.1983
4. Things I Do At School, January 1984
5. The Red Balloon, February 1954
6. At The Circus, February 1954
7. My Cousin And My Aunt March 1984
8. All About Myself March 1984
9. My Friends March 1984
10. My Weekend April 1984
11. The Magic Frog April 1984
12. Fall April 1984
13. Spring April 1984
14. My New Table May 1984
15. When We Went to the Young Author's Conference May 1984
16. My Trip To the Nature Center May 1984
17. Frog and Toad June 1984

Some Personal Thoughts on Writing

I probably did not think of myself as a writer until I participated in The Northeast Ohio Writing Project during the summer of 1985. The Writing Project is part of the National Writing Project which believes that teachers are the best teachers of other teachers. In addition to demonstration teaching, much reading and discussion of theory and research, we wrote every day for one hour and met in response groups for another hour. It was the first time I had ever shared my writing with other writers and allowed myself to be vulnerable. The support of the group encouraged me and gave me direction while leaving the authorship with me. Elementary teachers were in the minority; most of the participants were from area high schools. These were teachers who had chosen to teach English because they loved words and writing and literature. Not so with the elementary teachers. I had never thought about writing except as it was taught — with a heavy emphasis on grammar, diagraming sentences, correctness, and figuring out what the teacher wanted. I wrote a piece about my grandmother and her influence on my life. It was well-received, and I felt hopeful. I had revised and rewritten and revamped, but could I dare call myself a writer? The very word made me uncomfortable.

When I decided I might like to write a book for teachers, my college-age daughter said, "But can you write Mom?" Immediately on the defensive, I said, "I have no idea." She, a critical reader and writer, offered to read a few chapters and lend her opinion. Her excitement, surprise, and pleasure came through over the telephone as she told me she found the writing interesting and flowing. I breathed a sigh of relief. Could I write? I still wasn't sure.

Sitting down in earnest over the summer months to write the book, I found myself examining my behavior as a writer and relating it to what goes on in classrooms. I was so scared of just beginning that I used avoidance measures for days. I cleaned the house, wrote letters to friends, paid bills, put in a supply of my favorite ice cream, organized months of paper work. I wanted everything in my life organized so I could give writing my full attention. I had to get myself ready to write. (Do we allow students that readiness, avoidance time which may, in fact, be necessary to begin?)

When I finally did start, I could only work in spurts. I needed to get up and move around a lot. (I thought about the kids who ask to go to the bathroom often and students who cannot sharpen pencils after the bell rings. Some of them may just need to move about.) I needed my family and friends to listen to my thoughts, including my fears and frustrations, and give me helpful feedback. (I thought about quiet classrooms. Could I write if I couldn't bounce ideas off others?) I needed to reward myself with good food and snacks throughout the day. (I thought about no snacks in classrooms and kids who chew on pencils.) Perhaps what surprised me most was that I could not stick to one topic. I had several chapters going at one time. When I lost interest or got frustrated with one topic, I moved to another as a way of revitalizing my thinking. (I thought about students who must finish one piece before being allowed to start another.) And I thought about time. I had planned to write all morning, take an early afternoon break, write again before dinner and take the evening off. But my mind didn't cooperate with that nicely organized schedule. There were some mornings I couldn't get started. Some nights I couldn't sleep for thinking about a topic, and I would find myself at the word processor in the middle of the night. I was afraid that if I waited till morning, I'd forget the insight. (I thought about how we schedule writing periods and expect students to produce on cue and within a given time frame.)

Mostly, I thought about how hard it was to write and be a writer, how persistence and perseverance were necessary and how important the emotional climate of my working environment was. The process was scary and uplifting, agonizing and exhilarating, frustrating and fulfilling. I could not have done it without continuous support — my husband taking over most of the cooking and shopping and talking with me when I needed to talk, my son asking me daily, "How's it going, Mom?", fellow teachers reading and responding to drafts, friends and family listening to self-doubts and reassuring me. A supportive environment was what I needed most, and they gave it to me. I believe more strongly than ever that if students feel valued, encouraged, and supported, they will take on all that is necessary to develop their natural writing abilities. I also believe, based on my own writing experience and the insights I have gained, that teachers must begin to do some writing themselves if they are truly to understand and value the writing process.

Writing African folk tales.

7 The Reading-Writing Process
Moving into Grade 2

Second grade is a wonderful year for building confidence in reading-writing abilities. Students who are new to the school, or who have had a slow start, often make tremendous growth. This is a critical year, because after second grade, students who have not seen themselves as competent language learners may experience difficulty developing their full reading-writing potential.

Teachers and parents often ask, "What happens if students have to go back into a basal book program?" Our experience is that the students adjust. Having had the best possible first grade experience and feeling successful, they enter second grade as competent readers and are perceived as such. Parents usually try to exert some influence in bringing more literature into the classroom. Where there is more likely to be a problem is with writing; teachers unfamiliar with invented spellings may not appreciate the children's efforts and send them negative messages.

We were very fortunate. After our principal, Delores Groves, saw the success and confidence of our first grade children, she insisted that the literature program go on to second grade. We again had an uninterrupted block of language arts time which allowed for flexibility. We were able to get funds for books, and the second grade teacher and I were able to co-teach the reading-writing process the first year.

That constant conferring together was invaluable, as there were two perspectives, not only on how the teaching was going but also on getting to know each of the children. I was nervous all over again. We had no model and had to create our own.

The second grade teacher I was paired with, Joan Di Dio, was a highly skilled, creative, and humanistic teacher. Although she had been used to basals and workbooks, she had naturally gravitated towards literature — reading to her class and using thoughtful follow-up activities that promoted reading and writing, as well as human relations. I had anticipated that the first grade program would be extended with its emphasis on books and writing. I had also assumed there would be no workbooks or worksheets in second grade. When Joan told me she intended to use workbooks along with the literature because she needed to be assured the skills were being taught, I became very upset. I had failed to appreciate her needs in regard to the teaching of skills.

That summer before school started, we sat down together and listed all the "skills" the workbook and district curriculum guide specified. Then, as the months went by, we worked together on integrating the skills into our process teaching. Gradually, workbooks were used less and less as she became caught up in the "skills-through-literature" process. She came to recognize that the literature afforded ample opportunities for overall, effective reading instruction. As all teachers do, she had to have choices and ownership in her teaching. It was a significant insight for me, and one I have not forgotten.

The Reading Process in Second Grade

The range of reading levels in the classroom is wide at the start of the school year. We have proficient readers who can read anything and who are reading all the Beverly Cleary books along with such favorites as *Tales of a Fourth Grade Nothing* by Judy Blume and *Charlie and the Chocolate Factory* by Roald Dahl. Others are reading *The Littles* series by John Peterson. Still another group is reading difficult picture books such as the *Frances* books by Lillian and Arthur Hoban. Another bunch is reading 'I Can Read' books such as *Mouse Soup* and *Owl at Home* by Arnold Lobel, and then there are always some new students who are not reading at all. Meeting everyone's individual needs presents a real, ongoing challenge!

Most of the students come back to school having done some summer reading. Notices go home at the end of first grade on "Ways to Encourage Summer Reading". (See Appendix J). Some have even kept their own reading records at home, as well as summer journals. At least half a dozen have brought in books they have written and published at home as well as favorite books they wrote in first grade.

Lots of time is spent sharing over the first few weeks. Children are reading their own stories along with familiar favorites.

Shared Experiences and Literature Extension Activities

There is lots of whole class reading every day, the teacher reading aloud classic literature, as well as shared reading — not so much through the Big Books now, although those are still much enjoyed — but through chart poems and stories. Often the overhead projector is used. Students' attention is focused on the screen, and the overhead becomes a wonderful tool for cloze activities, drawing attention to the salient features of words, reinforcing one-to-one correspondence, for guided reading, and for visual modeling in mini-lessons. During this whole group time, students also share published works and completed projects and have involvement with the creative arts. A book may be performed as readers' theater; a class song might be written and sung; a poem might be dramatized during choral reading. Collaborative written responses to literature continue as in first grade and move beyond patterned text to summaries, original stories, and poems. As in first grade, and as is very common in New Zealand and Australia, many of these shared and individual pieces become "reading round the room" focuses for children to read and respond to.

After Lynn Cowen, a second grade teacher in our district, read *Otis Spofford* by Beverly Cleary to her class, the whole class discussed what a summary was and collaborated on summarizing the first section of the book on the overhead projector. Then the class was divided into groups, each with the task of summarizing specific sections of the book. Each group's draft was edited collaboratively by the class on the overhead projector. While the teacher printed out each text in enlarged print, each group worked on illustrations for their text. The whole endeavor was mounted in sequence as a wall story outside the classroom and was much enjoyed by students in many classes.

Lynn took advantage of creating another "reading the walls" activity when a bee "zoomed" into her classroom and disrupted the morning activities. The class gathered together, and with the teacher's guidance, wrote a descriptive story of what happened.

Poetry continues to be a well-loved activity, and some teachers continue the individual student anthologies into second grade. Some students choose favorite poems to memorize and recite, and some poems are learned whole class. Such poetry books as *Honey I Love* by Eloise Greenfield, *Every Time I Climb a Tree* by David McCord, and *If I Were in Charge of the World* by Judith Viorst are available in paperback in multiple copies and are a popular selection from the classroom library.

Thematic units are developed. For example, Joan Di Dio read aloud *A Toad for Tuesday* by Russell Erickson and used this delightful book — about an owl who has captured a toad and the development of their unlikely friendship — as a springboard for an ongoing unit on friendship. Her students wrote letters to the book characters, wrote original chapters to the book, wrote their own endings, did comparison and contrast illustrations on characters' traits, and read all the other *Warton and Morton* books in the series.

As a culminating activity, the children dramatized the story in the auditorium for the entire school, complete with original music and dance. Students, with the help of parent volunteers, also created costumes, props, and scenery. The literature-based dramatization afforded the children an increased sense of self-esteem, a sense of ownership in the literature, and an immeasurable sense of accomplishment. Every child had at least one speaking part, and each spoke confidently and expressively. Their teacher told me she still gets "goose bumps" at the memory of the second-graders spontaneously applauding Daniel's successful delivery of his lines. (Daniel had entered school at the end of first grade and was struggling with many severe learning difficulties.)

Other favorite books that dealt with friendship and that were extended through various activities and media included such favorites as *Me and Neesie* by Eloise Greenfield, *Sam, Bangs, and Moonshine* by Evaline Ness, and *Gabrielle and Selena* by Peter Desbarats. These books helped set the tone within the classroom for improving interpersonal relationships and promoting acceptance and kindness among the students.

A unit about Bill Peet and his wonderful books is a big hit every year. The fanciful illustrations and clever stories — some of them are completely in rhyme — captivate second-graders. Many of these are read aloud, discussed, and placed in the reading center; some are practiced in reading group for oral fluency; others are available for students to discover and read themselves for the first time. A videotape about Bill Peet ("Bill Peet in his Studio", Houghton Mifflin Company, 1982) where he is interviewed in his studio and does the narrating, allows students to see one way an author works. Bill Peet explains how he does his illustrations before he writes and how ideas for his writing may be suggested from his daily surroundings. Showing students what different authors do increases their options in writing and invites them to try new styles.

Activities to go along with Bill Peet have included: writing a final chapter to *The Whingdingdilly* before the actual ending was read, as well as illustrating an original Whingdingdilly; making posters advertising a favorite Bill Peet book; designing a new book cover for a favorite title; creating a diary written by one of the characters; making a mobile displaying favorite characters. In addition, letters each student wrote to Bill Peet were responded to by a letter he wrote to the class, and there is always great excitement when an author takes the time to answer students.

Literature is a wonderful stimulus for writing, and some of the writing we do emanates from picture books. After hearing and discussing *The Pain and the Great One* by Judy Blume, a humorous, realistic story of a middle child with a younger brother (the pain) and an older sister (the great one), I asked the children to write about "the pain" or "great one" in their lives. Even students without siblings had no difficulty thinking of someone in their lives who fits the description. We got some memorable writing, and students loved swapping stories. Because the focus was on the content and emotional honesty, first drafts were accepted, and the activity was completed in about 45 minutes. Even our low-ability students were successful. (See Figure 1.)

Dinosaurs, which are a favorite science focus in second grade, are incorporated into the language arts. All kinds of books are brought into the classroom. Students study the facts and ponder the fanciful. They write short reports on dinosaurs and create their own original dinosaurs based on the scientific knowledge they have. A favorite book from first grade, *If the Dinosaurs Came Back* by Bernard Most, is reread and is a wonderful stimulus for writing and illustrating about what would happen if dinosaurs were on earth today.

Rudyard Kipling's *Just So Stories*, as well as *How the Chipmunk Got its Stripes* by Nancy Cleaver and *Why Mosquitoes Buzz in People's Ears* by Verna Aardema, are jumping off points for speculating and collaborating on how animals got certain features and traits. Group and individual stories are composed.

Many of the activities that are part of independent work time evolve from shared experiences. A mystery unit developed after teachers read aloud several mystery stories and the class examined the features of a good mystery. With the librarian's assistance, teachers filled their rooms with all kinds of mysteries on all different reading levels. During independent work time, students read a classroom mystery book silently and kept a daily record of pages read. Each reading group was involved in discussing a mystery, and students wrote original mysteries (unedited but revised) and shared these with their peers.

Similarly, a biography unit was developed beginning with the teacher reading aloud a biography to the whole class. Students were all reading biographies silently in class as well as focusing on one biography in reading group. A final independent work project involved choosing a favorite biography and summarizing important early childhood and educational information, illustrating a favorite

Figure 1   A Story Inspired by **The Pain and the Great One**

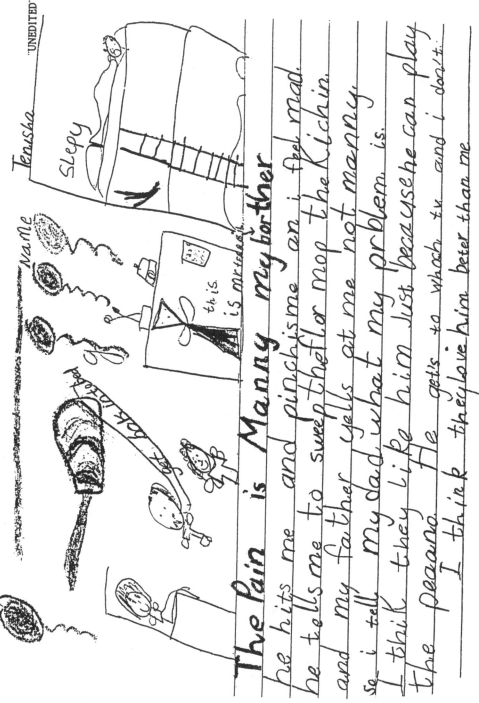

scene from the person's life, discussing important accomplishments and why they were significant, interpreting the effect this person had on other people's lives, and ways the book did or did not influence the student's life. In addition, students wrote their own autobiographies complete with family background and baby pictures.

Reading Groups

Checking WEB Reading (Independent reading): The first five to ten minutes of reading group are spent checking nightly reading. Realizing that students will continue to read if they are getting enjoyment and satisfaction out of the activity, focus is on understanding the story as a whole and fostering positive attitudes towards reading. The student need not read every word correctly to gain pleasure and meaning from print.

Students are expected to read for 20 to 30 minutes each day. Students come to group with their WEB book (*W*onderfully *E*xciting *B*ook), the name we use for their self-selected reading book. Most of the books are chosen from the classroom library. Since the teacher has read most of these, she can do a specific comprehension check. I do this daily: teachers do book check two to five days a week depending on their purposes and the group's needs, and spend up to several minutes per student. The student is asked to tell something about what he read, such as the part he liked best, the problem, what he thinks will happen next. High-level questions, such as "how" and "why" as opposed to "who" and "where" are encouraged. While it is important for teachers to keep in mind that questioning does not teach comprehension (which has already occurred or not occurred), guided questioning and response can help students refocus, recall, and make connections.

The teacher needs to emphasize that all students in the group listen during book check. This serves several purposes. Listening to a peer talk enthusiastically about a book often sells the book. It is not unusual for all members of a group to have read a book such as *How to Eat Fried Worms* by Thomas Rockwell or *Chocolate Fever* by Robert Kimmel Smith because of the excitement generated during discussion. Also, a student who has read the book being reported on may disagree with the student giving the report and ask his own question of the student. Students become critical listeners.

A student who is unable to answer the questions and is having trouble reading orally is asked to reread. If the book seems too difficult, the student is encouraged to choose another book. A student also exchanges a book if he doesn't like the selection after reading at least 30 pages. Teachers keep daily records on each child's reading (see *Lesson Plans* in Chapter 11), and students keep a written record of books completed with the title, author, and date completed. (See

Appendix F2.) Daily records make students accountable for their reading and aware of their daily progress. Occasionally, parents need to be contacted to lend their support to their student's efforts.

What Happens in Reading Group (guided reading): The purpose of reading group is reading together for pleasure while developing and reinforcing skills and strategies; emphasis is on understanding and appreciating the literature. (See *Recommended Literature, Grade 2*, Chapter 17.) Groups meet for about 30 minutes daily. Most of the time is spent between oral and silent reading for specific purposes and discussing the book. Story discussion focuses on using higher-level questions to consider author's purpose, predict plot, visualize setting, discuss and examine vocabulary in context, make connections to students' lives, etc. Students not in group are working on responding to literature through their reading response logs (see Chapter 12, Evaluation), through extension activities, silent reading assignments, WEB reading, or journal writing, and are expected not to interrupt the group.

Mostly, students have been grouped homogeneously as in first grade. Some teachers, however, are finding much success with heterogeneous grouping and report that low-ability readers are much more eager to read. The stimulation of being with higher level students has encouraged them. Keeping in mind that readers do not have to read every word to get the meaning, students are grasping concepts and gaining in confidence.

Elaine Weiner, a second grade teacher who tried heterogeneous grouping, notes:

> The slower readers were happy to join the more advanced groups, and there was a visible display of pride when they were asked to join. At the beginning, the slower readers found it somewhat difficult to "keep up" with their more advanced peers, but as the weeks went on, they showed marked improvement in comprehension and vocabulary development. They even became more proficient oral readers.
>
> By the end of the year, two of the four "slower" children could no longer be called low readers, and two were slightly below average in a group of very good to excellent readers. All were proud of their accomplishments. One child became an avid reader preferring reading to any other subject. Another became a very good reader with fine insights into story and comprehension. The other two began to enjoy reading far more than I had ever hoped.

If homogeneous grouping is used, it is important not to keep the children in the same grouping structure all year. Flexibility is necessary so children learn to interact with all their peers and so they do not become "slotted". In addition to ability grouping, children can be grouped on the basis of skills needs, interest, and peers they want to be with. A whole class reading group also works well and can be used occasionally. Students follow along in personal copies of a book as the teacher reads aloud, pair up to assist each other in assigned reading, and work in small groups on related literature activities. The disadvantage of whole class grouping on a regular basis involves discussion. With up to 30 students, typically, about one-third of the students do the talking and everyone else listens. Small groups, of say six to nine students, are necessary to have quality discussions where all students have the opportunity to participate and respond critically.

While second grade is the year that most students will move comfortably into more silent reading, students still gaining confidence in the reading process will need to do much oral reading to firm up their strategies. I keep a 9" x 12" blackboard at the reading table. When a student comes to a word he is unable to figure out and that is blocking his reading, I write it on the slate and write another word he knows under it to help him. These are students who have difficulty with phonics so it is important to help them relate what they already know to the unknown. For example, if the word causing difficulty is "sharpen", I might write the words "she" and "car" on the slate. The student would be asked to read the words and use the context of the sentence to make the connection to the correct word. As in first grade, the goal is to model for the student so he can help himself and eventually do this on his own. Emphasis is still on reading for meaning, but now that students are reading, more attention can be given to the graphophonic cueing system.

Even our low-ability readers know the purpose of reading is to get meaning from text, and they use meaning cues effectively. Notice the following examples from *Anna, Grandpa, and the Big Storm* by Carla Stevens; the reader has made substitutions that allow him to go on and to get the overall meaning. The reader's miscues are in italics.

"The wind is so fierce (*fast*) it's going to be hard to get a ladder up this high."

"The door opened and a fireman appeared (*approached*)."

"No one is to let go under any circumstances (*conditions*)."

In the sentence, "The wind was blowing up the avenue with the force of a h . . .", the reader hesitates briefly, then reads "hurricane" correctly using only the initial consonant and context. When students make meaningful substitutions, they demonstrate they are thinking as they read; they need to be congratulated and encouraged to go on.

Reading and writing are connected, even in reading group. Working with a group of high-ability students reading *The Adventures of Spider* and *More Adventures of Spider*, delightful African folk tales by Joyce Cooper Arkhurst, we analyzed how the stories were put together. Using a story map as a guide (see Appendix G), we collaborated on writing story maps for several tales. The story map is an excellent way for students to respond to literature because it requires a careful reexamination of the text. After working together as a group with teacher guidance and modeling, students worked with partners, choosing a tale and making a story map for it (see Figure 2). With good background knowledge of how the tales were put together, they confidently wrote their own African folk tales. While much of the writing was done during independent work time, responding to stories and revising was done with partners and within the small reading group. Final copes were typed by parent volunteers and bound into books that became popular reading in the classroom library.

Figure 2   A Story Map

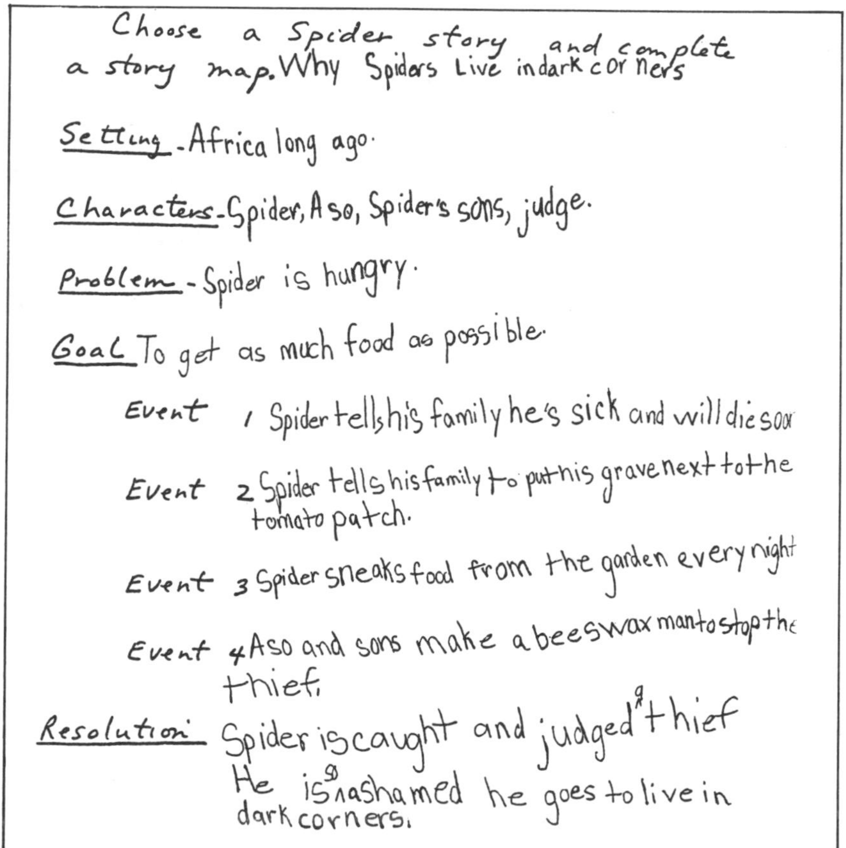

Choose a Spider story and complete a story map. Why Spiders Live in dark corners

Setting - Africa long ago.

Characters - Spider, Aso, Spider's sons, judge.

Problem - Spider is hungry.

Goal To get as much food as possible.

Event 1 Spider tells his family he's sick and will die soon

Event 2 Spider tells his family to put his grave next to the tomato patch.

Event 3 Spider sneaks food from the garden every night

Event 4 Aso and sons make a beeswax man to stop the thief.

Resolution Spider is caught and judged thief. He is ashamed he goes to live in dark corners.

In another interrelated activity, Linda Powers, a Grade 2 teacher in our district, read and discussed the format and content of the Big Book *The Musicians of Bremen* (retold by Brenda Parkes and Judith Smith). Through the school and public libraries, she located copies of seven other versions of the same tale. A group of students each read one tale and with individual teacher guidance noted descriptions of characters and storyline. The group then convened and shared the differences and similarities between the Big Book and their various retellings. Each student chose a character to illustrate, write about, and place along a cooperatively made road map from the farm to Brementown. The teacher noted:

> I was impressed that the students saw so many variations in language and description. I was surprised by the freedom in which they shared and the depth of their thinking. They went beyond what I would have expected from second-graders.

The Writing Process in Second Grade

Literature continues to influence second grade writers positively and naturally. We notice enriched vocabulary, greater attention to detail, improved grammatical structure and unexpected adaptations of an author's style as well as increased use of description and dialogue. One of the major differences we see between first and second grade writers is their capacity and willingness to do some specific work on revision, particularly in focusing on one topic, and ordering and structuring a piece. Second-graders are capable of a more sustained effort. For first graders, just the doing it — dealing with mechanics of spelling and handwriting — requires enormous effort. Second-graders have fewer physical constraints, and they have a sense of writing as an ongoing project. The skills students have acquired in first grade through daily writing allow them to write with a clear and authentic voice in second grade. Darlene, for example, used her writing to express her feelings about her grandmother.

Grand Mother

My grandmother is a nice lady because we play a lot of games such as: uno, sorry, and monopoly. Sometimes she lets me peal potatos and cor nand peass and take the steam off the turn ups and greens. When I was a little girl I lived with my grand panrents Because my mom had to get evey thing settell. Then sh came to get me.

Journal Writing

Journal writing using invented spelling continues on a daily basis, and teachers organize it and respond to it in various ways. Some teachers allow time for some daily sharing with the whole class; others promote sharing with a partner. Some use the concept of dialogue journals where the teacher responds regularly in writing to the students' writing. While it is not necessary to respond every day to students' writing, students need to know teachers will be responding in some regular fashion. While the conventional spelling of certain high utility words may be noted — as is done in first grade — red penciling and/or any kind of grading are never used in journal writing. Students' efforts are accepted and congratulated. Sloppy writing and poor efforts, however, are not accepted. Students are expected to comply with the standards the teacher and class set together. We expect our students to cross out as opposed to erasing, use a ∧ where information needs to be added, and to spell as best they can by stretching out the sounds they hear, quietly asking a neighbor, or by going back to a remembered source — such as a familiar book or environmental print around the room. The dictionary is not used during journal writing as it takes the focus off the writing and slows students down.

While most teachers continue to have students use the spiral notebook with the dating of daily entries, others like a three-ring notebook. Teachers find it practical and easier to snap out several pages to take home and read. They also like the possibilities for revision; it's easier to move pages around, add and delete pages, or add tabs for specific topics.

Especially at the beginning of the school year, the teacher will need to model and emphasize what is expected. I use the blackboard or overhead projector and demonstrate the writing process by thinking aloud and saying the words as I write them. I choose a topic that has meaning for me that day, for example, how my day got off to a bad start by my leaving some books I needed at home. I tell "what happened" and "how I felt about it." I also give detailed examples of other possible writing topics I know a lot about: our dog Tobi needing more attention with Peter off to college, my daughter Liz coming home to celebrate her 21st birthday, my garden needing attention, going to the local farmer's market and baking my husband Frank his favorite apple pie. Then I ask the students what they are going to write about, and we go around the room. Hearing other students' ideas gives reluctant writers suggestions for possible topics and reinforces the fact that everyone has a story to tell. I also tell the students that if they use words like "good", "bad", "fun", "nice", then they need to tell *why* the "party was fun" so the listener/reader can get a picture in his mind. Summaries of movies and television programs — which some students tend to overuse — are discouraged unless the show influenced or was important to the student in some way.

Occasionally, journal writing is extended to include teacher-suggested topics in academic areas. This is an effective way of letting the teacher assess what a student has gained from a lesson or activity, as well as a way of evaluating a lesson's overall effectiveness. What we teach is not always what students learn. After viewing a film on snakes or returning from a class trip to the art museum, students might be asked to write about what they learned that was significant to them. While the teacher has structured the topic, the student chooses the content and retains ownership. Some of the most enjoyable, memorable second grade writing experiences have resulted from "seize-the-moment" situations. For example, when a mini-earthquake occurred, the children were in school. Their many feelings were shared and related in detail in their journals immediately following the quake.

The Writing Folder

We introduced the writing folder in second grade and tried to teach writing process as described by Donald Graves and Lucy Calkins (see *Resources for Teachers*). In addition to daily journal writing, we scheduled three 50 minute time blocks each week for writing. The first year we co-taught, and even with two teachers in the room, we were extremely frustrated. Some children, given daily free-choice writing, did little writing and misused the time making it difficult for us to conference with others. Peer group conferencing did not work well with our second-graders, and we thought it was our fault. After a whole year, we never quite got it together. Looking back, we realize the children could have accomplished much more had we directed some of the writing topics, still allowing free choice in the actual writing with a topic that was real and relevant. It was all right to use one-to-one conferencing as we did in the first grade because that was what worked best for us. We would go around the room, moving a chair from student to student, and give lots of support and ask questions to keep the writing going. It wasn't until I heard Mary Ellen Giacobbe (who worked with Donald Graves) say that peer conferencing doesn't work well for her that I felt it was all right not to use it, no longer felt guilty, and began to trust my own judgments.

This writing process is difficult and challenging. Accepting the wide range of writing abilities, allowing enough time for brainstorming sessions, deciding what mini-lessons should be taught, and promoting class interaction and sharing, all take time and patience as well as trial and error. However, if we see ourselves as learners, along with the students, we will increase effective teaching and promote student respect. Joan Di Dio states:

> Even young second-graders recognize authenticity and honesty in a teacher, and they appreciate it. I would say to them, 'Well, kids, this idea didn't work very well yesterday, did it? So, today we're going to try something different.'

As in first grade, parent volunteers are an essential part of the process, especially with individual help in the revising and editing stages. Parents' help encourages the publishing process to flourish; the teacher does not get bogged down with lots of lengthy manuscripts that require final editing and typing. In some schools, parents have taken over the entire publishing process with an in-school publishing center that is open daily.

Spelling

While we do need to continue to teach spelling, current research in spelling does not support the heavy emphasis on drill and weekly spelling tests, which are prevalent in most classrooms. High scores on tests of word lists do not necessarily transfer to writing in context. What is recommended by research is lots of purposeful reading and writing in literate environments where children are encouraged to invent and try out as best as they can. (See *Resources for Teachers*, especially *Spell by Writing* by Wendy Bean and Chrystine Bouffler.) Like the language processes, spelling is developmental, and the child needs support for his approximations and risk taking. Through daily practice and teacher guidance, the child gradually moves towards conventional spelling.

High frequency words, such as "friend", "cousin", "when", "where", etc., that students are using in their daily writing become part of the required spelling program. Teachers, in reading the journals, note words that many students are inventing. A few teachers are taking all the spelling words from the journals and literature and individualizing for each child; others are compiling a weekly list. At this point, however, most of our teachers and administrators are still more comfortable using a formal spelling workbook program.

In our second grades, each student is requested to buy a *Spelling Reference Book* (Developmental Learning Materials, [Allen Texas], 1973). This handy booklet alphabetically lists the most common words middle elementary students use and leaves room for adding the student's personal words. It is easier and faster to use than a dictionary; definitions are not given, but homonymns are noted and explained with a clear example in the context of a meaningful sentence. This reference book is not used during journal writing; it slows students down to worry about spelling. It is heavily used in the editing process, and the booklet goes with students into third grade.

Parents need to be kept informed on how we are teaching spelling and what the research is that supports our teaching. A letter goes home to our parents with a very brief explanation of the reference book and the writing process. (See Appendix K.) Our Parent Teacher Association also stocks copies of *Spel... is a Four-Letter Word* (Gentry, 1987), a concise handbook written for teachers and parents that answers the questions most asked about spelling.

Adjustment of New Students

A Good Reader from the Basal Text

Jonathon was a student who entered our second grade after being in a first grade basal program. Jonathon had learned the mechanics of reading with the basal, but he did not associate pleasurable reading with school. Home reading of library books was something very different from the dull stories and many hundreds of worksheets at school. Interestingly enough, he was in the "average" reading group throughout first grade. While he could read virtually any book he chose from the library, he didn't read the basal as fluently. With all the pleasurable reading he was doing at home, school reading must have seemed like an irrelevant exercise. The example of Jonathon points up the fact that kids need to understand *why* they're learning what they are learning, and that what they are learning needs to be relevant. No doubt part of the problem was that the kindergarten teacher had put a heavy emphasis on phonics and skills — a common practice — so he would be "ready" for first grade reading.

With literature-based reading, Jonathon could now integrate all the things he liked about reading with school, and he blossomed. Over winter vacation, he completed all the books in the *Little House on the Prairie* series by Laura Ingalls Wilder, over 1000 pages of reading in two weeks. In the spring, after we read and discussed *Brighty of the Grand Canyon* by Marguerite Henry in reading group, he went to the school library and completed the entire series. He made lots of connections for himself; he understood how an author integrated factual material in a fiction book particularly as relates to natural setting; he recognized and appreciated a very descriptive style of writing; he asked questions about illustrators and their backgrounds.

Initially, he was quite bored with journal writing and seemed afraid to risk writing for his own purposes. Because he had no practice and experience with free choice writing, he was very guarded, and he did not understand the purpose of the activity. He tended to get into repetitive ruts, beginning each entry, "Yesterday, I..." or with some other boring formula. Gradually, he became more comfortable about revealing something about himself and starting with different leads.

By third grade, he was very expressive, and his mother and teacher noted the satisfaction he felt with the writing process.

A Poor Reader from the Basal Text

Jordan had entered first grade with excited anticipation. Although he showed no signs of being an early reader, he loved being read to. His nightly story time with his father was a favorite time of day for both of them. Jordan liked his first grade teacher very much, but he never saw himself as a reader. He was very conscious of the fact that he was in the lowest reading group, and he was frustrated by all the workbook pages. Based on the D's and F's he saw on some of his workbook pages, he told his father, "Dad, I think I'm going to fail reading." At the end of first grade he was reading on a Primer level and was showing some symptoms of anxiety. Despite a medical checkup which pronounced him physically fit, he was having to leave the room constantly — two to three times in an hour — to use the bathroom.

In second grade, he entered a literature-based reading-writing classroom. He heard stories all day long, and the room was filled with wonderful books. Despite the fact that he missed much of the first month of school due to illness, by late December he was reading beginning chapter books, *The Littles* series by John Peterson and *The Polk Street School* series by Patricia Giff. He pushed himself to read the books he liked and that other students were reading, and he attempted to read these books at home and at school. By late May, he had worked his way up to the highest-ability group and completed reading *Charlotte's Web* by E. B. White. All signs of tenseness were gone. He saw himself as a competent reader, and he had a sense of being able to do everything well at school. His total reading score on the Stanford Diagnostic Reading Test indicated a jump from second to sixth grade level, from October to May, in all areas of reading. His success with the best of children's books paved the way for personal and academic growth. Best of all, his confidence in all school areas increased; he saw himself as a successful student.

Joan Di Dio and second grade authors.

8 The Literature-Writing Process
Continuing in Grade 3

Cross grade sharing between third and fifth-graders.

What is most exciting about third grade is that this is the year the reading-writing processes merge to become totally interrelated. Students have acquired the habits of reading and writing daily for pleasure, and most are self-motivated and self-regulated in these behaviors. Reading continues to be an ongoing daily activity with many books brought in from libraries to supplement the classroom library and all curriculum areas. Reading includes reading aloud by the teacher, whole class shared reading and guided reading, reading groups, independent reading of self-selected books from classroom and school libraries, students reading to and with each other, and increased reading in content areas. The writing that goes on is interrelated to the reading and goes across the total curriculum. Besides self-selected writing which includes journal writing, stories, and messages to each other, focused writing includes letters, invitations, thank you notes, notices of important school activities, short reports, summaries of experiments, and reactions to books, filmstrips, films, field trips, and other classroom activities.

Most students begin the school year as confident readers and writers with a growing foundation of skills and strategies. The children are very eager to get into new books, reread old favorites, and continue responding to literature in various ways. Many enjoy reading all the books in a series, or all the books by one author. Reactions and extensions to books include much involvement with discussion, relevant vocabulary, the creative arts, and all types of writing — predicting events, forming opinions, summarizing, evaluating, making judgments. Children have become more aware of authors' styles and more readily adapt them into their own writing. They enjoy learning new words and playing with multiple word meanings. They are able to benefit from group conferencing, and are more willing to do significant revising and editing. By the end of the year, most students have moved primarily into conventional spelling, and many parents and teachers are relieved to see that transition take place. At the same time, parents and teachers continue to accept the students' need for some invented spelling.

Our lowest ability readers and writers are usually students new to the school. Students who have not acquired the reading-writing habit need special attention and encouragement as well as a clear understanding of what is expected. A new student was asked, "Would you lke to take out a WEB book?" Emphatically, he said "No." The teacher responded, "Let me rephrase that question. Which WEB book would you like to take out tonight?" Eventually, students pick up the motivation to read and write by being surrounded by good literature as well as peer and teacher models all day long: they want to belong to the "club" of readers and writers! We try to meet with new parents as soon as possible to describe the reading-writing processes, answer questions and concerns, and get the home-school connection going.

As in second grade, our principal, Delores Groves, was firm in making sure the literature program continued through the primary grades. For the reading-writing period, I was very fortunate to be paired with Linda Cooper, a talented, flexible, imaginative teacher with a traditional teaching background in almost all the elementary grades. Very open to new concepts and full of enthusiasm and ideas, she quickly took ownership of her teaching as we worked together developing the language arts program.

The Reading-Writing Process in Grade 3

Shared Experiences and Literature Extension Activities

Whole group time continues to be important for firming up reading and writing strategies, modeling by the teacher or other students, group discussion, and story enjoyment in a variety of ways. The class gathers together to hear wonderful books read aloud, for sustained silent reading, whole class reading of books, small group sharing, guided reading lessons, sharing of journal entries, published works and projects, and lots of mini-lessons as specific needs arise.

Reading aloud each day continues to be important in all grades, and teachers read for about 20 to 30 minutes at least once a day. Teachers select books that will extend students' literary appreciation, vocabulary, and enjoyment. Favorite books have included *Danny the Champion of the World* by Roald Dahl, *Indian in the Cupboard* by Lynne Reid Banks, and *The Hundred Penny Box* by Sharon Bell Mathis. Lots of predicting, discussion, and definitions of vocabulary in context go on. Vocabulary words, discussed around a book or topic, later may find their way into students' writing. Many literature extension activities, some of which are used as independent work when reading groups are meeting, develop from books read aloud. In fact, some of the best ideas have come from the children: making an original picture book from a chapter book and writing a play based on a book read aloud.

Uninterrupted sustained silent reading as a whole class takes place daily by teachers and students alike. We specify that WEB books or library books be read; comic books and magazines are not allowed at this time. With our students, we have found it beneficial to schedule this reading directly after lunch, and this serves as a quieting activity to get the children focused back on academics. No questions, discussion, or exchanging of books may take place during this time. The purpose is to get students into the habit of reading for pleasure. In addition, the surest way to get students to expand their vocabularies is through extensive reading. Seeing the teacher enjoying a book at the same time adds motivation and credibility to the activity.

Students use shared experiences time to "sell" books they have especially enjoyed. Students write short plays advertising a particular book with the goal of selling the book to potential readers. Like a readers' theater, the script is read and dramatized. Writers choose their own cast, depending on how many parts they have written. No costuming or props are needed: practice is minimal; students have ownership over a process; and they often see immediate results from their efforts. Students begin reading and asking questions about those specific books.

Cross-grade sharing of reading and writing takes place with much enthusiasm. Upper grade students have written and dedicated books to third-graders based on a pattern or theme. One year, fifth-graders wrote Halloween stories for our students. Those stories had gone through the entire writing process before they wound up as beautifully bound and illustrated books. Fifth-graders not only read the books to the students they were paired with; they showed students the messy, rough drafts and their revised and edited copies. Having another student as a writing model is often more powerful than having the teacher as model. Third-graders wrote thank you letters, and they were very specific and expressive in their comments. (See Figure 1.)

Extensions of literature through the creative arts are a high point of school for third-graders. When "Red Riding Hood" was professionally performed as an operetta for the whole school, different versions of the tale were first read and compared. Then another teacher, using a wolf puppet, came into the classroom and played the part of the "maligned" wolf to illustrate point of view. Students then wrote their own versions of "Little Red Riding Hood" from the wolf's point of view. We were also fortunate to get funds from the Parent Teacher Association to bring in a playwright for several mornings. He worked with the children on taking familiar nursery rhymes, rewriting them into short plays, and acting them out. (This activity could also be done without the presence of a professional playwright.) Depending on whom the student chose to be the main character, for example, Miss Muffet or the spider, points of view and outcomes varied. We assumed that students would be able to write in play form after the playwright's explanations and demonstrations. The children's first independent attempts showed a lack of understanding of the process, causing us to believe that the project might be too difficult for them. However, after reteaching the lesson — spending considerable time modeling the conventions, format, and style of playwriting, as well as collaborating on a play together — the students could do this independently. Once they got the hang of it, they loved selecting, writing, sharing, and acting out short play versions of nursery rhymes. It was a good lesson for us; we have found that when children are unable to do an activity it is usually because we have not defined it fully enough.

Poetry continues to be enjoyed, read, and reread by the children and teachers. Children remain very receptive to all kinds of poetry and enjoy memorization of favorite poems. Choral recitation — for peers, over the public address system for the whole school, and for themselves — brings pleasure and a feeling of "connectedness" and group comradery. Such books as *Piping Down the Valleys Wild* by Nancy Larick (ed.), *A Sky Full of Poems* and *Jamboree* by Eve Merriam, and *A Child's Garden of Verses* by Robert Louis Stevenson, as well as poetry books that have been enjoyed in first and second grade, are available in multiple copies in the classroom. Students enjoy putting together and sharing their own poetry booklets, selecting favorite poems to copy in their best handwriting, and creating original poems.

Specific poems can be the focus of a themed unit at the beginning of the school year. A unit on fall has included such poems as "Autumn Woods" by James Tippett, "The Mist and All" by Dixie Wilson, and

Figure 1 Appreciation of Other Students' Writing

Dear Sam,

I really liked The front picture of The book, *The Haunted House*, I Liked it because it is real colorful, and you put details in pictures. The book, has a good adventure in it. I Like the way you had Characters hav'ing a Conversation, and how you told The way old Joe Changed, and how they said It's Over for now."

Thank you for making this book for me.

Sincerely
Melanie

Dear Sara,

I like the book title *The Witch's Halloween Party.* I liked the part where a little girl screamed because she heard lightning crackling. I also liked the picture of stale candy. The best part was the part where they bob for candy witch hats. Thank you for the book.

Sincerely,
Shahidah

"Something Told the Wild Geese" by Rachel Field. Students enjoy emphasizing the "sound" words such as "sweeping" and "rushing". The latter poem was the impetus for a study of Canada geese. Geography, science, math, and vocabulary development were incorporated as students read and discussed the phenomenal flights of these geese.

Donna Brittain does a poetry reading-writing workshop with her third-graders. She fills the room with single and multiple copies of all kinds of poetry books and reads poetry throughout the day. Some of our former students proudly bring in their carefully illustrated poetry anthologies from first grade to add to the the collection. The children enjoy, discuss, and analyze types of rhythm, rhyme, patterns, free verse, and many varieties of poetry as well as the use of figures of speech such as similes, metaphors, and alliteration. At first, some of the children — especially those who had not been previously exposed to poetry — complained about reading and writing poetry, but as the daily workshop progressed, their enthusiasm grew to the point where their teacher commented, "I can't stop them from writing poetry. I am impressed with titles, the imagery, rhythm, and the quality of their work." Children wrote all manner of poems: couplets, quatrains, rhymes, limericks, haiku, and free verse. Immersed in delightful, inspiring poetry, they quickly picked up a natural love for reading and writing poetry.

The Use of Picture Books

Picture books are not just for beginning readers. Students of all ages delight in the clever illustrations, beautiful use of language, and appealing stories. Sometimes a message or theme is more poignant and powerful in a short, illustrated book than in a chapter book. We read and discuss many Caldecott and other award-winning books.

When the book is introduced, we read it at least twice. On the first reading the book is enjoyed in its entirety, and questioning is minimal so as not to interrupt the flow of the story. On the second reading which follows directly, we look for patterns and make comparisons with other books. The illustrations and text are carefully examined and discussed. Some of these picture books have intricate detail and sophistication that the older student can appreciate. A book such as *Crow Boy* by Taro Yashima is excellent for prediction, inferential questioning, and a discussion of prejudice and acceptance. Picture books such as *Round Trip* and *The Trek* by Ann Jonas are appreciated for their high quality, unique illustrations, and clever format. The award-winning African tales with their magnificent, colorful wood-cuts, *Arrow to the Sun, The Stonecutter: A Japanese Folk Tale* and *The Magic Tree: A Tale From the Congo* by Gerald McDermott afford opportunities for inferential comprehension and art appreciation.

Carefully selected picture books with outstanding literary quality also serve as wonderful models for short, specific, focused student writing. Another plus is that an entire lesson — reading and discussing the picture book as well as writing and sharing an original story — can be completed in a single time period. Our librarian keeps us abreast of outstanding new titles, and we attend children's literature conferences to find out about new books and to meet authors and get background on their stories and their lives. Telling students about the author and how the book was conceived and written makes the book come alive.

We do a unit on old people and read, discuss, and have available in the classroom multiple copies of such picture books as *Annie and the Old One* by Miska Miles, *Miss Rumphius* by Barbara Cooney, *Now one Foot, Now the Other* by Tomie de Paola, *Through Grandpa's Eyes* by Patricia MacLachlan, *Emma* by Wendy Kesselman, *My Grandson Lew* by Charlotte Zolotow, *I Know a Lady* by Charlotte Zolotow and *The Two of Them* by Aliki. All of these deal with some aspect of old age and are thought-provoking as well as beautifully written and illustrated. We talk about old people we know and what their lives are like. Then the children choose an old person they know and write about that person; their writing includes personal descriptions, perceptions, and activities shared with that person. Because of the prior discussion and the sensitive nature of the picture books which have been read, reread, and discussed, the portraits they write are also sensitive and genuine. These are illustrated, or actual pictures of the person are brought in.

One book we have had great success with at all grade levels, but which we introduce in third grade, is *William's Doll* by Charlotte Zolotow. This sensitively told story is about a boy who wants a doll. No one in his family understands or accepts his feelings until his grandmother comes to visit. Children are asked to apply the theme to something very personal, tangible or intangible, that they want but can't have. Students relate easily to this topic and have written on such topics as wanting special toys, a new lunchbox, bigger allowances, later bedtimes, or being allowed to go on special trips. Their writing is also sensitively done because it is heartfelt and personally significant and because of the wonderful model the book provides.

For this assignment, each child is given the following prompt with requirements clearly stated, numbered, and visible on the overhead projector and/or on an individual sheet passed out to him. We have found that stating expectations precisely and in writing assures better-quality work, gives students clear guidelines to refer to, and emphasizes the importance of following directions. A typical prompt is shown here:

> Include:
> 1. *What* you wanted (or want)
> 2. *When* you wanted it (how long ago)
> 3. *Why* you wanted it (or want it)
> 4. *What* happened, in detail
> 5. *How* you felt, (or feel) about what happened (how others feel)
>
> Be sure to:
> *Begin* each sentence with a capital.
> *End* each sentence with a period (or other punctuation).
> *Indent* each paragraph.

After the writing is completed, with permission of the students, we choose several writing examples and make transparencies for the overhead projector and model the revising and editing processes. Using colored pens, we also number each direction that has been followed. Each child then uses a colored pencil and adds numbers 1, 2, 3, 4, and 5 on his own paper to designate where he has included the "what", "when", "why", and "how" in the directions, which can be done in any order. This assignment can be accepted without further revision (in which case it would be stamped "unedited"), or additional revision and editing can take place.

When I Was Young in the Mountains by Cynthia Rylant is an exceptionally well-illustrated picture book written in lilting free verse. The author warmly recalls themes from her childhood in the mountains of West Virginia. We use this book as a model and springboard for students to recount memorable experiences from their own early childhoods. (See Figure 3 for an example.) Some of the most effective modeling comes from other students who volunteer to share parts of their writing. Kile, normally a macho, reserved writer who rarely risked sharing personal feelings, was asked:

> "Did Diane's story influence you?"
> "Yeah, a lot. Cause she wasn't embarrassed to tell her feelings."

For the teacher who has had some practice and training, storytelling is a way to make picture books come alive for students. Linda Cooper has successfully attempted several books that she has committed to memory, *The Mitten* by Alvin Tresselt and *The Great Big Enormous Turnip* by Leo Tolstoy, and she has shared these with her own students, as well as with younger and older students. Students' attention and comprehension is always high when they are focused solely on the teacher for hearing the story. Storytelling can be more than just an enjoyable listening activity. Follow-up role playing and acting out of scenes requires students to sequence events, recall

Figure 3   A Sample Page from a Student's Book

When I was young it was funny when my grandfather came home. He gave me piggy back rides, and we used to go to our favorite chair to sing the song "Ninety-nine Bottles of Beer on the Wall."

details, put in dialogue to help the plot unfold, and work together cooperatively.

A Whole Class Guided Reading Lesson

With one copy of a highly interesting book with fine illustrations, the teacher can effectively demonstrate and promote reading skills and strategies with the whole class at one time. Students have opportunities to predict text and vocabulary, integrate phonics with meaning cues, use oral and written cloze to predict words in context, predict and confirm events, and read orally and silently in a supportive group situation. As in shared book experience, emphasis is on enjoying a story together. Since most students are reading competently, attention can be given to the finer points of reading — specific vocabulary, word attack skills, inferential reasoning. Don Holdaway, the well-known New Zealand educator, developed the guided reading lesson and demonstrated his techniques when he visited our district (May 1986). An adaptation of his lesson follows:

- **introducing the story** to build background, interest, and motivation: making predictions from the title and pictures
- **reading aloud** the first pages of the story and asking prediction-type high-level questions
- **using the overhead projector for oral cloze.** The teacher makes a transparency of a story page. The teacher gradually exposes the text, word by word with a line marker, as the class reads orally and predicts words from initial letters and confirms or changes predictions. I use two overlapping 5″ x 7″ index cards, one to cover the text completely (print will not be visible on the screen, but the light coming through on the machine allows print to remain visible to the teacher) and a second card to expose the text progressively. The bottom card moves down the page line by line as the top card goes across the page word by word. This is an excellent technique for maintaining attention, predicting words and phrases, and for calling attention to particular features of print and specific words.
- **reading aloud** several more pages. The teacher continues to read the story with much expression and to ask the group to predict what will happen next. Possiblities are discussed, and attention is focused ahead.
- **whole group reading aloud.** A selected page is displayed on a transparency on the overhead projector. The group reads together for pleasure and to confirm predictions. As in shared book experience, students join in as best they can, and there is a relaxed group feeling in enjoying the book together.
- **guided silent reading.** Using a transparency on the overhead

and/or distributing individual copies, a page is read silently after the teacher has set purposes for reading. To keep faster readers on task, ask them to "find the specific words or the sentence that tells or shows..."

- **written cloze.** Each student is given a copy of several paragraphs or a page of text. The teacher uses "white-out" on her master copy so that only the beginning letters or letter cluster is visible. The teacher carefully chooses about 1 in every 15 words of text (or less if the meaning remains clear) to delete in this way and draws a line and leaves a space where the word is to be completed. For example:

"Good night," said the w___ to the pr_____ and "Good night," said the pr_____ to the w_____ and the one w___ for going one way and the other the other. But the dr._____ had his w___ about him s_____ enough, and before the old witch could get away he fl.___ the net that King Stork had given him over her h._____.

"Hi!" But you should have been there to see what h___ _____ for it was a great one-eyed r___, as bl ___ as the inside of the ch_____ that he had in his net.

Dear, dear, how it fl_____ its wings and struck with its great b___! But that did no good, for the drummer just wr___ its neck, and there was an end of it.

The student, working individually or with a partner, predicts and writes in what makes sense. Any response that fits in meaningfully should be accepted. Graphophonic generalizations the teacher wants to highlight can be reinforced in this manner. Meaningful substitutions are shown as useful for keeping the reading going. These pages can be collected and checked by the teacher or checked together by the whole class. If no time is available to complete the entire lesson, the teacher may decide to stop here and complete the cloze check and the book the following day.

- **whole group reading aloud.** Complete the story with unison reading on the overhead projector to end with an enjoyable, collegial atmosphere. The teacher may also choose to finish the last page(s) by reading it aloud.

The guided reading lesson is a highly motivating way to engage an entire middle grades class in a shared book experience. These techniques can be put in any order and format suitable to the individual teacher. I have found it useful to choose a highly interesting book with good vocabulary and a fast-paced plot, such as a fairy tale with which the children may be unfamiliar. Not all teachers may be aware that there are many fine picture books with challenging vocabulary and story line that are geared to older readers. Because of the sophistication of vocabulary and plot in these picture books, the book needs to be carefully chosen with a reading level appropriate to the majority of students. One such modern fairy tale our children have particularly enjoyed is *King Stork* by Howard Pyle. After the lesson, the book is available in the classroom and is always an instant favorite for many to reread. Extension activities, such as creating original illustrations (for pictures that were not shown) or writing a different ending, can be added to the lesson.

Thematic Units

Thematic units based on literature — books by William Steig, fables, poetry, fairy tales, animal stories — are developed. A unit on fables works well in third grade or above using *Aesop's Fables* and *Fables* by Arnold Lobel. Because very high-level thinking is required, this is a good unit to save for the latter part of third grade. Fables are action-filled tales about animals with human characteristics: the stories are intended to teach a lesson, and they end with a moral. Tales are read and discussed for storyline (literal level), discussed for the universal moral (interpretive level), and applied to a personal life situation (evaluation, critical level). The word and concept "personification" is introduced, and students use it and apply it to other literature. Usually, the fable is read up to the moral, and students are asked to give the moral. Sometimes, their morals and wording have seemed more appropriate than the original. For variety, the moral can be stated and discussed before the story is read; students are then asked to listen for the episodes that teach the lesson. Because fables are brief, usually not more than three or four paragraphs, hearing a fable and guiding discussion can easily take place as a quick stimulus at the start of the morning or language arts period. Our children hear many fables over many weeks, and there is always much modeling and discussion by teachers and students about the morals and how they may fit a present day situation. Students are then asked to choose several morals and use them as themes for writing original fables. They are expected to follow the structure of a fable: a one page story, animals acting like people as main characters, lots of action with a twist of the plot at the end, and the moral stated at the conclusion of the tale. With some classes, it may first be advisable for the class to collaborate on writing a fable or for the teacher to share orally and visually one that she has composed. Because the writing pieces are short, this a good assignment to take to final copy. A class book can then be put together, illustrated, and bound with each student's best, original fable. Enough copies can be made of each fable so that each student has a personal, bound copy to read and illustrate. We have not always concurred on what is a student's best piece of writing to be included, but the choice and final decision is always left with the author. Development of the child's sense of ownership remains primary.

We and the children particularly enjoy a WEB unit on William Steig. We reread *Dr. DeSoto* and *Sylvester and the Magic Pebble* and introduce the picture books *Amos and Boris, The Amazing Bone, Caleb and Kate, Gorky Rises, Solomon the Rusty Nail* and *Tiffky Doofky*. We also discuss his challenging chapter books *Dominic, Abel's Island,* and *The Real Thief* through the teacher reading aloud or group reading. Steig's challenging use of vocabulary and personification are two major focal points. With teacher guidance, these are excellent books for inferential comprehension, vocabulary development and literature extension. Students enjoy writing their own personification stories as well as letters to the author asking personal questions and giving reactions to his stories.

Integrating the Curriculum with the Language Arts

As much as possible, other content areas are integrated with reading and writing, along with reference skills. For example, we read aloud the book *Kid Power* by Susan Beth Pfeffer, the story of some kids who take the initiative and earn money through a business they start. This gave the opportunity to incorporate a complete unit on economics. Discussion included strikes, labor, management, compromise, and agreement and included work in math and social studies.

Linda Cooper has developed a unit, "Animal Research Reports", that connects the reading-writing processes with science, library research skills, art, and word processing. This two-month unit goes through the entire writing process from pre-writing to publishing and takes place during language arts time, science time, and throughout the day. To develop background information, a unit on animals with focus on care of the young is taught first. The teacher then puts many appropriate animal books on reserve in the library, and, with the aid of the teacher, librarian and parent volunteers, students choose and research their specific animals through books, magazines, and reference materials. Students begin their research by reading a specially chosen book about their animal. During the second reading, they record information describing the animal, its habitat, care of young, the adult animal, eating habits, and other information. Modeling is a very important technique for this long-term project, and using the animal she is also researching, the teacher carefully models each step of the process on the overhead projector: how to select out relevant facts, place information in the appropriate categories, take notes, put notes in paragraph form, conference, revise, and edit. As needed, additional modeling, to reteach and reinforce, will take place using students' research. During the reading-research-notetaking phase, several additional adult volunteers circulate throughout the classroom and offer assistance to individual students as needed.

After first rough drafts are written, response groups of five to eight students led by a teacher or adult volunteer, meet and adhere to a consistent format. (See Appendix L.) The writer reads his paragraph, and everyone listens attentively. He immediately reads it again, and each child takes notes on scrap paper so he can offer specific responses to the writer. Comments are then made, always beginning with a favorable comment such as "I liked the way you . . .", "The sentence I liked best . . .", "I learned . . ." Students are then directed to make their comments and questions constructive, such as, "I wasn't clear when you said . . . Did you mean . . . ?" Questions which do not help the flow of the writing (such as, "Does the animal have a tail?") are discouraged. Using a colored pencil, the writer jots down the questions and suggestions on his piece of writing; he can then refer to these as he rewrites. The writer decides what to include and what not to include as he writes a second rough draft in legible handwriting.

Second rough drafts are written, reviewed, edited, and word-processed with bibliographic information added. The editing process is first modeled on the overhead, and each student receives a guidesheet of editing marks. (See Appendix M.) As the junior editor, the student uses a colored pencil to mark all the mechanical errors he can find. All the misspelled words he can locate are circled, and he is expected to spell at least three of them correctly. Final editing — correctly spelling the remaining words, making other necessary corrections, and later, editing all discs — is done by a senior editor (the teacher or parent volunteer) using a different colored pencil or pen. The purpose is always to keep the focus on the writing process — in this case, editing — and not to frustrate the student by overemphasizing spelling or finding every error. Illustrations, hand drawn or taken from magazines and other sources, are added to the report along with a table of contents and title page. Final reports, bound with a graphically designed cover, are proudly shared with peers and parents.

Self-Selecting Writing

Third-grade writers still choose most of their topics from their daily lives, but some topics — especially as related to curriculum — will be suggested by the teacher. Even when the writing is prefocused, the student always has many open-ended options. Journal writing, in a spiral or three-ring notebook, continues at least three times a week with appropriate responding by the teacher. Mini-lessons are taught whole class and individually as needs become apparent, for example, paragraphing, writing interesting leads, and punctuating. In the beginning of the school year, a journal entry is modeled by the teacher with an emphasis on writing with a focus. For instance, if a student is writing about a trip he took, he is encouraged to "focus" in depth on one aspect of the trip that was significant to him as opposed to listing everything that happened. The writing folder also serves as a cumulative record of students' writing progress. Here, students have a choice as to the kind and color of paper they write on. They write only on one side of the page, skip lines (to add information and cut and paste), and cross out only (no erasures). Literature continues to have a strong influence on children's writing styles: story vocabulary and story elements become interwoven in original stories. Modeling and demonstrating continue to be of primary importance, not just for revision and editing, but for quality of writing. Teachers read descriptions of character, plot, setting, and opening passages from a book or selected student's writing and put them on the overhead projector for examination. Messy drafts by students and teachers are also shared so students see firsthand how to add, change, and move things around.

The writing process can be stopped at any stage. A particular piece of writing can be accepted as a rough draft, revised draft, or student-edited piece. Writing emphasis continues to be on the process, not the product. Taking writing to final copy needs to be done selectively. Since it is very time consuming, it tends to take away from focus on the writing quality. Where a final copy is desired, the teacher does the final editing of a writing piece after receiving the students' best editing efforts in his best handwriting. The student then recopies the piece noting all corrections. When we accept a piece of writing that is not in final copy, we stamp "rough draft" or "unedited" on the paper. As in second grade, a letter goes home to parents explaining the writing process and our procedures. Without effective communication, parents receiving a messy draft that is being evaluated only for content may feel the teacher hasn't done her job.

One-to-one conferencing remains important as a way to focus on individual needs, and parent volunteers are utilized to keep the publishing process going. Group conferencing and response groups, as previously described, continue. Once students have had extensive practice with conferencing, the adult is necessary only to keep the group on task; student comments and questions appropriately dominate.

Reading Groups

In grade 3, with so many competent readers, is is easy and advisable to vary the grouping structure. In addition to ability grouping, we also utilize whole class and interest grouping. It is always advisable for the teacher to read the books carefully before teaching them. We try to select books for reading group discussion that are of high literary quality, that require inferential reasoning, that promote vocabulary development, and that the student might not pick up on his own. For example, *Trumpet of the Swan* by E. B. White, and *Brighty of the Grand Canyon* by Margeuritie Henry take students a while to "get into" because of lengthy description of setting. Once immersed in the books, however, students become enthusiastic and opt to read other books by the same authors. Bobby told his teacher:

"I really don't like this book."
"That's your privilege, but we are going to finish it," she responded.

Upon completion of *Trumpet of the Swan,* he told her, "I'm glad you made me read this book. I didn't realize how much I would get to like it. It was great!"

On the other hand, books such as *The Chocolate Touch* by Patrick Skane Catling or *Tales of a Fourth Grade Nothing* by Judy Blume, have fast-paced plots which are easy for children to follow on their own. Such books sell themselves naturally and are encouraged for independent reading.

Rereading chapter books happens often and with positive results. If a student tells Linda Cooper that he has already read the selected reading group book independently, she says, "So have I." Really, the only part of the reading group he can't participate in is prediction; even here, students find it exciting to listen to all the different predictions by their peers. In fact, students usually tell us upon completing the book with the reading group that much has been learned, enjoyed, and savored through the second guided reading that was not gleaned or appreciated on the first reading. (See *Recommended Literature* for suggested titles for Grade 3.)

Whole Class Reading

Before reading groups get organized, several books are read whole class at the beginning of the school year with each student having a personal copy of the book. This can be done easily in grade 3, because with the exception of some new students who may be low readers and may have to be paired with better readers, most of our students enter with strong reading abilities. Reading a book together as a whole class, orally and silently, is a pleasurable, nonthreatening experience for the students as well as an opportunity for the teacher to make observations of her new class. Several favorite books we have used successfully are *The Velveteen Rabbit* by Margery Williams, and *The Comeback Dog* by Jane Resh Thomas. Both of these are short, 44 and 62 pages respectively, with a reading level that will be easy for most of the students. Such books give great opportunities for prediction and inferential reasoning, as well as building confidence and a group spirit. Activities to go along with the books have included creating original illustrations, dramatizing scenes, writing additional chapters, giving original titles to the numbered chapters, designing a new book cover, collaborating with a peer on rewriting a chapter as a scene in a play, making a book, writing a diary, and rewriting a chapter from the point of view of another character.

Interest Grouping

By presenting several titles and introductory information about several highly interesting books at the same time, teachers can give students an opportunity to group themselves according to the book they choose to read. Some of these books may have been heard previously as read alouds; this gives students extra confidence along with vocabulary and background knowledge that has already been provided. This flexible, voluntary grouping affords all students equal opportunities to read the same books, and is a welcome change to the usual homogenous grouping. Students, especially low-ability students, are always highly motivated when they have the chance to interact with other students and select a book they might not ordinarily read.

Paired reading, where a better reader is paired with a less able one, is an option that works well with class sets of one title or multiple copies of a book chosen by interest. We have found this reading arrangement works well for both readers. The proficient reader enjoys being in the position of helper and usually does this in a kind manner. The student having difficulty often responds well to guidance from a peer instead of the teacher. In addition to the positive social interaction, students learn to work together collaboratively.

What Happens in Reading Group

Checking WEB books (independent reading): Checking self-selected reading continues to take up the first part of reading group (no more than 10 minutes) with procedures for book check and sign out similar to second grade. Checking nightly reading becomes a habit; students rarely forget their books. We find when they do forget, they tend to pick up another book from home and come prepared to discuss what they have read. The teacher, or a student who has previously read the book, directs brief, challenging questioning. If a student is reporting on a library book or title unfamiliar to the teacher, certain general questions are appropriate:

> "What did you read last night?"
> "What is the problem in the story?"
> "How do you think the problem will be solved?"
> "Where were you surprised?"
> "Why do you think...?"
> "Is there a character in the story you particularly admire? Explain why or why not."
> "What are the clues so far in this mystery story?"

Favorite third grade books read independently have included *Charlotte's Web* by E. B. White, *The Adventures of Pinnochio* by Carlo Collodi, *Charlie and the Chocolate Factory* by Roald Dahl, *J. T.* by Jane Wagner, and *Big Red* by James Kjelgaard. Often, everyone in the group will complete a particular book because of the excitement that has built up from students reading and talking about the book. A full-length bulletin board at one end of the classroom says, "Don't leave third grade without reading..." About a dozen books are listed, and students write their intials on the posted book jackets after a book is successfully completed and checked for comprehension. The classroom library contains multiple copies of many selected titles for the children to check out, and most of these have been read first by the teachers. So that prediction strategies can be effectively utilized, books selected by the teacher for use in reading group are not available in the classroom library until reading groups have finished them. After WEB checking, the discussion of the reading group book follows.

Group Discussion and Follow Up Activities

For the most part, discussion is based on the silent reading that has been previously assigned. This is the time that predictions that were made the day before are confirmed or adjusted. Themes, points of view, character development, analysis of plot, sequence of events, and important vocabulary are strategically discussed. Questions are asked that encourage students to speculate and stretch their minds. Questions are also asked that make the students go back to the text for careful reexamination. For example, we might say, "What words can you find that show...?", or "Where does the author let us know that...?" Students get very good at using these techniques themselves. One morning, two boys were arguing over some details. Out of frustration, one said, "Wait a minute. I'll prove it!" He opened his book, found the passage he needed, and read it aloud.

Oral reading continues as an evaluative measure (see Chapter 12) and for enjoyment several times weekly. In addition, if the children have not grasped the meaning of a chapter, we may reread and discuss the entire chapter together. A semantic mapping technique can be used to interrelate story events and vocabulary. Students and teacher brainstorm ideas around a topic, add subtopics around a central theme, and represent everything in a graphic, visual map. The visual representation helps students see relationships and categories, aids comprehension, and can be used across the curriculum.

From talking and working with other teachers, I have found that guiding a high-level group discussion — asking questions that require making inferences and evaluating ideas — is one of the most difficult transitions for teachers to make. There is no guide giving teachers exact questions to ask, and typically, as teachers, we have had little training in facilitating critical discussion. While a few teachers can do this intuitively, most of us need some guidance to begin to use effective questioning. I have found the following sources particularly helpful for understanding and applying good questioning techniques: "Asking Appropriate Questions About Books Read", pp. 50-52, in *Towards a Reading-Writing Classroom* by Andrea Butler and Jan Turbill; "A Framework for Questioning", pp. 170-173, in *Booktalk* by Aidan Chambers; and "Guidelines for Questioning", pp. 16-29, in *Focus Units in Literature* by Joy F. Moss.

Vocabulary, unless it is essential to the story and cannot be figured out in context, is always discussed during and after the text reading, not before it. If a child comes across a word for which he does not know the meaning, he is encouraged to put in a meaningful substitution. I might say, "What other word could you put in the sentence that would make sense here?" In this way, the student learns that he can usually figure out words from the context and continue on with his reading. In choosing words to discuss in group, we highlight words that go across the curriculum and that are necessary to the understanding of the story. Vocabulary is not only discussed in context: it is recorded by the teacher so it can be reviewed orally on subsequent occasions. In *Helen Keller's Teacher* by Margaret Davidson, the following words were among those discussed: "laborer", "excursion", "poverty", "condescending", "mute", "isolation", "valedictorian", "concealed", "inquisitive", "unique", "conspicuous", "transform". Sometimes we dramatize words to help retain their meaning. When "condescending" was discussed, many students practiced condescending looks on their faces; when "conspicuous" was discussed, students acted or dressed in a conspicuous manner. When words are talked about beyond the initial use in context, and when students relate words to concepts they already possess, these words become a part of student's speaking and writing vocabulary. Some teachers also ask students to keep a self-selected list of vocabulary words from daily reading, perhaps five a week, and to use these words in the context of a phrase or sentence.

Depending on the book, students will be asked to respond in various ways. Sometimes, almost all the responding is through discussion, and this is true in all the grades. It takes some time not to feel "guilty" when there is no visible end-product and simply to enjoy and promote a high-quality discussion. Even when a written response is required in the reading response log (a notebook used to respond to books), it can be a free response and need not be lengthy. (See Figure 5 for typical examples of beginning third-graders' opinions of *The Great Quillow* by James Thurber and *Danny the Champion of the World* by Roald Dahl.

Figure 5   Third-graders' Written Responses to Literature

5a   THE GREAT QUILLOW

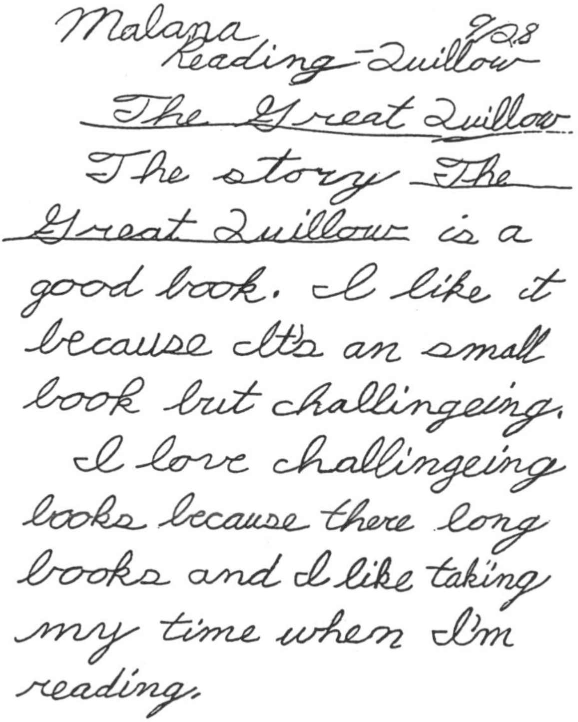

Malana   9.28
Reading - Quillow
The Great Quillow
The story The
Great Quillow is a
good book. I like it
because It's an small
book but challingeing.
I love challingeing
books because there long
books and I like taking
my time when I'm
reading.

Steve   9/29
  Reading
  I like this book it is very
very funny. Quilow is very smart.
Hisplan is very interesting. Hunder
is very gulabull. This book is
on my List of good books.

5b   DANNY THE CHAMPION OF THE WORLD

Anthony   Reading
            I like   the book
Danny.   I like   when Danny
and his father went pocking.
I like Sergeant Samways too.
I didn't like Captain Lancaster
when he hit Danny on his
hand. And I did't like
Mr. Hazell and his keepers because
of making the pit for people
who pocked in Hazell's woods.

Regina

            Reading
          I like the book Danny because
of the way Roald Dahl described the
characters and how he made every
chapter end in suspense. He made this
book adventurous by surprising us as
we read it. My reactions to this book:
that it is funny, surprising because
there scary characters as Captain Lancaster
and Mr. Victor Hazell, something new was
happening in every chapter, and funny
tricks were being played. The pictures
are beatiful because they look like
real life.

As an introductory activity for the book *Trumpet of the Swan* by E. B. White, students were asked to draw the setting as pictured in words on the opening pages. As a final activity, using a blank map of the United States students worked in pairs plotting Louis the swan's flight across Canada and the United States. Students may be assigned a written response in their reading spiral as a response to their WEB book or reading group book. Here it is important to give some structure to the assignment without burdening the students with the quantity of writing. They may be asked to write a story prediction, anticipate what will come next, what they like about the story so far, a short paragraph summary of what they read today, questions that came to mind while reading, a spontaneous personal reaction, several vocabulary words they figured out in context, or answer several questions specific to the story. In checking responses, teachers note sentence structure, punctuation, handwriting, and spelling along with content. While emphasis is on thoughtful responses, students are expected to be beginning and ending all sentences appropriately and spelling high utility words correctly.

Word Study Skills

A strong emphasis in third grade is word study skills with lots of work on reading multisyllable words. While most children are applying basic phonics generalizations by the end of grade 2, much work now goes into teaching syllabication and structural analysis (prefixes, suffixes, contractions, compound words), using dictionaries and reference materials, understanding multiple word meanings (synonyms, antonyms, and homonyms). These skills are practiced and reinforced in the context of the literature being read as well as taught in mini-lessons. Primary emphasis remains on getting meaning from print using all available cues interactively.

For instance, students are taught the basic syllabication rules (see Appendix N), and these rules are practiced in context. Students may be asked to find words that fit the rules from their reading book and write them in a syllabication booklet. By predicting and trying out while using meaningful context as a guide, students figure out most words that are already in their vocabulary. For words not in their speaking/reading vocabularies, they will need some assistance.

Independent Work

Students not in reading group are working individually or in small groups. They will be doing a silent reading assignment, writing a response to a book or question in their reading spiral, reading their WEB or library book, working on the computer, doing a literature extension, doing journal writing or other self-selected or focused writing. The first requirement of independent work time is always the reading group assignment — silent reading and/or answering a question in the reading spiral. Often, the idea for a literature extension project, which may take several weeks to complete, comes from a book read aloud to the whole class.

For example, after listening to and discussing the vivid description in *Danny the Champion of the World* by Roald Dahl, students were asked to choose six important scenes or characters that they would like to describe and write a paragraph for each using descriptive vocabulary and accompanying illustrations. As the book ends, Danny and his father are having a conversation about what they will do next. Students are also asked to describe two activities Danny and his father might elect to do, keeping in mind where they are (in England, living in a caravan) and their circumstances (no car, limited financial resources).

A table in a corner serves as a writing center where students may put together their own booklets and decide the format and number of pages. White and colored paper in assorted sizes, a long-arm stapler, a staple remover, and art supplies are available. While the teacher still models possibilities, third-graders are more involved in publishing and enjoy taking ownership in this process.

Instilling Lifelong Confidence

The reading-writing processes learned through the integrated curriculum continue in and out of school and positively affect students' self-worth. An education major from a local university, Maria Padovani, spent one semester with us student teaching in third grade. She spoke to me about the children's positive attitudes and confidence.

> Children don't seem to be afraid to try anything; they are very confident. They feel they can read anything, and teachers encourage them to try. They're not concerned about grade level. A child would never go into the library and say, "Where are the third grade books?" One group of kids was reading *The Magic Grandfather* by Jay Williams. I was surprised to see whole groups of children reading at that level of understanding and discussing complex language and plot.
>
> They also feel very confident about writing. They'll write about anything, and not being able to spell a word is not a limitation. Each child's story is unique. Often, kids will pull out their journals if there's something important that's happened to them, and they can't tell anybody at the time. The journal serves as a diary and a way to get to know the kids. These kids love writing. They write all the time. The publishing process gives such a sense of self-esteem and confidence. They show visitors to the classroom their work, and their pride in their accomplishments is evident. I was shocked to see third-graders complete Animal Research Reports and do such a thorough job.

We see our students as competent and able learners. We encourage them to take risks and support them for doing so. Our expectations are high, and the students usually meet them. We are constantly reading new books, trying out new ideas, and learning from each other and the children. Our confidence continues to grow along with the children's as our process teaching matures.

(*above*) *Karen Shiba taking a first grade guided reading lesson.*
(*opposite*) *A parent reading his son's published book with him.*

9 *Parent Involvement*
Communication

In setting up the learning environment, it was important to me that parents be involved from the start. As a parent of a former first-grader, I remembered how intimidated I felt coming into school to see what was going on and discuss concerns — and I was a teacher in the system! I knew it must be even more difficult for many of our black parents, some of whom had come up against discrimination in jobs and housing, to enter another institution — the school. My hope was that the classroom could belong to all of us — parents, teachers, and kids.

We have all become learners together. By observing and listening to children, by communicating with parents — who truly know their children best — and by gently advising and guiding each other, we have collaborated in the wondrous process of learning to read and write. Parents help us put together book projects, listen to children read, publish all of the children's books, and help with journal writing. We could not operate our program without them.

We start each year in first grade with an open house, before school begins, to let children and parents meet teachers, get a look at the unique classroom environment, ask questions, and possibly sign up to volunteer. We follow up the first month of school with individual interviews with each parent to find out more about the child's involvement with early literacy, present reading habits in the home, after school care, special concerns, etc. There is also an evening open house to describe the hows and whys of literature-based reading and writing, the rationale and philosophy, as well as the daily procedures in the classroom and suggestions for parallel follow-through at home. Beginning the first month of school, we also send home a weekly report on each child's learning and behavior. (Sample letters to parents, interview forms, and examples of our weekly communications are included in Appendix O.)

The importance of communicating with the family cannot be overstated. Many times, we have found that parent and teacher expectations are out of alignment, misinformation has been given, or specific incidents have occurred that affect the child's learning. In addition, our school district is well-known for its high academic achievement, and even though the racial and economic make-up of our school is atypical in the district, some parents feel that all they need to do is place their kids in the school system and the learning will be automatic. It is our job to bring these families into the educational system by making them feel they are a welcome and necessary part of the learning process. Some examples, where effective communication between home and school made a difference, are given below.

Maya was coming along quite well in her reading, but at mid-year she seemed less interested in signing out books to read at home. After talking with her mother, it was determined that the grandmother —who Maya was with after school each day — was insisting she sound out each word and then write those words she had difficulty with many times. Once we met with the grandmother and explained that the purpose of reading was for enjoyment, and once she understood our educational goals, procedures, and philosophy — all firmly rooted in current research — Maya returned to being an enthusiastic reader.

Marona was a very young and immature first-grader who had been recommended for kindergarten retention. (The parents had refused.) By late fall, she was severely deficient in all academic areas, off task much of the time, and did not take the learning process seriously. After a long conference with her father, where the emphasis was on the needed collaboration between home and school in efforts and expectations, Marona blossomed. Her parents began reading daily with her at home, and they began to expect much more from her in all academic areas. By the spring, she was reading above grade level, was delighted with her own progress, and was composing lengthy pieces in her journal.

And then there was Sharita — sad-faced, solemn, and silent at school's beginning. She struggled daily to write anything that seemed coherent, and there were times we wondered if she would ever learn to read and write. Although her parents did not become much involved in her learning, we were able to get her older sister to read with her and to her at home every day. By spring, she had broken through to literacy. With confidence and broad smiles, she took her writing journal with her daily when she went out to recess. Her outward demeanor was one of confidence and achievement, and she would proudly read to anyone who would listen to her.

Parents in the Classroom

Parents are invited to come into the classroom any day between 10:00 a.m. and noon to observe and participate in the learning process. Having the classroom open makes school seem like a friendly place, and parents see the learning process and their children's invovlement firsthand. We want parents to understand what we are doing so they can reinforce the learning at home, and we want and need their support. Many times, a parent's visit has had dramatic effects on a child's learning. Mostly, the parents are amazed at how well children are reading and writing, and they begin to raise their own expectation levels and their involvement with their child at home.

At first, parents in the classroom made the teachers uneasy. Closed doors, ownership, and privacy had been the norm for so long that this change, like most change, was unsettling. Quickly, however, the teachers' and childrens' complete involvement in the joy of literature made parents — and other visitors — no threat at all. Gradually, the teachers relaxed. The fun in learning through shared book experience, journal writing, published books, book projects, individual and group reading of favorite stories was contagious, and before long parents, grandparents, and toddlers were a familiar sight on any given morning. Children welcomed visitors as the norm and took pride in showing them around the room as well as having them as a personal audience for their reading and writing accomplishments.

Particularly wonderful are the fathers who have taken time to volunteer. So many of our children come from homes headed by women, that a male interested and involved in reading and writing makes a significant impact. Our first year, Robert's father came in weekly to read with children and take part in their learning. Some of the boys waited especially for him to read books and share stories they had written. Robert beamed with pride every time his dad was present. As a child who had failed to learn to read and write in first grade in another school, there is no question that Robert's remarkable success in reading and writing was influenced by his father's constant interest and support.

Joyce Pope, a first grade teacher in our district with a reading-writing classroom, uses her parents to help broaden the curriculum in a natural way. Each week, one of the parents (or grandparents or neighbors) of a child in her room is invited in to share something about their job or hobby with the children. Usually, parents talk about their work; sometimes they do a demonstration; occasionally, they just read a story. The goal is to get parents involved, to give children experiences in listening and asking good questions, and for students to see real life opportunities. Each visit is followed up by the children with journal writing, writing thank you letters by hand or on the computer, and the reading and discussing of related books. Joyce also takes polaroid pictures of each event, and these are used for class books, wall stories, and posters. Additionally, the photographs are sometimes Xeroxed for individual books so that each child can write their own booklet about the experience using the pictures as a sequential guide.

Some recent experiences that provided natural motivation for integration of the curriculum and led to investigative study in such areas as health, math, and science included a medical technologist who brought in culture samples and discussed the professions of nursing and medicine, a banker who talked about different currencies and how money is used in different countries, a grandmother who had participated in a national peace march, and a doll maker who invited the children to participate in the making of a doll. Not only do children begin to see the relevance of school to real life — with the need for reading, writing, math, and effective communication — they also develop their vocabulary and language skills tremendously.

Parents' Attitudes: Reactions to the Reading-Writing Program

It has been interesting to note that parents have accepted a literature-based reading-writing program more readily than most teachers. Sometimes teachers ask me, "Do the parents ever ask where the workbooks and worksheets are?" I respond truthfully. "No, they never do." When my own children were in school, I eventually tossed out all the hundreds of worksheets and completed workbooks they brought home. I know if they had brought home their own published and illustrated books and book projects, I would still have them today. The children's parents are our biggest supporters. Once they see how well their children are doing and how much they enjoy school, they become our partners in learning.

Because our parents are so involved in their children's learning, I wrote to them recently and asked for their thoughts on literature-based reading and writing in terms of their children's attitudes, self-esteem, or anything at all that seemed important to them. I wanted to know if and how they felt the program had impacted on their children. I share some of these responses with the hope that teachers will find some implications for their own teaching. The following responses were typical of many received.

> My child's attitude is the greatest; she loves to read and write... The more she has read, the better she enjoys it. Before, she didn't take a real interest in books, but now reading and writing is all she wants to do.

> Reading is without a doubt Jeffrey's favorite subject. He reads all sorts of things: the funnies, comics, signs, cereal boxes, the t.v. guide...

> At a time when there are so many people — young and older, who are unable to read or write, I am very grateful for Alana's success. I am thrilled that she can read and comprehend what she reads as well as she does. She loves reading and writing ... It has been a super influence on my son, two years old, in that he sees Alana reading and writing all the time, and there is an incentive for him to be interested in books.

> Michael is especially enthusiastic about reading, and he reads with understanding and surprising accuracy. Through such achievements, Michael has gained a sense of self-accomplishment, confidence, and esteem. He is sure of his ability and thus feels little to no sense of frustration or insecurity when presented with difficult reading tasks. Such "sureness" has spilled over into other areas of learning as well, whereby he is confident in his overall ability.
> Michael enjoys reading to anyone who will listen as well as reading to himself. He usually reads daily, often times to me or his father, and I read to him and his younger sister nightly. Sometimes he reads the bedtime story to us!...

> ... I personally loved the published books, and I am grateful to those who took the time and effort to make them so attractive.

> Allen enjoys reading all books at his level and at his sister's level — 4th grade. He has written little books on his various experiences at my friend Ron's house, losing his glasses, etc. The program has given him a positive attitude and approach toward reading and writing and more self-confidence. We enjoy the opportunity to read along with him at home.

I was particularly touched and surprised by Eddy's mother's response. In part, she wrote:

> "...he can communicate with his mother who is deaf by writing to her."

We knew, of course, that his mother was deaf, and Eddy's achievements in reading and writing had seemed all the more remarkable because of it, but we had no idea that this six-year-old was using daily writing at home to relay information to his mother.
Sharon's mother's letter is included in its entirety because Sharon struggled with the reading process but loved to write. It was through her writing that her confidence in her reading ability began to take shape. While we were aware of Sharon's obvious pleasure in writing,

we had no idea it was such an important part of her life at home as well as a way for her mother to get in touch with Sharon's feelings.

July 1, 1986

Dear Mrs Routman,

Sharon discovered an activity that became very tranquilizing and joyful for her, writing in her journal. We discussed her writing journal frequently, and there was always excitement in the house when Sharon was about to publish a new book. Sharon says that publishing books and writing in her journal was the most fun she had in first grade aside from gymnastics.

I noticed that during the end of the school year Sharon became more interested in reading books. Prior to that time, all she wanted to do was write in her journal. (She also started a journal at home.) We would often find Sharon in her bedroom alone, or behind the sofa on the floor in the living room, reading her selected books. She and I talked about the obvious pleasure she got from reading. Sharon informed me that she now reads so that she will get ideas for her journal, and eventually another published book.

Sharon expresses herself in many ways through writing in her journal and drawing pictures to further illustrate her feelings. I must confess that I have discovered things about Sharon by reading her journal.

I am extremely interested in doing whatever is necessary to further develop Sharon's interest in writing. If you have any suggestions, please let me know.

Sincerely,
Mrs. Joseph B. Brown

Jay was the lowest-ability reader in both first grades. He had a very difficult time learning graphophonic cues and letter sounds. He cried regularly the first months of school and constantly told us how hard everything was. On the last day of school, with a broad smile, he tugged on my skirt and said, "Please Mrs. Routman, can't we have reading group today?" He was reading close to grade level, but more important, was the pride and joy he felt in being able to read *Frog and Toad* books independently. His mother wrote:

At first he only wanted to be read to. I talked to him a lot, and now he is starting to read a lot. He still likes to be read to, but the last few months of school, he has shown so much improvement, and he likes reading. You have helped him a lot, he talks of you and is always telling us, 'Mrs. Routman says I am doing good Mommy'...

What is remarkable about Jay's achievement is that he was severely disabled in hearing sounds in words and in making that transition to the printed page in reading and in writing. Yet, here he was — our very poorest reader — bursting with pride at his abilities. And, despite his limitations in spelling, he did not act or feel limited. He could fill a whole page in his journal with meaningful language.

And lastly, there was Nathan — a large, awkward, hesitant boy. His parents were very anxious about him learning to read because the kindergarten teacher in another school had strongly suggested that he might have a learning disability. This judgment was supposedly made because of his difficulty completing phonics worksheets. Nathan clearly felt his parents' anxieties, and it was apparent he was worried about learning to read. His parents reported he was not verbal about what went on in school, and initially, he was not a risk taker in his reading or writing. Academics did not come easily for Nathan. His parents encouraged him with art activities where he could use his natural talents, and they also read to him regularly. They took our concerns about being involved parents very seriously, too seriously at first.

His father wrote:

> After a while we forgot reading should be a fun time. We as parents had to learn that, and you helped us. Once we relaxed, he did too.

Nathan's desire to read was very strong. He immersed himself in literature and all the opportunities books provided. His dad, finally quite pleased with Nathan's success, remarked:

> The thing I'm struck with is it was kind of a silent achievement. As we drove down the street, he read billboard signs, car dealers, everything. Something jelled all of a sudden, and he was reading everything. I was flabbergasted! I'm still struck by it all.

Nathan's mother commented on the writing opportunities:

> I think the approach — being able to integrate his reading with drawing that he already loved and felt competent at — influenced him. The nice thing with the writing was that he could create an entity — do writing and draw and do his own thing. He loved creating stories, publishing books, doing book projects, illustrating his poems.

In June, Nathan tested out at a beginning third grade level on a standardized reading test. He was a confident, expressive child, a risk taker who knew he could find meaning on the printed page even if he couldn't read every word. He was also, we thought, quite an extraordinary writer.

There is no question in my mind that Jay, Nathan, Sharon, Eddy, and many of our other students would have had a very difficult time learning to read and write, had they been in a basal book program with its isolated skill and sequence emphasis and overreliance on phonics. It was the joy and immersion in wonderful, meaningful children's books — along with a strong parent-teacher partnership —that made the difference.

And what a difference it has been!

(top) *A parent helping with a reading group.*
(above) *A parent putting together a book project.*
(opposite) *Karen Shiba taking a guided reading lesson.*

10 First Year Journals
Entries From Two Teachers

Karen Shiba and I co-taught the literature-language arts program for the first year, and she was instrumental in the successful implementation of our program. Karen had been a traditional classroom teacher with six years teaching experience in grades 2 and 4. She was comfortable with the basal text and workbooks but was very eager to try a new approach. Throughout the summer of 1983, she did much reading of articles and books supporting literature-based reading and whole language teaching. We had much discussion together as we mapped out plans for the beginning of a new school venture.

That first year, we each kept personal journals of what was happening in the classroom. It is hoped that by honestly sharing the daily happenings, frustrations and successes involved in teaching with literature for the first time, other teachers will have some feel for what this means and gain the courage to add literature and self-selected writing to their existing programs. We made and continue to make lots of adjustments in our teaching. We continue to work harder than we have ever worked and to enjoy teaching more than ever. Truly the hardest part was beginning for the very first time and taking that initial risk.

Many excerpts from the first three months of school in 1983 indicate high interest and excitement in literacy, our concerns about noise level and behavior, and insights about the children through the parents. Excerpts from both our diaries appear below; mine are in italic type.

Sept. 1, 1983

Karen and I alternate reading pages from our personal "I Like____" books. Attention of all is excellent. When we go through the books for a second reading, most kids join in orally from the pictures. Some questions are asked, "How did you know the word was winter?" "Because it begins with a 'w'." Good sound-symbol consciousness for beginning consonants. Group very enthusiastic. Karen has each child tell two things he/she likes. All do so successfully.

Then we begin making "I Like..." books. Children work enthusiastically cutting pictures out of magazines and pasting them into their personal books. We circulate to help them write in words to go with their pictures. Many write "I Like..." themselves from the blackboard. All write their name or part of it on the front cover. No one says, "I can't write my name." We have too many pages in their books. Still, 4 out of 23 complete their books.

Attention span too short for too many classroom rules. Students really enjoyed listening to our "I Like..." books. This project should ony be 6-7 pages long. Students loved the "September" poem, from **Chicken Soup With Rice** by Maurice Sendak. Students sang "The Other Day I Met a Bear". Students enjoyed **Clifford, the Small Red Puppy.**

Sept. 2

Three children who have completed "I Like..." books read them to group. They read every word correctly. Attention of all is excellent. Later on in the morning and in the afternoon, the rest work on completing their books, and 20 out of 23 finish by 3 p.m. Jamaar and Theo use invented spellings and do almost all their own writing. For those words we can't read, we lightly pencil in correct spelling underneath and they don't seem to mind.

We need to teach the children how to glue. Some of the books are messy because of too much glue. We are amazed so many finish and work so long in these books.

Karen does the "September" poem. (She did it yesterday afternoon at least 6 times!) The kids love it. She uses the pointer so the children see and hear the words at the same time. The boys read it, and then the girls read it without help. Karen copies the poem on a ditto, and we send it home in a folder to collect poems all year to read again at home.

*I read **Ebbie** by Eve Rice at about 10.30 a.m., and we talk about our names. Everyone listens to every word. Later, we collect all the train name tags and have each child stand as we* *show their name. We also do, "Would the other person whose name begins the same way stand up?" (Shahidrah, Sheila, etc.)*

We give each child a name card and a piece of paper to write a note, and we explain the use of the mailboxes. We are amazed that they all write. Karen adds "Dear" and "Love" to "I Like" on the board. Almost all space between words.

Mid-afternoon, I read the Big Book **Brown Bear, Brown Bear**. *It is 2.30 p.m. and they are tired. While attention is generally good, it is not as sustained as in the a.m. The children join in after several pages. We discuss why this is called a Big Book, and they talk about size of print, book, and pictures. Print awareness seems to be developing. When I ask at one point, how many think they can read already, almost every hand goes up.*

Overall, we are very pleased and exhausted about how the first two days have gone. Most of the children seem "turned on".

Peers were very attentive while "I Like..." books were being read. Students attacked "September" poem with "I know it" zest. All wanted "The Other Day I Met a Bear" sung again. I do a second reading of **Ebbie** — needs lots of discussion. Children stood when their train with their name was held in front of group. Students then took one train and drew a picture and/or wrote a note to that person and placed the note in the matching mailbox. Amazingly, all students wrote one word or more. We tell them spelling doesn't matter, that we know they can write. Students enjoyed the chart poem, "Pussycat, Pussycat..." and book **Clifford's Good Deeds** and Big Book **Brown Bear, Brown Bear**. First newsletter went home today.

Sept. 6
Four children read their "I Like..." books. Disappointingly, only a handful remember to return them from home. The chart poems "Pussycat, Pussycat", and "Mix a Pancake" are a hit. So is the book **Brown Bear, Brown Bear**. *Several children read the book independently in the reading area later on in the morning.*

Slow down! Not enough time has been spent on classroom rules. Only books that have been read should be displayed. Big Book **Grandpa, Grandpa** was a hit. In writing, we notice that children stop asking for spelling when we keep saying to write it the way they think it is written. They liked our discussion of their nicknames and the rereading of **Ebbie**. They continue to love chart poems.

Sept. 7
A delightful morning! More "I Like..." books came back from home and are shared. The class reads **Brown Bear, Brown Bear** *without any help. I call students up to find words with the*

pointer — good response. **Grandpa, Grandpa** *Big Book is reread. Rhyming words are discussed. Kids join in easily. New book* **Animals Should Definitely Not Wear Clothing** *is read and multiple copies are placed in the reading center.*

Karen and I go over rules with the kids and have a demonstration of proper reading behavior in the reading center —how to handle books, place back in same place, noise level, etc. We should have done this sooner.

We have a serious discussion about proper behavior in the reading center. All students stepped out of center while a few demonstrated how to behave properly. Very effective!

Students **love** Big Books! Students are very entertained by photos and tellings of Regie's vacation at the beach. She brings in shells and mussels, and they seem to relate to **Grandpa, Grandpa** even more now.

While some finished work in the afternoon, others worked or drew pictures to friends to put in mailboxes. They are starting to understand the mailboxes and seem to like them a lot. They write notes to each other in their spare time.

Sept. 12
We have five parent interview/conferences this week. We learn that Darlene does not eat breakfast (even when Mom fixes it) and that she is an only child who spends most of her time with Mom. We suggest that Dad come to our Open House. We learn from Max's mom that little time at home is spent reading and that she does not belong to the public library. We encourage her to join. We also suggest less television after school with more letter writing and reading taking place.

We begin listening to children read. Adrienne reads **Brown Bear, Brown Bear**. *We record it on her reading record. She takes the book home to read to her family. We need parent volunteers. Everyone wants to read to us!*

Sept. 13
Writing journals are introduced today. I am very nervous that someone will say they can't or won't write, but that doesn't happen. Overall, it goes better than we expect. More invented spellings are showing up. Theo writes a whole sentence about her broken leg. She can read what she writes. Britt copies "Trees are nice" from the person next to her. Lynn writes two sentences about her brother, and she is a lot more comfortable with invented spelling. Some seem unable to put down anything. They draw a picture. Max puts down "r" "k" for his racing car picture. Adrienne, with much encouragement, writes, "I like b-ks". I think the writing will be a hit.

We do the Big Book **Yes Ma'am** *again. We read* **A Apple Pie** *and* **Apple Pigs** *to go along with a whole group phonics lesson on short a. We also eat apples. I'm not sure yet how whole* *group phonics will work out. I'm still worried too about how reading groups will be organized so kids are doing meaningful activities during all of reading time.*

Parent conferences indicate the poems are a big hit. Theo's mom says Theo knows all five poems by heart and says and sings them over the phone to relatives and friends. Another mother said, "She reads them to anyone who will listen."

Parent conferences are very informative. Parents have questions about proper bedtime, what children should do besides watching t.v., and the use of the public library. Parents appear willing to come in and listen to children read. One parent did come in and was impressed with the children's "involvement". Most parents mention how much the children enjoy the books in class and the poems sent home on Friday. They also like my weekly letters.

Sept. 14
We chant the song "This Old Man", and the kids sing enthusiastically. They also love "Who Stole the Cookie from the Cookie Jar?", and it's great for teaching names and getting to know other kids. We need to meet with the music teacher and tie in enlarged print reading with singing. These kids love to sing.

*We introduce the Big Book **Hairy Bear**. They like it! We read it five times throughout the day. **Yes Ma'am** is done alone by the class. Karen is reading at least 5 to 7 books a day, some old, some new, certainly not too much. All books read are placed in the reading center with multiple copies.*

We do journal writing for the second day. What excitement! The kids write more freely than the first day. They all seem to like it and need little coaching on topics.

We are wrestling a lot with classroom management. What is noise, and what is the creative sound of children working? Can we expect kids to create, write, and read books and be silent? We're not sure yet. The noise level is too high for some and doesn't seem to bother others. One thing is evident. These kids are happy and enjoying school.

Sept. 16
*Our alphabet WEB unit which we concluded today was not a success. The alphabet books we had the children make were forced, and we wouldn't do it again. The children did not enjoy making these the way they did the **I Like** books. **A Apple Pie** was a big hit.*

It will be helpful when we get regular parent volunteers coming in to listen to the children read.

We had 19 parent conferences this week — exhausting! But worth it. We know the kids a lot better. All the parents tell us how much their children enjoy school.

Sept. 21

*I read **Little Red Riding Hood** (de Regniers) all in rhyme. Using the cloze technique, I pause at the end of the line, and they are able to fill in the predictable rhyming word. They love this book and this activity, and attention is excellent. Karen does new poems and the Big Book **The Longest Journey in the World** two times in the morning and twice more in the afternoon. Mike Thaler's **Hippopotamus** books are enthusiastically received, especially **A Hippopotamus Ate the Teacher. Leo the Late Bloomer** is much enjoyed.*

Writing continues to excite most of the children. Lynn is giving a blow by blow description of a neighbor's house being robbed. Adrienne moves beyond "I Like..." entries to write about her brother. Robb, with teacher encouragement, writes a sentence about why he is crying, and he seems surprised that he can do it.

Traditional "bell work" (where the teacher has a before school assignment for all children) is unnecessary. Children come into the classroom and immediately are busy reading by themselves or to each other, drawing or writing notes, or writing in their journals. Shahidrah wrote a note to Oscar saying how much she liked him and could he come over.

Kids continue to love Big Books and chart poems. Mrs. Hise, the music teacher, started putting songs on chart paper. She said it was great. Kids are working on their own **Grandpa, Grandpa** books. They have to put in the illustrations to match the text. They love this project. ABC unit was not successful. We are gathering books for Bear unit to start next week.

Whole group phonics with enlarged print is very successful. The brighter kids help the others remember. It is quick and fun, and there is no pressure.

Sept. 26

A colleague, Debbie Powell, visits from Indiana University and gives us a wealth of ideas. She is a wonderful resource person.

*When the children enter at 8.45, she notes that all are either reading a book at their desk or in the reading center or writing a note to someone. Although it's noisy, everyone is productively involved in reading or communicating for some purpose. We are relieved to hear her say that... We do **Hush Little Baby** again. I sing it, and they join in. We tape record it, and they listen to themselves singing. It is very quieting for them.*

Debbie Powell from Indiana is visiting today. She read a homemade Big Book entitled **One Bright Monday Morning**... We then wrote a class book, **One Cloudy Monday Morning**... on chart paper. It started out as "One morning on my way to school, I saw..." The kids had lots of ideas, and they will illustrate their pages later.

We introduced the Bears unit by reading aloud **Bears, Bears, Bears.** Then the children chose an animal, and with the help of the other students, they thought of rhyming sentences. One was, "Cats, cats, cats. Sleeping in hats. Running with bats. Cats, cats, cats." Regie and I wrote what the kids said in a large group on the bottom of drawing paper. The kids will illustrate these later, and we will put them all into a class book.

Students continue to make progress in their writing journals. Robb wrote 5 or 6 sentences on Friday! And they were well written.

New student to make 24 this morning. It continues to be difficult to get used to a nontraditional classroom. I **will say** — language development is surely taking place!

Sept. 27

Victor and Franklin are the first to publish books from stories they have written in their writing journals. They work one-to-one with Mrs. Lawrence, a volunteer who will be helping us with this publishing process three mornings a week and will also be teaching some parents how to make book covers for us. The boys are so excited about being published! Franklin is repeating first grade. (He came here from another school as an LD student and a nonreader.) He can read every word in his book, and he is thrilled!

I write today in my journal with a group of children around the reading table. This modeling of writing behavior seems to motivate some kids. There seems to be even more interest in writing now that the class sees what it means to be a published author.

Sept. 28

Karen and I note that the children are reading/seeing/hearing at least six books a day plus poems.

*We do the Big Book **Lazy Mary**. They sing it well, having already done it in music. We read the Big Book **One Cold Wet Night** and introduce a new Big Book, **The Bus Ride** which has been beautifully illustrated by my son Peter.*

Our Bear Web has begun, and we are reading several bear books a day. We have over 50 bear books in the classroom, signed out from the school library and the public library.

*Mrs. Groves, our principal, takes the class after lunch. They go to the office and read **Grandpa, Grandpa** to Jean, the secretary, and mistakenly, the public address system is on all over the building. The kids love the attention, and I think Mrs. Groves is quite impressed with their reading. Students are still enjoying working daily on the individual **Grandpa, Grandpa** books and illustrating them with magic markers.*

Children are signing out books daily now to read at home. Reading groups have begun to meet every day. The lowest-

ability students have read **Brown Bear, Brown Bear**. *The highest-ability students have read* **Hairy Bear** *and will finish* **More Spaghetti I Say** *today.*

Whole group phonics is getting easier. Andrew, Todd, and Matthew are having trouble keeping up.

In free time, kids are writing letters to Mrs. Powell about her visit.

Sept. 29

A teacher from another school visits to observe. Lynn's mom Mrs. Babbin visits and stays; she has her baby with her. Yesterday Robb's mom stayed all morning. We are getting used to visitors and distractions.

Brad finally writes a sentence in his journal — about his trip to Canada. We met with his mom yesterday afternoon, and that was helpful. She was expecting perfect spelling of individual words, and he was afraid to make a mistake.

Several children write letters to my son, Peter, thanking him for making the Big Book **The Bus Ride**.

Open House last night was a real success. 19 of the 24 parents showed up, and many of them brought aunts, uncles, and grandparents. The video tape of the children should have showed more of the children reading and less of us teaching.

The children loved reading **The Bus Ride** and **Boo-hoo** Big Books today, and they are enjoying reading and discussing lots of books about bears. We reread **One Bright Monday Morning** as well as our own versions **One Cloudy Monday Morning** and **One Windy Tuesday Morning**.

When Regie mentioned writing in their journals today, the kids cheered loudly. They love to write!

Sept. 30

We read **The Bus Ride** *again and several children sign out our small copies. This book is a favorite. Karen notes that the children seem to enjoy the second and third readings even more than the first reading.*

Children are doing well in their writing journals, although it is still very noisy during this time. They are talking to each other, exchanging ideas, helping each other with spelling, and reading their writing to each other. We are still not comfortable with the noise level.

In art, the art teacher Linda Rozman is showing slides of bears, and the children will be making pastel chalk bears. In music, Mrs. Hise is doing **The Bear Went Over the Mountain** *to go along with our Bear* WEB. *We need to talk with our librarian to coordinate in their library time also.*

We are working at a frantic pace in the morning. It's exhausting, but it's getting easier. Our Shared Book Experience time lasts about 50 minutes, from 10.00 a.m. to 10.50 a.m. The children's attention is getting better during this time. Then we generally have a brief recess followed by writing journal time and reading groups. There is never enough time for everything. I worry about the kids who aren't getting enough attention.

Our October and November entries indicate sustained interest in writing, excitement about books and reading progress, our growing comfort level as routines become established, lots of parent involvement, concern about individual students, differences in ability levels and rates of progress.

Oct. 3
Wes's mom came in all morning. He is one we've been concerned about, and I think it was helpful that she saw how he was functioning. He wrote more this morning with her here.

*Karen introduced several new poems including "October" from **Chicken Soup With Rice**. We read the Big Books **The Bus Ride** and **Boo Hoo**. I read **Edyth and Mr. Bear**, a long book (10 min.), but attention was excellent.*

Writing is going well. There is interest in being published. Kristy asked me, "Will you help me today because I want to be published?"

Oct. 4
We had two parent vounteers plus Mrs. Lawrence doing the publishing. Can we continue to come up with things for our volunteers to do? They seem to feel so good about feeling welcomed. I wonder what they think about the noise level in the room. The kids continue to love writing in their journals.

Oct. 6
*Karen and I both feel this morning is a breakthrough. **The Carrot Seed** is read by the whole class without our chiming in. We manage to meet with all the reading groups. The highest-ability readers are almost done with **The Magic Fish**, and the lowest-ability readers are reading **Rosie's Walk**. The room is orderly. Children seem to know the routines and our expectations. It looks like the program will work well. It's the first time things seem to run really smoothly.*

Liz Lawrence, our great volunteer, comes in and finishes another book. Jamaal is published and can read every word of his story.

Oct. 10
*We check books. Kids already know what books they want to sign out next. Victor and Adrienne want to keep their books, **The Magic Fish** and **Nobody Listens to Andrew** until they can read them perfectly. Lynn is still working on **Apple Pigs**. It's been two weeks now, and she is determined to master it. Nicky is doing beautifully. She, over a period of days, wrote a story*

about herself: "On Monday, I...", "On Tuesday, I..." It was only after checking her on **One Bright Monday Morning** *that I realized she was imitating the book's pattern while changing the activities. She can read every word. Her spelling is amazingly correct. She is thriving.*

Oct. 11
Parent volunteers help with checking books, writing journals, and getting book projects assembled. Mrs. Lawrence helps Ebby publish a book, and she can read it. Amazing! She is in the lowest ability reading group. Her book, about her aunt, is well done.

I am beginning to read most of the kids' writing without their help. Two parents are in today. I am able to meet with reading groups comfortably now. Parents that did not come to Open House to hear about the nightly take home of books and other procedures are the parents of kids who have trouble with reading. Next year we may want to call each family personally.

Oct. 13
Darlene's dad stops in, and we tell him what a difference his input has made in her behavior. Kile's father stops in to say he will be in two mornings next week to volunteer. Mrs. Jones comes in for the morning.
  Several of the children can read the entire sheet of "Bear Facts" the class has written. The children illustrate their three poems for the week plus "Bear Facts".
  The Biggest Sandwich Ever *is requested again, and I read it with oral cloze, letting the class fill in the rhyming words. They love it, and do so successfully. This is a book to possibly make into a Big Book.*
  Oscar, one of our lowest ability readers signed out **A Hippopotamus Ate the Teacher**. *I am amazed that he is able to read it!*

Oct. 17
We begin our Halloween-spooky stories WEB *today and have about 50 books from the school and public libraries. Mrs. Lund comes in with lots of book covers she made over the weekend, and several more kids publish books.*
  I call Max's mom (he is moving along so slowly) to ask her to spend more time with him at home. Also, I speak to Oscar's mom to thank her for spending time with him. Although he's in the low reading group, he has been self-selecting challenging books for independent home reading and reading them. I am impressed. This kid has potential.
  Our top group begins **Little Red Riding Hood**, *in rhyme, and they love it. The low group is completing* **One Cold Wet Night**. *Andrew, Max, and Todd still do not quite have the one-to-one*

correspondence for pointing to each word as it is read, but they are enjoying the rhythm of the story.

Oct. 19
The children write Halloween spooky stories. They do very well. Franklin can hardly wait to get started. He writes un- interrupted, a whole page, for twenty minutes and ignores talking around him. What a good story. He begins, "There once was a witch. She was so little an ant could eat her." It's obvious Franklin loves to write.

Charley writes a whole sentence in his journal without help. He is beginning to believe he can do it.

Adrienne reads her published book to the class. She took it home yesterday to practice it. Her illustrations are carefully done.

Jamaar is a great reader. He read **Ebbie** to me without a mistake.

Karen does two more Halloween poems. They love the books **Humbug Witch** and **The Goblins Will Get You If You Don't Watch Out**.

Yesterday's project, a flip book, "All About Me" got done so quickly and easily we decide to do it earlier next year.

Oct. 20
I spoke to Jamaar's mom about his excellent reading but not so excellent behavior. Jamaar was not reading when school started, and he reads fluently now. She was not aware of what a good reader he is.

Shelia's mom spent the morning with us. She said repeatedly she was "shocked" to see how well the kids read. She said she was taking the many toys and t.v. out of Shelia's room and putting in a book shelf. This mom really needs help parenting. She is only 23.

We did a new big book **Woosh!** Many could figure out the title before I read it. We also read **Clifford's Halloween, Over in the Meadow** (in preparation for the Big Book to begin in art class on Friday), and **The Goblins Will Get You If You Don't Watch Out**, along with some requested Halloween stories.

Max, our lowest-ability student, writes every day in his journal about how he misses his father. Charley is beginning to be more comfortable with writing. More children are beginning to spell words correctly in their writing journals. Franklin spelled "then" and "good" correctly. Nicky is spelling most words correctly. Britt, who has been writing all words with the beginning consonant only, wrote today with some conventional spelling.

Oct. 25
We begin to flash sight vocabulary words in enlarged print, the nonphonetic words from the Dolch list. We are surprised that

most seem to already know the words. In phonics, we again do consonant-vowel-consonant words such as "mend". Whole group phonics with enlarged print seems to be working very well.

Both of Victor's parents came in today to volunteer. They listen to kids read, and help with journal writing. That makes three fathers who have been in to observe and help.

Karen says at least five children can read all the names of the children and can pass out papers.

Oct. 26

I feel so guilty for not writing. The pressure is on! The kids came into the reading center the other day and saw the Big Book **Woosh!** and said the name instantly. Big Books are read quickly now. Many students are beginning to spell correctly and write on the notebook lines in their writing journals. Discipline is under control now. The weekly Good Citizen reports seem to help. We started a new project today based on **The Seven Little Monsters**, and the kids loved it.

We opened the WEB room (small room adjacent to classroom) to the students yesterday for free choice activities for students who are working well. The kids all have library pockets on the front of their manila folders (where they keep their book projects). In the pocket they have their name on an index card. They use this card to place in one of the envelopes posted on the back of the book case marked, for example, Computer (2 students), WEB room (4 students) and Reading Center (5 students). During whole group time, we explain all the activities in the WEB. The kids **love** to go in there, and they have learned to use the tape recorder — and love the stamps and puzzles.

The kids are **really** learning to read, and they **love** school. So do I — but I'm so tired. Delores wants us to present a 10 minute "thing" to the Board of Education in a week or so — **pressure**.

The kids write in their writing journals before school and write to each other. Their notes to each other have become quite lengthy.

Nov. 2

The classroom is quiet before school. Kids have settled into the routine of writing a letter, writing in their journal, or reading a book by themselves or with a friend.

*I read **Tight Times** yesterday as part of our new WEB unit on feelings. The room is silent; they loved this sensitive story. Karen also read **Nobody Listens to Andrew**.*

An interesting note — On Halloween, Karen passed out some old Halloween dittoes she had. There was little interest and no excitement in doing this project.

*Today, in addition to Big Books and poems we read **Do Not Open, Dan the Flying Man, Who is My Mother?** and **The Hating Book**.*

In writing journals, more phonetic spelling is occurring. When Lynn wrote "her" for "here", I asked her what was missing from the word, and she could say "e" herself.

Nov. 3
*Going along with our feelings unit, Karen read **I Don't Care** and **Pierre**. They spontaneously joined in on "I don't care" in **Pierre**.*

Mr. Hall came in for the morning and read with lots of the kids. He is really good with them and seems to enjoy it.

*Nicky and Lynn will both be publishing another book today. Robb and Kile finished publishing their books with Mrs. Lawrence, and they are thrilled. Jamaar did a page in our class big book of **Seven Little Monsters**.*

*In **The Bus Ride** which we read as a Big Book again this morning, I pointed out the use of "!" after "Then!" Nicky and Franklin incorporated exclamation marks into their writing today.*

Nov. 4
The Seven Little Monsters projects are not well done. We did not give enough guidance. The fact that we had no Big Book as a large model for reading made it difficult for kids. Also we didn't give enough explanation of what we expected. All the monsters look the same; most pictures have no background, and are not carefully colored.

Model writing for writing journals is important every once in a while. If we hurry them, they don't write much, and quality is poor. Make time!

Nov. 8
Parent conferences went well. Parents expressed enthusiasm for the program and appreciation of our hard work. It was very comfortable to have met all the parents previously and already have established a relationship. Parent communication is good.

*Karen introduced **Three Little Ducks**. Since it is so easy, we thought there might be lack of interest. Quite the contrary. After Karen read it first, the group read it through with no help. No memorization here — real reading!*

*Highest-ability readers were able to read **Noisy Nora** with little help. Lowest-ability readers did well on **Three Little Ducks**.*

Karen does an experience chart on fall and really pulls a lot from the kids. What they write is excellent. Adrienne's writing is poetic at times. Friday she wrote all about the seasons.

Nov. 9
Lynn used the "?" and "!" correctly. Britt attempted the "." Several days ago, I held up large cards with these punctuation marks and explained how each was used. We found examples

in **Noisy Nora** of the different punctuation marks. I thought perhaps more students would have been ready to use these punctuation marks. More and more correct spelling is appearing. The daily phonics seems to be aiding the transition from invented to conventional spellings. Britt has gone, almost overnight, from using one letter (the beginning consonant) to represent each word with no spacing to complete sentences with correct spacing of words and many correctly spelled words. I think sitting across from Jamaar, a good writer, has positively influenced her.

The classroom has really settled down. There is a quiet hum in the morning as children write and read and know exactly what they can do.

Nov. 10
The children are so excited about all the different activities in the room. We opened up a new book shelf to hold published books, **Clifford** books, and **Monster** books. The feelings unit is a success. **Grandpa and Me** is a favorite, along with **Noisy Nora** and **Pierre**.

Nov. 11
There is never enough time... Parent volunteers didn't show too much this week, and we missed them. We have very little personal time. We're sending home **Seven Little Monsters** projects after going over them in a large group. The children know this week's four poems very well. Less and less are asking what the poems say and are reading them on their own.

Nov. 15
Conferences go well. Parent support makes a difference. Oscar's dad, Mr. Greer, came in at 8.00 a.m. When we show him that Oscar is doing well in all areas except written language where he has not put down a thought or sentence but just copies words and names, he talks to Oscar before he leaves. Later that morning, Oscar writes a complete sentence with good sound-letter association. A breakthrough!

Nov. 17
High-ability readers complete **There's No Such Thing as a Dragon**. Lowest-ability readers complete **The Happy Egg**. Both groups take the books home to read to their families. This week's poems are illustrated including a collaborative class poem about fall.

Ebby's mom came in for the morning. This should make a difference in Ebby's progress, as she now knows what Ebby can do and what our expectations are. For example, her mom said she was writing **for** Ebby at home. She was surprised to see that Ebby could write on her own using invented spelling.

Franklin's dad came in again. He's been coming weekly to help and really seems to enjoy being in the classroom.

Nov. 28
*In shared book time we introduce two new chart poems and the Big Book **Too Much Noise**. By the second reading, most are reading it well. We sing the class made Big Book **Over in the Meadow**. The high-ability readers have completed **Heather's Feathers**. The low-ability readers have finished **Yes Ma'am**.*

Almost all the children checked out and successfully read two books over the Thanksgiving holiday.

Dr. Horoschak (our superintendent) came in and stayed about twenty minutes. He came in when the children were writing and seemed interested in what was going on. (I chewed his ear off!) We were delighted he took the time to come into our classroom.

Charley, who was the only child who really seemed to feel he couldn't write, now is writing decently and with less and less teacher input. What an improvement!

Reflecting back after the first three months of school in 1983, Karen and I noted that we were happy with the way things were going although we still had concerns about the "noisy" classroom. Enthusiasm and involvement of parents, teachers, and students were high. We had already read and reread over 30 Big Books, over 50 poems, and more than 250 picture books! With the help of our parent volunteers, the children had published more than 40 books!

Selected excerpts from December through May indicate growing confidence in reading and writing and continued parent involvement.

Dec. 6
Nicky is in the hospital with pneumonia, and we are all upset. The children will write letters to her today, and I'll pay her a visit late afternoon.

The letters they write are wonderful! There is more substance and length than we usually get in their journals, and a lot of warm feelings are expressed. What good writers they are! Here, where there is a specific purpose, they really shine.

*We read and discuss **The Red Carpet, Alexander and The Terrible, Horrible, No Good, Very Bad Day, I'll Fix Anthony**, two favorite Big Books, and our chart poems. Many of the children are reading the **Monster** books on their own.*

Dec. 8
*Top readers finished **Alexander and The Terrible, Horrible, No Good, Very Bad Day**. It is remarkable how well they are reading! We will read the book again from start to finish on Friday and then send it home. The reading level is probably second grade, and after hearing the story once, most could read it fairly easily,*

*and not word-by-word reading either. Adrienne read "invisible" without a hesitation. We see this happening a lot; Kids read multisyllable words easily in the context of the story. Karen has seven children reading **Apple Pigs**. I feel confident that we will reach our goal of half of our children testing out in May at the district average of beginning third grade reading level.*

*We have many easy-to-read books in multiple copies that the children have not heard yet. Karen and I add new books to the shelves today. After introducing them, we put out the **Thunder the Dinosaur** series, **Indian Two Feet and His Horse**, and **I Was Walking Down the Road**. Because we are crammed for book space, we take out some of the easy titles that almost all of the children have read and reread like **Fire! Fire! Said Mrs. McGuire** and **One Cold Wet Night**.*

Jan. 4

*Over winter vacation I began Donald Graves **Writing: Teachers and Children at Work**. I thought about Charley who would not sit even for five seconds without guidance during writing time the first three months. Now he writes on his own for fifteen minutes or more. Looking back, he didn't know he had something to say. He needed to be convinced that he knew about his life and could tell about it.*

I also realized after reading Graves' suggestions about making a list from memory of each child plus telling something about that child's life that is of interest to him, that I still didn't know some students well — Matthew, Theo, Kile.

*We are just about out of commercial Big Books, and Karen and I are now making our own at a stepped up pace. There is a need for more Big Books with more difficult — though not necessarily lengthier — content, if only for motivation. The kids love these books. I completed making **I Can't Said the Ant** and the words for **Pierre**. (Fifth and sixth grade volunteer artists will do the illustrations.) Karen is working on a book from all the photos taken the day of the **Over in the Meadow** assembly. The kids have written the text and are excited about their Big Book.*

We're back from vacation. Is it possible that the kids are better writers? Their journals were terrific today. About half the room can fill at least half of the page or more. They all want what they write to be read. We need to continue to be careful that we comment and ask questions about what they write while leaving the choices to them.

We got another new student today. That makes the fifth new student since September. We're losing another student tomorrow. My — after all the effort and caring we put into these students — it sure is a heartbreak. That also makes five students we've lost.

Feb. 7
Some of the children are publishing books weekly now and getting the idea of a continuous story. Stories are lengthier with better spacing of words. The use of dashes for unknown letters has all but disappeared. More correctly spelled words appear. Writing is more legible. Almost all of the children are spacing words. Capitals and punctuation are still rare. The sense of sentence is present. Almost all write complete sentences. "It is fun."; "It is nice." still appear often. We are encouraging more detail and descriptive words by pointing out and discussing the language from the picture books we read.

The high-ability readers have completed **Freckle Juice, The One in the Middle is the Green Kangaroo**, *and* **Ping**. *The low-ability readers have just completed* **Nobody Listens to Andrew**.

Feb. 21
I have been amazed that after completing **The Littles** — *a chapter book of about 70 pages — in reading group, each of the seven members has voluntarily begun another* **Littles** *book in the series. They are not put off by the length and fewer pictures. Low-ability readers finish* **The Magic Fish** *today.*

March 19
Derrick, a new student, arrived last week unable to read and write. He signed out **How to Catch a Ghost** *and was able to read it perfectly after three days. (He had heard it as a Big Book and had been practicing it over and over with his mom.) His whole demeanor changed. He was happy and smiling.*

He is unable to write, but interestingly enough, he is the fastest copier (from the board) in the room. When Karen put up Open House invitations to be copied, his was done quickly — an indication he did lots of board copying, an infrequent activity for our children.

Debbie Powell, who just visited for several days, noted that the energy level and sometimes perceived behavior problems are at least in part due to the confidence and high self-concepts the children have. They feel free to take a risk.

Ebby, one of our lowest-ability readers, continues to progress beautifully. She is breezing through the **Little Bear** *series. She tells everyone who comes in the room, "I can read!" and is all but bursting with enthusiasm.*

Max, probably our lowest reader, showed he is able to think when he figured out a solution to a problem in the book **That's What Friends Are For**, *which was read to the whole class. When asked how the elephant, who had a bad foot, could get to the lion on the other side, he offered "bring a wagon to take her there."*

Thinking skills are constantly evident in all the children. When a child finishes reading his published book to the class, he asks the group several questions. All can do this now.

April 23
The low-ability readers have completed **Red Riding Hood** *in rhyme and will start reading* **Stone Soup**. *The high-ability readers will finish* **Jenny and the Cat Club** *this week and then begin* **Charlotte's Web**. *Many in this group are reading full length chapter books with ease. Three have read* **The Little House in the Big Woods**, *over 200 pages. All have read at least several* **Littles** *books.*

The music teacher reports kids reading out of the song book. She says it's the first time first-graders have done this.

Derrick still cannot write. Even with encouragement, he seems afraid to take a risk.

Ebby's mother came in. When I told her how well Ebby was doing, she admitted that she thought our expectations were too high at first, but now that she has seen what Ebby can do and how confident she is, she has raised her expectations as a parent. What a different that has made!

Looking back, we found our own journal writing valuable as a personal way of noting what was taking place in the classroom and zeroing in on successes, concerns, and problem areas. We would highly recommend that teachers getting started in similar directions keep a log that includes daily happenings as well as teacher insecurities. Noted areas of concern can be discussed at weekly/monthly support group meetings.

When a traditional teacher, used to the basal and worksheets, joined Karen and me as a first grade teacher in an adjacent classroom, she initially had a difficult time moving into process teaching that was very different from the controlled management system she was used to. It looked to her as if Karen and I had it all "together" and that our expectations for children were unrealistic. She was clearly frustrated and did not like asking for help. I gave her my first year journal to read which honestly expressed some similar beginning frustrations. She read it overnight and felt greatly relieved. She also admitted to having a greater understanding of the total process from being able to view aspects of an entire year.

Everyday Concerns
11 Organization and Classroom Management

A corner of the WEB.

Paperback Books
Selecting Books

Use the bibliographies in this book plus your own personal favorites to get started. For Grades 1, 2, and 3, a • indicates a high priority book, that is, a book that has proved itself to be particularly suitable for whole class or group reading and would be a good title to order first. Consult your school librarian for suggestions. Use *The Read Aloud Handbook* and *For Reading Out Loud! A Guide for Sharing Books With Children* (see *Resources for Teachers*) for suggested titles for all grades. A book that is a great 'read aloud' is already a proven children's favorite and is usually a book rich in literary style. Check book reviews in journals and magazines for teachers. Also, go regularly to local book stores to find out what's new; they stock the latest books in paperback before your local or school libraries. For teachers feeling overwhelmed at the prospect of selecting titles, "core" libraries from reputable publishers such as Richard C. Owen Publishers, Rigby Education, Scholastic Inc., and The Wright Group may be a good way to begin.

Once our district made a commitment to a whole language

philosophy, the ordering and selection of books was facilitated by a reading committee made up of teachers, librarians and administrators. The first year the total school district was involved, six titles were carefully selected for each grade level to serve as a beginning core collection. (Kindergarten and first grade had more.) The Library Media Center ordered enough books for teachers to use the books whole class if they chose to do so. The Center also coated the covers with plastic for increased durability.

When selecting new titles, we use common sense, the book's appeal, and evaluation criteria. (Criteria for predictable books for beginning readers have been discussed in Chapter 4.) For more difficult books, children enjoy fast-faced plots, a setting so detailed you can visualize it, and a satisfying ending. They particularly appreciate warmth in the characters — that they like each other, express their feelings, and act selflessly. We look also for a worthwhile theme — the underlying idea that ties the plot, setting, and characterization together, and for style — the way language and point of view are used to develop the story. In addition, we try to balance our collection; besides fiction of all types, we look for quality books of poetry, nonfiction, and books that deal with the black experience. Finally, we always try to choose books that are worth the children's time and attention.

Ordering Books

Although you will be ordering titles from many publishing companies, find a jobber or wholesale distributor who will take your entire order. Your school librarian or central library office should be able to give you the names of some reliable book suppliers. You may receive a 25% to 40% discount depending on the size of the order, particularly if you are ordering multiple copies of the same title. You may need to allow several months for processing and delivery.

You may also want to check with your local bookstore to see if they are interested in dealing with your school system and handling the order. One school district elected to purchase all titles that way because of the extra amenities provided by the bookstore. Although the discount was only 20%, teachers could browse through the shelves and examine the books. Service was personal and friendly, and special orders and requests were accommodated quickly.

We have found it desirable to order ten copies of any book that we plan to use with a reading group. With any chapter book used in a reading group, we set aside one copy as a "Teacher Edition", and the teacher pencils in prediction questions at the end of a chapter leading into the next chapter. Review questions at the beginning of a chapter serve as springboard for discussion and recall. Notes in the margin of the book recall specific concepts to be highlighted and examples of skills taught. Specific vocabulary words to be discussed are underlined. All this helps the teacher recall key points and vocabulary she wants to highlight; it also provides the substitute teacher with some guidelines.

Some of our classrooms have their own libraries, and for these we order three copies of books to be read independently. We use the school and local libraries to supplement our WEB units and classroom collections. The general rule is that a class of thirty students should have a minimum of 100 books in its classroom library.

Finding Money for Books

Fortunately, paperbacks can still be purchased fairly inexpensively. The average book, with a discount, costs about $3.00. Your district may be willing to give you some money for books if you convince them of the need. Approach your building principal first. Some teachers have been successful in being awarded grant money from private local foundations. Check with your administration for possible sources and guidelines for writing grants. If you are working with Chapter 1 students, available federal funds can be used for book purchase. If you are no longer using workbooks, it is possible that the money that previously went for their purchase can be put toward books. You may also be able to charge your students for one or several books, which gives the students the added advantage of being able to write in the books. National book clubs such as "Scholastic" and "Trumpet" offer significant discounts to students on selected titles. In addition, your Parent Teacher Association may be willing to sponsor a fund raiser. We were able to purchase additional books and book spinners that way.

Finally, if monies are not available, use the libraries. Our district Library Media Office listed the number of titles held in each elementary building for books listed in *The Read Aloud Handbook* by Jim Trelease and *For Reading Out Loud! A Guide for Sharing Books With Children* by Margaret Mary Kimmel and Elizabeth Segal. By letting our librarian know a week or so in advance, she could borrow enough titles for group reading of a book. Also, if you let local and county libraries know you will need certain titles, they are very cooperative about getting them for teachers and making special arrangements for keeping the books beyond the due dates.

Organizing the Book Collection

Housing the books: We house all the books in a room we call the WEB. In one school, it is a room adjacent to the first grades; in another building, it is a large book room with floor to ceiling shelves. Our own collection numbers over 1000 titles in multiple copies. The books are separated by grade levels, and the shelves are so marked. In the first grade section, they are arranged from easiest to hardest using our color-coded leveling system, and a corresponding leveling chart is posted for teacher reference. The first grade area also has a non-fiction section and shelves for Big Books — both commercial and teacher-made. In the second and third grade sections, picture books, biographies, and chapter books are arranged separately by these categories. There are also sections of poetry as well as professional books and resources for teachers.

All the books are stamped "Moreland School Literature Collection", which helps lost books get returned and avoids confusion with the school library. In addition, all books are numbered on the inside cover. This is to ensure that the student returns the same book he has signed out or that has been assigned to him for reading group. The first year we had not numbered the books, and some students would pick up a book from the classroom library and return that copy. There was no way for us to tell the difference.

Every book is available in one central place for any teacher in the school to sign out and use. This is very important. Because all the books are available to everyone equally, there is no feeling of possessiveness on the part of a teacher, and a fine sense of community develops. The books also get maximum use and circulation. A third grade teacher with a new student who is a poor reader can find appropriate books at the first grade level. At the beginning of the school year, second grade teachers sign out books from the more difficult section of the first grade collection. A first grade teacher who needs more challenging books for an advanced reader can find them. Books are also signed out by the Chapter 1 teacher and special education teachers for their students, as well as by tutors and parent volunteers.

In the classroom, where there are many titles in multiple copies, the teacher assigns one or more students to be in charge of keeping the books organized by title on the shelves and book spinners. In the first grade, where there are so many books, the teachers have former students serve as after-school librarians to keep the books neatly together by title.

Organizing Sign-out Procedures: Every book in our collection is listed alphabetically by title in a large spiral bound book. The suggested grade level, type of book (Big Book, fiction, poetry, etc.), recommendation as a reading group book, and number of copies is listed. Teachers sign out books noting their initials and grade level, number of copies taken, and date, recorded in a grid of boxes next to the title. (See Figure 1.) A teacher looking for a specific book can see immediately who has it and how long it has been out. On returning

Figure 1 Book Borrowing Record

MORELAND SCHOOL LITERATURE PROGRAM PAPERBACK BOOK COLLECTION

Grade Level	Title	Qty.	Type	Teacher's Initials	Number of books	Date out	Date in	Teacher's Initials	Number of books	Date out	Date in	Teacher's Initials	Number of books	Date out	Date in	Teacher's Initials
First	A, B, C Bunny (The)	3	Fiction													
Second	Abe Lincoln Gets His Chance	8	Biography													
Third	Abel's Island	10	William Steig													
Second	Abraham Lincoln	7	Biography													
Second	Accident (The)	7	Fiction													
First	Across the Stream	3	Fiction													
Second	Admiral Richard E. Byrd	3	Biography													
Second-Third	Adventures of Spider	10	Fiction													
Third-Fourth	Adventures of Tom Sawyer	3	Fiction													
Third	Aesop's Fables	10	Fiction													
Second	Air	1	Nonfiction													
First	Akimba and the Magic Cow	6	Fiction													
Third	Aladdin and the Wonderful Lamp	10	Fiction													
Second-Third	Aldo Applesauce	6	Fiction													
First	Alexander and the Terrible, Horrible.... Day	8	Fiction													
Third	Alexandra the Great	1	Fiction													
First-Second	All Ears	2	Little Trolley													
First-Second	All Eyes	2	Little Trolley													
Third	All-of-a-Kind Family	2	Fiction													
First-Second	Almost Awful Play (The)	3	Fiction													
Second-Third	Amazing Bone (The)	7	William Steig													

books, teachers note the date and number of copies returned. Teachers also assume the responsibility for any necessary repair and return the books in good condition.

We have been fortunate to have a teacher, Sue Walker, volunteer to do the time-consuming task of putting all titles on her computer using a data base and updating the listing each year. In addition to the alphabetical listing of books, the data base allows for easy categorizing. We have separate sheets listing all our Big Books, poetry books, Beverly Cleary books, William Steig books, Bill Peet books, teacher resources, etc. In addition, every teacher in our school has the complete list — reduced in size — with all available titles and categories for easy reference.

One general rule we follow is that books designated by the district reading committee or particular building for one grade level may not be used by a lower grade level. A higher grade level could, however, use the title. For example, *Trumpet of the Swan* is designated for third grade. While a second grade teacher would not use this book in a reading group, a fourth grade teacher could elect to do so.

Book Repair, Replacement, and Inventory: After four years of very hard use by many teachers and students, most of our original collection is still intact. We use parent volunteers and upper grade students to keep our books repaired using book tape on the cover and binding and scotch tape for inside pages. Most teachers assign one students to check the books regularly for needed repair. With new paperbacks, you may want to consider reinforcing the cover and binding with clear "Contac" or plastic coating and reinforcing the pages next to the front and back covers with scotch tape.

If a student loses a book, he is obliged to purchase a new book or pay $3.00 so we can replace it. A large manilla envelope is kept in a secure place in the WEB, and teachers note the book lost, the student's name, and the money paid. Students and parents know that if the book turns up, the money will be refunded. At the end of the school year, we replace lost books when we order new titles. A large envelope is also kept in the WEB for teacher suggestions of new and additional books recommended for purchase and the number of copies desired.

The last week of school, parent volunteers make an inventory of the entire book collection, complete book repairs as necessary, change the number of copies of a book available if there is a discrepancy, and alphabetically list new additions to the collection. This is a time-consuming task and one that would be very difficult to accomplish without volunteer help. Sue Walker has also graciously updated our collection over the summer, and new printout sheets are bound into a book for the new school year. All books are stored in the WEB over the summer months.

Big Books

Buying Big Books

Big Books are commercially available from the following reputable companies and range in price from about $13.00 to $30.00. You are likely to get a better price if you order them in sets with the accompanying little books.

Holt, Rinehart & Winston, Inc.
383 Madison Avenue
New York, New York 10017

Rigby Education
PO Box 797
Crystal Lake, Illinois 60014

Scholastic Inc.
904 Sylvan Avenue
Englewood Cliffs,
New Jersey 07632

The Wright Group
10949 Technology Place
San Diego,
California 92127

Making Big Books

Since commercially available Big Books are limited in number, as well as costly, most of our books are made by teachers using 18" x 24" oaktag. Because we introduce at least one new Big Book each week, while continuing to read old favorites, a large supply is needed. To increase our supply of Big Books, we take apart worn copies of favorite paperbacks, using the original illustrations and printing the words ourselves. For some books, an enlarging machine is used to get sizable black and white illustrations. As well, we use individual children's illustrations from the first grade class for original and favorite stories, and our own limited artistic talent to make reasonable facsimiles. The Big Book Club of 5th and 6th graders which meets weekly at noon is of great assistance here. Some teachers also make use of the overhead and opaque projectors in tracing and drawing illustrations. They use heavy duty paper, staple the binding, and use colored binding tape to make an attractive, sturdy finish. Parent volunteers have also made some beautiful Big Books for teachers. Because of the number of teachers who became interested in making Big Books, our district Library Media Center was able to purchase a machine for spiral binding. Prior to that we were having our books spiral bound by a local printing company for about $5.00 per book. Our library media center also has a laminating machine and laminates all book pages before binding.

In making Big Books, the teacher needs to make the print sizable and clear enough to be seen by the entire class, and the visual layout needs to be the same as the original book. Considerations need to be given to careful spacing between words and lines. Color can be used to emphasize and highlight dialogue and repetitive refrains. Illustrations can be done by the children; elaborate illustrations are unnecessary for the purposes of enlarged text reading. According to the United States Copyright Law (1976), permission to make Big Books would fall within the definition of "fair use" which allows reproduction "for nonprofit educational purposes".

Storing Big Books

We store our Big Books in a free-standing upright book case. This works well for us because the books are readily accessible to the children. Books which have not yet been introduced are stored in a cupboard. Other teachers also use skirt hangers on a circular rack (as found in a clothing store) or rods suspended on a bar from the ceiling to hold individual Big Books.

Supplies Needed by Teacher

Easel, for reading of Big Books.

We use an existing art easel. Our custodian cut the height of the easel by several inches and inserted a wood strip where the painting jars used to go. The wood strip, inserted flush with the height of the open paint well, allows the book to rest evenly on the stand so pages turn easily.

Pointer, for reading of Big Books, class stories and poems.

We cut a ½" wooden dowel, purchased at a hardware store, to a comfortable size and stain it brown. For the point on the end of the dowel, we use the bright orange top from a container of Elmer's glue and paste it in. This is my husband's bright idea, and it works beautifully.

Book spinners, to hold and display books. (These are commercially available book stands for paperbacks, as used in libraries and book stores.) To accommodate most of our picture books, which are larger than the standard library book, our custodian has used a wire cutter to make a wider holder from two smaller ones.

Book shelves, for paperbacks, library books, and children's published books.

We have used whatever we can find in our building, from standard book cases to portable, free-standing folding racks. Check the newspaper for stores going out of business. Stationery stores and discount stores have wonderful display cases to hold cards, books, and miscellaneous items. Some resourceful teachers have been able to purchase these at very low prices.

Mailboxes. Anything your imagination conjures up will work here

— circular oatmeal containers, shoe boxes, milk cartons, cardboard storage units from a discount store.

Three-hole punch, for individual copies of poems for poetry anthologies.

Sturdy chart paper, for copying poems in enlarged print and collaborating on stories.

Chart stand, for hanging poems and stories.

Clotheslines and clothes pins, for displaying projects in classroom that are accessible to the children.

Book mending tape, for book repair, especially of cover binding. Sturdy tape is available in various widths through a library supply company. Check with your librarian for a source. Our school district stocks this tape in the warehouse so it is readily available.

Listening post center. Tape recorders and ear phones for books with cassettes.

Reading table. Kidney-shaped or circular table for small group reading.

Area for reading center. Use existing furniture and possibly a carpet remnant to designate a whole class reading center. Old bean bag chairs, cushions, and pillows work well here for free reading in a comfortable setting.

Rocking chair, old-fashioned wooden. We bought ours used, and love the comfort for storyreading.

Author's chair. Designate a sturdy chair, next to the rocking chair, as the place where authors share their writing with the class.

Supply basket. With process teaching, there is little time spent sitting at a desk. Karen Shiba gave up her desk and keeps a picnic basket full of necessary supplies: paper clips, stapler, pencils, etc.

Overhead projector, transparencies and magic markers, for modeling, whole class teaching, and visual cloze activities.

School book stamp. We stamp every paperback, "Moreland School Literature Program" with a rubber stamp ordered from a local printing company.

"Unedited" stamp, "Revised" stamp, "Draft" stamp. From the local printing company, we ordered these stamps for every teacher in our school who wanted one. For writing not taken to final copy, we stamp "unedited", "revised", and/or "draft". (You can get by with just an "unedited" stamp.)

Spiral notebooks. We keep a supply of these bought at a discount, for writing journals, and charge the children when they need one. Advance purchasing in quantity keeps the price down and allows us to have control of the notebook size and line spacing.

Art supplies. Budget for tempura paints, water colors, pastel chalk, magic markers, construction paper for project covers, large paper for murals, assorted papers for self-selected writing, and fadeless roll paper in assorted colors for comparison charts, vocabulary charts, and thematic displays of children's work. (Order from a school supply company.)

Supplies Needed by Students

Waterproof book bag, for transporting WEB book back and forth to school daily. Some teachers also ask students to use a "zip-loc" bag for extra security.

Three-ring notebook, for poetry anthology or journal writing.

Writing folder, for record and storage of student writing.

Cassette tapes, for taping oral reading.

Magic markers, colored pencils, for illustrating books and projects.

Fine-tipped colored markers or pencils, for revising in writing process.

Organizing the Publishing Process

Setting Aside a Place for Publishing

We use part of the WEB, the room where the literature collection is housed, for an in-school publishing house. A circular table and chairs in the center of this small room, shelves with bookmaking supplies, and a "hot pot" with instant coffee and tea make it a welcome place for parents to make book covers, work one-to-one with students, and put together book projects for teachers. A chart on the wall gives pictorial and written directions for making wallpaper books. (See Appendix P). Having supplies in a central place and having that place available to everyone promotes a feeling of cooperation. It is not unusual for a volunteer parent from one classroom to work with students from other classrooms and grade levels. Parents transcribe stories by hand, type stories, help with final editing, help students with the layout of their books, make Big Books, and assemble book projects from models the teacher has provided. Some teachers also set up their own in-class publishing centers by designating an area of the classroom for that purpose. Bookmaking supplies and various papers and media are available to students.

Training Parent Volunteers for Book Publishing

Publishing is a key component of our program, but it is a labor-intensive endeavor that can be overwhelming for a classroom teacher to handle alone. Our district has recently initiated a formal parent volunteer program to help first grade teachers with the publishing process. This support allows teachers to concentrate on their roles as coaches of writers and writing. Teachers are encouraged to identify two or three parents in their classrooms whom they feel would work well with children and their writing. These parents then meet with our volunteer coordinator, Marianne Sopko, for a two-hour orientation.

In a typical orientation session, Marianne uses her own son's journals to show the parent volunteers the process he made through his first grade year and shares with them some insights she gained by working for two years with children's publishing.

Key elements that she then covers with parents are:

- **invented spelling**

   Most of our parents have been introduced to invented spelling by their children's former kindergarten teachers.

- **the journal writing process**

   Many parents later spend some time in the classroom observing and helping with journal writing to give them a feel for how it works.

- **the spectrum of both mechanical competence and content that parents can expect to see**

   Mechanics can range from beginning sounds standing for words to nearly perfect spelling, while content can range from very simple "Things I Like To Do" books to accounts of family trips and experiences, retellings of familiar stories or original stories, and books conveying all the information a child knows about a particular topic.

- **the importance of keeping the ownership of writing with the child**

   Here our coordinator explains that the role of the parent editor is to use standard English grammar and spelling but to keep as close to the child's language as possible. If changes and reorganization of material seem necessary for clarification, the parent editor always asks the child's permission.

- **the professional relationship implied in assisting the teacher and child**

   Sometimes children write or share sensitive information that requires our careful respect and discretion.

- **the "nuts and bolts" of publishing**
  - How to make the wallpaper books
  - Where the supplies are
  - A sample format for the books (This can vary from school to school.)
  - Some method of record keeping. In most instances, this is an entry at the back of the child's journal listing the title of the book and date of publication. (Refer to Figure 3, Chapter 6.) The volunteer also helps the classroom teacher keep track of the publication process by making a chart that includes each child's name with spaces to denote the dates of publication, completion of illustrations, and the reading of the book to the class.

Marianne then models the process for the parents by bringing in a child who is ready to publish and following the procedure described in Chapter 6. Even after the parents take over the process, Marianne continues to stay in touch with the teachers and volunteers making sure that materials are available and answering questions and concerns.

Colorful, wallpaper book jackets are available for children to select for their books. This time-consuming task is handled by our parents. The room mother may set up a time when a group of parents can get together to make book covers, or a parent may offer to do this at home. Some working parents appreciate the chance to be able to volunteer outside of school hours. One year, we had a grandmother who beautifully made over 200 book covers for us.

Supplies Needed

Paper cutter. You can quickly cut various shapes for making projects and books.

Mimeograph paper, white and assorted colors. All the colors of the rainbow are available and are used for projects and books.

Long-arm stapler. This extra-long stapler allows booklets and books to be easily fastened together with several staples in the centerfold. Order from a school supply company.

Wallpaper books. Outdated sample books can be secured free of charge from stores that sell wallpaper. The book is cut apart into individual rectangular sheets which are used as book covers. Book covers can also be made from fabric, Contac paper, or whatever you have available.

Cardboard. Any stiff paper, such as the cardboard inside pressed shirts from the dry cleaner, or tagboard, can be used as a backing for the book covers.

Rubber cement. Rubber cement, or another suitable paste, is used with a wide paint brush to paste the covers securely. Rubber cement works well because excess paste is rubbed away cleanly.

Masking tape. Any size masking tape is used to place the cardboard on the wallpaper to secure it and leave space for a flexible binding.

Construction paper. Assorted colors are cut to fit the inside and outside book jackets to give a clean finish to the book covers.

Labels. We keep a supply of assorted self-stick blank labels that we use to write the title and author on the front cover of the book.

Scissors, black marking pens, pens, pencils, crayons, rulers, paint brushes.

Planning Your Program

Scheduling

Time

See if you can arrange with your building principal to have an uninterrupted block of language arts time. Also try to request a common time when all the teachers at your grade level have specials (art, music, gym) so that you all have a common planning time. That common time allows for sharing of ideas and materials and promotes collegiality. At the same time, see if the master schedule can be worked out with "grade level blocks", time when no one has specials so teachers have flexible time for teaming, coaching, and sharing lessons.

Reading Groups

Try shortening up your reading group and independent work time and lengthening direct instruction time. Incorporate whole class lessons where all students are exposed to the same book and questioning through some type of guided reading lesson. Set up interest centers. Vary your grouping structure. With the traditional three reading groups, try having students do independent "seat work" for only one period; the other period they are not with a reading group, let them read with a partner, listen to a tape, work on a mural, work with a partner to rewrite a story into a play, or work on or plan some other literature extension activity. Try having reading groups only four days a week. The fifth day, meet with students one-to-one to take running records, conference about a book, discuss concerns, etc. Or, skip reading groups all together for a while and have an individualized reading program. (See *Resources for Teachers*, especially *Read On: A Conference Approach to Reading* by David Hornsby, Deborah Sukarna and Susan Hill (eds.) for organizing an individualized reading program.)

Students Needing Remediation

As the reading specialist, I go into the classroom and work inside the room, or adjacent to it, at the same time as the classroom teacher is meeting with students in reading. I become teacher of record for the students I teach, and I also serve as a resource person for the classroom teacher. By my going into the classroom, direct instruction time is maximized by reducing the time necessitated for independent work, and students don't suffer the stigma that is sometimes associated with having to leave the room for special classes. Students who qualify for Chapter 1 service may receive additional instruction. As much as scheduling allows, this takes place during the language arts period.

Lesson Plans

In addition to written lesson plans (See Appendix B for samples from Grade 1 and Grade 3), we keep a file box and the reading group books on the reading table. The 5″ x 7″ file box contains the list of students in each reading group, a record of the WEB books for each, the names of the book being discussed in each group, key vocabulary being focused on, procedures for checking WEB books, general reading group procedures, and a brief explanation of the writing process.

For chapter books being discussed, the "Teacher's Edition" copy of the reading group book — a designated copy we write in, mentioned earlier in this chapter — is also available in the file box or on the reading table.

For the checking of WEB books (books read independently), we keep a file card on each student. On each card, we note the book title and date signed out. At each book checking session, we note the date and the page number the student is on, so from session to session we can see how much reading the student is doing. We also make brief notations in regard to the student's progress and assigned expectations for a book, such as: "book returned — too difficult", "excellent recall of details", "needs to reread Chapter 3 for better comprehension", "assigned to reread pp. 16-18 for fluency", "forgot book", "has completed all the books in this series". These notations are also useful for parent conferences and for the substitute teacher.

Literature Extension Activities

Over the years, we have gradually pooled our resources by working together to develop files for specific books. These are not "packets";

these are higher level thinking activities. In each file (for grade 2 and above), we keep the "Teacher's Edition" copy of the book, activities we have used successfully with the book, Xeroxed samples of children's work to use as models, related books and activities for a "thematic web", and a possible comprehension test.

Recently, teachers across our district have begun meeting by grade levels to brainstorm and share ideas/activities and develop webbing strategies for specific books. Our administration and library media office have promoted this collaboration by providing some release time for teachers to work together as well as typing and collating the resulting ideas for each book, and having them available in folders in each building for teachers' use.

Many good sources for helping teachers to develop activities to go along with literature are described in *Resources for Teachers*. See *Literature Extension Activity Resources*.

Planning for a Substitute

The first time you need a substitute in a reading-writing process classroom can be unnerving. Substitutes, used to traditional classrooms, can have difficulty adjusting and understanding your routines. We try to line up substitutes familiar with and supportive of our program, and after a while, this is easy to do. With at least two teachers at a grade level, either I or the classroom teacher who is present initially take some time to help orient the substitute and answer questions. We also have a brief explanation of our language arts program in the substitute folder. The file box — with its explanatory notes — and the reading books, both prominently placed on the reading table, give procedures and expectations along with the lesson plan book.

Arranging Your Classroom (See Figure 2.)

Try to arrange your room so you have a designated spot where the whole class can gather for a shared book time or collaborative writing effort. Have a blackboard, or chart stand with chart paper, available at that spot so you can easily model, demonstrate, make a teaching point, write collaboratively, highlight particular words and conventions from print, etc. To promote students "languaging" with one other, experiment with desks and students in different, adjacent groupings. Think about setting up a cozy corner for reading, a writing center, and interest centers that extend the literature and integrate the curriculum.

Figure 2   Floor Plan from Karen Shiba's First Grade Classroom

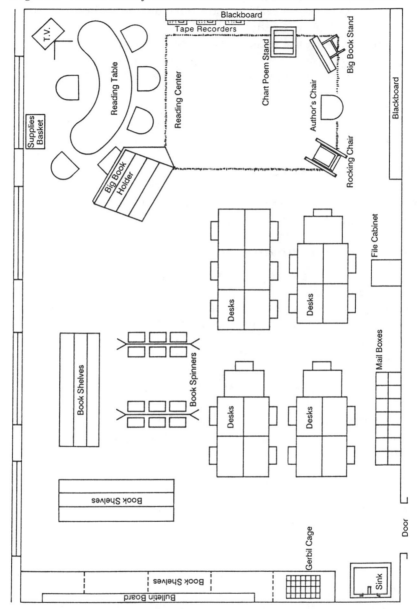

Finally, take a good look at your bulletin boards and walls. In a process-oriented, whole language classroom where children are continually reading, writing, thinking, creating, collaborating, and making choices, one expects to see all manner of children's art work, writing, and responses to literature around the room for children to read, respond to, and celebrate.

Evaluation
12 Evaluating the Process as well as the Product

A student publishing a book, aided by parent volunteer Marianne Sopko.

I had a mother of a second-grader tell me that she wasn't impressed with our reading program. "I hear all you do is sit around and talk about books. What about the skills?" She was a Chapter 1 teacher in a metropolitan area, working with students who scored below the 36th percentile in some area of reading. She used worksheets and drill to teach such "subskills" as phonics, main idea, sequencing, locating supporting details, cause and effect, drawing conclusions and vocabulary — all out of context, all in isolation, and all requiring specific, time-consuming directions. She could easily measure her results. She charted students' daily progress with percentages of short answers correct on their various workbook pages. She was teaching what she knew and what she had always taught.

Nervously, I invited her in to observe and participate in her daughter's reading group. I also gave her Dorsey Hammond's article, "Common Questions on Reading Comprehension" (*Learning*, January 1986). I was working with high-ability second graders, and we were reading and discussing *The Story of Martin Luther King: I Have a Dream* by Margaret Davidson. In doing so, we were also working on comprehension skills. I started off by having several of the students tell about what we had read and discussed so far. They *summarized*

Dr. King's early life. I asked why he had decided to become a minister. They talked about the influence of Ghandi, Martin Luther King Sr., and Jesus. They were *understanding cause and effect*. I asked them to discuss the events that led up to the Montgomery bus boycott. They were *sequencing* and *noting details*. I asked them to tell what non-violent resistance and sit-ins were and what part they played in the civil rights movement. They were *understanding vocabulary in context, paraphrasing ideas,* and *interpreting purposes*. I asked them what they thought it meant when Dr. King received the Nobel Peace Prize and he said, "I have been to the mountaintop, and I have seen the promised land." They were *interpreting figurative language*. I asked them why Dr. King refused to retaliate when his house was bombed. They were *analyzing character traits and motivation*. I asked what would happen next in the civil rights movement. They were *predicting outcomes*. We read a current news article recounting the story of Rosa Parks who refused to give up her bus seat to a white person and how the Montgomery bus boycott had followed. Students were *thinking about and discussing cause and effect*. We discussed inequalities blacks still face today. They were *relating the past to the present*. We talked about how and why prejudice still affects the lives of blacks today. They were *evaluating* an issue. I asked them to read several pages silently to find out what happened when blacks decided to march for freedom. They were *reading for specific purposes*. Several days each week, the students went back to class with a question or two to answer in their reading spiral. One was, "What do you think was Dr. King's greatest contribution to society? Give reasons why you think so." They had to *give an opinion with supporting facts, make judgments,* and *draw conclusions*. Another question was, "Describe what the march on Washington would have seemed like if you had been there. Tell what happened throughout the day, and how you would have felt." They had to *understand point of view* and events.

Comprehension skills and subskills can be effectively taught in the context of good literature as well as through mini-lessons for reinforcement. Attention to these skills occurs within the whole meaningful context, never in isolation. Inferential questions and discussion help students to analyze, focus, recall, rethink, and gain new insights. Students' comprehension is measured through their oral contributions in group discussion and their occasional written responses to thoughtful questions.

I received a short note from the visiting mother. She wrote:

> Thank you for allowing me to be part of my daughter's reading group. I was very impressed with the high level of discussion. All the children were on task for the whole 30 minutes and all seemed excited and involved in what was going on.

I was relieved. I do believe much of the concern about the skills not being taught comes from a lack of understanding and how parents remember they learned to read. "Skills" and "subskills" most often are used to denote word attack abilities, but on the highest level, "skills" can refer to abilities used to integrate meaningful aspects of print in a strategic manner. That mother became one of our biggest supporters and went on to try using some real literature and good questioning strategies with her own students. Parents and administrators need to be continually welcomed and invited into our classrooms; we need their support and understanding.

The whole area of evaluation can create anxiety and pressure. Teachers — held accountable by parents, administrators, and boards of education for students' learning — tend to stay with the conventional mode of evaluation through testing and collecting end products because it is safe, accepted, and convenient for reporting to parents and administrators. However, because our teaching methods and philosophy are changing, we need to look at evaluation in broader terms — beyond what is product-focused to what is process-focused. Beyond that again, we need to consider the affective domain because evaluation has far-reaching effects on a student's attitudes about himself and learning.

One hopeful sign is that several states are presently making attempts to assess reading and writing more wholistically; humans are actually scoring original written passages, and reading assessment is using more relevant material and more open-ended questions. Michigan and Illinois are in the process of developing and implementing tests consistent with good classroom teaching. Rather than multiple-choice questions that measure skills and subskills based on short passages out of context, the new tests include complete stories and long selections from literature and text books, and focus questions on important ideas and themes, as well as students' attitudes towards reading.

What is Evaluation All About?

Evaluation involves two steps: first, collecting data, and, secondly, making judgments about all aspects of teaching and learning for both students and teachers. I believe that evaluation should be consistent with the teacher's philosophy and the way the children have been taught. Consequently we evaluate the process, the product, and attitudes.

Often, many of the required evaluation procedures we teachers are asked to follow do not match with the way we teach and, therefore, do not serve the teacher's needs or the children's best interests. We need to incorporate informal and ongoing procedures for evaluation as well as formal procedures, and children need to be evaluated in relation to themselves. Where was the child last month? Where is he now? Where do we expect him to be next month? Always, the total child needs to be looked at and we need to be asking, "Is the curriculum fitting the child?" If not, we need to adjust it to meet the child's needs. The remainder of this chapter will look at meaningful evaluation procedures, issues in standardized testing, and teacher and student attitudes.

Meaningful Evaluation

Alternatives to Standardized Testing and "Skills" Evaluation

While standardized testing has its place in evaluation, we need to be sure that we do not overfocus on mechanical accuracy and detail. At best, standardized testing gives an individual's performance on a given day in a group situation and in comparison to other children. Such results need to be used cautiously. The use of standardized tests is acceptable as long as they are not the only means of assessment; a balance is needed. It is important to use other means of evaluation which focus on meaningful communication in the language processes — listening, speaking, reading, and writing — and the individual's day to day progress. Such focus relies on careful teacher observation and teacher judgment and implies trust in teachers as professionals. Such focus encompasses the broader definition of "active literacy" and requires the children to ask themselves, "What do I want to know?"; "What choices can I make?"; "How can I find that out?"

There is no question that teachers are under enormous pressure from both administrators and parents to be more and more accountable for students' progress. However, there are workable alternatives to multiple choice and "fill in the blank" graded assignments. Valid measures of progress through process evaluation can substantiate a grade and yield valuable information for instructional needs. Teachers who are judged by their class's performance on standardized tests need to share alternative means of evaluation with parents and administrators. I would like to share with you some alternative methods of meaningful evaluation. All of these methods look at individual progress and give the teacher specific information on individual instructional needs and growth.

• **Running Records:** Some teachers are beginning to take "running records" of students' oral reading to assess what strategies they are using. Running records were developed by New Zealand educator Marie Clay as a way to observe, record, and carefully analyze what the child does in the process of reading. Learning to take a running record will give teachers valuable information and insight about a child's reading behaviors. In approximately five minutes, a teacher can take a running record on any page of any book. Using about a hundred to two hundred word sample, the teacher notes the child's exact oral reading — repetitions, substitutions, insertions, omissions, self-corrections, and where the child has needed and received help in order to proceed. With much practice and careful attention to instructions, teachers can learn to take running records and quickly gain specific reading information that is qualitative as well as quantitative. While the procedure seems confusing initially, with practice it becomes a simple task and an excellent diagnostic and analytical tool. (See *Resources for Teachers,* especially *The Early Detection of Reading Difficulties* by Marie Clay, for exact procedures.)

• **Tape recording oral reading:** Some teachers tape record students' oral reading several times during the school year to show progress. These oral records can be shared with parents and the students themselves as a way of noting increased fluency and phrasing as well as overall reading gains.

• **Oral responses:** The way students respond in oral discussion, as well as the kinds of questions students ask, gives information as to their language processing and thinking. A child's reading strengths and responses to literature can be observed in many situations. Asking a child to retell a story orally through daily book check gives information about his skills in sequencing, summarizing, para-phrasing, and interpreting, as well as about his memory for text and recall of details. Most teachers work out their own systems to record information briefly. Student participation in shared book experience, whole class and individual cloze activities, and group discussion give insight into the child's understanding and appreciation of literature.

• **Oral Reading:** Oral reading can also be used evaluatively. Unlike the old "round robin reading" of the basal where the goal was word-perfect reading and "sounding out" without regard to meaning, process teachers use oral reading to determine the reading strategies the child is using and then guide the child towards more strategic reading. (See Chapter 3.)

One teacher has students recite a poem each week, from memory or by reading it. She tape records each student and goes back to the tape to note expression and fluency. Another teacher uses oral reading to gain insights into the child's thinking. Students in reading group are asked to go back through a chapter that has already been read silently and discussed and to choose a favorite part to read aloud. At first, they choose lengthy selections. Gradually, they become more discerning and choose paragraphs that make a particular point or that are especially well-written in terms of description, characterization, or humor.

• **Reading Records:** Reading records, folders, and notebooks can be used to document reading progress from month to month; they will indicate how extensively the child reads, as well as a student's reading habits and preferences. Looking at the child's reading record (See Appendix F for samples) shows the quantity and difficulty level of books read from month to month.

• **Reading Response Logs:** A look at the reading log or reading spiral demonstrates the child's written ability to synthesize and interpret information from silent reading and oral discussion, as well as give an opinion about the book. (See Figure 1. See also Figures in Chapter 8.) The reading notebook, which we use from Grade 2 up, can be used to evaluate students' written responses to literature.

A Page from a Reading Response Log, Grade 2

DEC. 5 Nathan

I liked how Droofus the Dragon Lost his Head because the pikers were good and I liked the story. I think the 2 best parts are wine at the end The King has en idea ya that Droofus did not loos his Head He gust stuk it there in a windo and at the bigining when He was 4 and He lost his famLy in a big cloud.

Students can be asked to write predictions before reading a chapter silently, write a brief summary, answer a question the teacher has posed, give their opinion of the book (why they liked or disliked it), describe a character, write a letter to a character, keep track of some difficult vocabulary they want to learn, or just write their personal reactions and comments to what has been read. It is important to keep the emphasis on enjoying and appreciating the literature and to stay away from the lengthy written assignments and mandatory book reports which tend to turn students off reading.

Some teachers favor having students respond to the book through letter writing — dialogue journals — which focuses on personal reactions to the book. The teacher responds to the students' comments in return letters with her own personal comments and questions. (See Nancie Atwell, *Resources for Teachers*, for procedures.)

• **Writing Journals:** The student's unedited, daily writing about personal experiences or topics he chooses to write about, shows how well the student is organizing his thoughts, what conventions of print he is using, handwriting and spelling development, and knowledge of phonics and the English language, as well as giving the teacher insight into the student's thinking and what is important to him. Dated samples of children's writing concretely reveal the child's language development, interests, and perceptions. Journals, as well as writing folders, and occasional dictation, can be used to demonstrate movement from stages of invented spelling to more conventional spelling as well as to show conventions of print and writing skills the child is mastering. (See Martin's writing samples, Chapter 6 and see Appendix Q for Nathan's journal entries on Halloween in first, second and third grade for growth in vocabulary and expressive language development.)

• **Writing Folders:** The writing folder, with the student's weekly work throughout the year, includes drafts, revisions, final copies, work in progress, possible future writing topics, skills the student holds himself accountable for and vocabulary he is using. The writing folder is even acceptable in a court of law as a valid means of documenting writing progress. (See Appendix R for an Editing Checklist used in Grade 2. Also see Donald Graves and Lucy Calkins, *Resources for Teachers*, for specific use of the writing folder.)

• **Conferencing:** Some teachers are beginning to use a conference approach as the main method of evaluating their students' reading and writing behaviors and progress. (See in *Resources for Teachers, Read On: A Conference Approach to Reading* and *Write On: A Conference Approach to Writing* for suggestions and specific advice on how this can be done.)

Conferencing with students allows us to analyze the kinds of errors made, the problems the students may be encountering, the strategies they are using — giving valuable information on how the child is organizing his language and pointing up specific needs for instruction.

When we conference with parents, we go through the child's journal, response log, and folder and examine the writing for progress in handwriting, use of mechanics such as periods, capitals, and paragraph indenting, spelling, number of drafts, revision and editing, clarity of thought, complexity of sentences, ability to synthesize information, use of descriptive detail, choice of topics. Parents can easily see their child's growth. Students, too, enjoy going back through their journals and folders noting their own progress and accomplishments. Sharing a child's writing records with administrators is a convincing way to demonstrate writing and reading progress.

• **Written Tests:** Because almost all our comprehension activities center around oral discussion and higher-level thinking through active questioning, we sometimes give a written test after a book has been completed in group. Students are expected to write in complete sentences. Questions are thoughtful and open-ended and will center around key issues that have already been discussed. For example, some test questions from *The Story of Martin Luther King: I Have a Dream* were: "How did the bus boycott in Montgomery, Alabama affect the lives of white and black people?"; "What are sit-ins? What part did they play in the civil rights movement?"; and "What do you think were Dr. King's greatest contributions to society? Why do you think so?" Responses will differ greatly and reflect individual interpretations: the student is evaluated on how thoughtfully and completely he has answered the questions. (See Appendix S for a test on *The Comeback Dog* by Jane Resh Thomas.)

• **Responding in Writing for Real Purposes:** When students are able to respond in writing to real-life situations — such as writing an account of what happened, writing a necessary letter, or writing a letter requesting specific information — then the writing that has gone on in school has been relevant. By contrast, the student who has only written for the teacher's or textbook's purposes may have difficulty.

Our principal, Delores Groves, became convinced that the children were writing better than ever when she saw the results first hand. These days, when children get into a fight or have a disagreement necessitating her involvement, her policy is to have them write their version of what happened before speaking with them. In particular, she has been impressed with how well first-graders can express themselves — the descriptions they use and the volume of writing they easily produce. She notes that children of all grades who have been in the literature/writing program include the "what", "how", and "why" of the situation with lots of supporting details. By contrast, students who have not been immersed in literature and process writing just state the facts briefly and dully and are unable to go into detail.

• **Extension Activities:** Book projects, collaborative writing, and original activities that children come up with in response to the literature, all indicate the level of understanding and appreciation that has taken place. The way children respond to literature through art, drama, and music demonstrates their perceptions and interpretations.

• **Self-evaluation:** Self-evaluation is evaluation of the highest level. Observing the child's predicting, confirming, self-correcting strategies tells us whether or not the child is in charge of his own reading. A child who consistently self-corrects and self-monitors is reading for meaning. When the child is allowed to self-select much of what he reads and writes and to keep his own reading and writing records, he is also involved in evaluating what he can and wants to read and write.

Issues in Standardized Testing and "Skills" Evaluation

Knowing that our children are required to take standardized tests and that they, and we, will be judged by the results, we spend some necessary time in preparation. We give instruction and practice in test-taking formats, typical questions, and ways to figure out an unknown answer. Neither we, nor the children, enjoy these procedures, but they are necessary in a culture that places so much emphasis on tests. Our children test better than ever, especially in reading comprehension. On some skills subtests, where they have to relate letter sounds to word parts or words in isolation, their results are average. My own belief is that the only place in life where they will ever have to do this task is on this test, so I don't worry about it very much. The Report of the Commission on Reading (*Becoming a Nation of Readers*, 1985, p. 100) supports this: "If scores on the reading comprehension subtest are acceptable, the scores on the other subtests need very little attention." If the child does well in reading comprehension, that indicates that he is integrating cueing systems and using appropriate strategies to make sense of print. He is reading for meaning.

Unfortunately, a teacher who is preoccupied with "skills" and subtests can send very negative messages to a competent reader. Jolene was a proficient reader who made sense out of print despite her difficulty with using phonics cues. On the district-administered standardized reading test, she scored in the 99th percentile in reading comprehension. By late fall of second grade she had completed *Charlie and the Chocolate Factory* by Roald Dahl, *Charlotte's Web* by E. B. White, *Mr. Popper's Penguins* by Richard and Florence Atwater, and at least a dozen more challenging chapter books. She loved to read, and she read for meaning. In December, she moved and was placed in a classroom with a phonics-based teacher. The teacher was unimpressed with Jolene's reading: she *was* concerned with her inability to complete phonics worksheets. She referred the child to the reading specialist who worked with her daily to improve her phonics. What concerns me most is the message Jolene was getting — not what a wonderful reader she was but what a poor decoder she was. The effect that this focus on Jolene's phonetic weaknesses, as opposed to the focus on her meaningful strengths, has had on her long range reading and self-esteem can easily be imagined.

Emphasis on standardized testing often tends to focus on what children *can't do*, as opposed to what they *can* do. Learning-disabled children are particularly affected by this. They do miserably on the phonics subtests and word lists, and their individual education plans are written to give attention to those deficits. If reading assessment is going to continue to focus on parts, then I would like to see a standardized reading test that tests words in isolation and then uses those same words in a meaningful passage. If the child could read the words in context — which would mean he was using meaning and higher-level strategies — then the word test and phonics test would not be significant.

What About Report Cards?

Teachers who move into process teaching have legitimate concerns about giving letter grades to students. Evaluation and grading are not the same thing. Grades do not indicate our individual strengths nor do they diagnose weaknesses. They emphasize comparison and foster competition. When grading is required, it is preferable for the teacher to incorporate many of the evaluative measures that yield information helpful to individual instruction.

Our district uses a check list and narrative format in kindergarten through grades 3, and letter grades after that. Process teachers use lots of writing and reading samples from journals, folders, and reading spirals (or reading response logs) to substantiate the grades they must give, and they share these samples with parents at conferences. Among other things, they look to see, "Did the student get the concept?"; "Can he defend the point he is making?"; "Did he follow the directions given?"; "Is there evidence of revising in the writing?" They let students know what their criteria for grading is and what assignments will and will not be graded. The child is not graded in comparison to other students; instead, the process teacher looks at the child developmentally. "Where was he before, and what is he doing now?" One teacher says, "If I have a child who shows superb understanding and effort, even if his mechanics are poor, he gets an A. I never give an F (there are some Ds) unless the student fails to turn in assignments."

Teachers report that once they move to a system of teaching that is no longer broken into subskills, the old scoring system is no longer appropriate. By speaking knowledgably and by coming up with alternatives to grades, some teachers have been successful in getting their school systems to move into more meaningful ways of reporting to parents — using checklists along with narratives for specific cognitive and affective behaviors. For example, in evaluating reading progress, reading attitudes, knowledge about print, use of strategies and comprehension, participation in shared book experience, and selection of books are all noted. Report cards in our district are not yet consistent with our process teaching, but we are working on moving towards more relevant reporting. An example of a more appropriate "Reading Report for the Primary Grades" appears as Appendix T.

Changes in Attitudes

Teachers' Atttitudes

Teachers who move from the basal text and worksheets into process teaching and children's books report on their excitement and joy as well as their frustrations and concerns. Many teachers particularly note that one of the greatest benefits of shared experiences and self-selected reading and writing has been the way it has allowed them to get to know the children and feel close to them. Teachers' attitudes about teaching reading and writing reflect shifts in their thinking, learning, and expectations of what they and children can accomplish. Coments from teachers follow.

Marie Hobart taught for 28 years as a traditional first grade teacher, and had used just about every basal series. The last two years before retiring she moved into process teaching. She says she was ready for the transition "because the opportunity and necessary support were present, and I never really liked the basal." She observed two major differences in her last two years of teaching.

> I liked the fact that each child had success. Finally, they were no longer judging themselves against other children. Also, the children were now freed to write from a very young age. Before, they didn't really write. Now they created their own stories without worrying about

spelling. Looking at their writing and projects was a lot more interesting than that insipid seat work, and revealed a lot about the child.

June Bailey, a retired first grade teacher, taught upper elementary grades and then two years in first grade as a traditional teacher before moving into literature-based reading and writing for two more years. She comments about the frustrations she used to feel with workbooks and describes her present feelings:

> I used to have to spend almost the whole reading period explaining and interpreting the directions on the workbook pages. Though I'd already explained it to the whole group, there was no way they could remember what to do on four different pages. I wanted the kids to feel good about themselves, and the only way that could happen was if we did the workbook pages together. If I did that, then there was no time for anything else and no way to reach individual learners.
>
> With the literature I felt so comfortable teaching reading. I could approach the job the way I did mothering. Learning went on in a natural, self-exploratory way, and kids were encouraged to move at their own pace.
>
> This kind of teaching is very hard and takes more time than I've ever spent before, but I didn't mind the work because I knew it was valuable and meaningful.

Barbara Broiche, a traditional teacher with seven years experience with at-risk students in a "prescribed first grade", moved into a literature-based program with some skepticism, especially about writing and skill development. After her first year she commented:

> At the in-service workshops I thought, "Don't bother me with all that writing." Initially, I wasn't interested in writing at all, but as the year went on, I could see how the reading-writing processes complement each other. I used to think, "How can you expect first-graders to write when they can't even form the letters?" I didn't realize they could write pictures, use invented spellings, and that we could take dictation. Children were much more capable than I'd ever anticipated.
>
> With skills, I used to believe they all had to be taught in a specific sequence. I would spend the entire year covering the basal and all the workbook pages. I felt so pressured! Going on to second grade was tied to finishing the basal texts. My whole philosophy of reading was, "Get them through the basal text." I was so locked into getting them through all the materials, I never had time to do interesting things with kids.
>
> Now 95% of my time is spent in real reading and talking about books with kids. One of the greatest things that has come out of this is the closeness I have developed with the children. Whole group time has allowed me to really get to know the kids well, and it's a wonderful feeling. Before, they were just kids sitting at desks doing skill sheets.
>
> There were periods throughout this past year when I was very

discouraged and tired. Although I loved doing the planning, it took lots of time. It's certainly easier to look at a basal manual. At first, I wasn't sure if I was doing things right. I did not have the feedback the skills tests provided, and it was hard not to have those guidelines. But all of a sudden, I'd see children pick up books and read them. I think, too often, teachers' opinions aren't trusted, especially if what they say is not supported by the tests.

Kate Walley, a substitute on a long-term assignment in a second grade reflected:

I liked the pleasure of reading and sharing and the freedom to use the knowledge and strengths I had. All the things I felt were important professionally, I could incorporate. I could create along with the children. When I feel like that, that I'm learning and expanding, that rubs off on the children. They feel they can learn and expand too. The excitement and anticipation of having choices in reading made it fun.

Sue Walker, a former first grade teacher presently working as a math specialist, comments on the writing, accountability, and children's accomplishments:

The writing was the toughest part for me. The hardest thing is to understand the process that goes into the invented spelling. It was hard to accept that not all the children will do it in the same way. I finally got comfortable when I started to do some mini-lessons. Then I felt I was doing something to add to their writing. I wasn't ready to let go of some responsibility for their finished product.

I never thought kids would be able to sit for an hour of shared book time, but they do, because they're so involved and excited. I was amazed at what low readers could do. Who would have thought they would have read over 100 books?

Accountability was a hangup for me the first year. All I knew was what I observed. Where was my concrete evidence without standardized test scores? I never became comfortable assigning a reading level based on just my observations.

Donna Brittain, an experienced traditional teacher with high energy and enthusiasm, was asked by our principal to move into literature-based reading in the third grade, and she reflects:

It took a while before I was convinced that teaching reading through literature was the way to go. My greatest concern was that skills development would suffer without a basal guide telling me when to teach the skills. I was fortunate to have the opportunity to team teach with Linda Cooper and also to have the support of Regie, our reading specialist. I learned many techniques and experienced the rebirth of a love that I had for reading in my elementary years. (I was taught in grades 5 and 6 through a whole language approach.) Three years later, it all seems so natural. I wouldn't want to teach reading any other way.

And finally, a student teacher noted:

Teaching with literature gives teachers options. The basal tells you exactly what to teach. Here, teachers see what kids' needs are and plan direct instruction. Not everything that's taught can be prescribed in advance. Through discussion and observation, the teacher is a learner also. This approach gives better information as to where the problems lie because you see immediately where the trouble spots are.

Students' Attitudes

What are first grade children's attitudes to literacy after a year of immersion in a literature-based reading and writing program? I decided to ask them. Some years ago I heard an educator say that if you want to know what is really going on in your classroom, ask the children what reading and writing are.

The children's oral responses on the last day of school in first grade in 1984 were reassuring about the kind of teaching we were doing. In fact, what was astounding was the very first response to the question, "What is reading?" It was, "Reading is writing." We had never verbalized this, but a six-year-old had made the connection! (He evaluated the program.) The second response to the question, "What is writing?" was "Writing is reading." Once again I was amazed. The children's oral responses to those questions, which we ask each year of the literature program, have focused on books, stories, pleasure, learning, and creating. There has been no mention of sounding out words, correct spelling, or grades. What also comes through are the positive attitudes and self-concepts, pride in accomplishments, and joy of learning. Responses to the questions, "What is Reading?" and "What is Writing?" are listed in the order given on the last day of school in first grade.

What is reading?
Reading is writing.
Reading is words put together that mean something.
Reading is reading books.
Reading is when you read a book and you read it over again and you practice it, and then you can read it well.
Reading is something very special. There are lots of words.
Reading is thinking.
Reading is reading real hard books like "Stone Fox".
Reading is learning.
Reading is sitting in a quiet place with a book.
Reading is when you decide what you're going to write in a book.
You need silence for reading.
Reading can get you moving into the grades.
Reading is fun.
Reading is enjoyment.

What is writing?
Writing is words.
Writing is reading.
Writing is words that you think of in your mind, and then you write them down.
Writing is something like writing a book.
Writing is looking into the future and telling about your life.
Writing is important.
Writing is fun because if you don't have a book you can write a book.
I made a book myself, and my friend and I are writing a book together.
Writing is writing sentences.
Writing is letters.
Writing is when you write a book.
Writing is writing about your life and your friends in your writing journal. Writing is publishing books.
Writing is kind of hard.
If you keep trying to write, you'll get better and better.
Writing is thinking about your life or a story and writing it down.
Writing is publishing a book after you have worked hard.

Figure 1   What is Reading?

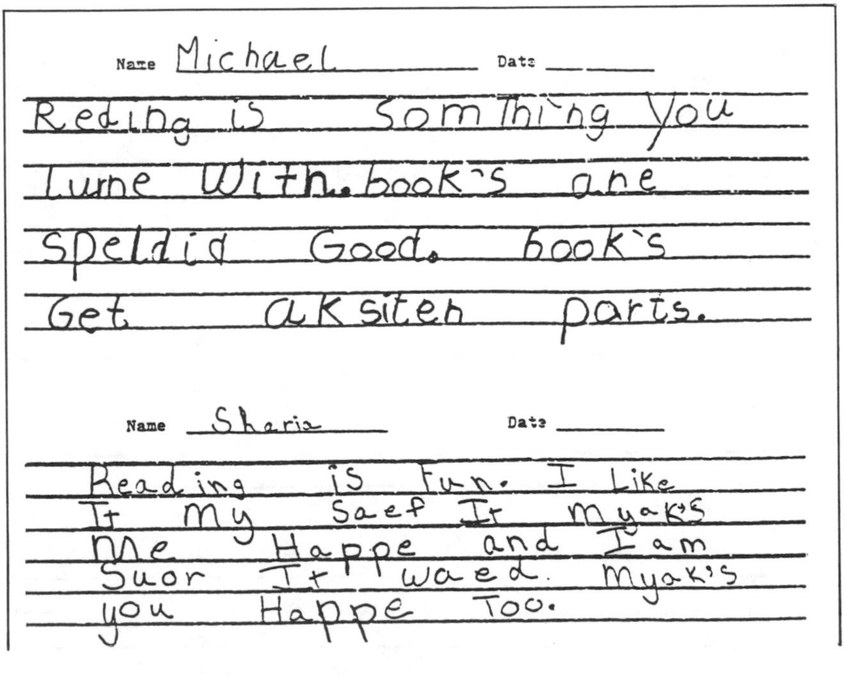

Name Michael   Date _____

Reding is som Thing you Turne With. book's are speldid Good. book's Get a k siteh parts.

Name Sharia   Date _____

Reading is fun. I Like It my saef It myaks me Happe and I am Suor It waed. myaks you Happe Too.

Name *Erica*   Date *6/10/86*

Reading is Books to read
and it is fun.

Name *Chasity*   Date *6-10*

Reading is Graet Because you
lron a lot you can lran a loo
thigs and you can a loryr and
a Doter the End

Name *JOHN*   Date *6-12-86*

READING IS WOT YOU DO WEN YOU
OPEN A Book A Book IS SOMThen
SHAPT LIKA SKWeR AND HAS
WRDS AND PIKSHS IN IT

Figure 2   *What is Writing?*

Name *KEITh*   Date *6-10-86*

I Love Wring
IT IS The Bg
Teg Of all and
When Fou gro
uP Fou Wll
Be Smrt LiKe
me.

Name *Sharia*   Date *6-12-86*

Writing is fun all you
have to do is peak

> Up your pensoll and puaet
> It on a peas of paper
> and move It arond on
> the paper. and Writing iS
> Wut you dow Wen you are
> Bord !

During the last week of school in a recent June, I again asked the first-graders: "What is reading?", "What is writing?" This time I asked for written responses so their thoughts would be truly their own. There was no prior discussion, and these are abstract questions, so it was a difficult assignment. I was awed at the profoundness in the simplicity of their answers. (See Figures 1 and 2, this chapter.)

I was particularly struck by Sharia's response on writing because it expresses some understanding about a concept I have only recently grasped. That is, one writes to discover meaning and to figure out what one wants to say. Along with the children's definitions, what consistently come through are the feelings of confidence and success — even though they are all at different developmental stages in their reading and writing. This, too, is part of evaluation.

I was also curious about their sense of story in their writing. It was obvious they had it, judging from their writing, but could they verbalize it? I asked them orally to tell me, and these were some of the responses.

What makes a good story?
Think of a story; keep on thinking about it, and then you write it down.
Practice.
When you try and work really hard.
If you can't think of a story, you can look in a picture book and get some
*   ideas.*
Get ideas from your life.
You need details in your story and expression.
You need periods and spaces.
Sometimes I make pictures to get ideas for a story.
If you get a book with no words, you can put your own words in.
If you read lots of books, you get ideas for your own stories.

Choosing to Read and Write

Perhaps, the reading test with more validity than any other is whether or not children read as a free choice activity. The standardized reading test which tells us which children *can* read does not tell us which children *will* read on their own. Children who can read but who don't read are, in fact, nonreaders. Children, however, do establish the reading habit naturally and pleasurably when they are exposed to good literature in a supportive environment. Our children read all the time — because they want to.

In our third grades, children cheer and applaud when we bring armloads of books into the classroom library and talk about the books. A student teacher comments:

> The thing I was struck with is the kids come in before school, and right away, they pick up a book. They're so engrossed in their reading, you can't even question them. Kids have two and three books in their desks. This reading is a continuous thing; in other schools I haven't seen that. Here, reading is books and all things that interest kids. Reading is incorporated into everything — writing, social studies, science. It's not a separate subject like it is with the basal. Reading is not just in a group; it's all day long. It's all their free time. In other schools, kids would be doing dittoes and seat work. Whenever these kids are not doing something, they'll pick up a book and read. That's really unusual.

A principal from a neighboring district spent the morning with me recently moving from class to class and observing the reading behaviors of children excited about books. She reported that her students did well on standardized tests and had mastered reading skills, but they did not choose to read in their leisure time. This is a sad but typical commentary in many classrooms. The basal textbook and accompanying workbook pages do little to foster a love of reading. Only exposure to the best of children's books can do this.

Our students love to come to school. They feel successful about being able to read and write, and that self-confidence spills over into other academic and social areas. Parents report all the time on their children's eagerness for learning. School and local librarians report increased numbers of books being borrowed during school months and throughout the summer. Because the learning environment promotes risk taking and congratulates approximations, students become very confident and willing to try new tasks across the curriculum. In addition, their positive view of literacy reflects the supportive, rich literary environment in which they have been immersed.

By looking beyond the end products of evaluation to how the child feels about himself and school, it becomes obvious that school is making a positive, long-term difference in these children's lives.

(opposite) The first week of school, 1983: Regie Routman and a first-grader sharing a book project.

13 *Making Changes*
The Need for Teacher Support

The majority of school districts in this country are very traditional; that is, most teachers follow lesson plans based on textbooks, teacher manuals, skills sheets, and periodic testing. There are small pockets of innovative change, but most of us continue to work in isolation using "tried and true" methods and materials. As long as the test scores are "decent" and the students are "quiet", no one complains. Constructive changes are difficult to make and involve enormous time and commitment along with excitement and anticipation. The process of change causes pressure, conflict, disagreement, and frustration. The stakes are high, and the incentives have been few for taking risks and trying new procedures, so we play it safe and stay with what we know and have always done. In addition, over recent decades the value attributed to the profession of teaching has declined. Therefore, the motivation of teachers to change has spiraled downward.

Changes in moving into process reading have come about more slowly than transitions into process writing. As teachers, we have long felt uncomfortable about the way we teach writing, so that change has been easier for most of us to accept. However, we have long felt quite competent and comfortable teaching reading, and high comfort level is not conducive to making change. Making the transition from traditional, basal book teaching to process teaching with the best of children's literature happens very gradually over a period of years. It requires lots of questioning, observing, reading, reflecting, and trying out along with continuing in-service, staff development and teacher support.

Our school district adopts a new reading series every six or seven years. In the past, all the major basal book companies have come in and done elaborate presentations. Selection of a series was made, and then — based on the reading series adopted — a statement of philosophy and goals was written. I am pleased that this year a reading committee, consisting of teachers, librarians and administrators, was formed with the primary task of creating a statement of philosophy that reflected current research on the language processes. We wanted to be sensitive to the fact that while many teachers were moving towards whole language theory and literature-based teaching, some teachers were more comfortable with the basal. We read, argued, and discussed. We wrote, revised, and rewrote. It took the better part of the school year to write a one page statement! Now we are ready to begin to think about curriculum and staff development needs.

It is difficult and lots of hard work to move away from the basal towards an integrated, whole language classroom, but it is worth the struggle. Participating with a group of young children excitedly discussing a favorite book and making new insights makes the teacher feel, "This is worth it." Observing and coaching a child's writing development and seeing the child's pride as an author, is exhilarating. Discussing philosophy and ideas with colleagues is stimulating and enriching. Taking responsibility for our teaching and learning — and sharing that responsibility with students — empowers and frees us to be continually learning and making our own decisions as responsible educators. The anxiety that is inherent in taking more responsibility can be directed into new, high energy. This chapter will discuss some of the necessary factors and issues inherent in effective educational change.

Becoming a Knowledgable Teacher

A Teacher Who Reads

Before one can make changes, a strong understanding of philosophy and rationale and current research must be present. I strongly believe that one of the main reasons teachers are not viewed as professionals equal to doctors and lawyers and other professional groups is that as a group we don't read. As a whole, we are not well-informed about the latest research and current educational trends, and most of us do not attend meetings for professional growth. When we hear about something new, the first questions are often, "Where can I buy it?"

and, "How much does it cost?" We have been conditioned to view learning in terms of prepackaged programs.

There is no question that teachers are overburdened with too many children, too many lesson plans, too much accountability, too many secretarial-type duties, and too little time. Many dedicated teachers put so much effort into being well-planned and well-prepared for their daily teaching that the thought of professional reading and reflection seems an overwhelming burden. Nonetheless, if we are to be truly effective and knowledgable practitioners, we must find the time to make personal educational growth a high priority. We must personally demonstrate that we hold "knowledge" — the product we work so hard to promote and produce — in the highest regard. The reading of professional journals/texts doesn't need to entail lengthy reading sessions; it does need to be consistent. One article from a journal, and/or one chapter from a text per week or even per month, is better than no reading at all.

Recently, at the close of a workshop I conducted with a colleague, a woman who later identified herself as a college teacher asked, "Where did you learn all that psycholinguistic theory? Who were your professors?" She was taken aback when we explained we had learned through reading, thinking, and observing children. Similarly, at a reading convention where I was a speaker, I was introduced by a colleague, a college professor who said, "... And Regie is very knowledgable about the research that supports her work. She has read many books..." I was surprised by those remarks. I know they did not intend to be condescending, but I felt insulted as well as flattered. Was a well-informed teacher who reads and reflects such a rarity? Was that domain left only to the universities?

In order to be credible to administrators, parents, and other teachers as well as ourselves, it is necessary to stay well-informed. Reading and discussing current journal articles and books is a great place to start. If I had to begin with one article, it would be "Shared Book Experience: Teaching Reading Using Favorite Books" by Don Holdaway, and if I had to begin with one book it would be Don Holdaway's *Foundations of Literacy*. If I had to choose one beginning place to start reading about teaching writing, it would be *No Better Way to Teach Writing!* by Jan Turbill (ed.) If I had to choose one book to start me thinking about educational philosophy, it would be Frank Smith's *Essays Into Literacy*. (See *Resources for Teachers* for other recommended reading. I have marked (•) the ones other teachers and I have found particularly useful in getting started.)

If you are serious about making changes in your classroom, you must convince your administrators that you know what you are doing. Share articles; invite them into your classroom; share samples of children's work you are excited about; show them your anecdotal records and evaluation procedures. No program can succeed without administrative backing. You will be more likely to win the support of your administrators as well as your parents if you and they are kept well-informed.

After my proposal to teach first-graders to read through literature was accepted, my principal let me know that the basal textbooks would also be in the classroom. There was some assumption that these needed to be there for the students and to reassure the parents. But after I gave her a lengthy article I had written detailing the extensive research that supported teaching with literature, she told me, "You've convinced me. You don't have to have the basals in the room. Go with just the books." She was able to relax and lend me her full support when it was clear to her that there was a solid research and educational base for what we were about to do.

Attending Professional Meetings

One excellent way to stay abreast of national trends, innovations in education, and the latest research — as well as to continue growing professionally — is to attend and participate in professional meetings and in-service workshops. Even though it is difficult to get the classroom and lesson plans organized for a substitute, as well as making necessary family arrangements, it is well worth the extra effort. Such participation affords opportunities for collegial inter-action, information on techniques and teaching strategies and insights into our own teaching and learning. When possible, it is a good idea to participate with a colleague from your school. That provides an automatic support group and stimulus for brainstorming, making clarifications, and trying out new ideas once you return. It is also important to join and support national and local reading and writing organizations such as the International Reading Association and the National Council of Teachers of English, and to subscribe to their journals. These organizations sponsor excellent local and national meetings.

In the spring of 1981, I attended the International Reading Association annual meeting in New Orleans. It was the first reading conference I had ever attended, and it changed my professional life. Until that time, I had worked mostly isolated in my small room and had little opportunity to share, discuss, and interact with colleagues.

I shall always be grateful to the administration in my school district for the opportunity I was afforded to expand my thinking. I left the meeting inspired, refortified, and refueled. In addition to the outstanding speakers I heard, I was struck by the number of bright young women knowledgable in their field and confident of the direction in which they were heading. The conference helped me realize there were possibilities beyond my structured, pull-out, small group teaching. I have continued to attend the I.R.A. annual meeting each year, and it continues to keep me professionally vibrant. Even though I often arrive burned out and exhausted, I always return refreshed and revitalized.

Exciting things were happening at I.R.A. in 1981. Ken Goodman had just completed his presidency, and he was the first president in over 20 years who was not pro-basal. Writing was beginning to be talked about in connection with reading. I heard some powerful speakers at my first convention. Shirley Haley-James reported on what research said about writing and stated there was very little support for the teaching of formal grammar before junior high. She advocated self-selected writing, exposure to good literature for understanding sentence structure, and using high utility words from children's writing for spelling. Roach Van Allen, who referred to himself as the "grandfather" of the language experience approach, was inspiring in his talk on the need for reading aloud daily. Among some memorable quotes, he said, "Read one author enough so the child can write in that author's language", and "Efficiency in reading is dependent on prediction and decreasing dependence on visual cues." John Warren Stewig spoke of ways to use children's literature as motivation for writing. Yetta Goodman discussed print awareness and literacy in very young children. William Teale reported on the effects of home storybook reading (and parent interaction with children) leading to the natural development of literacy. Vera Milz spoke about her work with first and second-graders in learning to read and write in a literate environment. Bill Martin Jr. spoke of all children being "natural language learners". I was reaffirmed in much of what I was already trying to do in my small group work; new questions about literacy were raised and left unanswered.

One of the highlights of professional meetings has been educators who have given so generously of their time. At my second I.R.A. meeting, I met Don Holdaway and was like a stage-struck school girl. In our conversation, I mentioned to him that I was doing a presentation, and he said he would come and show his support. I never expected him to show up, but he did! I was both embarrassed and exhilarated. When I spoke to Dorsey Hammond after his excellent presentation on teaching reading comprehension, he invited me to attend a local workkshop as his guest. Vera Milz graciously took the time to meet with me and answer lots of my questions on process teaching in the first grade. And I shall never forget the generosity of Barbara Watson, present Director of Reading Recovery in New Zealand. She spent three hours with a colleague and myself meticulously teaching us how to take a running record (a record and analysis of a child's oral reading). These were educators who valued and respected teachers enough to give unselfishly of their time. It left a lasting impression on me. As teachers we must willingly and generously share our knowledge with other teachers.

Establishing Support Networks for Teachers

Coaching

While reading professional literature, understanding theory and research, and providing in-services and supportive environments are all necessary for personal change, "coaching" — which will be defined as one-to-one expert modeling, support and feedback — is critical if actual change is to reach the implementation stage. Ideally, this coaching requires another teacher, but videotapes of teachers in actual classrooms can provide models of excellent process teaching. Coaching also requires an actively involved principal who supports cooperative learning and teaching.

The first year of our process teaching in first grade, second grade, and third grade, I co-taught with another teacher. That opportunity allowed for demonstration lessons, constant conferring, trying things out, closer observations of children, and increased confidence to take a risk. Such peer coaching fosters collegiality, intellectual stimulation, and eventually self-sufficiency. While there were initially two teachers in the classroom, daily coaching made it possible for the classroom teacher confidently to assume total responsibility the second year. Karen Shiba in first grade, Joan Di Dio in second grade, and Linda Cooper in third grade, have each gone on to coach other teachers in classrooms and to present in-service workshops for teachers in other districts.

One effective method of coaching has been used successfully by Linda Cooper who invites the same grade level class into her room for demonstrations in whole class reading and process writing. There are no discipline problems with two teachers in one room. The visiting teacher is able to observe lessons, participate when comfortable, ask questions and get a dialogue going, and later try out procedures in the privacy of her own classroom. Eventually, she will be asked to teach a lesson to both classes with her coach observing and cheering her on. Sometime that day, the two teachers will meet and the coach will give feedback, make suggestions, give encouragement. The apprentice teacher gradually becomes a coach for another teacher. In schools where everyone is an apprentice (which is how we all started), teachers can still try out lessons and give each other feedback by putting their two classes together for a lesson. Teachers teaching teachers has become a powerful vehicle for effective change.

Continuing Support After In-service

Much in-service tends to be a "one shot" deal with a guest presenter coming in for hours or days and teachers then being left with lots of good ideas and inspiration but without the necessary, continuous support for implementation. Ongoing daily and weekly support is necessary if teachers are to make lasting innovations.

In June 1986, I conducted workshops in another district for thirty teachers and five administrators; the goal was to implement literature-based reading and writing into four first grades and four second grades. The eight pilot teachers were paired from four buildings; this allowed and encouraged working partnerships with exchanging of ideas, materials, and concerns. Carl Walley, the elementary consultant responsible for curriculum development and teacher in-service, coordinated the workshops and taught a writing strand.

While the workshops gave a lot of information on theory, research, and practical application, without Carl there to support the teachers daily during the school year, the program would have faltered. He secured block grant funding and organized the selection and ordering of paperbacks, Big Books, and supplies. He established a support group for the eight pilot teachers, and every two weeks they met for one hour to share ideas and discuss concerns. In the beginning months, he carried ideas and books and personal support to each teacher on a weekly basis. He arranged for parent meetings to educate and train parent volunteers. He kept administrators informed as to student and teacher progress. The year was an enormous success for the entire school district. Anticipated problems with parents and administrators never materialized. Community support, understanding, and appreciation were at an all-time high. Children had never shown as much enthusiasm or success in reading and writing. The following summer eight more teachers of first, second, and third grades were in-serviced. The original eight pilot teachers conducted the workshops for their district as well as in-servicing teachers in other districts. Teachers teaching teachers was spreading.

Inviting Other Teachers In

I have come to realize that a school is a community, and it works well for all the members only if all have equal access to materials, methods, and programs. I have received tremendous pleasure in sharing what we have accomplished, and how we have done it, with anyone who is interested. At first this was painful; I wanted to go and set up the program my way. Now it is quite easy and pleasurable; I have come to realize that teachers must have ownership of their teaching. I might be part of the catalyst for change, but the change that results is personal and individual and different for each teacher. There is no one way or best way to teach anything.

In my own building, the first year of our literature-based reading program was apparently so threatening that neither second grade teacher (they were next door and across the hall) ever set foot in the classroom or asked any questions about what was going on. All they understood about Big Books were that they were big and that the children read in a loud voice (they could hear them). Their main concern was how they would know what basal to put the children in the following year. Our principal was insistent that these children continue in a literature program, and both second grade teachers elected to leave second grade rather than move into this new reading program.

Looking back, I see there were things the first grade teacher and I could have done to raise their comfort level. We could have invited them, welcomed them in to our classroom to demonstrate what was going on. We could have asked them if they had any questions and concerns and tried to get a dialogue going. We could have kept our doors open figuratively as well as literally. We could have enticed them into being part of the process by sharing our excitement with them. But since they didn't ask, we didn't offer. I think too, we felt a sense of ownership and not wanting to share. This was our special, original project; we enjoyed the exclusivity and local attention the program was getting, and we felt possessive. Part of the learning process has been giving up possessiveness and control of materials and ideas, not only with students but with teachers as well. When this happens, teachers have the opportunity of ownership which is due them. Our process teaching community has grown steadily each year as all students and teachers are invited in.

Educating Parents

Whenever there is a change of curriculum plan, parents — along with teachers — need to be informed of the changes and provided with some basic understanding of the program. Parents relate their child's education to their own school experience. If they wrote misspelled words ten times each, that's what they ask their child to do at home. If they "sounded out" every word, they encourage their child to do the same. In order for them to reinforce and support what is going on in school, they need to be brought into the process. Inviting them into the classroom to view activities from their child's perspective is very effective but does require a certain comfort level for the teacher. Newsletters and parent education evenings can serve well. Some of the topics and terminology that need to be explained are developmental learning, invented spelling, process writing, process reading, upgraded papers, and the absence of worksheets. Parents also need to be helped to recognize signs of progress other than through workbooks, report cards, and standardized tests. Writing journals, writing folders, independence and fluency in reading, attitudes and self-confidence can be used as alternative measures of progress. Parents are powerful agents for change and teacher support if they are included as part of the educational process. Our parents have been our biggest supporters; in fact, they have understood the benefits and joys of literature-based reading and writing much faster than most teachers and administrators.

Establishing a Teacher Support Group

Teachers in our building meet monthly to discuss interesting articles and books we have read, strategies and activities that have worked, as well as concerns and frustrations. We have found this opportunity to talk together informally an absolutely essential ingredient for continued professional growth and for making innovative changes in our teaching. We have met once a month at lunch break in the school library and the alternate month for an evening meeting at someone's home. We initially began several years ago with a small group of teachers talking together informally over coffee. We found the comradery and support so invigorating, we decided to meet on a regular basis. Early meetings included such activities as sharing of book projects for independent work, conferencing procedures attempted, and viewing of professional videotapes of the writing process. Our meetings have remained unstructured unless a specific agenda, such as a report by colleagues from a conference, has been set. While there is no official leader, generally the person hosting the meeting monitors the time so each member gets an equal opportunity to paticipate.

In addition to our regular meetings, we are supportive of each other as professionals. If a teacher has a specific problem, for example, with response groups, she feels comfortable enough to call several members of the group together informally to brainstorm alternatives. When one of us comes across an excellent journal article, newsletter, children's book, or teaching idea we try to circulate a copy through the building(s). We continually try to validate one another through encouragement and celebration of each person's attempts and accomplishments. We have found sharing our beliefs, concerns, ideas, and philosophy with other colleagues to be as valuable as any "expert" coming in to present ideas. As interest in process teaching has continued to grow, our group has expanded to include all interested teachers and administrators in our school district at monthly, evening meetings. Some plans for the coming year include bringing in speakers to give information on spelling and evaluation in process teaching.

Taking a Risk

Knowledge reflecting current research, educational theory, and how children learn, is powerful. This knowledge can be used to influence educational agencies, boards of education, and commercial publishers that make decisions affecting children. We can begin to apply pressure for more relevant courses in teacher education. Many teachers today still have no exposure to alternative approaches such as shared reading, literature-based reading and writing, language experience, writing as a process, and guided questioning procedures. It is not surprising then, that they automatically continue teaching in a basal text, product-oriented classroom. We need to be persuasive in getting adequate time and support for staff development. As knowledgable teachers, we need to demand high-quality reading materials and genuine literature. We need to stop accepting inferior packaged materials and start questioning publishers and educators about what they are preparing for children. We need actively to become part of the teaching/learning process and contribute to it. Greater knowledge and active decision making increases our self-esteem along with our public esteem. Teachers can lead the way once we realize we have the power, right, and responsibility to do so. Trusting ourselves and our students with self-chosen responsibility has far-reaching effects beyond the classroom.

However one is currently teaching reading and writing, there are approaches that can be integrated into the existing program. Reading aloud to children daily, shared reading, guided whole class reading, poetry, higher-level questioning, shared writing, journal writing, literature extension activities, publishing children's writing, and self-selected reading are components that have been discussed in this book which can easily be added to the language arts program. It is not difficult to start by adding one or more of these components. Many teachers have found adding poetry and journal writing a very workable way to begin. As teachers, we need to begin to make educated choices about how and what we are teaching and to trust ourselves and the children. Even a teacher "stuck" with the basal may have the option not to buy the workbooks and not to read the selections the students have always found boring. We must start practicing our own three Rs — reading, risking, and reflecting. Well-prepared, well-educated teachers with a positive belief and acceptance of children as natural learners can choose a variety of approaches in teaching. We must provide successful reading and writing experiences for all children, regardless of ability levels. Process teaching with children's literature offers optimal choices, pleasure, and satisfaction for everyone involved in the educational process.

14 *Any Questions?*

Following workshop presentations, teachers have gone back to their classrooms excited about the possibilities of literature and writing. These are some of the typical questions teachers have later written to me or asked me about regarding specific concerns.

General Questions

Did you have an outline of your schedule, goals, objectives, and materials prior to beginning that first September?

We had a general outline of the reading program, enough books to begin with, and a tentative schedule. The first grade teacher and I worked throughout the summer getting ready — making Big Books, choosing poems, developing book projects and WEB units, planning parent involvement. We had the first month roughed out, but we were constantly modifying and experimenting to fit our purposes.

Approximately how much money did you spend on books, and where did the money come from?

We initially spent about $4000.00 on books and supplies. Most of that was money secured through Chapter 1 funds, but some was block grant money that the district applied for.

Did your lowest achievers get additional help from a Chapter 1 program?

By going into the classroom during reading group time, I serve as the reading teacher and the teacher of record for the lowest-ability students. Our school does have a full time Chapter 1 teacher, but in only one year out of the four did we find it necessary for her also to service these students.

What happens to the Learning Disability students?

We keep almost all the LD students for reading/language arts. (These are students that have already come to us as LD through the district LD kindergarten.) It has been our experience that the LD children do exceptionally well with the literature program, probably because it is not phonics based and is so meaning centered. Many find immediate success with the writing process and do their first reading with their own published books. We have even been able to phase out some of these students permanently, an unusual occurence in LD programs. We have been fortunate that the LD teacher has gradually become convinced that teaching reading with books is the best way to go. In fact she states, "After years of trying different basal and skill approaches, I have had the best reading results by far with the literature approach." Although we are finding that many fewer first-graders need to be referred for LD evaluation, the small percentage that still qualify and need to be seen by the LD teacher are being taught to read and write in similar ways to all other first-graders in our school.

Do the children enter a traditional second grade with basal textbooks? If so, how do you suggest placement in books? In my building, teachers have such concern for exactly how far kids got in the basal, and where they will fit in the fall. How do kids make such a transition smoothly?

I used to worry about this exact problem a lot. In our building, our principal insisted that the literature-based reading program would be the only program in grades 1-3, but this has not been the case in some other schools. Some students do go into a basal in second grade. Two things have happened. The parents have begun to apply pressure to the administration for the literature program to continue, and this is beginning to have some effect. Also, teachers are relaxing a bit after they see how well the children do read. Records of the books read orally by the teacher, independently by the students, and in reading group, follow students from grade to grade so teachers do get information on students' wide reading background. Some teachers, however, complain about a child's phonics skills in isolation even though the child might be a very fluent reader. We need to let these teachers know what it means to be a good reader and share some of the current research with them. We also need to realize that even if a child does have to go back into a basal, the child has had the best possible beginning reading/writing experience in the first grade, and that this early success will enable him to cope with any program.

Since the children have not been exposed to worksheets, are they at a disadvantage when they have to take a standardized test?

Before testing, we give the children lots of practice on the format of a test by doing practice sheets with them. In particular, we give attention to the word attack skills section which is phonics heavy and uses words in isolation. Our children score particularly well on the comprehension subtests where they can use meaning cues. My personal feeling is that if they can read in context, I'm not overly concerned about a lesser showing on word analysis in isolation. Since the tests are geared to the basal text format, I question their validity for our students.

Do the children have homework?

The only reading activity we expect and highly encourage the children to do daily is to practice reading the book(s) they have signed out. Usually, the children choose books they can read fairly easily, so we are talking about ten minutes a night. We encourage the children to read the book as many times as they need to for fluency. They understand that fluency means smoothness and having it sound like a story. We also encourage the parents to read to and with their children daily. We emphasize that this should be a pleasurable activity, not a stress time. If the child is struggling with the book, it is too difficult and needs to be exchanged for an easier one.

What exactly do the parents do when they are in the classroom? How do you organize this so it is helpful and not a source of interruption?

At first, parents just observed the reading and writing processes. We quickly found, however, that we could use the extra help and that parents felt highly valued when they were included in the educational process. We also felt more comfortable when parents were actively involved with children as opposed to passively watching our teaching. Parents walk around the room with us during writing journal time and individually conference with and encourage students in their writing. Parents read one-to-one with a child who needs reinforcement and practice on a particular book or who just needs some extra attention. Sometimes a parent will take over a reading group — freeing the teacher to work with a student individually. (Since reading group involves reading a book for pleasure and practice, a parent with good management skills can do this effectively.) Parents also give assistance and support to students working on book projects.

Questions Concerning Reading

I'm concerned about sight word development. Using Big Books, other predictable books and printed poems, what activities do you engage the children in to learn sight vocabulary?

The first few years, we were very concerned that the children would only pick up sight vocabulary if we taught it and reinforced it in isolation with flash cards. Our own research in the classroom supports a growing body of research which demonstrates that children pick up the basic sight vocabulary naturally through repeated readings of predictable books. We no longer "teach" sight vocabulary. Through lots of reading practice on easy familiar books, children pick up sight vocabulary effortlessly.

No one will be able to convince you that this is true until you see it happen yourself. I was ready to stop teaching words in isolation after two years of our literature program, but the first grade teacher was not comfortable doing this until after three years of teaching reading with books. Another first grade teacher who joined us went along with us but was not convinced the children were really learning basic sight words until she had a parent volunteer test all her children individually. She was amazed at how many words they knew. Certainly the children suffered no damage the years we taught the sight words separately, but now we have that time for more meaningful activities.

If kids take a book home each night to read, how do you check each child on reading their book the next day? It seems impossible to reach each child.

We use time before school starts when children are reading to themselves and with each other or involved in writing activities. I am also available at this time to check books. (At the beginning levels, this is primarily a fluency check since the book has already been discussed during whole group time.) Some teachers prefer the very last part of the day while students are finishing up work or free choice activities. Teachers say this one-to-one activity is relaxing and enjoyable at the end of the day and a good way to get to know their students. In addition, we sometimes use older elementary students and parent volunteers to help us. While it sounds very time consuming, the process moves quickly and requires only a few minutes per student. In the second and third grades, this book check is done at the beginning of reading group time.

How do you check comprehension? Workbooks provide vast numbers of pages to check children on making inferences, drawing conclusions, recalling facts, etc. How do you address these things in your program?

When a child is reading fluently and monitoring his reading behavior with self-corrections, he is reading for meaning, and we see this daily. When a child does an oral retelling of a book or a written retelling in his journal, it is clear he has understood the story. We are constantly asking prediction-type questions where students hypothesize and then listen or read on for confirmation. In addition, the book projects the children work on independently require careful thought processing and extended writing. These are all high-level comprehension activities that demand more than a one-word answer. In the second and third grades, we sometimes give a written comprehension test at the completion of a book read in reading group. The emphasis on these tests is on the interpretive and critical levels with "why" and "how" questions as opposed to "what", "when", and "who".

When I am in reading group, if children are not doing worksheets and workbooks, what activities should they be doing?

This is often the first and most critical question to teachers moving away from the basal. It certainly is easier to assign a workbook page, but the question to keep in mind is, "Is the activity purposeful and meaningful?" It has been our experience that as our own philosophy and understanding of process-whole language teaching has grown, activities have begun to emerge quite naturally from the literature. From year to year, the activities change depending on the particular group of students and the way they and the teacher respond to the literature.

Our students in grade 2 and above always have a silent reading assignment and some type of literature extension activity. They may be answering a specific question or writing a reaction or prediction based on what they have just read. They may be working as author and illustrator on a story based on a book that has been read aloud to the class or read in group. (For example, after completing *The Stories Julian Tells* by Ann Cameron, a book where ordinary happenings have become exciting events, our third-graders were asked to write their own "Stories ———— Tells" relating personal, past experiences to the literature.) Individually or in a small group, they may also be doing an art-literature related activity such as a diorama, poster, literary comparison chart, or mural. If all work is completed, students are expected to have a book to read independently — from school, home, or classroom library. Once teachers take sufficient time to clearly set up expectations during independent worktime, students become very self-directed, do not interrupt reading group, and quietly assist and collaborate with each other.

I am uneasy teaching vocabulary with literature-based reading. If the students don't have to look up and write meanings of unknown words, how do you know they are really learning the necessary vocabulary?

The meaningful teaching of vocabulary seems to be a particularly difficult shift for teachers used to the basal and lots of word exercises. If you keep in mind what adult readers do, what we're talking about is really common sense. When I read a novel of several hundred pages, I do not stop to look up words in the dictionary as I am reading. For the most part, I figure out the words in context or skip over them while still getting the overall meaning. If, at the completion of the book, I have learned several new words, I consider that quite good. I certainly would not want to be responsible for giving the definition of fifty words or more, and yet, that is what we often do to students.

I, and other teachers, have found that students learn vocabulary best when they can choose the words they want to know. Typically, we ask students to select several words they want to learn from the chapter that has been assigned for silent reading. Students write down each word in their reading spiral, the page it is on, the context in which it is used, and what they think it means. When the reading group convenes, students have a lively discussion on the meanings of these words. For those words students are still unsure of, the dictionary is consulted. Teachers usually find that the words they would have asked students about have been selected. Words the teacher deems important that have not been brought up are also discussed. For those words that have come up over and over again and are words that seem useful for knowing, we write them in enlarged print and post them on a wall, bulletin board, or window shade. As much as possible, we use these words over and over again in daily classroom conversation. In one second grade class, the following words came from a group discussion: "ambled", "emphatically", "persistent", "coaxing", "unfamiliar", "mumbled", "anxious". The teacher then used these words repeatedly while she was talking to students. When these words find their way into their own conversation and writing — and they do — then we know students "own" the words and have not just memorized definitions. Students enjoy learning vocabulary in this contextualized manner and seem to do it effortlessly. Teachers find that allowing students to share the responsibility of selecting their own words makes students highly interested and involved in learning new words.

At the beginning of the reading process, parents often comment that their child has memorized the book and is not really reading. How do you respond to those parents?

It is important that parents understand that reading is a memory process, and that this memorizing of easy patterned text is a desirable early reading behavior. The child receives confidence and pleasure while gaining fluency and control of the text. This is an early stage, and the child should be praised for his efforts so he views himself as a reader right from the start.

One way to check if the child has moved beyond the memorization stage is to copy several sentences from the book the child is reading. The teacher cuts up the sentences and makes a new, original sentence using the same words. If the child can read it, he is reading words in a new context.

Questions Concerning Writing

Do you model daily the process of writing through class-inspired chart stories? If not, how do the kids learn to put this act together?

Through daily journal writing and conferencing and through hearing the language of books throughout the day, children quite naturally pick up a sense of story. While their first writing is almost always a personal topic, they eventually move into story writing with beginnings, middles, and endings, characters, conversation, chapters, etc. Seeing how books work, by being immersed in different authors' language and styles and having access to hundreds of books, seems to aid the whole writing process. We don't teach what a sentence is, and yet, they write in complete sentences.

When kids write letters to other people, do they do this completely on their own, and do you send them with their own spelling and punctuation? If it is not easily read, do you pencil in words so the receiver can make sense of it?

While the students do the writing on their own, brainstorming and some modeling always takes place first. The expected format of the letter would be on the board as well as some difficult words (such as art museum, guide, tapestry) that the writer might be likely to use. We would expect their best handwriting, but the letter would be sent as the child wrote it. Invented spellings difficult to read would have the conventional spellings penciled in. By third grade, when students are used to revising and editing for real purposes, letters would be sent in correct form.

Are your students in a textbook spelling program? If not, how do you address spelling instruction? How do you evaluate and grade spelling if not through traditional weekly tests?

We have no formalized spelling program in the first grade. The children use invented spellings, and a careful look at their daily journal writing shows the gradual progression to conventional spelling, especially of high utility words. As we walk about the room and conference individually with the children daily on their journal entries, we do call their attention to words we feel they are ready to spell correctly by penciling in above their spelling. A first grade teacher, who was worried that her students were not learning to spell, gave them a test on basic sight words and was relieved and surprised to find they could spell more words than she thought. Parents express some concern too about their children's spelling and need reassurance. We have found that by the end of third grade these children are proficient spellers, and current research on invented spelling supports this. In the meantime, content has not been sacrificed for over concern with perfect form. Again, you will not be convinced by reading it here. You will have to immerse yourself in the process to see what children can accomplish.

Spelling instruction above Grade 1 is an area parents and teachers are concerned about. We are beginning to examine and refine our techniques of teaching spelling strategies.

*(above) A literature extension project modeled after **Meanies** by Joy Cowley.*
(opposite) A fifth-grader checking a first-grader's nightly reading.

15 Postscript
Transitions

It has taken at least ten years to get to where I am in my process teaching, and I am still very much in transition. I continue to question, try out, observe, learn, and adjust my thinking and teaching. My teaching has moved beyond literature-based reading to language-based learning with a more natural integration between the reading-writing processes. Although I am becoming more comfortable calling myself a whole language teacher, I am aware of many areas that I still need to address: teaching spelling strategies, continuing to develop more relevant evaluation procedures, using more non-fiction, adding a greater emphasis to listening and speaking, integrating more subjects across the curriculum, and educating parents effectively. These are my goals for the coming years, and new transitions will surely occur.

In the fall of 1987, as the writing of this book was being completed, our school district implemented its reorganization effort. Due to declining enrollments and racial imbalance, four elementary schools — including Moreland School where our program was based — closed. The remaining five elementary buildings were consolidated into grades kindergarten through four, while all fifth and sixth-graders were grouped together in self-contained classrooms in a separate facility. At the same time, the district made a formal, long-range commitment to a whole language approach to reading and writing and implementing literature-based reading and writing process. A reading committee made up of teachers, librarians, and administrators had met throughout the summer to identify selected titles at each elementary grade, to begin to develop strategies and procedures to use with those titles, and to make plans for on-going in-service and staff development for the next five years. The district Library Media Office ordered the books, reinforced the covers and binding with plastic, and distributed them among the buildings. A slide presentation and lecture, which described the evolution of whole language in our district and focused on the integration of the language processes as it is occurring in various classrooms across the district, was presented to the Board of Education for approval. The First Grade Literacy Program at Moreland School — which moved to Mercer School — was recognized as a Center of Excellence by the National Council of Teachers of English for 1987-1989, and I was asked to assume the role of assisting and supporting teachers in the transition to process-whole language teaching in the K-4 buildings. In addition, Marianne Sopko, who had published books in our first grades for two years, became the parent volunteer coordinator to support the publishing process in the first grades across the district.

As I reflect on these changes, I am most struck by the fact that they came about district-wide, largely because of what two teachers started with the support of our principal and parents in one classroom. Whole language teaching spread as other teachers caught the enthusiasm and began reading professionally, attending workshops, and discussing and trying out new ideas. Parents observed and participated in the excitement and success of children learning to read and write naturally with quality literature, and they began to push teachers and administrators to implement the program across the grades for all children. By trusting and observing what children could accomplish and by constantly conferring with and assuring ourselves and parents, we all became even more convinced that literature to literacy was the most meaningful teaching and learning we had ever done.

Working with teachers in our various buildings, I am impressed that we as teachers are a very hard working, dedicated, professional group with a sincere desire to do an excellent job. I am pleased to see administrative support and involvement on all levels. Teachers who have used basal textbooks and workbooks throughout their teaching careers are asking questions about whole language-process teaching and requesting resource materials to read, demonstration lessons to observe, and time to talk with and observe other teachers and share ideas and concerns. Teachers and administrators are beginning to look at reading as a meaning-centered activity emphasizing semantics and syntax as well as phonics. Teachers are examining the relevance and connection of everything they are doing to activities in the real world. They are using their classroom as a cooperative community instead of a teacher-dominated one. They are looking at learning from whole-to-part instead of part-to-whole and teaching specific skills as the need arises. They are experimenting with more flexible grouping, trying out journal writing with their students, questioning accepted evaluation procedures, and responding critically to literature with their children. They are beginning to trust themselves and the children — allowing more choices and freedom for both.

My belief, that teachers will make the transition to more natural, meaningful teaching if they are supported, has been verified. The anxiety that is inherent in taking on more responsibility for one's teaching is being channeled into new energy and excitement as children, parents, teachers, and administrators discover the enormous enjoyment that comes with teaching literacy through quality literature. We are all reading, risking, and reflecting together while supporting each other in a life-long commitment to active literacy. It continues to be one of the most challenging and rewarding experiences of my life.

A first-grader's first published book.

16 *Resources for Teachers*

Professional Books

These lists are not meant to be all-inclusive but rather to be used as a guide. A • before a title indicates resources that other teachers and I have found particularly useful in getting started in process-whole language teaching. All titles, unless noted otherwise, are available in paperback. (Year listed is latest publication or reprint date.)

• Anderson, Richard C., et al. *Becoming a Nation of readers: The Report of the Commission on Reading.* Champaign, Illinois: University of Illinois, Center for the Study of Reading, 1985.

This book, the result of a two-year study funded by the National Institute of Education, summarizes the research on the nature of reading as it has been practiced in the United States. Some of the topics discussed include literacy, environmental influences, teaching techniques, materials, testing, phonics, beginning reading, teacher education. Specific recommendations are given to teachers, parents, administrators, and text book publishers. Despite some minor flaws, this is must reading for all responsible educators.

Atwell, Nancie. *In the Middle. Writing, Reading, and Learning with Adolescents.* Portsmouth, New Hampshire: Boynton/Cook Publishers, 1987 (Heinemann Educational Books, Inc.)

This is a beautifully written, inspiring book that demonstrates the power of a workshop approach to reading and writing and the importance of reading for writing. Nancie Atwell, an eighth grade English teacher, shares her students' and her own interactions in a classroom where students have plenty of time to read and write, the freedom to choose their books and topics, and many opportunities to respond to printed text. Students are guided to look at reading from a writer's point of view (as in "insider") and at their own writing from a reader's point of view (as in "outsider"). The explanations and procedures of the writing workshop — which includes the mini-lesson, "status-of-the-class conference", writing, conferencing, and "group share" — are clearly defined. The theory and practice described are applicable and transferable to the elementary grades.

Bean, Wendy and Chrystine Bouffler. *Spell by Writing.* Portsmouth, New Hampshire: Heinemann Educational Books, 1988.

This excellent resource stresses the importance of teaching spelling — like all language — in context. The authors argue for an integrated reading and writing program as an alternative to memorizing word lists and rules. Language strategies that children use to spell are identified. Strategy lesson plans that include rationale, learner suitability, materials required, and procedure are clearly articulated and very useful to the teacher ready to look at spelling as part of the whole language process.

Bissex, Glenda. *GYNS at Work: A Child Learns to Read and Write.* Cambridge, Mass: Harvard University Press, 1980.

This careful documentation and discussion of one child's writing and reading from age five to eleven has important implications for how we teach. A parent, acting as researcher in observing her son Paul's growing literacy, reports in detail on his natural development of generalizations about spelling, vocabulary, and reading in a supportive, print-rich environment. Using invented spelling at home, where his errors were regarded as positive, informational sources which could be used to further his knowledge, Paul's writing was varied, frequent, spontaneous, and imaginative. In school, where his writing was mostly assigned and expected to be correctly spelled and formed, the writing was monotonous and repetitious. Much of Paul's learning and use of multiple strategies in reading and writing appeared to be "constructive" with the child using his knowledge and experience to make sense of print, as opposed to "instructive" where the main source of knowledge comes from the teacher or parent.

Boomer, Garth. *Fair Dinkum Teaching and Learning: Reflections on Literacy and Power.* Portsmouth, New Hampshire: Boynton/Cook Publishers, 1985. (Heinemann Educational Books, Inc.)

'Fair Dinkum' means genuine, true, and real. This collection of first person, literary essays by a respected

Australian educator causes the reader to reflect on issues in literacy and "teaching actions", and each article is followed by a response by an educator. I found the following articles useful for reflecting on my own theories and actions: "A Parent's Guide to Literacy", "Literacy: Where Should Australia Be Heading?", and "The Wisdom of the Antipodes: What's Working for Literacy in Australia?"

Busching, Beverly A. and Judith J. Schwartz (eds.) *Integrating the Language Arts In the Elementary School*. Urbana, Illinois: National Council of Teachers of English, 1983.

This book supports efforts of teachers who want students to experience meaningful language learning. Nineteen contributors, almost all of whom are university level, discuss more theory and some practice of integration across the curriculum. Two chapters on language play with singing and games, as well as chapters that include the use of specific books to extend the curriculum and creative arts, may be particularly helpful to teachers.

• Butler, Andrea and Jan Turbill. *Towards a Reading-Writing Classroom*. Portsmouth, New Hampshire: Heinemann Educational Books, Inc., 1984.

This practical, excellent handbook (90 pages) by Australian educators/language consultants takes you inside teachers' classrooms that closely link reading and writing in theory and practice. The authors provide the theoretical framework and give immediate practical application in the classrooms. Inter-relationships between the reading and writing processes are clearly delineated. Teachers will find many workable ideas and suggestions for setting up routines and classroom organization, shared book experience, creating "big books", publishing, and many other daily reading and writing practices.

Butler, Dorothy. *Cushla and Her Books*. Boston: The Horn Book, Inc., 1980.

An inspiring study of how the very early immersion in picture books remarkably affected the cognitive development and quality of life of a handicapped child. Despite medical pronouncements of physical and mental retardation, a determined child surrounded by a loving, supportive family and wonderful books learns to read naturally and develops a love of words and language. The author, Cushla's grandmother, concludes:

"Seven years ago, before Cushla was born, I would have laid claim to a deep faith in the power of books to enrich children's lives. By comparison with my present conviction, this faith was a shallow thing. I know now what print and picture have to offer a child who is cut off from the world, for whatever reason. But I know also that there must be another human being, prepared to intercede, before anything can happen. . . ."

Calkins, Lucy McCormick. *The Art of Teaching Writing.* Portsmouth, New Hampshire: Heinemann Educational Books, Inc., 1986.

This comprehensive book (over 300 pages) by a well-known researcher brings the reader inside the writing process. Major chapters deal with the writing process at each grade level, conferencing techniques, and reading-writing connections students make as "insiders". Teachers will have clear guidelines on setting up and carrying out the "writing workshop" in the classroom. Particularly helpful are the sections on conferencing, "mini-lessons", and authorship.

Cambourne, Brian and Jan Turbill. *Coping with Chaos.* Portsmouth, New Hampshire: Heinemann Educational Books, 1987.

Don't be put off by the title! This is a short (70 pages) useful handbook that focuses on whole class settings in 'process writing' classrooms. Eight conditions are described as essential: immersion, demonstration, expectations, responsibility, approximation, practice, engagement, and response.

Chambers, Aidan. *Booktalk: Occasional Writing on Literature and Children.* London: The Bodley Head Ltd., 1985.

This challenging collection of essays, lectures, and articles by an English writer and teacher of literature discusses literature, children, and education in ways that give new, thoughtful insights into all three. Some of these discussions are titled: "The Role of Literature in Children's Lives", "Teaching Children's Literature", "Whose Book is it Anyway?", and "Tell Me: Are Children Critics?" I find the latter particularly helpful for understanding and utilizing a questioning framework that moves beyond the usual emphasis on the content of the book to higher levels of "booktalk" that have "critical direction". The teacher acts as facilitator and guide to help children, who Chambers views as capable critics, see patterns, make connections, and discover new meanings.

Some quotes to stimulate your thinking:

"Whenever possible put the teacher-student through exactly the same experience as the teacher will ask the child-pupil to go through." (p. 118)

"Certainly, in my experience the people who have the most interesting things to say about children's literature are also those who read and think about adult literature." (p. 122)

". . . there can never be a definitive reading *of a text* (my italics), but only additional readings, all of them in some way revealing. . ." (p. 127)

"The act of reading lies in talking about what you have read." (p. 141)

"Understanding about meaning is arrived at naturally as the more specific and practical questions about 'what happened to us as we read?' and 'how is the story told?' are discussed. Thus we can say that content and meaning are best approached through exploration of form and pattern." (p. 173)

Clark, Margaret M. *Young Fluent Readers. What Can They Teach Us?* Portsmouth, New Hampshire: Heinemann Educational Books, 1976.

Thirty-two children who enter school at age 5 as fluent readers are studied as they progress through school, and all aspects of their reading are analyzed in a total language context. Some major factors seen as contributing to their reading fluency are: parent involvement and encouragement in the reading process, parent respect and valuing of education, regular library use, repetition of stories, and the encouragement of children to make choices in their lives.

Clay, Marie M. *The Early Detection of Reading Difficulties.* Third Edition. Portsmouth, New Hampshire: Heinemann Educational Books, Inc., 1985.

This text, based on the extensive research of New Zealand psychologist and educator Marie Clay, describes the Reading Recovery procedures for the early assessment, intervention, and observation of at risk beginning readers. Teachers willing to take the time to read and reread this very explicit text carefully will gain an understanding of how to observe reading behaviors and guide young readers in the acquisition of reading strategies. The procedures for taking a

Running Record on a child's oral reading of any book passage are valuable for evaluating the child's strengths and weaknesses and establishing instructional purposes.

Clay, Marie M. *Observing Young Readers: Selected Papers.* Portsmouth, New Hampshire: Heinemann Educational Books, Inc., 1982.

In a series of scholarly papers, the author presents extensive research and observations on learning to read in cross-cultural groups. The longitudinal studies that led to the development and implementation of Clay's Reading Recovery program are described. Educators will gain a broader knowledge of the beginning reading process and recognize the importance of good first teaching as the best deterrent to reading failure.

Clay, Marie M. *What Did I Write?* Portsmouth, New Hampshire: Heinemann Educational Books, Inc., 1987.

This short volume (75 pages) will prove especially useful to kindergarten and grade 1 teachers who recognize the importance of a self-directed early writing program. (Writing vocabulary is known to be a good predictor of reading progress.) The author observes and analyzes writing samples and progress of five-year-olds and makes theoretical links between early writing behaviors and reading.

• Cochrane, Orin; Cochrane, Donna; Scalena, Sharen; and Ethel Buchanan. *Reading Writing & Caring.* New York: Richard C. Owen Publishers, Inc., 1985.

The authors, Canadian educators, present a clear, well-organized explanation of the reading, writing, thinking processes and how to set up a classroom environment to foster these processes. An explanation of miscue analysis: ". . . an in-process system of assessment and evaluation of oral reading" and how to do it, is useful. The section on Reading Comprehension, particularly the model lesson of how children are guided by the teacher's questions to use their own prior knowledge to predict, is outstanding. The goals and curriculum of a writing process program, including insights into helping children develop spelling abilities, are clearly detailed. The final chapter, "Teaching Strategies for Whole Language Classrooms", includes very specific objectives and procedures that elementary teachers will want to incorporate. This is an excellent book for understanding and incorporating meaningful teaching in a whole language classroom.

● Cullinan, Bernice E. (ed.). *Children's Literature in the Reading Program.* Newark, Delaware: International Reading Association, 1987.

Well-known, respected educators give their interpretations and rationale for using literature in the reading program. Primary grades, intermediate grades, and upper grades (6 to 8) are separated by sections. A useful overview is presented along with some specific ideas and recommended children's books. Informal writing style and book format make this book a readable introduction for interested teachers.

Education Department of Victoria (Australia). *Beginning Reading.* Crystal Lake, Illinois: Rigby Education, 1987.

For the kindergarten and first grade teacher new to helping children learn to read and write naturally, this 40 page booklet, written by teachers, outlines a meaningful, balanced beginning reading approach. Through a classroom environment that encourages playing, talking, listening, reading, writing, observing, thinking, and doing, children become readers and writers. Lots of useful activities that promote language learning are briefly presented.

Education Department of Victoria (Australia). *Reading On.* Crystal Lake, Illinois: Rigby Education, 1987.

This booklet (68 pages) is a clear, concise, well-organized introduction to beginning reading in a whole language framework. Topics covered include what happens in the reading process, how competent beginning readers develop, how a language-rich reading program is planned, what reading and writing activities are appropriate, and evaluation. Lots of good, basic information for the teacher wanting an overview of beginning reading using meaningful approaches.

● Fader, Daniel. *The New Hooked on Books.* New York: Berkley Publishing Corporation, 1982.

Fader looks at what has gone wrong in the teaching of literacy and offers inspiration and solutions. The author speaks convincingly of the benefits of self-selected reading and recommends "saturation" — surrounding students with newspapers, magazines, and a wide variety of paperbacks, and "diffusion" — making literacy necessary, attractive, and pleasurable for all students. Appendixes recommend paperback wholesalers by states and list many paperback books by themes. Inspiring, recommended reading!

- Fehring, Heather and Valerie Thomas for the Ministry of Education of Victoria. *The Teaching of Spelling*. Crystal Lake, Illinois: Rigby Education, 1987.

  This practical, concise handbook (34 pages) gives lots of specific suggestions and activities for planning a meaningful spelling program that focuses on children's own writing to help children develop a basic spelling vocabulary and spelling strategies (such as identifying and correcting misspellings and using resources to find correct spellings). "*Learning to spell* is not simply a matter of learning how to spell individual words. It entails learning how our written language works. In order to learn this, children need to be exposed to many activities that involve written language: reading, word games and extensive writing." (p. 5) Teachers who want to begin to teach spelling without a workbook program will find support and information here. This booklet also includes two pages of useful references for additional resources and more information on spelling and writing.

- Gentry, Richard R. *Spel. . . is a Four-Letter Word*. Portsmouth, New Hampshire: Heinemann Educational Books, Inc., 1987.

  This easy to read "parent/teacher guide", 54 pages, is chock full of useful information on learning to spell. The author cites his own experiences as well as research in making specific recommendations on spelling instruction. Myths about spelling are cleared up; invented spelling is clearly explained, and strategies for teaching spelling are presented.

- Goodman, Ken. *What's Whole in Whole Language?* Portsmouth, New Hampshire: Heinemann Educational Books, Inc., 1986.

  This "parent/teacher guide", 79 pages, answers many basic questions and clearly explains what whole language teaching is all about. Ways to make language learning easy are given; the learning theory behind whole language teaching is discussed; principles of whole language instruction and learning are listed; implementation objectives and specifics are concisely noted. The last section of the book discusses whole language policy in the United States and other countries and invites teachers to make the transition to whole language teaching.

Goodman, Kenneth S.; Smith, E. Brooks; Meredith, Robert; and Yetta M. Goodman. *Language and Thinking in School: A Whole-Language Curriculum.* Third Edition. New York: Richard C. Owen Publishers, Inc., 1987. (hardcover)

This comprehensive text (416 pages) provides a theoretical understanding of the nature and development of language and thought and its application and expansion through a whole language curriculum. "A key premise is that development of language and thought are interdependent: language is the medium of thought, learning, and communication, and it is learned best in the process of its use." (p. 386.) What is meant by a whole language approach in reading, writing, spelling, and handwriting is clearly defined by rationale, key principles, and instructional strategies. Educators who believe that a solid base of knowledge and theory is necessary to make intelligent decisions for students will eventually want to read this challenging book.

Goodman, Yetta M.; Watson, Dorothy J.; and Carolyn L. Burke. *Reading Miscue Inventory.* New York: Richard C. Owen Publishers, Inc., 1987.

By learning how to use miscue analysis techniques, professional educators and researchers have a valuable evaluation tool that provides information on how readers use language, knowledge, and strategies in the process of reading. Miscue analysis enables the teacher/researcher to note the sampling, predicting, and confirming strategies the reader is using, to interpret the miscues made, and to determine the suitability of the reading material. A complete reading miscue analysis includes the marked typescript of the reading passage, the Coding Sheets, the list of repeated miscues, the reader's retelling of the passage, the teacher's written comments, the Reading Interview, and the "Reader Profile" summary. While the information is very useful, this qualitative and quantitative analysis is very time-consuming and complicated. For teacher/researchers desiring more information on research, theory, whole language instruction, and strategy lessons, the book concludes with an extensive bibliography and references.

Goodman, Yetta M. and Carolyn Burke. *Reading Strategies: Focus on Comprehension.* New York: Richard C. Owen Publishers, Inc., 1985.

This comprehensive resource text advocates a comprehension-centered reading curriculum with focus on reading evaluation. The authors recommend that teachers evaluate readers' use of strategies by examining students' miscues ("unexpected responses" in oral reading that demonstrate the readers' strengths and weaknesses) and then by providing reading-strategy instruction. "The purpose of reading-strategy instruction is to make students consciously aware of the language and thought cues available to them as readers and to support their developing use of reading strategies." (p. 27) Using meaningful selections, strategy lesson plans are provided for furthering readers' uses of the three cueing systems: semantic, syntactic, and graphophonic. Particularly useful are the questions for discussion, excellent examples of how to stimulate high-level discussion and promote comprehension. This text has two parts: "A Theoretical Framework" and "Reading-Strategy Lessons" and is recommended for the teacher who already has a good understanding of the reading process.

Gordon, Naomi (ed.). *Classroom Experiences. The Writing Process in Action.* Portsmouth, New Hampshire: Heinemann Educational Books, Inc., 1984.

Seven teachers describe their successes and frustrations of moving into process writing. Each chapter deals with specific grade levels. The writing is honest, personal, and very supportive to teachers ready to take a process approach. Lots of good suggestions for organization and conferencing.

Graves, Donald. *Writing: Teachers and Children at Work.* Portsmouth, New Hampshire: Heinemann Educational Books, Inc., 1983.

This thorough, practical text (326 pages) on learning and teaching writing takes the reader through the process of children's development as writers and gives teachers confidence, understanding, and strategies to support children in their writing development. Much of the book is based on Graves' three-year study of children's writing with Lucy Calkins and Susan Sowers at Atkinson Academy, a public school in New Hampshire. As such, the clear voice of teachers and children throughout the book gives authenticity and many concrete examples from writing process classrooms. Guidelines are presented for helping children in choosing topics, sharing writing, publishing, teacher modeling, organizing the classroom for writing, composing with the children and in front of the children, conferencing principles, revising principles, using the "writing folder", keeping records, communicating with parents, listening to children for the author's voice, and many other areas. Teachers have found Graves' chapters on answers to questions teachers ask about writing and conferencing especially helpful.

Hall, Mary Anne. *Teaching Reading as a Language Experience.* Third Edition. Columbus: Charles E. Merrill Publishing Company, 1981.

The language experience approach, which uses children's oral language and experiences to create personal reading materials, is described from a theoretical and mostly practical point of view. Texts that the child creates become highly predictable and engaging reading material. Very helpful to the teacher are: the organization of the classroom for individual, small group, and large group instruction as well as into centers for reading, listening, writing, and art activities; development of sight words and vocabulary through the use of word banks; and the suggested, annotated, reading at the end of each chapter.

Hancock, Joelie and Susan Hill. (eds.) *Literature-based Reading Programs at Work.* Portsmouth, New Hampshire: Heinemann Educational Books, Inc., 1988.

Australian teachers discuss the setting up and organization of their individualized, literature-based reading programs and present practical ideas for extending children's responses to books. Specific suggestions are offered for a student reading survey, conducting a reading conference and keeping records in an individualized reading program, shared book experience, thematic use of literature, poetry, and biography. Many workable, practical ideas for a literature program.

• Hansen, Jane; Newkirk, Thomas; and Donald Graves (eds.). *Breaking Ground: Teachers Relate Reading and Writing in the Elementary School.* Portsmouth, New Hampshire: Heinemann Educational Books, Inc., 1985.

This well-written book is unique in that it totally connects the teaching of writing with reading, and most of the chapters are written by classroom teachers. Teachers use their knowledge and practice of writing process to examine their traditional teaching of reading and modify it so it complements the writing process. Articles deal with such topics as: immersion in reading as preparation for writing, creating opportunities for writing across the curriculum, how daily self-selected writing promotes natural reading development, the power of literature as an integral part of a writing program, how children's reading and rereading of their own writing to themselves and others helps their developing reading skills, how writing stories helps students relate to stories of other authors, and the kinds of stories that young writers compose.

Hardt, Ulrich H. *Teaching Reading with the Other Language Arts.* Newark, Delaware: International Reading Association, 1983.

Teachers ready to integrate the teaching of reading with all the language arts will find theoretical and practical support in this text. The section on "Classroom Practices" is especially useful and is full of examples of meaningful activites for effective language learning and teaching. The following articles from that section are particularly recommended: "Bringing Together Reading and Writing" by Dorothy J. Watson, "Organizing the Elementary Classroom for Effective Language Learning" by Lynn K. Rhodes, "Literature in the Language Arts Program" by Ulrich H. Hardt, "Literature and the Language Arts for Middle Grade Students" by Arlene M. Pillar, and "Evaluation in the Holistic Reading/Language Arts Curriculum" by Richard Ammon.

Harste, Jerome; Woodward, Virginia; and Carolyn Burke. *Language Stories and Literacy Lessons.* Portsmouth, New Hampshire: Heinemann Educational Books, Inc., 1984.

Through reading this theoretical text (252 pages) about literacy and literacy learning, the teacher/researcher gains new insights into how children's language experiences contribute to their growing literacy. The authors have observed and analyzed "language stories" — vignettes of conversation, scribblings, invented spellings, art work — from preschool children aged three to six, to understand the "literacy lessons". Using the "child-as-informant", this research study indicates that young children know far more about reading and writing than teachers and beginning reading and writing programs assume, and that the decisions young writers make are highly organized and meaningful.

This text urges us to examine the current instructional assumptions we make as teachers and to make the school environment a place that promotes the expansion and exploration of the written language experiences children enter school with. Implicit is the necessity of uninterrupted time for reading and writing with the child taking ownership of the language learning processes.

- Holdaway, Don. *The Foundations of Literacy.* Portsmouth, New Hampshire: Heinemann Educational Books, Inc., 1979.

  Based on research and theory in how children develop literacy as well as on educational practice in New Zealand, this magnificent book (232 pages) is an invaluable resource to teachers who want to understand and promote early literacy learning. Holdaway believes the job of teachers is to ". . . induce appropriate activity in literacy tasks rather than provide instruction. . . the complex work of learning is carried out by the individual learner in a self-regulatory manner. . ." (p. 81). To this end, Holdaway gives many examples of how to induce the development of basic literacy strategies through shared book experiences and integrating various approaches that respect the developmental learning model, especially as it occurs in children's acquisition of spoken language. Written with humility, humor, clarity, and great intellect, this practical book is mandatory reading for gaining a foundation in understanding language learning and fostering it through a strategy oriented style of teaching.

Holdaway, Don. *Independence in Reading.* Portsmouth, New Hampshire: Heinemann Educational Books, Inc., 1980.

  This text focuses on procedures in teaching reading and will give the teacher specific strategies for individualized reading, teaching sight words in sentence context, word study skills, reference skills, understanding, and evaluation. Teachers will find the appendixes "A Simplified Progression of Word Recognition Skills" and "Sequential Development of Reading Skills" very useful for descriptions of skills and strategies to be taught and appropriate age-level expectations.

Holdaway, Don. *Stability and Change in Literacy Learning.* Portsmouth, New Hampshire: Heinemann Educational Books, Inc.; and London, Ontario, Canada: The University of Western Ontario, 1984.

  This is a short (64 pages) philosophical, enlightening book that discusses literacy in terms of research, common sense, environment, programs, and teaching. Perhaps most valuable to teachers is the detailed description of what actually happens in a developmental learning environment. This is must reading to fully understand how shared book experience can work, how phonics can be taught within the context of books, and how follow-up independent language and related arts activities are organized.

Hornsby, David; Sukarna, Deborah; with Jo-Ann Parry. *Read On: A Conference Approach to Reading.* Portsmouth, New Hampshire: Heinemann Educational Books, Inc., 1988.

This practical handbook gives lots of good ideas to go along with children's books including procedures for reading conferences, sample questions, activities for teaching skills and strategies, record keeping folders, evaluation forms. Teachers desiring more information on implementing a literature-based reading program will find lots of specifics here.

Howgate, Lynn. *Building Self-Esteem Through the Writing Process.* Berkeley: University of California, The National Writing Project, 1982.

The title does not do justice to the wealth of practical ideas for teachers on understanding and using the writing process through the grades. Specific guidelines and examples are given for prewriting activities, free writing, journal writing, dictation, drafting, revising, group conferencing, proofreading, poetry, and publication. An appendix of about 100 pages gives samples and excerpts of lesson plans, students' writing, and cross grade sharing. A very useful handbook!

Huck, Charlotte S.; Hepler, Susan and Janet Hickman. *Children's Literature in the Elementary School.* Fourth Edition. New York: Holt, Rinehart, and Winston, Inc., 1987. (hardcover)

This updated edition of an acclaimed text (753 pages) should be readily accessible to all teachers and librarians as it is one of the most comprehensive reference books on children's literature. Part 1 discusses the value of literature and gives guidelines for evaluation of literature. Chapter 2, "Understanding Children's Response to Literature", is valuable for understanding, observing, encouraging and examining what goes on between a book and its reader. In Part 2, all types of literature are discussed in depth: books to begin on including wordless books, ABC books, and concept books; picture books; traditional literature including folk tales, fables, myths, legends, and the Bible; modern fantasy; poetry; contemporary realistic fiction, historical fiction; biographies and informational books. Some of these are complete enough to stand as individual anthologies. Part 3 focuses on developing a literature program in the school. The specific suggestions and examples for guiding in-depth studies of books with webbing and questioning techniques are especially helpful. At the end of each of the thirteen chapters are "Suggested Learning Experiences" which give ideas that can be adapted to the classroom; "Related Readings" with a brief description of each reference cited; and "References" with recommended book titles specific to each topic.

Hudson, Colin and Mary O'Toole. *Spelling: A Teacher's Guide.* Revised Edition. Crystal Lake, Illinois: Rigby Education, 1987.

Written by an Australian language consultant, this book views spelling as part of the total language development process and gives lots of practical ideas to help children become competent spellers. Believing that children learn to write and spell by writing (and not by memorizing word lists), the teacher's role is seen as assisting children to form spelling generalizations through their own writing. Most of the book is devoted to developing spelling strategies through activities such as modeling, building up word collections, wall stories, "the look, cover, write and check procedure", chunking words, noting words within words, letter clusters, morphemic knowledge, mnemonics, "have a go", dictation, knowledge of sound-symbol relationship, listing related words, etc.

Jewell, Margaret Greer and Miles V. Zinz. *Learning to Read Naturally.* Dubuque, Iowa: Kendall/Hunt Publishing Company, 1986.

This is a well-organized, lengthy, comprehensive text that discusses the research, theory and practice of the development of natural readers. Instructional practices and issues are detailed including shared book experience, oral language development, activities for the classroom, desirable reading materials and environments. Each chapter concludes with a brief summary and extensive list of references. The book ends with a complete glossary of educational terms. Writing, as it relates to reading, is basically not discussed.

Kimmel, Margaret Mary and Elizabeth Segal. *For Reading Out Loud! A Guide to Sharing Books With Children*. New York: Delacorte Press, 1983. (hardcover)

This helpful guidebook for adults who read aloud to children encompasses the benefits of reading aloud, ways to make time to read aloud at home and at school, and a carefully selected list of 140 books of high literary quality for reading aloud to children from kindergarten through eighth grade. For each book listed there is a description of the plot and theme, the estimated time and number of sessions it will take to read the book aloud, and the suggested listening level by grades. This book can also be used to help teachers select books for group discussion; a book that is great read aloud can also be an excellent choice for guided reading.

• Meek, Margaret. *Learning to Read*. Portsmouth, New Hampshire: Heinemann Educational Books, Inc., 1986.

This is one of my favorite books to give to parents and teachers for understanding the natural reading process and its developmental stages, especially the emergent and beginning stages. Meek is convincing and inspiring in her sensible viewpoints on learning to read. She is particularly helpful to parents on what they can and must do at home in spite of a nonsupportive school learning environment.

Melser, June. *The Story Box Teachers' Book: No Failing!* San Diego: The Wright Group, 1983.

Although much of this handbook (42 pages) outlines a commercial reading program for beginning readers, the first part gives easy to read suggestions and excellent illustrations involving emergent literacy. Very helpful as a guide to beginning process teachers.

Newkirk, Thomas and Nancie Atwell (eds.). *Understanding Writing: Ways of Observing, Learning, and Teaching*. Second Edition. Portsmouth, New Hampshire: Heinemann Educational Books, Inc., 1988.

Classroom teachers/researchers write about their careful observations of their students' writing development. Teachers will gain a greater understanding of writing process instruction and be able to apply many insights into their own teaching. Susan Sower's article, "Six Questions Teachers Ask About Invented Spelling", is very informative and reassuring. "Squeezing from the Middle of the Tube" by Susan B. Bridge gives workable specifics for conferencing with the young writer at the drawing stage. "Young Writers as Critical Readers" by Thomas Newkirk suggests that ". . . a writing program that constantly asks students to make judgments as to clarity, completeness, order, interest, and consistency will have a beneficial effect on all reading." "A Writer Reads, A Reader Writes" by Mary Ellen Giacobbe follows one first-grader's writing development. "Using Writing Folders to Document Student Progress" by Anne Bingham is a very helpful article that clearly discusses how to document writing progress.

Newman, Judith. *Whole Language: Theory in Use.* Portsmouth, New Hampshire: Heinemann Educational Books, Inc., 1985.

This informative text, written by Canadian "whole language" educators, give elementary teachers a lot of theory and practice about what a whole language curriculum means in a context of language and language learning. The dichotomy between how many teachers instruct (with emphasis on word analysis) and what research studies support and teachers say they do when they read (with emphasis on getting meaning with ". . . a transaction between the print cues and knowledge supplied by the reader . . ." p. 56) is discussed. These teachers share their experiences with children's spelling and writing development through letter writing, journal writing, message writing, and conferencing: Particularly informative for understanding reading and writing in a whole language framework are the articles by Judith Newman: "Insights from Recent Reading and Writing Research and Their Implications for Developing Whole Language Curriculum", "Using Children's Books to Teach Reading", and "What About Reading?"

• New Zealand Department of Education. *Reading in Junior Classes.* New York: Richard C. Owen Publishers, Inc., 1985.

This well-organized handbook, originally published for teachers by the New Zealand Department of Education to go along with the "Ready to Read" series, is an outstanding guide for understanding what it means to teach beginning reading in a meaningful way. How children learn and develop language at home is applied to how children learn to read books and continue to develop language at school. The book describes what happens in the process of skilled reading and applies it to teaching. Some of the major areas

the book deals with are: developing reading strategies —
sampling, predicting, confirming, self-correcting; the why
and how of observing and monitoring children's reading
progress, including the use of Running Records; building a
sight vocabulary through meaningful context; the various
approaches in a balanced reading program — reading to
children, language experience, shared reading, guided
reading, independent reading, and writing; and organizing
the classroom environment for instruction and learning.

Norton, Donna. *Through the Eyes of a Child. An Introduction to
Children's Literature.* Second Edition. Columbus: Charles F.
Merrill Publishing Company, 1987. (hardcover)

This is an absolutely wonderful resource that you will
want to have access to. While the book is "... designed for
children's literature classes taught in the departments of
English, Education, and Library Science..." this valuable,
comprehensive text (691 pages) is for anyone interested in
all aspects of children's literature. The organization of the
book is unique. The content includes such topics as history
of children's literature, selecting and evaluating literature,
artists and their illustrations, picture books, traditional
literature including folktales, fables, myths, and legends,
modern fantasy, poetry, contemporary realistic fiction,
historical fiction, and multi-ethnic fiction. Following each
chapter on the characteristics, history, and discussion of
books for each genre is a chapter on involving children in
that genre. These chapters present many activities and
strategies for webbing and extending and appreciating the
literature and give teachers lots of terrific, practical ideas for
use in the classroom. Also unique to this text are the
controversial issues raised in each chapter, the personal
portraits and statements by well-known authors and
illustrators about themselves and their books, and the
illustrated flashbacks which highlight significant people,
books, and events in the history of children's literature.
Each chapter also ends with a summary, suggested activities,
references, and an annotated bibliography of children's
literature with approximate reading level by grade and
interest level by age. Useful appendixes to the text include
book selection aids, professional reading, notable children's
films and filmstrips, and a bibliography of book awards.

Parkes, Brenda and Judith Smith. *Beginnings: Contexts for Early Language Learning.* Crystal Lake, Illinois: Rigby, 1987.

This extremely practical handbook, by two experienced teachers who are also accomplished creative writers, is designed for use with children prior to the introduction of formal literacy learning. Providing many interesting demonstrations of authentic language use, and exploring a wide range of language contexts, *Beginnings* is both a good starting point for new teachers and a valuable source of information and inspiration for those who are already working with whole language.

It includes imaginative ideas for using the Rigby *Beginnings* program and Traditional Tales, and, although originally published in Australia, has many American bibliographic references.

Parry, Jo-Ann and David Hornsby. *Write On: A Conference Approach to Writing.* Portsmouth, New Hampshire: Heinemann Educational Books, Inc., 1988.

This practical book gives the teacher lots of ideas, presented mostly in a list or informal outline form, on beginning a process writing program. Included are activities/ suggestions for prewriting, drafting, revising, conferencing, publishing, organizing the classroom for writing, record keeping, evaluation, and reading activities in the writing program. The section on "Spelling in the Writing Classroom" is very useful to teachers ready to move away from textbook programs. Spelling strategies and procedures are given for organizing a meaningful spelling program.

Peeton, Adrian. *Shared Reading: Safe Risks with Whole Books.* Richmond Hill, Ontario, Canada: Scholastic-TAB Publications, Ltd., 1986.

This easy-to-read booklet (32 pages) describes useful strategies to help less able readers in grades 2-6 respond to and enjoy chapter books together.

Sampson, Michael (ed.). *The Pursuit of Literacy. Early Reading and Writing.* Dubuque, Iowa: Kendall/Hunt Publishing Company, 1986.

The chapter by Don Holdaway, "The Structure of Natural Learning as a Basis for Literacy Instruction", is the most comprehensive I have read for gaining an understanding of how children learn naturally and how that knowledge can be applied in teaching. Other chapters, by well-known educators, offer insights and suggestions for effective literacy learning.

- Sloan, Peter and Ross Latham. *Teaching Reading Is* . . . Crystal Lake, Illinois: Rigby Education, 1987.

  This excellent, comprehensive, well-organized book (269 pages) by Australian reading educators gives numerous specific strategies, techniques, and procedures for reading aloud, word identification, individual and group language experience, oral reading, silent reading, individualized reading, using the library as a resource, classroom organization, and more. For the teacher who wants to develop readers' comprehension strategies (sampling, predicting, selecting, confirming/disconfirming) and learn how to teach reading effectively, (and without the basal), this book is extremely useful and applicable with lots of step-by-step activities to enhance and extend reading. The procedures for language experience activites (". . . a method of teaching reading that is based on the language generated orally by the reader"), oral reading activities (but not "round robin reading"), and using silent reading activities to develop comprehension are particularly useful. While the focus of the book is on the teaching of reading, activites on how to promote writing, listening, and speaking as part of an integrated language arts approach are included. Teachers who want to teach reading as a meaning-getting, problem-solving process, but who have not had the experience, knowledge, and training to do so, will find this book invaluable.

- Smith, Frank. *Essays into Literacy.* Portsmouth, New Hampshire: Heinemann Educational Books, Inc., 1983.

  This book is must reading for forming your own philosophy about teaching and learning. I reread it every few years. Frank Smith uses language in a way no other writer does, and he forces the reader to think. One of his chapters is titled, "Twelve Easy Ways to Make Learning to Read Difficult". I give some of his quotes from different parts of the bok to entice you.

  "Students of weak ability who are interested in reading and writing will always have the hope of improvement. But those who detest the activities are lost; they have learned from the wrong demonstrations." (p. 115)

"Teachers are an endangered species. While being given less and less freedom to teach, they are being held more and more accountable." (p. 115)

"The collaborative nature of the teacher-learner relationship in literacy does not require deliberate instruction or that children should work everything out independently. It is a mutual undertaking, the nature of which has not yet been fully examined by researchers." (p. 145)

Smith, Frank. *Insult to Intelligence*. Portsmouth, New Hampshire: Heinemann Educational Books, Inc., 1988.

Smith discusses the current preoccupation with programmed instruction, computers, and testing in language education and offers suggestions for meaningful learning in collaborative, cooperative environments where students are invited into "learning clubs" with "no grades", "no coersion", "no restrictions" and "no status". This book gives teachers ammunition and support for responsible decision making and educational change.

Smith, Frank. *Joining the Literacy Club*. Portsmouth, New Hampshire: Heinemann Educational Books, Inc., 1988.

Smith's second collection of literacy essays thoughtfully explores language, learning, and education and the importance of "joining the club" of literate individuals. By the "literacy club", Smith refers to the social nature of literacy learning and children's natural desire to be part of the community of learners. The teacher's role is viewed as critically important in facilitating entrance into the reading and writing clubs; it is up to the teacher to foster apprenticeships and collaborations — partnerships in joint enterprises — and to demonstrate the advantages of club membership. Smith claims that learning takes place easily and naturally when it is worthwhile, relevant, interesting, meaningful, and accessible; it is only difficult when it is irrelevant, boring, and nonsensical to the learner.

Smith also discusses the importance of students observing teachers discussing together, the dangers of programmatic instruction, the negative consequences of evaluation and emphasis on grades, and the pitfalls and the possibilities of the computer. I found the following essays particularly enlightening: "Joining the Literacy Club", "Collaboration in the Classroom", and "How Education Backed the Wrong Horse".

Smith, Frank. *Reading Without Nonsense.* Second Edition. New
York: Teachers College Press, 1985.

This is a thought-provoking, theoretical and practical
book that argues for sensible, meaningful reading material
along with a supportive teacher. Smith examines what good
readers do with an unknown word — they skip it, predict
from context, use phonics (last choice). "In natural, out-of-
school surroundings, printed words exist not to be
associated with sounds but with sense."

Smith, Frank. *Understanding Reading.* Third Edition. Hillsdale,
New Jersey: Lawrence Erlbaum Associates, Publishers, 1986.

In the preface, Smith writes, "It is the wisdom and
intuition of teachers that must be trusted, provided that
teachers have the basic understanding necessary for the
classroom decisions that only they should make." This book,
about how reading is learned (not how it is taught) provides
that deep understanding of reading as an "experience-
constructing" (not an "information-acquiring") activity.
The book provides a theoretical analysis of all aspects of
reading — linguistic, psychological, social, and physiological
— based on current research and Smith's own brand of
brilliant thinking. Teachers wanting to function as
facilitators and guides (not managers of programs) will find
much support here along with an increased base of
knowledge about the learning process.

Smith, Frank. *Writing and the Writer.* Hillsdale, New Jersey:
Lawrence Erlbaum Associates, Publishers, 1982.

This scholarly, theoretical text provides valuable insights
into what happens in the act of writing. Composition is
viewed as a natural, creative activity that will develop if it is
nurtured and not inhibited. "Writing is fostered rather than
taught, and what teachers require is not helpful advice about
'methods' of writing instruction, not an outline of
appropriate 'programs', but an understanding of the task a
child faces in learning to write." (p. 200).

Smith believes that conventions of writing, which have to
be learned, will be worked out by the child implicitly if
teachers demonstrate what writing can do and help children
do it themselves. The kind of learning environment teachers
need to provide and the necessary conditions for learning
anything ("demonstration", "engagement", and
"sensitivity") are discussed. Educators will gain a clearer
understanding of the importance of reading for writing, the

registers of language, intentions and conventions of writers, specifications for a text, prewriting, revising, editing, writing blocks, and aspects of transcription (handwriting, spelling, punctuation and grammar).

Somerfield, Muriel; Torbe, Mike; and Colin Ward. *A Framework for Reading. Creating a Policy in the Elementary School.* Portsmouth, New Hampshire: Heinemann Educational Books, Inc., 1985.

For teachers and administrators who want to sort out and determine how to approach the teaching of reading, this well organized, easy to read guide (120 pages) gives a valuable framework for constructing a "language policy" and getting a dialogue going concerning the issues of literacy education. The book, based on successful classroom practices and current research, is a very helpful resource to all who want to think about, revamp, and evaluate the components and principles of the elementary school reading curriculum.

Temple, Charles A,; Nathan, Ruth G.; Burris, Nancy A.; and Frances Temple. *The Beginnings of Writing.* Second Edition. Boston: Allyn & Bacon, 1988.

The authors focus on and analyze the writing development and the composing process of children aged four to eight. Using many writing samples, children's early efforts from scribble to invented spelling to standard spelling are examined in detail. Teachers will find this guide very helpful in understanding the principles of early writing and the importance of invented spelling for enabling young children to begin to gain control over their writing.

Trelease, Jim. *The Read-Aloud Handbook.* New York: Penguin Books, 1985.

This deservedly inspiring, popular handbook for parents and teachers talks about the importance and joy of reading aloud to children of all ages and the positive influence of an adult who loves books, talks enthusiastically about them, and reads aloud regularly. The first half of the book deals with the need to read aloud to children and how and when to begin and carry through. The influence of television, "... the largest stumbling block to reading enjoyment and achievement in this country...", the importance of public and home libraries, and sustained silent reading are also discussed. The second half of the book is the "Treasury of

Read-Alouds", a listing and brief description of recommended titles from picture books to novels that also includes poetry books and literature anthologies.

• Turbill, Jan (ed.). *No Better Way to Teach Writing!* Portsmouth, New Hampshire: Heinemann Educational Books, Inc., 1982.

I recommend this book to teachers as the first book to read on how to teach writing process in the classroom. The book (96 pages) is basically written by dedicated primary teachers in Australia who took part in a year long 'process-conference approach' to writing based on the inspiration and research of Donald Graves. Teachers tell how they got started, how they worked out classroom organization, conferencing, publishing, and other aspects of writing. Teachers honestly share their problems and insecurities along with their successes and the children's growing confidence. Written in a straightforward, practical, and encouraging manner, this book gives confidence and lots of information to teachers who want to get started on the 'conference approach' to writing.

Turbill, Jan. *Now, We Want to Write!* Portsmouth, New Hampshire: Heinemann Educational Books, Inc., 1983.

This sequel to *No Better Way to Teach Writing!* follows up two more years of teachers' experiences with the 'process-conference approach' to writing and is an easy-to-read, short (72 pages) book for all the elementary grades. The book deals in practical terms with what children and teachers say about their involvement with the approach, how to get started, classroom management, questioning techniques in a "roving conference", conferencing — peer, individual, group, and whole class — the teacher's role in "writing workshop", and dealing with spelling, publishing, and evaluating.

Walshe, R. D. (ed.) *Donald Graves in Australia — "Children want to write..."* Portsmouth, New Hampshire: Heinemann Educational Books, Inc., 1982.

This 120 page book includes articles by researchers and teachers involved in Donald Graves' research on children's writing. Articles by Donald Graves, Susan Sowers, Lucy Calkins, Mary Ellen Giacobbe, and others are informative, lively, easy-to-read, and give the teacher the necessary background and understanding to try writing process in the classroom.

• Walshe, R. D. *Every Child Can Write!* Crystal Lake, Illinois: Rigby Education, 1987.

This is an absolutely terrific book — wonderfully practical, highly specific, and backed by solid research. Teachers will clearly understand and be able to implement multiple aspects of the writing process in the classroom. A wealth of ideas for drafting, revising, editing, publishing, evaluating, choosing topics, journals, poetry, conferencing, publishing, teaching grammar, spelling. Everything you ever wanted to know about writing is here in an organized, useful format.

• Wells, Gordon. *The Meaning Makers. Children Learning Language and Using Language to Learn.* Portsmouth, New Hampshire: Heinemann Educational Books, Inc., 1986.

This powerful, clearly written text has such important implications for how we teach and interact with children that I view it as *must* reading for understanding the facts that contribute to literacy development at home and at school. Based on fifteen years of longitudinal research investigating the language development of a representative sample of children in Bristol, England from age fifteen months through the end of elementary school, a quantitative and qualitative analysis was made from samples of naturally occurring conversations at home and at school. The study found that in the home, parents naturally and intuitively encouraged collaboration in conversation and activities of mutual interest to the parent and the child. By contrast, at school, the teacher did most of the talking and decision making and asked the kinds of questions that actually limited children's participation in conversation. Perhaps, the most important finding in terms of literacy at school was that listening to stories read aloud at home was the best predictor of school achievement — confirming the importance of reading stories aloud to children from an early age.

Among some of the important recommendations that Wells makes throughout the book are: provide more opportunities for children to initiate and sustain topics of conversation; promote collaborative interaction between students and teachers including curriculum negotiation; recognize the value of oral language skills in literacy development as well as skills in reading and writing.

Some thought-provoking quotes to think about:

" . . . compared with homes, schools are not providing an

environment that fosters language development. For *no* child was the language experience of the classroom richer than that of the home — not even for those believed to be 'linguistically deprived'." (p. 87)

"When adults are determined at all costs to develop the meaning that *they* see in the situation, there is little chance of achieving that collaboration in meaning making which is so essential for successful conversation." (p. 100)

"What I want to suggest is that stories have a role in education that goes far beyond their contribution to the acquisition of literacy. Constructing stories in the mind — or *storying*, as it has been called — is one of the most fundamental means of making meaning. As such, it is an activity that pervades all aspects of learning." (p. 194)

Wilson, Lorraine. *Write Me A Sign: About Language Experience.* Crystal Lake, Illinois: Rigby Education, 1987.

This book is a good introduction to language learning in young children and is based on the premise that language is best learned through its use. Teachers will find many ideas and activities for setting up a classroom environment that supports and fosters language development, primarily through a language experience approach, ". . . an approach for developing children's language (listening, speaking, reading, and writing), out of their first-hand experiences."

Journal Articles

Allington, Richard. "If They Don't Read Much How They Gonna Get Good?" *Journal of Reading*. October 1977. pp. 57-61.

The author observes that remedial readers spend most of their time in isolated skill instruction and almost no time at all reading in context without interruption. (These findings remain true today.) To become a reader, one has to spend time reading continuous, meaningful text.

● Butler, Andrea. "Guided Reading". Crystal Lake, Illinois: Rigby Education, 1988. (nominal charge).

The Guided Reading lesson, where a group of children come together with the teacher's assistance to share their responses to a book, is expanded upon in a suggested sequence of six steps: planning the possibilities, setting the scene, reading the text, returning to the text, responding to the text, and sharing responses. Teachers will find the general discussion questions especially useful in this thorough, twenty-five page booklet.

● Butler, Andrea. "Shared Book Experience". Crystal Lake, Illinois: Rigby Education, 1987. (nominal charge).

Teachers will find this an extremely useful article for understanding the rationale and procedures of Shared Book Experience for younger and older children. A typical shared book session is described in detail. Step-by-step procedures are presented along with follow up activities and how to develop strategies and conventions of print.

Cohen, Dorothy H. "The Effect of Literature on Vocabulary and Reading Achievement". *Elementary English*. Vol. 45 (February 1968), pp. 209-213, 217.

This often-quoted study of low socio-economic second-graders who were read to daily demonstrated a significant increase in vocabulary and reading comprehension over a control group that were only read to occasionally or not at all.

● Deford, Diane. "Literacy: Reading, Writing, and Other Essentials". *Language Arts*. Vol. 58 (September 1980), pp. 157-162.

Deford's research clearly demonstrates how the reading

materials/instruction children receive influences their
writing development. The author calls for meaningful
programs that integrate the reading-writing processes and
encourage children to make explorations into literacy.

DiStefano, Philip P. and Patricia J. Hagerty. "Teaching spelling at
the elementary level: A realistic perspective". *The Reading
Teacher.* January 1985, pp. 373-377.

In place of a spelling series, the authors recommend a
spelling program that starts with invented spelling and
moves to using high frequency word lists and spelling by
meaning.

Durkin, Delores. "Testing in the Kindergarten". *The Reading
Teacher.* April 1987, pp. 766-770.

A year-long study of kindergarten programs revealed a
high emphasis on developmental and academic tests to
determine the instructional programs, and many of the
programs included "inordinate attention" to phonics;
". . . practically no evidence was found that any test was
given for the purpose of learning whether programs were
suitable. Instead, the children had to adapt to programs."

Goodman, Kenneth S. "Basal Readers: A Call for Action".
Language Arts. Vol. 63 (April 1986), pp. 358-363.

Goodman points out the knowledge gaps between present
research and learning theory relating to literacy development
and basal readers. "The current state of American basal
readers is unnecessary and intolerable. . ." Share this
powerful article with your administrators.

Goodman, Kenneth and Yetta Goodman. "Reading and Writing
Relationships: Pragmatic Functions." *Language Arts.* Vol.
60 (May 1983), pp. 590-599.

This article makes some important points concerning the
interrelationships between reading and writing in the
development of literacy in the young child and suggests the
kinds of personal and relevant writing experiences that need
to occur in the schools.

Graves, Donald and Jane Hansen. "The Author's Chair".
Language Arts. Vol. 60 (February 1983), pp. 176-183.

By becoming immersed in the writing-reading-publishing
cycle in the classroom, children develop a sense of

authorship. The Author's Chair, where children sit to read their own published books and trade books to the class, is symbolic of children's understanding of the author concept.

Hammond, W. Dorsey. "Common Questions on Reading Comprehension". *Learning*. Vol. 14 (January 1986), pp. 49-51.

   Through answers to questions posed by teachers, a reading professor discusses how to help students develop comprehension strategies through use of prior knowledge, reading for meaning, and effective questioning.

• Holdaway, Don. "Shared Book Experience: Teaching Reading Using Favorite Books". *Theory into Practice*. XXI, No. 4 (Autumn 1982), pp. 293-300.

   This excellent article gives the history, research, rationale, and procedures of "shared book experience" by the educator who helped develop it. Natural literacy learning and its application to classroom teaching is clearly discussed.

• Huck, Charlotte. "I Give You the End of a Golden String". *Theory into Practice*. XXI, No. 4 (Autumn 1982), pp. 315-321.

   Huck persuasively advocates using the power of literature — which develops children's imagination as well as their insights and understandings about themselves and the world — as the mainstay of all reading programs.

Koeller, Shirley. "25 Years Advocating Children's Literature in the Reading Program". *The Reading Teacher*. February 1981, pp. 552-556.

   Among other findings, Koeller, in reviewing past research studies, found that the amount of reading done by a student affects growth in reading as well as reading comprehension and attitudes.

• Milz, Vera. "First Graders Can Write: Focus on Communication". *Theory into Practice*, XIX, No. 3 (Summer 1980), pp. 179-185.

   Milz describes how she uses writing interactively with reading, speaking, and listening to foster whole language development in her first grade classroom and gives lots of useful information on how writing is used for meaningful communication.

Pearson, P. David. "Changing the Face of Reading Comprehension Instruction". *The Reading Teacher*. April 1985, pp. 724-738.

Using recent research, Pearson urges the necessity for changes in the way we ask questions, teach vocabulary, teach comprehension skills, view the role of the teacher, and use and choose materials. This important article calls for a reading comprehension model that is "active, constructive, and reader-based" as opposed to "passive, receptive, and text-based".

Rhodes, Lynn. "I Can Read! Predictable Books as Resources for Reading and Writing Instruction". *The Reading Teacher*. February 1981, pp. 511-518.

The characteristics of predictable books and specific examples of how to use them with beginning readers and writers are discussed. A useful bibiography of predictable books is included.

● Rich, Sharon. "Restoring Power to Teachers: The Impact of 'Whole Language'." *Language Arts*. Vol. 62 (November 1985), pp. 717-724.

This inspiring article describes what happens to teachers as they move towards a whole language approach and demonstrates what "whole language" means for the teacher and the child.

Russell, Connie. "Putting Research into Practice: Conferencing with Young Writers". *Language Arts*, Vol. 60 (March 1983), pp. 333-340.

A sixth grade teacher describes how she skeptically applied Lucy McCormick Calkins' methods to change the way she taught writing. This is a very helpful article for understanding how a teacher can bridge the gap between current research and actual classroom practice.

● Smith, Frank. "Demonstrations, Engagements, and Sensitivity: A Revised Approach to Language Learning". *Language Arts*. Vol. 58 (January 1981), pp. 103-112.

Smith discusses how we naturally learn the complex conventions of language unless certain contrived or instructional situations cause the brain not to learn. When the environment is set up for "demonstrations" (showing how something is done), "engagement" with a demonstration, and "sensitivity" (expecting learning to occur), the brain learns easily. (For a fuller discussion by the author, see *Writing and the Writer*.)

Squire, James R. "Composing and Comprehending: Two Sides of the Same Basic Process". *Language Arts*. Vol. 60 (May 1983), pp. 581-589.

In this scholarly article based on current research, the author argues for the importance of teaching composition and comprehension as interrelated, thinking processes as opposed to teaching isolated skills which do not promote language learning.

Stotsky, Sandra. "Research on Reading/Writing Relationships: A Synthesis and Suggested Directions". *Language Arts*. Vol. 60 (May 1983), pp. 627-642.

The author explores research studies that investigate the relationships between reading achievement and writing ability, the influence of writing upon reading, and the influence of reading upon writing. Among the findings are ". . . that reading experience may be as critical a factor in developing writing ability as writing instruction itself."

Valencia, Sheila and P. David Pearson. "Reading assessment. Time for a change." *The Reading Teacher*. April 1987, pp. 726-732.

Because reading assessment is not consistent with current reading theory, research, or practice, the authors convincingly argue not only for new tests but for ". . . a new framework for thinking about assessment ..." This article gives educators some direction for making changes in reading assessment.

Journals

Language Arts
8 issues per year/Subscription: $35.00 annually
National Council of Teachers of English (NCTE)
1111 Kenyon Road
Urbana, Illinois 61801

> This official journal of the National Council of Teachers of
> English contains well-written, literary articles in various
> formats on all areas of language and language learning. Each
> monthly journal is themed — addressing an issue in
> language arts education — and also contains reviews of
> children's and professional books as well as information,
> announcements, and publications from NCTE.
>
> NCTE sponsors an annual convention in late November
> ". . . to discuss issues currently affecting the profession"
> and a spring conference ". . . devoted to improving English
> and language arts instruction". State and local affiliates also
> sponsor meetings of interest to English/language arts
> teachers at all levels. Additionally, NCTE publishes *English
> Journal* (for junior and senior high school teachers), *College
> English,* and hundreds of professional publications for
> teachers.

The New Advocate
4 issues per year/Subscription: $25.00 annually
The New Advocate
P.O. Box 809
Needham Heights, MA 02194-0006

> This relatively new journal (first issue January 1988)
> advocates and gives suggestions for teaching with children's
> literature. The first issues included thought-provoking
> articles and interviews by and about well-known educators,
> children's writers, and illustrators as well as practical
> teaching ideas and book and media reviews, and important
> reflections on children's literature and reading.

• *The Reading Teacher*
9 issues per year/Subscription $30.00 annually
International Reading Association (IRA)
800 Barksdale Road
P.O. Box 8139
Newark, Delaware 19714-8139

This official elementary school journal of the International Reading Association deals with issues and ideas devoted to the improvement of reading instruction and promotion of reading. While research is sometimes included, this is mostly a very practical journal for teachers that includes teaching ideas and approaches as well as reviews of children's books, professional books, tests, and computer software. Subscribers also receive "Reading Today", a bimonthly newspaper on news and activities in the reading profession.

I.R.A. sponsors a national convention, a World Congress every two years that is held outside of North America, and state, local, and special conferences. I.R.A. also publishes the *Journal of Reading* (for secondary, college, and adult levels), the *Reading Research Quarterly* (for current reading research), and *Lectura Y Vida* (a Spanish-language journal). Additionally, I.R.A. publishes many books for teachers.

Newsletters

The Five Owls
published bi-monthly/Subscription $18.00 annually
The Five Owls, Inc.
2004 Sheridan Avenue South
Minneapolis, MN 55405

> This publication is intended ". . . for readers personally and professionally involved in children's literature." In-depth articles and features encourage and give lots of information on reading, literacy, and activities with books. A full section is devoted to reviews of books.

• *Teachers Networking: The Whole Language Newsletter*
4 issues per year/Subscription: $12 annually
Richard C. Owen Publishers, Inc.,
Rockefeller Center, Box 819
N.Y., N.Y., 10185

> Articles by leading whole language educators are featured along with recommended reviews of children's and professional literature, strategies for implementing whole language techniques in the classroom, and other issues of concern and interest to parents and educators. Teachers who want to feel connected to the whole language movement will want to read this newsletter.

•*The WEB: Wonderfully Exciting Books*
4 issues per year/ Subscription: $10 annually
The Web, Ohio State University College of Education
200 Ramseyer Hall, 29 West Woodruff
Columbus, Ohio 43210-1177

> Comprehensive current book reviews, including teaching ideas and group activities, are presented by teachers and librarians who have field tested the ideas. Teachers find the center spread in every issue, a teaching web focusing on activities built around a book or a theme, especially helpful for integrating the curriculum with literature.

The Whole Idea
4 issues per year/free of charge
The Wright Group
10949 Technology Place
San Diego, California 92127

    The purpose of this newsletter is to assist teachers who are becoming involved with whole language by presenting many ideas for process teaching. The publication also serves as an "idea exchange" for teachers.

Whole Language Newsletter
4 issues per year/Subscription: $7 annually
Whole Language
123 Newkirk Road
Richmond Hill, Ontario, CAN L4C 3G5

    The editor and professional educators — including teachers — talk about many aspects of whole language teaching including what it is, ideas and information for working with parents, professional and children's books, and many ideas for teaching. This is a well-done, supportive newsletter.

Writings in reading and language arts
Ginn Occasional Papers
free of charge
Ginn and Company
P.O. Box 2549
Columbus, Ohio 43216

    This series of about twenty papers by respected educators offers some valuable insights. Some notable papers (some are not) include: "Changing the Face of Reading Comprehension Instruction" by P. David Pearson (appeared first in *The Reading Teacher*, April 1985), "Asking Questions About Stories" by P. David Pearson, "Balanced Decoding and Comprehension in a Good Reading Program" by Roger W. Shuy, "Three Sound Strategies for Vocabulary Development" by Dale D. Johnson, and "Reading and Writing Revisited" by Roselmina Indrisana.

Literature Extension Activity Resources

Baskwill, Jane and Paulette Whitman. *Whole Language Sourcebook.* Ontario, Canada: Scholastic-TAB Publications Ltd., 1986.

This resource is written by two Canadian whole language teachers who developed the activities described as a guide for teachers of grades 1 and 2 (actually most useful for kindergarten and grade 1). The major focus is on thematic units which are organized around bears, monsters, farms, mice, rain, sea, space, dogs, houses, and frogs. Three ring notebook format so teacher can add to it. Well organized and very useful for specific guidelines and resources cited. Expensive.

Bosma, Bette. *Fairy Tales, Fables, Legends, and Myths.* New York: Teacher's College Press, 1987.

The teacher is given very specific and useful information for developing units on folk literature. The book is filled with lots of thoughtful teaching ideas that respect reading and writing as interactive processes.

Cochrane, Orin. (ed.) *Reading Experiences in Science.* Winnipeg: Peguis Publishers Limited, 1985.

A delightful set of eight booklets of about 16 pages each — Frogs, Apes, Beavers, Bees, Dinosaurs, Spiders, Whales, and Bats — can be used to tie literature and science together. Each booklet includes a poem and story about the animal, factual information, illustrations, "Reading with Minimal Clues" (a visual cloze activity), and a play, dramatization, or choral reading. Suitable for grades 2-4.

Cutting, Brian and Helen Depee. *Language is Fun. Teacher's Book* Level 1. San Diego: The Wright Group, 1987.

Geared to children up through first grade, this resource focuses on the theme "This is My Life" to develop language through varied oral and written language experiences in the classroom. While some of the activities go along with specific books in a reading series, most activities are applicable across the curriculum. Lots of workable ideas and extensions of literature are presented using a multimedia format. Particularly helpful are the many colorful illustrations and examples from New Zealand classrooms.

Dunn, Sonja with Lou Pamenter. *Butterscotch Dreams. Chants for Fun and Learning.* Portsmouth, New Hampshire: Heinemann Educational Books, Inc., 1987.

This short collection of original chants can be added to shared book experience to reinforce reading and enjoyable group participation through chanting — rhythmical reading. Some suggestions for movements, original patterns, puppets, drama, and music are also introduced with the chants.

Fox, Mem. *Teaching Drama to Young Children.* Portsmouth, New Hampshire: Heinemann Educational Books, Inc., 1987.

"I have written this book to show teachers how children learn through drama and play, and to give people who have never taken a drama lesson before the confidence to teach drama to youngsters." The book is arranged in five sections: song and dance, word families, the world around us, our community and where we live, and happenings. Lessons are clearly defined and well-organized with lots of practical, fun ideas to develop children's imagination, confidence, language, letter-sound knowledge, and general knowledge. Many tie-ins to favorite storybooks are included.

• Hopkins, Lee Bennett. *Pass the Poetry, Please!* Revised Edition. New York: Harper & Row, Publishers, 1987.

The author presents wonderful ideas to help incorporate poetry into the total curriculum. Guidelines and suggestions are presented for getting children to love poetry, for reading poetry aloud, and for "sparking" children to write various forms of poetry. One section of the book is devoted to acquainting children with about twenty notable poets; bibliographic profiles and poetry references are included for each poet. The final section, "A Potpourri of Poetry Ideas", gives many specific poetry-related activities. Appendixes include "Poetry Reflecting Contemporary Issues", "Poetry in Paperback: a Selected List", "Sources of Educational Materials...", and "Mother Goose Collections".

• Huck, Charlotte and Janet Hickman (eds.). *The Best of the Web.* Columbus: The Ohio State University, 1982.

This publication takes the six most often requested Webs from "The WEB", 1976-1982. Several selections included are "Learning to Read Naturally", "Folk and Fairy Tales", and "Sharing the Art of Picture Books". Book titles, reviews, and articles, along with "A Web of Possibilities", give teachers many activities grouped around a theme.

Johnson, Terry and Daphne Louis. *Literacy Through Literature.* Portsmouth, New Hampshire: Heinemann Educational Books, Inc., 1987.

The authors present many tried and original activities for developing skills and comprehension through literature. Some examples include the preparation and use of story maps, structured writing forms, literary report cards, literary journals, literary news reports, small group discussions, and dramatizations.

Koch, Kenneth. *Wishes, Lies, and Dreams: Teaching Children to Write Poetry.* New York: Harper & Row, Publishers, 1980.

Based on his experiences teaching New York City school children to write poetry, the author gives suggestions and guidelines to help children find their voice as poets. He believes that good teaching of poetry means allowing children to discover a natural talent they already have. The book is full of poems by children on some of the following: wishes, comparisons, noises, dreams, lies, colors, metaphors. "A poetry idea should be easy to understand, it should be immediately interesting, and it should bring something new into the children's poems." (p. 14)

McCaslin, Nellie. *Creative Drama in the Primary Grades.* New York: Longman Inc., 1987 (hardcover)

Teachers who feel insecure and inexperienced with the theater arts, but who realize the potential of creative dramatics, can use this practical handbook to bring movement, rhythm, pantomine, improvision, puppetry, story dramatization, and "possibilities in poetry" into the classroom. Each activity is clearly described and includes objectives and suggestions for the teacher. (There is also a handbook for grades 4, 5 and 6, *Creative Drama in the Intermediate Grades.*)

McCracken, Marlene and Robert. *Themes.* Winnipeg: Peguis Publishers Limited, 1984-1987.

Individualized activity books on various themes —Myself, Halloween, Animals, Fantasy, the Sea, Celebrations, Fall, Winter, and Spring — give the early primary teacher many ideas for integrating the language arts across the curriculum.

Manna, Anthony L. (ed.) "Drama and Language: Learning in Action." *English Language Arts Bulletin.* Ohio Council of Language Arts, Fall 1985. (Available through the National Council of Teachers of English)

A series of articles by respected educators demonstrates that active involvement through drama in the classroom can be used to enhance literature, language, communication, and the total curriculum by providing opportunities for expansion and growth in language, thinking, and social-personal development.

Massam, Joanne and Anne Kulik. *And What Else?* San Diego: The Wright Group, 1986.

A beautifully illustrated activity book (42 pages) visually demonstrates the classroom setting, shared experiences, and many possible literature extensions for very young readers. More pictures than text focus on the visual and creative arts.

Moss, Joy F. *Focus Units in Literature: A Handbook for Elementary School Teachers.* Urbana, Illinois: National Council of Teachers of English, 1984.

The author has developed "focus units" as expansive literary experiences for children. Each focus unit is clearly detailed around a theme and includes objectives, stories to read aloud, sample questions to guide comprehension, comparative study and analysis of stories and literary forms, books for independent reading, writing activities, and activities that include the creative arts. Focus units for grades 1 and 2 include: "Toy Animals", "Pig Tales", "The Night", "Friendship", "Heroes and Heroines", and author "Roger Duvoisin". There is a focus unit for grades 2 and 3 on "Giants" and units for grades 3 and 4 on "Folktale Patterns" and "Dragons". "The Sea" is a unit for grades 4 and 5, and "Japan" and "Survival Tales" are the focus units for grades 5 and 6. Questioning, as a strategy for teaching thinking, is rightfully given high priority. An entire chapter is devoted to "Guidelines for Questioning" and is particularly helpful for the kinds of questions that can promote comprehension and thinking. (Before we can expect students to ask good questions before, during, and after reading, we need to be able to model these questions ourselves.) This guidebook is extremely helpful for understanding what critical responding to literature means and for meaningfully extending a literature program.

Pied Piper Media. Glendale, California.

Quality filmstrips and videocassettes are available for favorite stories, authors, poems, and nonfiction. Many books are Newbery and Caldecott award favorites.

Prelutsky, Jack. (selected by) *The Random House Book of Poetry For Children*. New York: Random House, Inc., 1983.

A wonderful anthology of poems children delightedly respond to are separated by topics/themes such as "Nature Is", "The Four Seasons", "Dogs and Cats and Bears and Bats", "The Ways of Living Things", "Some People I Know", "Nonsense! Nonsense!", "Where Goblins Dwell", and others. The collection is illustrated by Arnold Lobel.

In the introduction, Prelutsky writes...

"I've begun to understand the kinds of poems to which children respond — poems that evoke laughter and delight, poems that cause a palpable ripple of surprise by the unexpected comparisons they make, poems that paint pictures with words that are as vivid as brushstrokes, poems that reawaken pleasure in the sounds and meanings of language."

Public Broadcasting Service and other instructional television stations.

Check with your librarian for times and listings of "Reading Rainbow", "Wonderworks", and other special programs and dramatizations for children.

Rhodes, Lynn, (ed.). *L.I.N.K.* (Language Instruction Natural to Kids). Lakewood, Colorado: The Language Company, 1986.

"Link Paks" have been developed as structured extensions for specific titles. A synopsis of the book is given along with activities for reading the book, reading other versions, sequencing, comparing, and writing. Most useful are other related books which can be used for comparison.

Roettger, Doris. *Reading Beyond the Basal*. Logan, Iowa: The Perfection Form Company, 1987.

Study guides and reproducible activity pages are included for 25 titles. While many of the activities are over-structured, the author information page and annotated bibliography of related books is very useful.

Roettger, Doris and Darrell Bentz (eds.) *Book Pros* Program.

Ankeny, Iowa: Heartland Educational Agency. 1986.

Teaching guides for selected novels are available by middle to upper elementary grade level. Each guide is divided into four sections: Before Reading, During Reading, After Reading, and The Web. There are some workable ideas for extensions following the reading of the book. Very few suggestions are given for guided reading discussion. Expensive.

Somers, Albert B. and Janet Evans Worthington. *Response Guides for Teaching Children's Books.* Urbana, Illinois: National Council of Teachers of English, 1984.

Response guides are provided for twenty-seven quality book titles for the elementary grades. Each guide is meant to be a very basic foundation only; it will need to be supplemented by the teacher. Among other topics for each book, there is a brief summary, discussion questions, activities involving the creative arts and dramatics, and instructional resources.

Tway, Eileen. *Writing is Reading: 26 Ways to Connect.* Urbana, Illinois: National Council of Teachers of English and ERIC Clearinghouse on Reading and Communication Skills, 1985.

A 48 page pamphlet ties reading and writing together with theory and research and uses the 26 letters of the alphabet to give specific teaching ideas with related books; A — alphabet books; B — bookmaking, C — character development, etc.

• Watson, Dorothy J. (ed.) *Ideas and Insights: Language Arts in the Elementary School.* Urbana, Illinois: National Council of Teachers of English, 1987.

This valuable resource book (244 pages) of meaningful teaching activities to promote whole language teaching and thinking is written by practicing teachers and educators and gives specific ideas for language arts activities such as author study, the use of journals, comparison of similar stories, thematic units with literature, examination of illustrations, biographies, extending literature across the curriculum, and all kinds of relevant writing activities. For teachers who say, "I'd like to use literature, but I don't know how and what activities to plan without workbooks and worksheets", this is a much-needed book. Along with the hundreds of activities are some useful bibliographies — wordless books, picture books, predictable books, sing-along books, children's magazines. Chapter 9 is full of suggestions for effectively communicating with parents and making them part of their child's learning process. Chapter 10 presents some useful forms of evaluation.

The one disadvantage I found to this book is that by using "The List of Teaching Activities..." at the end of the book (there is no index), you can't always tell what's included in this book. For example, in a section on "Extended Literature" in Chapter 2, *"Literature Points the Way"*, an activity titled "Friends Can Help" is listed, but it does not say that this is an activity based on *Amos and Boris* by William Steig. Where the activity listed is general, I have written in specific notations (as I was reading) for my own future reference.

Weston Woods. *Weston Woods Motion Pictures*. Weston, Connecticut.

These top quality motion pictures include animated versions of the best of children's books and may be booked for preview, rental or purchase. Check with your librarian for titles already available in your school.

Wuertenberg, Jacque. *Helping Children Become Writers at Home and At School*. Tulsa: Educational Progress, 1982.

Each page in this spiral bound books has three 3″ x 5″ index cards; the book is made to be taken apart and organized in a file box. While extensions described are quite brief, the teacher who likes lots of variety and visual samples will get some new ideas for illustrating, writing, and publishing based on specific book titles.

Videotapes

Butler, Andrea. A sequential four-part staff development series on Whole Language. Crystal Lake, Illinois: Rigby Education, 1987.

> Series consists of four videos, written handouts and reference reading. Titles of videos are:
> 1 "Conditions of natural learning".
> 2 "Application of these conditions to the classroom".
> 3 "Components of a Whole Language classroom".
> 4 "Shared book experience".
> Contact Rigby Education for purchase information.

Edelsky, Carol. "Theory and Practice in Two Meaning-Centered Classrooms." New York: Richard C. Owen Publishers, Inc., 1986.

> A tour of two meaning-centered classrooms is visually and mentally informative through interviews and discussions with an inner city sixth grade teacher and a suburban kindergarten teacher in Phoenix, Arizona. Available for rental or sale. Expensive.

Harste, Jerome. (developer). "The Authoring Cycle: Read Better, Write Better, Reason Better." Portsmouth, New Hampshire: Heinemann Educational Books, Inc., 1986.

> This series of eight programs on specific aspects of process writing balances theory and practice with well-known educators discussing writing amidst film footage from various primary classrooms. There are some valuable ideas for teachers new to writing process. Available for rental or purchase individually or as a series. Expensive.

Richard C. Owen Publishers, Inc. New York. "Horrakoptchkin", 1987.

> This video dicusses and describes the "Ready to Read" series, a "natural language text program" developed by the Department of Education in New Zealand. Although a specific program is being described, there is useful information and a good foundation for implementing literature. Available on loan free of charge.

Powell, Deborah A. (project director). "Relating Reading/Writing Theory to Practice in the Elementary and Middle Grades." Newark, Delaware: International Reading Association, 1988.

This is a complete staff development package of six video-cassettes, a participant's guide, and a leader's handbook. Teachers and administrators just beginning the reading-writing process approach will find the classroom examples and professional resources very valuable. Contact IRA for rental, purchase information.

17 Recommended Literature

Classified by Grade and Literary Style

- Recommended as a high priority book to have in your collection.
- ★ Suitable for very beginning readers.
- † Also available as a Big Book with enlarged print format.
- (c.o.p.) currently out of print.

Year listed is year of publication, or most recent reprint, as listed in *Paperbound Books in Print*, (New York: R. R. Bowker Company), spring 1987, and/or most recent publication/ reprint date from publisher and/or distributor.

For Beginning Readers

Rhyme, Rhythm and Repetition

●★ Ahlberg, Janet and Allen. *Each Peach Pear Plum*. New York: Scholastic Inc., 1985.

●★ Aliki. *Hush Little Baby*. Englewood Cliffs, New Jersey: Prentice-Hall, Inc., 1968.

●★† Allen, Pamela. *Who Sank the Boat?* Crystal Lake, Illinois: Rigby Education, 1987.

●★† Arno, Ed. *The Gingerbread Man*. New York: Scholastic Inc., 1985. (c.o.p.)

●★ Barchas, Sarah. *I Was Walking Down the Road*. New York: Scholastic Inc., 1988.

★ Becker, John. *Seven Little Rabbits*. New York: Scholastic Inc., 1985.

●★† Bonne, Rose. *I Know An Old Lady*. New York: Scholastic Inc., 1985.

●★ Brown, Margaret Wise. *Goodnight Moon*. New York: Harper & Row, Publishers, 1984.

Brown, Margaret Wise. *Where Have You Been?* New York: Scholastic Inc., 1986.

●★† Cairns, Scharlaine, *Oh No!* Crystal Lake, Illinois: Rigby Education, 1987.

★ Cauley, Lorinda Bryan (Illus.). *The Three Little Kittens*. New York: G. P. Putnam's Sons, 1987.

★ Cowley, Joy. *The Jigaree*. San Diego: The Wright Group, 1987.

●★† Cowley, Joy. *Mrs. Wishy-Washy*. San Diego: The Wright Group, 1987.

● Fox, Mem. *Arabella the Smallest Girl in the World*. New York: Scholastic Inc., 1987.

★ Ginsburg, Mirra. *Across the Stream*. New York: Penguin Books (Puffin Books), 1985.

★ Goss, Janet L. and Jerome Harste. *It Didn't Frighten Me!* New York: Scholastic Inc., 1988.

★† Green, Robyn; Pollock, Yevonne and Bronwen Scarffe. *When Goldilocks Went to the House of the Bears*. New York: Scholastic Inc., 1987.

●★ Kraus, Robert. *Whose Mouse Are You?* New York: Macmillan Publishing Co. (Aladdin Books), 1972.

★ Langstaff, John. *Frog Went A-Courtin'.* New York: Harcourt Brace Jovanovich, Publishers, 1972.

●★ Langstaff, John. *Over in the Meadow.* New York: Harcourt Brace Jovanovich, Publishers, 1973.

●★† Littledale, Freya. *The Magic Fish.* New York: Scholastic Inc., 1986.

●★† Martin, Bill, Jr. *Brown Bear, Brown Bear, What Do You See?* Toronto: Holt, Reinhart & Winston, Inc., 1982.

●★† Martin, Bill, Jr. *Fire! Fire! Said Mrs. McGuire.* Toronto: Holt, Rinehart & Winston, Inc., 1982.

★† Martin, Bill, Jr. *Monday, Monday, I Like Monday.* Toronto: Holt, Rinehart & Winston, Inc., 1983.

●★† Melser, June and Joy Cowley. *Grandpa, Grandpa.* San Diego: The Wright Group, 1987.

●★ Melser, June and Joy Cowley. *Hairy Bear.* San Diego: The Wright Group, 1987.

★† Melser, June and Joy Cowley. *Yes Ma'am.* San Diego: The Wright Group, 1987.

★† Parkes, Brenda and Judith Smith. (retold by) *The Three Little Pigs.* Crystal Lake, Illinois: Rigby Education, 1986.

●★† Parkes, Brenda. *Who's in the Shed?* Crystal Lake, Illinois: Rigby Education, 1986.

★ Patrick, Gloria. *A Bug in a Jug and Other Funny Rhymes.* New York: Scholastic Inc., 1981. (c.o.p.)

●† Sendak, Maurice. *Chicken Soup with Rice: A Book of Months.* New York: Scholastic Inc., 1986.

● Sendak, Maurice. *Pierre, a Cautionary Tale.* New York: Scholastic Inc., 1983. (c.o.p.)

★ Sendak, Maurice. *Seven Little Monsters.* New York: Harper & Row, Publishers, 1977.

●★† Wells, Rosemary. *Noisy Nora.* New York: Scholastic. Inc., 1986.

Rhyme

Buckley, Richard. *The Greedy Python.* Natick, Massachussetts: Picture Book Studio USA, 1985.

Cameron, Polly. *I Can't Said the Ant.* New York: Scholastic Inc., 1981. (c.o.p.)

★ Causley, Charles. *"Quack" Said the Billy Goat.* New York: Harper & Row, Publishers, 1986.

Child, Lydia Maria. *Over the River and Through the Wood.* New York: Scholastic Inc., 1987.

Craft, Ruth and Erik Blegrad. *The Winter Bear.* New York: Macmillan Publishing Company (Aladdin Books), 1979.

de Paola, Tomie. *The Comic Adventures of Old Mother Hubbard and Her Dog.* New York: Harcourt Brace Jovanovich, Publishers, 1981.

● de Regniers, Beatrice Schenk. *May I Bring a Friend?* New York: Macmillan Publishing Company (Aladdin Books), 1974.

● de Regniers, Beatrice Schenk. *Red Riding Hood.* New York: Macmillan Publishing Company (Aladdin Books), 1977.

Eichenberg, Fritz. *Ape in a Cape. An Alphabet of Odd Animals.* New York: Harcourt Brace Jovanovich, Publishers, 1973.

★ Einsel, Walter. *Did You Ever See?* New York: Scholastic Inc., 1980. (c.o.p.)

★ Gag, Wanda. *The ABC Bunny.* New York: Putnam Publishing Group, 1978.

●★† Gardner, Majory, et al. (Illus.) *Time for a Rhyme.* Crystal Lake, Illinois: Rigby Education, 1987.

●★ Gelman, Rita Golden. *The Biggest Sandwich Ever.* New York: Scholastic Inc., 1984. (c.o.p.)

★† Gelman, Rita Golden. *Cats and Mice.* New York: Scholastic Inc., 1985.

★ Gelman, Rita Golden. *Leave it to Minnie.* New York: Scholastic Inc., 1987.

●★† Gelman, Rita Golden. *More Spaghetti I Say.* New York: Scholastic Inc., 1987.

Gelman, Rita Golden. *Mortimer K. Saves the Day.* New York: Scholastic Inc., 1985. (c.o.p.)

Gelman, Rita Golden. *Pets for Sale.* New York: Scholastic Inc., 1986.

★† Gelman, Rita Golden. *Why Can't I Fly?* New York: Scholastic Inc., 1986.

●★† Glusac, Randy et al. (Illus.) *Time for a Number Rhyme.* Crystal Lake, Illinois: Rigby Education, 1987.

★ Hayes, Sarah. *This is the Bear.* New York: Harper & Row, Publishers, 1986.

★ Kraus, Robert. *Ladybug, Ladybug.* New York: E. P. Dutton (Windmill Books), 1957. (c.o.p.)

★ Krauss, Ruth. *Bears.* New York: Scholastic Inc., 1985. (c.o.p.)

★ Lear, Edward. *The Owl and the Pussycat.* New York: Putnam Publishing Group, 1986 and New York: Scholastic Inc., 1986.

Lord, John Vernon. *The Giant Jam Sandwich.* Boston: Houghton Mifflin Company, 1987.

★ Lüton, Mildred. *Little Chicks' Mothers and All the Others.* New York: Penguin Books (Puffin Books), 1985.

★ Mark, Jan. *Fur.* New York: Harper & Row, Publishers, 1986.

† Martin, Bill, Jr. *The Happy Hippopotami.* Toronto: Holt, Rinehart & Winston, Inc., 1983.

★† Melser, June and Joy Cowley. *Boo-hoo.* San Diego: The Wright Group, 1987.

★† Melser, June and Joy Cowley. *Obadiah.* San Diego: The Wright Group, 1987.

★† Melser, June and Joy Cowley. *Poor Old Polly.* San Diego: The Wright Group, 1987.

★† Melser, June and Joy Cowley. *Woosh!* San Diego: The Wright Group, 1987.

● O'Neill, Mary. *Hailstones and Halibut Bones. Adventures in Color.* New York: Doubleday & Company Inc., 1961.

● Orbach, Ruth. *Apple Pigs.* New York: Putnam Publishing Group (Philomel Books), 1981.

● Slepian, Jan and Ann Seidler. *The Hungry Thing.* New York: Scholastic Inc., 1980. (c.o.p.)

★† Smith, Judith and Brenda Parkes. *Gobble Gobble Glup Glup.* Crystal Lake, Illinois: Rigby Education, 1986.

Zolotow, Charlotte. *The Hating Book.* New York: Scholastic Inc., 1980. (c.o.p.)

Repetition

Asch, Frank. *Happy Birthday, Moon.* New York: Scholastic Inc., 1982.

★ Baum, Arline and Joseph. *one bright Monday morning.* New York: Knopf Pantheon, 1973. (c.o.p.)

Brandenberg, Franz. *I Wish I Was Sick, Too!* New York: Penguin Books (Puffin Books), 1982.

●★ Brown, Margaret Wise. *The Runaway Bunny.* New York: Harper & Row, Publishers, 1977.

★ Brown, Ruth. *A Dark, Dark Tale.* New York: Dial Books for Young Readers, 1984.

●★ Carle, Eric. *The Very Hungry Caterpillar.* New York: Scholastic Inc., 1987

●★† Chase, Edith Newlin. *The New Baby Calf.* New York: Scholastic Inc., 1984.

Clarke, Mollie. *Congo Boy: An African Folk Tale.* New York: Scholastic Inc., 1965.

●★† Cowley, Joy. *Greedy Cat*. New York: Richard C. Owen Publishers, Inc., 1988.

★† Cowley, Joy. *Meanies*. San Diego: The Wright Group, 1987.

★† Cowley, Joy. *Number One*. New York: Richard C. Owen Publishers, Inc., 1987.

★ Cowley, Joy. *Old Tuatara*. New York: Richard C. Owen Publishers, Inc., 1987.

★ Cowley, Joy. *The Red Rose*. San Diego: The Wright Group, 1987.

★ Cutts, David. *The House that Jack Built*. Mahwah, N. J.: Troll Associates, 1979.

Ets, Marie Hall. *Just Me*. New York: Penguin Books (Puffin Books), 1978.

★ Ets, Marie Hall. *Play With Me*. New York: Penguin Books (Puffin Books), 1983.

★ Flack, Marjorie. *Ask Mr. Bear*. New York: Macmillan Publishing Company. (Aladdin Books), 1986.

Gag, Wanda. *Millions of Cats*. New York: Putnam Publishing Group, 1977.

● Galdone, Paul. *The Gingerbread Boy*. Boston: Houghton Mifflin Company, 1985.

★ Galdone, Paul. *Henny Penny*. Boston: Houghton Mifflin Company, 1984.

● Galdone, Paul. *The Little Red Hen*. Boston: Houghton Mifflin Company, 1985.

●★ Galdone, Paul. *The Three Bears*. New York: Scholastic Inc., 1984.

●★ Galdone, Paul. *The Three Billy Goats Gruff*. Boston: Houghton Mifflin Company, 1981.

★ Gomi, Taro. *Coco Can't Wait*. New York: Penguin Books (Puffin Books), 1985. (c.o.p.)

★ Graboff, Abner. *Old MacDonald Had A Farm*. New York: Scholastic Inc., 1985.

●★ Guilfoile, Elizabeth. *Nobody Listens to Andrew*. New York: Scholastic Inc., 1973.

●† Handy, Libby. *Boss for a Week*. New York: Scholastic Inc., 1982.

Heide, Florence Parry and Sylvia Van Clief. *That's What Friends Are For*. New York: Scholastic Inc., 1971. (c.o.p.)

★ Hutchins, Pat. *Don't Forget the Bacon*. New York: Penguin Books (Puffin Books), 1978. (c.o.p.)

●★ Hutchins, Pat. *The Doorbell Rang*. New York: Scholastic Inc., 1987.

★ Hutchins, Pat. *Happy Birthday, Sam*. New York: Penguin Books (Puffin Books), 1985.

★ Hutchins, Pat. *1 Hunter*. New York: William Morrow & Co. (Mulberry Books), 1986.

★ Hutchins, Pat. *You'll Soon Grow Into Them, Titch*. New York: Penguin Books (Puffin Books), 1985.

●★ Kent, Jack. *The Fat Cat*. New York: Scholastic Inc., 1987.

●★ Krauss, Ruth. *The Carrot Seed*. New York: Scholastic Inc., 1984. (c.o.p.)

★ Krauss, Ruth. *The Happy Egg*. New York: Scholastic Inc., 1983. (c.o.p.)

Kuskin, Karla. *Just Like Everyone Else*. New York: Harper & Row, Publishers, 1982.

★ Kwitz, Mary DeBall. *Little Chick's Story*. New York: Scholastic Inc., 1983.

● Lobel, Arnold. *A Treeful of Pigs*. New York: Scholastic Inc., 1981. (c.o.p.)

●★ Long, Earlene. *Gone Fishing*. Boston: Houghton Mifflin Company (Sandpiper Books), 1987.

● McGovern, Ann. *Stone Soup*. New York: Scholastic Inc., 1986.

●★ McGovern, Ann. *Too Much Noise*. New York: Scholastic Inc., 1984.

●★ Mayer, Mercer. *If I Had*. New York: Dial Books for Young Readers, 1977.

★† Melser, June and Joy Cowley. *The Big Toe*. San Diego: The Wright Group, 1987.

●★† Melser, June and Joy Cowley. *In a Dark Dark Wood*. San Diego: The Wright Group, 1987.

★† Melser, June and Joy Cowley. *Lazy Mary*. San Diego: The Wright Group, 1987.

★† Melser, June and Joy Cowley. *One Cold Wet Night*. San Diego: The Wright Group, 1987.

★† Melser, June and Joy Cowley. *Sing A Song.* San Diego: The Wright Group, 1987.

Merriam, Eve. *Do You Want to See Something?* New York: Scholastic Inc., 1965. (c.o.p.)

●† Morris, William Barrett. *The Longest Journey in the World.* Toronto: Holt, Reinhart & Winston, Inc., 1982.

● Most, Bernard. *If the Dinosaurs Came Back.* New York: Harcourt Brace Jovanovich, Publishers, 1984.

★† Parkes, Brenda and Judith Smith. (retold by) *The Gingerbread Man.* Crystal Lake, Illinois: Rigby Education, 1986.

●★† Parkes, Brenda and Judith Smith. (retold by) *The Enormous Watermelon.* Crystal Lake, Illinois: Rigby Education, 1986.

★† Parkes, Brenda and Judith Smith. (retold by) *The Little Red Hen.* Crystal Lake, Illinois: Rigby Education, 1985.

★† Parkes, Brenda and Judith Smith. (retold by) *The Three Little Pigs.* Crystal Lake, Illinois: Rigby Education, 1985.

Pienkowski, Jan. *Dinnertime.* London: Gallery Five Ltd., 1981 and Los Angeles: Price/Stern/Sioan Publishers, 1981.

Preston, Edna M. *The Temper Tantrum Book.* New York: Penguin Books (Puffin Books), 1976.

● Rose, Anne. *Akimba and the Magic Cow.* New York: Scholastic Inc., 1981. (c.o.p.)

★ Ruwe, Mike. *Ten Little Bears.* (Reading Unlimited Program) Glenville, Illinois: Scott, Foresman and Co., 1976. (c.o.p.)

★† Smith, Judith and Brenda Parkes. (retold by) *The Three Billy Goats Gruff.* Crystal Lake, Illinois: Rigby Education, 1986.

Sueling, Barbara. *The Teeny, Tiny Woman: An Old English Ghost Tale.* New York: Penguin Books (Puffin Books), 1978. (c.o.p.)

★ Shulevitz, Uri. *One Monday Morning.* New York: Macmillan Publishing Company (Alladin Books), 1986.

●† Slobodkina, Esphyr. *Caps for Sale.* New York: Scholastic Inc., 1984.

Sonneborn, Ruth A. *Someone Is Eating the Sun.* New York: Random House, Inc., 1974. (c.o.p.)

★ Szeghy, Joe. *The Lion's Tail.* (Reading Unlimited Program) Glenview, Illinois: Scott, Foresman and Company, 1976. (c.o.p.)

★ Tafuri Nancy. *Have You Seen My Duckling?* New York: Penguin Books (Puffin Books), 1986.

Tolstoy, Alexei and Helen Oxenbury. *The Great Big Enormous Turnip.* London, England: Pan Books, Ltd. (Piccolo Picture Books), 1983. (c.o.p.)

Viorst, Judith. *The Tenth Good Thing About Barney.* New York: Macmillan Publishing Company (Aladdin Books), 1975.

●★ Wagner, Justin. *The Bus Ride.* (Reading Unlimited Program) Glenview Illinois: Scott, Foresman & Company, 1976. (c.o.p.)

★ West, Colin. *Have You Seen the Crocodile?* New York: Harper & Row, Publishers, 1986.

★ West, Colin. *"Pardon?" Said the Giraffe.* New York: Harper & Row, Publishers, 1986.

★ Wildsmith, Brian. *All Fall Down.* Toronto: Oxford University Press, 1985.

★ Wildsmith, Brian. *Cat on the Mat.* Toronto: Oxford University Press, 1986.

★ Wildsmith, Brian. *Giddy Up.* Toronto: Oxford University Press, 1987.

★ Wildsmith, Brian. *If I Were You.* Toronto: Oxford University Press, 1987.

★ Wildsmith, Brian. *The Island.* Toronto: Oxford University Press, 1984.

★ Wildsmith, Brian. *Toot, Toot.* Toronto: Oxford University Press, 1985.

★ Wildsmith, Brian. *What a Tale.* Toronto: Oxford University Press, 1986.

★   Wood, Leslie. *Bump, Bump, Bump.* Toronto: Oxford University Press, 1986.
★   Wood, Leslie. *A Dog Called Mischief.* Toronto: Oxford University Press, 1985.

Predictability and High Interest

Alexander, Martha. *Nobody Asked Me If I Wanted a Baby Sister.* New York: Dial Books for Young Readers, 1981.

Alexander, Martha. *When the New Baby Comes, I'm Moving Out.* New York: Dial Books for Young Readers, 1981.

Aliki. *We are Best Friends.* New York: William Morrow & Co. (Mulberry Books), 1987.

• Asch, Frank. *Turtle Tale.* New York: Dial Books for Young Readers, 1980.

•★ Barchas, Sarah. *Janie and the Giant.* New York: Scholastic Inc., 1978. (c.o.p.)

Barrett, Judi. *Animals should definitely **not** act like people.* New York: Macmillan Publishing Company (Aladdin Books), 1980.

Barrett, Judi. *Animals should definitely **not** wear clothing.* New York: Macmillan Publishing Company (Aladdin Books), 1980.

★   Barton, Byron. *Buzz, Buzz, Buzz.* New York: Penguin Books (Puffin Books), 1985. (c.o.p.)

Bate, Lucy. *Little Rabbit's Loose Tooth.* New York: Scholastic Inc., 1984.

★   Bauer, Caroline Feller. *My Mom Travels a Lot.* New York: Penguin Books (Puffin Books), 1985.

Benchley, Nathaniel. *Red Fox and His Canoe.* New York: Harper & Row, Publishers, 1985.

• Bishop, Claire Huckey and Kurt Wiese. *The Five Chinese Brothers.* New York: Scholastic Inc., 1982. (c.o.p.)

Blance, Ellen and Ann Cook. *Monster Books.* Series I & II. Glendale, CA: Bowmar Noble Publishers, 1981.

• Bridwell, Norman. *Clifford Books.* New York: Scholastic Inc., 1984-1986.

† Bridwell, Norman. *Clifford's Family.* New York: Scholastic, Inc., 1985.

Bridwell, Norman. *Crazy Zoo.* New York: Scholastic Inc., 1980. (c.o.p.)

Bridwell, Norman, *Kangaroo Stew.* New York: Scholastic Inc., 1984. (c.o.p.)

Bridwell, Norman. *A Tiny Family.* New York: Scholastic Inc., 1980.

Brown, Marc. *Arthur Books.* New York: Avon Books and Boston: Little, Brown and Company, 1979-1986.

• Bulla, Clyde Robert. *Daniel's Duck.* New York: Harper & Row, Publishers, 1982.

Byars, Betsy. *Go and Hush the Baby.* New York: Penguin Books (Puffin Books), 1982.

Caines, Jeanette. *Just Us Women.* New York: Harper & Row, Publishers, 1984.

•★ Carle, Eric. *The Secret Birthday Message.* New York: Harper & Row, Publishers, 1986.

• Carlson, Nancy. *Harriet Books.* New York: Penguin Books (Puffin Books), 1985.

Cohen, Miriam. *Best Friends.* New York: Macmillan Publishing Company, 1976.

Cohen, Miriam. *The New Teacher.* New York: Macmillan Publishing Company, 1974.

Cohen, Miriam. *Will I Have a Friend?* New York: Macmillan Publishing Company, 1971.

Cook, Ann and Herb Mack. *Robot Books.* New York: Dell Publishing Co., 1982.

Cooney, Nancy Evans. *The Blanket That Had to Go.* New York: Putman Publishing Group, 1981.

★   Crews, Donald. *School Bus.* New York: Penguin Books (Puffin Books), 1987.

Delton, Judy. *Two Good Friends.* New York: Crown Publishers, Inc., 1986.

●   de Paola, Tomie. *Bill and Pete.* New York: Putnam Publishing Group, 1978.

●   de Paola, Tomie. *Oliver Button is a Sissy.* New York: Harcourt Brace Jovanovich, 1979.

Elkin, Benjamin. *Six Foolish Fisherman.* New York: Scholastic Inc., 1984.

●   Elting, Mary and Michael Folson. *Q is for Duck: An Alphabet Guessing Game.* New York: Clarion Books, 1980.

●   Freeman, Don. *Corduroy.* New York: Penguin Books (Puffin Books), 1983.

Freeman, Don. *Dandelion.* New York: Penguin Books (Puffin Books), 1977.

●★ Friskey, Margaret. *Indian Two Feet and His Horse.* New York: Scholastic Inc., 1984. (c.o.p.)

●   Galdone, Paul. *The Three Little Pigs.* Boston: Houghton Mifflin Company, 1984.

Giff, Patricia Reilly. *Today was a Terrible Day.* New York: Penguin Books (Puffin Books), 1980.

★   Ginsburg, Mirra. *Good Morning Chick.* New York: Scholastic Inc., 1980. (c.o.p.)

★   Ginsburg, Mirra. *Where Does the Sun Go At Night?* New York: William Morrow and Company, Inc., (Mulberry Books), 1987.

Graham, John. *I Love You Mouse.* New York: Harcourt Brace Jovanovich, Publishers, 1978.

Graham, Margaret Bloy. *Harry the Dirty Dog.* New York: Harper & Row, Publishers, 1976. (c.o.p.)

Hargreaves, Roger. *"Mr. Men"* Books. Los Angeles: Price/Stern/Sloan Publishers, 1982.

Hazen, Barbara Shook. *The Gorilla Did It.* New York: Macmillan Publishing Company (Aladdin Books), 1978.

●   Hazen, Barbara Shook. *Tight Times.* New York: Penguin Books (Puffin Books), 1983.

●   Hoban, Lillian. *Arthur's Honey Bear.* New York: Harper & Row, Publishers, 1982.

Hoban, Lillian. *Arthur's Prize Reader.* New York: Harper & Row, Publishers, 1984.

●   Hoban, Russell. *Frances* Books. New York: Harper & Row, Publishers, 1976.

Hoff, Syd. *Danny and the Dinosaur.* New York: Harper & Row, Publishers, 1978.

●★† Hutchins, Pat. *Rosie's Walk.* New York: Scholastic Inc., 1987.

●★ Hutchins, Pat. *Titch.* New York: Penguin Books (Puffin Books), 1985.

Johnson, Crockett. *Harold* Books. New York: Harper & Row, Publishers, 1981.

Jonas, Ann. *Round Trip.* New York: Scholastic Inc., 1985.

★   Jonas, Ann. *When You Were A Baby.* New York: Penguin Books (Puffin Books), 1986.

★   Joyce, William. *George Shrinks.* New York: Harper & Row, Publishers, 1987.

Keats, Ezra Jack. *Louie.* New York: Scholastic Inc., 1983. (c.o.p.)

Keats, Ezra Jack. *Peter's Chair.* New York: Harper & Row, Publishers, 1983.

●   Keats, Ezra Jack. *The Snowy Day.* New York: Scholastic Inc., 1987.

Keats, Ezra Jack. *The Trip.* New York: William Morrow & Co. (Mulberry Books), 1987.

Keats, Ezra Jack. *Whistle for Willie.* New York: Penguin Books (Puffin Books), 1977.

Kellogg, Steven. *Can I Keep Him?* New York: Dial Books for Young Readers, 1976.

- Kent, Jack. *There's No Such Thing as a Dragon.* New York: Western Publishing Co. (Golden Press), 1975.

  Kessler, Ethel and Leonard. *What's Inside the Box?* New York: Scholastic Inc., 1976. (c.o.p.)

  Klein, Lenore. *Brave Daniel.* New York: Scholastic Inc., 1980. (c.o.p.)

★ Klein, Lenore. *Silly Sam.* New York: Scholastic Inc., 1969. (c.o.p.)

  Krasilovsky, Phyllis. *The Man Who Didn't Wash His Dishes.* New York: Scholastic Inc., 1982. (c.o.p.)

  Kraus, Robert. *Leo the Late Bloomer.* New York: Windmill Books, 1971. (c.o.p.)

  Kraus, Robert. *The Littlest Rabbit.* New York: Scholastic Inc., 1982. (c.o.p.)

- Littledale, Freya. *The Boy Who Cried Wolf.* New York: Scholastic Inc., 1986.

  Littledale, Freya. *The Snow Child.* New York: Scholastic Inc., 1986.

- Littledale, Freya. *Snow White and the Seven Dwarfs.* New York: Scholastic Inc., 1987.

- Lobel, Arnold. *Frog and Toad* Books. New York: Harper & Row, Publishers, 1979, 1981 and New York: Scholastic Inc., 1983-1985.

  Lobel, Arnold. *How the Rooster Saved the Day.* New York: Penguin Books (Puffin Books), 1981. (c.o.p.)

- Lobel, Arnold. *Mouse Soup.* New York: Harper & Row, Publishers, 1986.

- Lobel, Arnold. *Mouse Tales.* New York: Harper & Row, Publishers, 1978.

  Lobel, Arnold. *Owl at Home.* New York: Harper & Row, Publishers, 1987.

  Lobel, Arnold. *Small Pig.* New York: Harper & Row, Publishers, 1976. (c.o.p.)

  Lobel, Arnold. *Uncle Elephant.* New York: Scholastic Inc., 1986.

  Logan, Dick. *Thunder-the Dinosaur* Books. Glendale, CA: Cypress Publishing Corp., 1977.

  McPhail, David. *The Bear's Toothache.* New York: Penguin Books (Puffin Books), 1986.

  Margolis, Richard J. *Big Bear, Spare That Tree.* New York: Scholastic Inc., 1980. (c.o.p.)

- Marshall, James. *George and Martha* Books. Boston: Houghton Mifflin Company (Sandpiper Books), 1982.

★ Mayer, Mercer. *Just Me and My Dad.* New York: Western Publishing Co. (Golden Press), 1977.

●★ Mayer, Mercer. *There's a Nightmare in My Closet.* New York: Dial Books for Young Readers, 1976.

  Miles, Miska. *Small Rabbit.* New York: Scholastic Inc., 1977. (c.o.p.)

- Minarik, Else Holmelund. *Little Bear* Books. New York: Harper & Row, Publishers, 1979.

  Murphy, Jill. *Peace at Last.* New York: Dial Books for Young Readers, 1982.

  Myers, Bernice. *My Mother is Lost.* New York: Scholastic Inc., 1987.

★† Noodles. *How to Catch a Ghost.* Toronto: Holt, Rinehart and Winston, Inc., 1983.

  Parish, Peggy. *Too Many Rabbits.* New York: Scholastic Inc., 1985. (c.o.p.)

★ Peppe, Rodney. *Odd One Out.* New York: Penguin Books (Puffin Books), 1975. (c.o.p.)

  Piper, Watty. *The Little Engine That Could.* New York: Scholastic Inc., 1985.

  Rey, Margaret. *Pretzel.* New York: Harper & Row, Publishers, 1984.

  Rice, Eve. *Ebbie.* New York: Penguin Books (Puffin Books), 1978. (c.o.p.)

★ Rice, Eve. *Goodnight, Goodnight.* New York: Penguin Books (Puffin Books), 1983.

  Rice, Eve. *New Blue Shoes.* New York: Penguin Books (Puffin Books), 1983.

  Rice, Eve. *Oh, Lewis!* New York: Penguin Books (Puffin Books), 1979. (c.o.p.)

  Rice, Eve. *Sam Who Never Forgets.* New York: William Morrow & Co. (Mulberry Books), 1987.

★ Robison, Deborah. *Anthony's Hat.* New York: Scholastic Inc., 1980. (c.o.p.)

† Rose, Gerald. *Trouble in the Ark.* New York: Scholastic Inc., 1984. (c.o.p.)

● Sendak, Maurice. *Where the Wild Things Are.* New York: Harper & Row, Publishers, 1984.

Sharmat, Marjorie Weinman. *I Don't Care.* New York: Dell Publishing Co., 1977. (c.o.p.)

Slepian, Jan and Ann Seidler. *The Cat Who Wore a Pot on Her Head.* New York: Scholastic Inc. 1987.

Stevens, Carla. *Hooray for Pig.* New York: Scholastic Inc., 1984. (c.o.p.)

Stevenson, James. *Could Be Worse!* New York: Penguin Books (Puffin Books), 1979.

● Tarcov, Edith. (retold by). *Rumpelstiltskin.* New York: Scholastic Inc., 1973.

● Thaler, Mike. *A Hippopotamus Ate the Teacher.* New York: Avon Books (Camelot Books), 1981.

Thaler, Mike. *There's a Hippopotamus Under My Bed.* New York: Avon Books (Camelot Books), 1978.

● Viorst, Judith. *Alexander and the Terrible, Horrible, No Good, Very Bad Day.* New York: Macmillan Publishing Company (Aladdin Books), 1976.

● Viorst, Judith. *I'll Fix Anthony.* New York: Macmillan Publishing Company (Aladdin Books), 1983.

Viorst, Judith. *My Mama Says There Aren't Any Zombies, Ghosts, Vampires, Creatures, and Demons.* New York: Macmillan Publishing Company (Aladdin Books), 1977.

● Waber, Bernard. *Ira Sleeps Over.* Boston: Houghton Mifflin Company (Sandpiper Books), 1975 and New York: Scholastic Inc., 1984.

● Wagner, Jenny. *John Brown, Rose and the Midnight Cat.* New York: Penguin Books (Puffin Books), 1986.

● Weiss, Leatie. *Heather's Feathers.* New York: Avon Books (Camelot Books), 1978.

Wells, Rosemary. *Benjamin and Tulip.* New York: Dial Books for Young Readers, 1980.

★ Wildsmith, Brian. *My Dream.* Toronto: Oxford University Press, 1986.

★ Wood, Leslie. *The Frog and the Fly.* Toronto: Oxford University Press, 1985.

★ Wood, Leslie. *Tom and his Tractor.* Toronto: Oxford University Press, 1986.

Zolotow, Charlotte. *Mr. Rabbit and the Lovely Present.* New York: Harper & Row, Publishers, 1977.

For Grade 2

Aardema, Vera. *Why Mosquitoes Buzz in People's Ears.* New York: Dial Books for Young Readers, 1978.

Aliki. *The Two of Them.* New York: William Morrow & Co. (Mulberry Books), 1987.

Andersen, Hans Christian. *The Ugly Duckling.* New York: Scholastic Inc., 1987 and New York: Macmillan Publishing Company (Aladdin Books), 1987.

Andersen, Hans Christian. *The Snow Queen.* New York: Atheneum, 1986.

● Arkhurst, Joyce Cooper. *The Adventures of Spider.* New York: Scholastic Inc., 1987.

Arkhurst, Joyce Cooper. *More Adventures of Spider.* New York: Scholastic Inc., 1987.

Babbitt, Natalie. *The Something.* New York: Farrar, Strauss, & Giroux, 1987.

● Bang, Molly. *The Paper Crane.* New York: William Morrow and Co. (Mulberry Books), 1987.

Barrett, Judi. *A Snake is Totally Tail.* New York: Macmillan Publishing Company (Aladdin Books), 1987.

• Blume, Judy. *The Pain and The Great One.* New York: Dell Publishing Co., Inc., 1985.

Brinckloe, Julie. *Fireflies!* New York: Macmillan Publishing Company (Aladdin Books), 1986.

Brown, Marcia. *Cinderella.* New York: Macmillan Publishing Company (Aladdin Books), 1981.

Bulla, Clyde R. *A Lion to Guard Us.* New York: Thomas Y. Crowell Co., Inc., 1981. (c.o.p.)

• Bulla, Clyde R. *The Shoeshine Girl.* New York: Scholastic Inc., 1975. (c.o.p.)

Calhoun, Mary. *Cross-Country Cat.* New York: William Morrow & Co. (Mulberry Books), 1986.

• Carrick, Carol. *The Accident.* Boston: Houghton Mifflin Company (Clarion Books), 1976.

Carrick, Carol. *Ben and the Porcupine.* Boston: Houghton Mifflin Company (Clarion Books), 1985.

Carrick, Carol and Donald. *Sleep Out.* Boston: Houghton Mifflin Company (Clarion Books), 1982.

Catling, Patrick S. *The Chocolate Touch.* New York: Bantam Books, Inc., 1984.

Cavanah, Frances. *Abe Lincoln Gets His Chance.* New York: Scholastic Inc., 1986.

Christopher, Matt. *Touchdown for Tommy.* Boston: Little, Brown, and Company, 1984.

• Cleary, Beverly. *The Mouse and the Motorcycle.* New York: Dell Publishing Co., Inc., 1980.

Cleary, Beverly. *Ramona* Books. New York: Dell Publishing Co. Inc., 1982-1985.

• Cleaver, Nancy. *How the Chipmunk Got its Stripes.* New York: Scholastic Inc., 1981. (c.o.p.)

Cousins, Margaret. *The Story of Thomas Alva Edison, Inventor.* New York: Random House, Inc., 1981.

• Dahl, Roald. *The Enormous Crocodile.* New York: Bantam Books, Inc., 1984.

• Dahl, Roald. *Fantastic Mr. Fox.* New York: Bantam Books, 1978.

Dahl, Roald. *The Twits.* New York: Bantam Books, 1982.

• Dalgliesh, Alice. *The Courage of Sarah Nobel.* New York: Macmillan Publishing Company (Aladdin Books), 1986.

Margaret. *Five True Dog Stories.* New York: Scholastic Inc., 1987.

• Davidson, Margaret. *The Story of Martin Luther King. I Have a Dream.* New York: Scholastic Inc., 1986.

de Paola, Tomie. *The Legend of Bluebonnet.* New York: Putnam Publishing Group, 1983.

de Paola, Tomie. *Nana Upstairs and Nana Downstairs.* New York: Penguin Books (Puffin Books), 1978.

de Paola, Tomie. *Now One Foot, Now the Other.* New York: Putnam Publishing Group, 1981.

de Paola, Tomie. *Strega Nona.* Englewood Cliffs, New Jersey: Prentice-Hall Publishing Co., 1975.

• Desbarats, Peter. *Gabrielle and Selena.* San Diego: Harcourt Brace Jovanovich, Publishers, 1974.

• Erickson, Russell. *A Toad for Tuesday* (and other Warton and Morton books in the series). New York: Dell Publishing Co., Inc., 1976. (c.o.p.)

Feajles, Anita. *Casey the Utterly Impossible Horse.* New York: Scholastic Inc., 1980. (c.o.p.)

Friedman, Tracy. *Henriette, the Story of a Doll.* New York: Scholastic Inc., 1986.

Gennett, Ruth S. *My Father's Dragon.* New York: Random House, Inc., 1986. (c.o.p.)

Graeber, Charlotte. *Mustard.* New York: Bantam Books, Inc., 1983. (c.o.p.)

Green, Nancy. *The Bigger Giant.* New York: Scholastic Inc., 1972.

Greenfield, Eloise. *First Pink Light.* New York: Thomas Y. Crowell Co., Inc., 1976. (c.o.p.)

● Greenfield, Eloise. *Honey I Love and Other Poems.* New York: Harper & Row, Publishers, 1986.

● Greenfield, Eloise. *Me and Neesie.* New York: Harper & Row, Publishers, 1984.

Hazen, Barbara. *Tight Times.* New York: Penguin Books (Puffin Books), 1983.

Hoban, Russell and Lillian. *Frances* books. New York: Harper & Row, Publishers, 1976-1986.

●† Hoberman, Mary A. *A House is a House for Me.* New York: Scholastic Inc., 1986.

Hurwitz, Johanna. *Aldo Applesauce.* New York: Scholastic, Inc., 1983.

● Lamorisse, Albert. *The Red Balloon.* New York: Doubleday Inc., 1987.

Lexau, Joan M. *Striped Ice Cream.* New York: Scholastic Inc., 1971.

Littledale, Freya. (retold by) *The Little Mermaid.* New York: Scholastic Inc., 1986.

● McCloskey, Robert. *Blueberries for Sal.* New York: Penguin Books (Puffin Books), 1976.

McCloskey, Robert. *Lentil.* New York: Penguin Books (Puffin Books), 1978.

● McCloskey, Robert. *One Morning in Maine.* New York: Penguin Books (Puffin Books), 1976.

● McCord, David. *Every Time I Climb a Tree.* Boston: Little, Brown and Company, 1980.

● McGovern, Ann. *Wanted Dead or Alive: The True Story of Harriet Tubman.* New York: Scholastic Inc., 1977.

MacLachlan, Patricia. *Through Grandpa's Eyes.* New York: Harper & Row, Publishers, 1983.

Mirkovic, Irene. *The Greedy Shopkeeper.* San Diego: Harcourt Brace Jovanovich, 1980. (c.o.p.)

Moore, Eva. *The Story of George Washington Carver.* New York: Scholastic Inc., 1971. (c.o.p.)

● Ness, Evaline. *Sam, Bangs, and Moonshine.* New York: Holt, Rinehart and Winston, Publishers, 1987.

●† Odgers, Sally Farrell. *Elizabeth.* Crystal Lake, Illinois: Rigby Education, 1988.

Ormondroyd, Edward. *Theodore.* Boston: Houghton Mifflin Company, 1984.

●† Parkes, Brenda and Judith Smith. (retold by) *The Hobyahs.* Crystal Lake, Illinois: Rigby Education, 1988.

† Parkes, Brenda. *McBungle's African Safari.* Crystal Lake, Illinois: Rigby Education, 1988.

† Parkes, Brenda and Judith Smith. (retold by) *The Musicians of Bremen.* Crystal Lake, Illinois: Rigby Education, 1988.

Patrick, Skene Catling. *The Chocolate Touch.* New York: Bantam Books, 1981.

● Peet, Bill. All titles. 25-30 are in paperback. Favorites include: *Chester the Worldly Pig, How Droofus the Dragon Lost His Head, Kermit the Hermit, The Whingdingdilly,* and *The Wump World.* Boston: Houghton Mifflin Company, 1961-1986.

● Peterson, John. *The Littles* series. New York: Scholastic Inc., 1971-1986.

Rey, H. A. and Margret Rey. *Curious George* Books. Boston: Houghton Mifflin Company, and New York: Scholastic Inc., 1973-1985.

Rockwell, Thomas. *How to Eat Fried Worms.* New York: Dell Publishing Co., Inc., 1975.

Saunders, Susan. *The Golden Goose.* New York: Scholastic Inc., 1987.

Schwartz, Amy. *Bea and Mr. Jones.* New York: Penguin Books, 1983.

Scribner, Charles Jr. *Hansel and Gretel by the Brothers Grimm.* New York: Charles Scribner's Sons, 1975. (c.o.p.)

Slote, Alfred. *My Robot Buddy.* New York: Harper & Row, Publishers, 1986.

Smith, Robert K. *Chocolate Fever.* New York: Dell Publishing Co. Inc., 1978.

Stevens, Carla. *Anna, Grandpa, and the Big Storm.* New York: Penguin Books (Puffin Books), 1986.

Turkle, Brinton. *Do Not Open.* New York: E. P. Dutton & Co., Inc., 1985.

Viorst, Judith. *If I Were in Charge of the World. . .* New York: Macmillan Publishing Company (Aladdin Books), 1984.

Viorst, Judith. *Rosie and Michael.* Macmillan Publishing Company (Aladdin Books), 1979.

- White, E. B. *Charlotte's Web.* New York: Harper & Row, Publishers, 1952.
- Williams, Margery. *The Velveteen Rabbit.* New York: Putnam Publishing Group, 1987.

York, Carol B. *The Witch Lady Mystery.* New York: Scholastic Inc., 1977.

For Grade 3

Andersen, Hans Christian (pictures by Susan Jeffers) *Thumbelina.* New York: Dial Books for Young Readers, 1985.

Andersen, Hans Christian (pictures by Susan Jeffers) *The Wild Swans.* New York: Dial Books for Young Readers, 1987.

Arnold, Elliott. *Brave Jimmy Stone.* New York: Scholastic Inc., 1974. (c.o.p.)

- Atwater, Richard and Florence. *Mr. Popper's Penguins.* New York: Dell Publishing Co., Inc., 1986.
- Banks, Lynn Reid. *The Indian in the Cupboard.* New York: Avon Books (Camelot Books), 1982.

Bond, Michael. *A Bear Called Paddington.* New York: Dell Publishing Co., Inc., 1968.

●† Butler, Andrea. (compiled by) *Shuffle Shuffle Rhyme Chime.* Crystal Lake, Illinois: Rigby Education, 1988.

Byars, Betsy. *The Cartoonist.* New York: Dell Publishing Co., Inc., 1981.

Byars, Betsy. *The Summer of the Swans.* New York: Penguin Books (Puffin Books), 1981.

Cameron, Ann. *The Stories Julian Tells.* New York: Alfred A. Knopf, 1987.

●† Cochrane, Orin. *The Great Gray Owl.* New York: Richard C. Owen Publishers, Inc., 1987.

- Collodi, Carlo. *The Adventures of Pinocchio.* New York: Putnam Publishing Group, 1982.

Cooney, Barbara. *Miss Rumphius.* New York: Penguin Books (Puffin Books), 1985.

- Dahl, Roald. *Charlie and the Chocolate Factory.* New York: Bantam Books, Inc., 1986.

Dahl, Roald. (adapted by Richard George). *Charlie and the Chocolate Factory: A Play.* New York: Penguin Books (Puffin Books), 1983.

- Dahl, Roald. *Danny the Champion of the World.* New York: Bantam Books, Inc., 1978.
- Dahl, James. *James and the Giant Peach.* New York: Bantam Books, Inc., 1981.

Dana, Barbara. *Zucchini.* New York: Bantam Books, Inc. 1984.

Davidson, Margaret. *Five True Horse Stories*. New York: Scholastic Inc., 1987.

• Davidson, Margaret. *Helen Keller's Teacher*. New York: Scholastic Inc., 1972.

Du Bois, William Pene. *The Twenty-One Balloons*. New York: Penguin Books (Puffin Books), 1986.

• Estes, Eleanor. *The Hundred Dresses*. San Diego: Harcourt Brace Jovanovich, Publishers, 1974.

Fitzhugh, Louise. *Harriet the Spy*. New York: Dell Publishing Co., Inc., 1986.

• Gardiner, John R. *Stone Fox*. New York: Harper & Row, Publishers, 1983.

Giovanni, Nikki. *Spin a Soft Black Song*. Revised Edition. New York: Farrar, Strauss and Giroux, 1987.

Grimm, Jacob and Wilhelm (pictures by Susan Jeffers) *Hansel and Gretel*. New York: Dial Books for Young Readers, 1986.

Hague, Kathleen and Michael. (retold by) *East of the Sun and West of the Moon*. San Diego: Harcourt Brace Jovanovich, Publishers, 1980.

Hall, Donald. *The Ox-Cart Man*. New York: Penguin Books (Puffin Books), 1983.

• Henry, Marguerite. *Brighty of the Grand Canyon*. New York: Rand McNally and Company, 1985.

Holling, Holling C. *Paddle to the Sea*. Boston: Houghton Mifflin Company (no date listed).

Hopkins, Lee Bennett. *The Sky is Full of Song*. New York: Harper & Row, Publishers, 1983.

Jukes, Mavis. *Like Jake and Me*. New York: Alfred A. Knopf, 1987.

King-Smith, Dick. *Pigs Might Fly*. New York: Scholastic Inc., 1984.

Kipling, Rudyard. *Just So Stories*. New York: New American Library, 1974.

Kjelgaard, James. *Big Red*. New York: Bantam Books, Inc., 1976.

Lang, Andrew (retold by) *Aladdin*. New York: Penguin Books (Puffin Books), 1983.

• Larrick, Nancy. *Piping Down the Valleys Wild*. New York: Dell Publishing Co., Inc., 1986.

Le Cain, Errol (Illus.) *The Twelve Dancing Princesses*. Penguin Books (Puffin Books), 1983.

Lewis, Naomi. (translator) *Hans Andersen's Fairy Tales*. New York: Penguin Books (Puffin Books), 1983.

• Lobel, Arnold. *Fables*. New York: Harper & Row, Publishers, 1983.

• MacLachlan, Patricia. *Sarah Plain and Tall*. New York: Harper & Row, Publishers, 1985.

McClosky, Robert. *Homer Price*. New York: Penguin Books (Puffin Books), 1976.

McClosky, Robert. *More Homer Price*. New York: Penguin Books (Puffin Books), 1976. (c.o.p.)

• Mathis, Sharon B. *The Hundred Penny Box*. Penguin Books (Puffin Books), 1986.

• McGovern, Ann. (retold by) *Aesop's Fables*. New York: Scholastic Inc., 1965.

• Merriam, Eve. *Jamboree*. New York: Dell Publishing Co., Inc., 1984.

• Merriam, Eve. *A Sky Full of Poems*. New York: Dell Publishing Co., Inc., 1986.

† Merriam, Eve. *That Noodle-head Epaminondas*, Crystal Lake, Illinois: Rigby Education, 1988.

• Miles, Miska. *Annie and the Old One*. Boston: Atlantic Monthly, 1971.

• Milne, A. A. *Winnie the Pooh*. New York: Dell Publishing Co., Inc., 1970.

Mowat, Farley. *Owls in the Family*. New York: Bantam Books, Inc., 1981.

† Odgers, Sally Farrell. *How to Handle a Vivid Imagination*. Crystal Lake, Illinois: Rigby Education, 1987.

Pyle, Howard. *King Stork*. New York: Little, Brown and Company, 1986.

Rogasky, Barbara. (retold by) *Rapunzel From the Brothers Grimm*. New York: Holiday House, 1986.

● Rylant, Cynthia. *When I Was Young in the Mountains*. New York: E. P. Dutton and Co., Inc., 1985.

Sendak, Maurice (Illus.) *King Grisly-Beard: A Tale from the Brothers Grimm*. New York: Farrar, Strauss, & Giroux, 1987.

● Smith, Doris. *A Taste of Blackberries*. New York: Scholastic Inc., 1976.

● Steig, William. *Abel's Island*. New York: Farrar, Strauss, & Giroux, Inc., 1987.

● Steig, William. *The Amazing Bone*. New York: Farrar, Strauss, & Giroux, Inc., 1977.

Steig, William. *Caleb and Kate*. New York: Farrar, Strauss, & Giroux, Inc., 1977.

Steig, William. *Dominic*. New York: Farrar, Strauss, & Giroux, Inc., 1972.

Steig, William. *Gorky Rises*. New York: Farrar, Strauss, & Giroux, Inc., 1986.

Steig, William. *The Real Thief*. New York: Farrar, Strauss, & Giroux, Inc., 1973.

Steig, William. *Solomon the Rusty Nail*. New York: Farrar, Strauss, & Giroux, Inc., 1987.

● Steig, William. *Sylvester and the Magic Pebble*. New York: Windmill Books, 1969.

Steig, William. *Tiffky Doofky*. New York: Farrar, Strauss, & Giroux, Inc., 1987.

Stevenson, Robert Louis. *A Child's Garden of Verses*. New York: Random House, 1978.

● Thomas, Jane Resh. *The Comeback Dog*. Boston: Houghton Mifflin Company, 1981.

● Thurber, James. *The Great Quillow*. San Diego: Harcourt Brace Jovanovich, Publishers, 1984.

Thurber, James. *Many Moons*. San Diego: Harcourt Brace Jovanovich, Publishers, 1973.

● Wagner, Jane. *J. T.* New York: Dell Publishing Co., Inc., 1971.

● White, E. B. *Stuart Little*. New York: Harper & Row, Publishers, 1973.

● White, E. B. *Trumpet of the Swan*. New York: Harper & Row, Publishers, 1973.

● Wilder, Laura Ingalls. *The Little House on the Prairie* series. New York: Harper & Row, Publishers, 1986.

● Williams, Jay. *The Magic Grandfather*. New York: Scholastic Inc., 1976. (c.o.p.)

Wolkstein, Diane. *The Magic Wings*. New York: E. P. Dutton and Co., Inc., 1986.

● Yagawa, Sumiko. (retold by) *The Crane Wife*. William Morrow & Co. (Mulberry Books), 1987.

Yashima, Taro. *Crow Boy*. New York: Penguin Books (Puffin Books), 1976.

Yolen, Jane. *The Girl Who Loved the Wind*. New York: Harper & Row, Publishers, 1987.

Zolotow, Charlotte. *William's Doll*. New York: Harper & Row, Publishers, 1985.

Books Classified by Levels of Difficulty

For Beginning Readers
(Early through mid Grade 1)

Books for the beginning months of first grade have been leveled progressively from easiest to more difficult with small colored circles as a guide for teachers, not for students. (Numbers are used here for clarification only.) At no time do we ever state that a student is on "green level" and is to choose green level books.

These levels are to be used as a starting point guide only. It is not *the* list. When we find a book does not work at one level, we change it. Teachers will need to do the same and make adjustments according to their students' reactions.

Most of the books noted in "Recommended Literature —classified by grade and literary style" are listed here in levels 1-7. Levels 8-12 reflect books from about a high first grade level to a mid second grade level. Because many paperback books regularly go in and out of print, those titles currently out of print (c.o.p.) are included.

Level 1

> Cowley, Joy. *Old Tuatara*. New York: Richard C. Owen Publishers, Inc., 1987.
> Hutchins, Pat. *1 hunter*. New York: William Morrow & Co. (Mulberry Books), 1986.
> Maris, Ron. *My Book*. New York: Penguin Books (Puffin Books), 1987.
> Martin, Bill Martin Jr. *Brown Bear, Brown Bear, What Do You See?* Toronto: Holt, Rinehart & Winston, 1982.
> Tafuri, Nancy. *Have You Seen My Duckling?* New York: Penguin Books (Puffin Books), 1986.
> Wagner, Justin. *The Bus Ride*. (Reading Unlimited Program) Glenview, Illinois: Scott, Forseman & Company, 1976. (c.o.p.)
> Wildsmith, Brian. *All Fall Down*. Toronto: Oxford University Press, 1985.
> Wildsmith, Brian. *Cat on the Mat*. Toronto: Oxford University Press, 1986.
> Wildsmith, Brian. *Giddy Up*. Toronto: Oxford University Press, 1987.
> Wildsmith, Brian. *The Island*. Toronto: Oxford University Press, 1984.
> Wildsmith, Brian. *My Dream*. Toronto: Oxford University Press, 1986.
> Wildsmith, Brian. *Toot, Toot*. Toronto: Oxford University Press, 1985.
> Wildsmith, Brian. *What a Tale*. Toronto: Oxford University Press, 1986.
> Wood, Leslie. *Bump, Bump, Bump*. Toronto: Oxford University Press, 1986.
> Wood, Leslie. *A Dog Called Mischief*. Toronto: Oxford University Press, 1985.
> Wood, Leslie. *The Frog and the Fly*. Toronto: Oxford University Press, 1985.
> Wood, Leslie. *Tom and his Tractor*. Toronto: Oxford University Press, 1986.

Note on Level 1 books:

This first level is the most difficult one to find books for. A number of the books listed, especially those by Brian Wildsmith and Leslie Wood, do not have a consistent, predictable language pattern. Nonetheless, because children always hear and see the books repeatedly before reading them, and because the simple text matches so well with the illustrations, we have found them to work very well at this level with most students.

However, for a small percentage of students, these books will be too difficult to begin with. The teacher may need to start with very simple pattern books (such as "I like..." or "I can...") of three or four pages of the child's own language which is the most predictable text of all. In addition, some commercial publishers (Developmental Learning Materials, Richard C. Owen Publishers, Inc., Rigby Education and The Wright Group) offer "little books" of about 8 pages. While many of these are not really "literature" some students will need to begin with the very limited, simple text they provide.

Level 2

Aliki. *Hush Little Baby*. Englewood Cliffs, New Jersey: Prentice-Hall, Inc. 1968.

Barchas, Sarah. *I Was Walking Down the Road*. New York: Scholastic Inc., 1988.

Cairns, Scharlaine. *Oh No!* Crystal Lake, Illinois: Rigby Education, 1987.

Cowley, Joy. *The Jigaree*. San Diego: The Wright Group, 1987.

Cowley, Joy. *Mrs. Wishy-Washy*. San Diego: The Wright Group, 1987.

Crews, Donald. *School Bus*. New York: Penguin Books (Puffin Books), 1987.

Fox, Mem. *Arabella The Smallest Girl in the World*. New York: Scholastic Inc., 1987.

Ginsburg, Mirra. *Across the Stream*. New York: Penguin Books (Puffin Books), 1985. (c.o.p.)

Green, Robin; Pollick, Yevonne and Bronwyn Scarffe. *When Goldilocks Went to the House of the Bears*. New York: Scholastic Inc., 1987.

Hutchins, Pat. *Rosie's Walk*. New York: Scholastic Inc., 1987.

Hutchins, Pat. *Titch*. New York: Penguin Books (Puffin Books), 1985.

Jones, Ann. *When You Were A Baby*. Penguin Books (Puffin Books), 1986.

Krauss, Ruth. *Bears*. New York: Scholastic Inc., 1985. (c.o.p.)

Krauss, Ruth. *The Happy Egg*. New York: Scholastic Inc., 1983. (c.o.p.)

Mark, Jan. *Fur*. New York: Harper & Row Publishers, 1986.

Martin, Bill, Jr. *Monday, Monday, I Like Monday*. Toronto: Holt, Rinehart & Winston, Inc., 1983.

Melser, June and Joy Cowley. *The Big Toe*. San Diego: The Wright Group, 1987.

Melser, June and Joy Cowley. *In a Dark Dark Wood*. San Diego: The Wright Group, 1987.

Melser, June and Joy Cowley. *Lazy Mary*. San Diego: The Wright Group, 1987.

Melser, June and Joy Cowley. *Sing a Song*. San Diego: The Wright Group, 1987.

Patrick, Gloria. *A Bug in a Jug and Other Funny Rhymes*. New York: Scholastic Inc., 1981. (c.o.p.)

Ruwe, Mike. *Ten Little Bears*. (Reading Unlimited Program) Glenville, Illinois: Scott, Foresman and Co., 1976. (c.o.p.)

West, Colin. *Have You Seen the Crocodile?* New York: Harper & Row, Publishers, 1986.

West, Colin. *"Pardon?" Said The Giraffe*. New York: Harper & Row, Publishers, 1986.

Wildsmith, Brian. *If I Were You*. Toronto: Oxford University Press, 1987.

Level 3

Allen, Pamela. *Who Sank the Boat?* Crystal Lake, Illinois: Rigby Education, 1987.

Brown, Ruth. *A Dark, Dark Tale*. New York: Dial Books for Young Readers, 1984.

Cauley, Lorinda Bryan. (Illus.) *The Three Little Kittens*. New York: G. P. Putnam's Sons, 1987.

Causley, Charles. *"Quack" Said the Billy Goat*. New York: Harper & Row, Publishers, 1986.

Cowley, Joy. *Meanies*. San Diego: The Wright Group, 1987.

Cowley, Joy. *Number One*. New York: Richard C. Owen Publishers, Inc., 1987.

Cowley, Joy. *The Red Rose*. San Diego: The Wright Group, 1982.

Flack, Marjorie. *Ask Mr. Bear*. New York: Macmillan Publishing Company (Aladdin Books), 1986.

Gelman, Rita Golden. *Cats and Mice*. New York: Scholastic Inc., 1985.

Ginsburg, Mirra. *Good Morning, Chick*. New York: Scholastic Inc., 1980. (c.o.p.)

Ginsburg, Mirra. *Where Does the Sun Go at Night?* New York: William Morrow & Co., (Mulberry Books), 1987.

Gomi, Taro. *Coco Can't Wait*. New York: Penguin Books (Puffin Books), 1985. (c.o.p.)

Goss, Janet L. and Jerome C. Harste. *It Didn't Frighten Me!* New York: Scholastic Inc., 1988.

Graboff, Abner. *Old MacDonald Had a Farm*. New York: Scholastic Inc., 1985.

Hayes, Sarah. *This is the Bear*. New York: Harper & Row, Publishers, 1986.

Hutchins, Pat. *Happy Birthday, Sam*. New York: Penguin Books (Puffin Books), 1985.

Joyce, William. *George Shrinks*. New York: Harper & Row, Publishers, 1987.

Kraus, Robert. *Whose Mouse Are You?* New York: Macmillan Publishing Co., 1972.

Krauss, Ruth. *The Carrot Seed*. New York: Scholastic Inc., 1984. (c.o.p.)

Long, Earlene. *Gone Fishing*. Boston: Houghton Mifflin Company (Sandpiper Books), 1987.

Melser, June and Joy Cowley. *Boo-hoo*. San Diego: The Wright Group, 1987.

Melser, June and Joy Cowley. *Grandpa, Grandpa*. San Diego: The Wright Group, 1987.

Melser, June and Joy Cowley. *Hairy Bear*. San Diego: The Wright Group, 1987.

Melser, June and Joy Cowley. *Obadiah*. San Diego: The Wright Group, 1987.

Melser, June and Joy Cowley. *One Cold Wet Night*. San Diego: The Wright Group, 1987.

Melser, June and Joy Cowley. *Poor Old Polly*. San Diego: The Wright Group, 1987.

Melser, June and Joy Cowley. *Woosh!* San Diego: The Wright Group, 1987.

Melser, June and Joy Cowley. *Yes Ma'am*. San Diego: The Wright Group, 1987.

Noodles. *How to Catch a Ghost*. Toronto: Holt, Rinehart and Winston, Inc., 1983.

Parkes, Brenda and Judith Smith. (retold by) *The Enormous Watermelon.* Crystal Lake, Illinois: Rigby Education, 1986.

Parkes, Brenda. *Who's in the Shed?* Crystal Lake, Illinois: Rigby Education, 1986.

Sendak, Maurice. *Seven Little Monsters.* New York: Harper & Row, Publishers, 1977.

Level 4

Ahlberg, Janet and Allen. *Each Peach Pear Plum.* New York: Scholastic Inc., 1985.

Arno, Ed. *The Gingerbread Man.* New York: Scholastic Inc., 1985.

Bonne, Rose. *I Know an Old Lady.* New York: Scholastic Inc., 1985.

Bridwell, Norman. *A Tiny Family.* New York: Scholastic Inc., 1980.

Carle, Eric. *The Secret Birthday Message.* New York: Harper & Row Publishers, 1986.

Carle, Eric. *The Very Hungry Caterpillar.* New York: Scholastic Inc., 1987.

Chase, Edith Newlin. *The New Baby Calf.* New York: Scholastic Inc., 1986.

Cowley, Joy. *Greedy Cat.* New York: Richard C. Owen Publishers, Inc., 1988.

Elkin, Benjamin. *Six Foolish Fishermen.* New York: Scholastic Inc., 1984.

Ets, Marie Hall. *Play With Me.* New York: Penguin Books (Puffin Books), 1983.

Friskey, Margaret. *Indian Two Feet and His Horse.* New York: Scholastic Inc., 1984. (c.o.p.)

Galdone, Paul. *The Three Bears.* New York: Scholastic Inc., 1984.

Galdone, Paul. *The Three Little Billy Goats Gruff.* Boston: Houghton Mifflin Company, 1981.

Gardner, Marjory et al. (Illus): *Time for a Rhyme.* Crystal Lake, Illinois: Rigby Education, 1987.

Gelman, Rita Golden. *More Spaghetti I Say.* New York: Scholastic Inc., 1987.

Gelman, Rita Golden. *Why Can't I Fly?* New York: Scholastic Inc., 1986.

Glusac, Randy, et al. (Illus): *Time for a Number Rhyme.* Crystal Lake, Illinois: Rigby Education, 1987.

Guilfoile, Elizabeth. *Nobody Listens to Andrew.* New York: Scholastic Inc., 1973.

Hutchins, Pat. *Don't Forget the Bacon.* New York: Penguin Books (Puffin Books), 1978. (c.o.p.)

Hutchins, Pat. *The Doorbell Rang.* New York: Scholastic Inc., 1987.

Hutchins, Pat. *You'll Soon Grow Into Them, Titch.* New York: Penguin Books (Puffin Books), 1985.

Kent, Jack. *The Fat Cat.* New York: Scholastic Inc., 1987.

Klein, Leonore. *Brave Daniel.* New York: Scholastic Inc., 1980. (c.o.p.)

Kuskin, Karla. *Just Like Everyone Else.* New York: Harper & Row, Publishers, 1982.

Lüton, Mildred. *Little Chicks' Mothers and All the Others.* New York: Penguin Books (Puffin Books), 1985.

McGovern, Ann. *Too Much Noise.* New York: Scholastic Inc., 1984.

Martin, Bill Jr. *Fire! Fire! Said Mrs. McGuire.* Toronto: Holt, Rinehart, & Winston, Inc., 1982.

Mayer, Mercer. *If I Had.* New York: Dial Books for Young Readers, 1977.

Mayer, Mercer. *There's a Nightmare in My Closet.* New York: Dial Books for Young Readers, 1976.

Parkes, Brenda and Judith Smith. (retold by) *The Three Little Pigs.* Crystal Lake, Illinois: Rigby Education, 1986.

Seuling, Barbara. *The Teeny Tiny Woman. An Old English Ghost Tale.* New York: Penguin Books (Puffin Books), 1978. (c.o.p.)

Smith, Judith and Brenda Parkes. *Gobble Gobble Glup Glup.* Crystal Lake, Illinois: Rigby Education, 1986.

Smith, Judith and Brenda Parkes. *The Three Billy Goats Gruff.* Crystal Lake, Illinois: Rigby Education, 1986.

Szeghy, Joe. *The Lion's Tail.* (Reading Unlimited Program) Glenville, Illinois: Scott, Foresman and Company, 1976.

Wells, Rosemary. *Noisy Nora.* New York: Dial Books for Young Readers, 1981.

Level 5

Asch, Frank. *Turtle Tale.* New York: Dial Books for Young Readers, 1980.

Barton, Byron. *Buzz, Buzz, Buzz.* New York: Penguin Books (Puffin Books), 1985. (c.o.p.)

Baum, Arline and Joseph. *one bright Monday morning.* New York: Knopf Pantheon, 1973. (c.o.p.)

Becker, John. *Seven Little Rabbits.* New York: Scholastic Inc., 1985.

Benchley, Nathaniel. *Red Fox and His Canoe.* New York: Harper & Row, Publishers, 1985.

Blance, Ellen and Ann Cook. *Monster Books.* Set I. Glendale, CA: Bowmar Noble Publishers, 1981.

Bridwell, Norman. *Kangaroo Stew.* New York: Scholastic Inc., 1984. (c.o.p.)

Bridwell, Norman. *Clifford* Books. New York: Scholastic Inc., 1984-1986.

Bridwell, Norman. *Crazy Zoo.* New York: Scholastic Inc., 1980. (c.o.p.)

Brown, Margaret Wise. *Goodnight Moon.* New York: Harper & Row, Publishers, 1984.

Brown, Margaret Wise. *The Runaway Bunny.* New York: Harper & Row, Publishers, 1984.

de Regniers, Beatrice Schenk. *May I Bring a Friend?* New York: Macmillan Publishing Company (Aladdin Books), 1974.

Elting, Mary and Michael Folsom. *Q is for Duck. An Alphabet Guessing Game.* New York: Clarion Books, 1980.

Gag, Wanda. *The ABC Bunny.* New York: Putnam Publishing Group, 1978.

Galdone, Paul. *Henny Penny.* Boston: Houghton Mifflin Company, 1984.

Gelman, Rita Golden. *The Biggest Sandwich Ever.* New York: Scholastic Inc., 1984. (c.o.p.)

Graham, John. *I Love you Mouse.* New York: Harcourt Brace Jovanovich, Publishers, 1978.

Hoff, Syd. *Danny and the Dinosaur.* New York: Harper & Row, Publishers, 1978.

Keats, Ezra Jack. *The Snowy Day.* New York: Scholastic Inc., 1987.

Keats, Ezra Jack. *The Trip.* New York: William Morrow & Co., (Mulberry Books), 1987.

Logan, Dick. *Thunder-The Dinosaur* Books. Glendale, CA: Cypress Publishing Corp., 1977.

Minarik, Else Holmelund. *Little Bear* Books. New York: Harper & Row, Publishers, 1979.

Morris, William Barrett. *The Longest Journey in the World.* Toronto: Holt, Rinehart & Winston, 1982.

Rice, Eve. *Goodnight, Goodnight.* New York: Penguin Books (Puffin Books), 1983.

Rice, Eve. *Sam Who Never Forgets.* New York: William Morrow & Co., (Mulberry Books), 1987.

Sendak, Maurice. *Chicken Soup With Rice: A Book of Months.* New York: Scholastic Inc., 1986.

Smith, Judith and Brenda Parkes. *Jack & the Beanstalk.* Crystal Lake: Rigby Education, 1987.

Thaler, Mike. *A Hippopotamus Ate the Teacher.* New York: Avon Books (Camelot Books), 1981.

Wells, Rosemary. *Benjamin and Tulip.* New York: Dial Books for Young Readers, 1980.

Level 6

Asch, Frank. *Happy Birthday, Moon.* New York: Scholastic Inc., 1982.

Alexander, Martha. *I'll Be the Horse if You'll Play With Me.* New York: Dial Books for Young Readers, 1980.

Alexander, Martha. *Nobody Asked Me if I Wanted a Baby Sister.* New York: Dial Books for Young Readers, 1981.

Alexander, Martha. *When the New Baby Comes I'm Moving Out.* New York: Dial Books for Young Readers, 1981.

Brandenberg, Franz. *I Wish I Was Sick Too!* New York: Penguin Books (Puffin Books), 1982.

Cohen, Miriam. *Best Friends.* New York: Macmillan Publishing Company, 1976.

Cohen, Miriam. *The New Teacher.* New York: Macmillan Publishing Company, 1974.

Cohen, Miriam. *Will I Have a Friend?* New York: Macmillan Publishing Company, 1971.

Cutts, David. *The House That Jack Built.* Mahwah, New Jersey: Troll Associates, 1979.

de Paola, Tomie. *The Comic Adventures of Old Mother Hubbard and Her Dog.* San Diego: Harcourt Brace Jovanovich, Publishers, 1981.

de Regniers, Beatrice Schenk. *Red Riding Hood.* New York: Macmillan Publishing Company (Aladdin Books), 1977.

Galdone, Paul. *The Gingerbread Boy.* Boston: Houghton Mifflin Company, 1985.

Galdone, Paul. *The Little Red Hen.* New York: Houghton Mifflin Company, 1985.

Gelman, Rita Golden. *Mortimer K Saves the Day.* New York: Scholastic Inc., 1985. (c.o.p.)

Heide, Florence Parry and Sylvia Van Clief. *That's What Friends Are For.* New York: Scholastic Inc., 1971.

Highlights for Children, Inc. *The Highlights Book of Nursery Rhymes.* Columbus: 1974.

Keats, Ezra Jack. *Louie.* New York: Scholastic Inc., 1983. (c.o.p.)

Keats, Ezra Jack. *Peter's Chair.* New York: Harper & Row, Publishers, 1983.

Keats, Ezra Jack Keats. *Whistle for Willie.* New York: Penguin Books (Puffin Books), 1977.

Langstaff, John. *Over in the Meadow.* San Diego: Harcourt Brace Jovanovich, Publishers, 1973.

Littledale, Freya. *The Boy Who Cried Wolf.* New York: Scholastic Inc., 1982.

Littledale, Freya. *The Magic Fish.* New York: Scholastic Inc., 1986.

McGovern, Ann. *Stone Soup.* New York: Scholastic Inc., 1986.

McPhail, David. *The Bear's Toothache.* New York: Penguin Books (Puffin Books), 1986.

Margolis, Richard. *Big Bear, Spare That Tree.* New York: Scholastic Inc., 1980. (c.o.p.)
Murphy, Jill. *Peace at Last.* New York: Dial Books for Young Readers, 1982.
Myers, Bernice. *My Mother is Lost.* New York: Scholastic Inc., 1987.
Nicoil, Helen and Jan Pienkowski. *Meg* Books. New York: Penguin Books (Puffin Books), 1982.
Peppe, Rodney. *Cat and Mouse.* New York: Penguin Books (Puffin Books), 1982.
Peppe, Rodney. *Odd One Out.* New York: Penguin Books (Puffin Books), 1975. (c.o.p.)
Rand, Ann and Paul. *I Know a Lot of Things.* San Diego: Harcourt Brace Jovanovich, Publishers, 1980.
Sendak, Maurice. *Pierre.* New York: Scholastic Inc., 1983.
Slobodkina, Esphyr. *Caps For Sale.* New York: Scholastic Inc., 1984.
Stevens, Carla. *Rabbit and Skunk* Books. New York: Scholastic Inc., 1976.
Wagner, Jenny. *John Brown, Rose and the Midnight Cat.* New York: Penguin Books (Puffin Books), 1986.
Zolotow, Charlotte. *The Hating Book.* New York: Scholastic Inc., 1980.

Level 7

Aliki. *We Are Best Friends.* New York: William Morrow & Co. (Mulberry Books). 1979.
Benchley, Nathaniel. *The Strange Disappearance of Arthur Cluck.* New York: Harper & Row, Publishers, 1979.
Bridwell, Norman. *Clifford's Family.* New York: Scholastic Inc., 1985.
Caines, Jeanette. *Just Us Women.* New York: Harper & Row, Publishers, 1984.
Cameron, Polly. *I Can't Said the Ant.* New York: Scholastic Inc., 1981. (c.o.p.)
Clarke, Mollie. *Congo Boy.* New York: Scholastic Inc., 1987.
Delton, Judy. *Two Good Friends.* New York: Crown Publishers, 1986.
Gelman, Rita Golden. *Pets for Sale.* New York: Scholastic Inc., 1986.
Goodspeed, Peter. *A Rhinoceros Wakes Me Up in the Morning.* New York: Penguin Books (Puffin Books), 1982.
Graham, Margaret Bloy. *Harry the Dirty Dog.* New York: Harper & Row, Publishers, 1976. (c.o.p.)
Gross, Ruth Belov. *Hansel and Gretel.* New York: Scholastic Inc., 1974.
Hazen, Barbara Shook. *The Gorilla Did It.* New York: Macmillan Publishing Company (Aladdin Books), 1978.
Hoban, Lillian. *Arthur's Honey Bear.* New York: Harper & Row, Publishers, 1982.
Kent, Jack. *Clotilda's Magic.* New York: Scholastic Inc., 1981.
Krasilovsky, Phyllis. *The Man Who Didn't Wash His Dishes.* New York: Scholastic Inc., 1982.
Langstaff, John. *Frog Went A-Courtin'* New York: Harcourt Brace Jovanovich, Pubishers, 1972.
Littledale, Freya. *The Snow Child.* New York: Scholastic Inc., 1978.
Lobel, Arnold. *Frog and Toad* Books. New York: Harper & Row, Publishers, 1979, 1981 and New York: Scholastic Inc., 1983-1985.
Lobel, Arnold. *Mouse Soup.* New York: Scholastic Inc., 1986.
Lobel, Arnold. *Mouse Tales.* New York: Harper & Row, Publishers, 1978.
Lobel, Arnold. *Owl at Home.* New York: Harper & Row, Publishers, 1987.
Lobel, Arnold. *Small Pig.* New York: Harper & Row, Publishers, 1976. (c.o.p.)
Lobel, Arnold. *Uncle Elephant.* New York: Scholastic Inc., 1986.

Nixon, Joan Lowery. *The Boy Who Could Find Anything*. New York: Harcourt Brace Jovanovich, Pubishers, 1978.

Parish, Peggy. *Too Many Rabbits*. New York: Scholastic Inc., 1985. (c.o.p.)

Rey, Margaret. *Pretzel*. New York: Harper & Row, Publishers, 1984.

Rice, Eve. *Ebbie*. New York: Penguin Books (Puffin Books), 1978. (c.o.p.)

Rice, Eve. *Oh, Lewis!* New York: Penguin Books (Puffin Books), 1979. (c.o.p.)

Rice, Eve. *New Blue Shoes*. New York: Penguin Books (Puffin Books), 1983.

Rose, Ann. *Akimba and the Magic Cow*. New York: Scholastic Inc., 1981. (c.o.p.)

Rose, Gerald. *Trouble in the Ark*. New York: Scholastic Inc., 1984. (c.o.p.)

Rubel, Nicole. *Sam and Violet* Books. New York: Avon Books (Camelot Books), 1982.

Stevens, Carla. *Hooray for Pig*. New York: Scholastic Inc., 1974.

Tarcov, Edith. (retold by). *Rumpelstiltskin*. New York: Scholastic Inc., 1980.

Thomas, Lewis. *Hill of Fire*. New York: Harper & Row, Publishers, 1984.

Viorst, Judith. *I'll Fix Anthony*. New York: Macmillan Publishing Company (Aladdin Books), 1983.

Weiss, Leatie. *Heather's Feathers*. New York: Avon Books (Camelot Books), 1978.

Wiseman, B. *Morris Goes to School*. New York: Harper & Row, Publishers, 1983.

Zolotow, Charlotte. *Mr. Rabbit and the Lovely Present*. New York: Harper & Row, Publishers, 1977.

For late Grade 1 through mid Grade 2

Level 8

Brenner, Barbara. *Wagon Wheels*. New York: Harper & Row, Publishers, 1978.

Brown, Marc. *Arthur's Eyes*. New York: Avon Books (Camelot Books), 1981.

Brown, Marc. *Arthur's Nose*. New York: Avon Books (Camelot Books), 1981.

Brown, Marcia. *Stone Soup*. New York: Charles Scribner's Sons, 1975.

Buckley, Richard. *The Greedy Python*. Natick, Massachussetts: Picture Book Studio, 1985.

Bulla, Clyde Robert. *Daniel's Duck*. New York: Harper & Row, Publishers, 1982.

Byars, Betsy. *Go and Hush the Baby*. New York: Penguin Books (Puffin Books), 1982.

Carlson, Nancy. *Harriet* Books. New York: Penguin Books (Puffin Books), 1985.

Cromic, William J. *Steven and the Green Turtle*. New York: Scholastic Inc., 1970.

de Paola, Tomie. *Oliver Button is a Sissy*. San Diego: Harcourt Brace Jovanovich, Pubishers, 1979.

Faulkner, Matt. (Illus.) *Jack and the Beanstalk*. New York: Scholastic Inc., 1986.

Freeman, Don. *A Rainbow of My Own*. New York: Penguin Books (Puffin Books), 1984.

Gantos, Jack. *Rotten Ralph*. Boston: Houghton Mifflin Company, 1976.

Giff, Patricia Reilly. *Today Was a Terrible Day*. New York: Penguin Books (Puffin Books), 1984.

Hogrogian, Nonny. *One Fine Day*. New York: Collier Books, 1971.

Keats, Ezra Jack. *Apt. 3*. New York: Macmillan Publishing Company (Aladdin Books), 1971.

Kent, Jack. *There's No Such Thing as a Dragon.* New York: Western Publishing Co. (Golden Press), 1975.

Littledale, Freya. *Snow White and the Seven Dwarfs.* New York: Scholastic Inc., 1987.

Lobel, Arnold. *How the Rooster Saved the Day.* New York: Penguin Books (Puffin Books), 1981. (c.o.p.)

Lobel, Arnold. *A Treeful of Pigs.* New York: Scholastic Inc., 1981. (c.o.p.)

Lord, John Vernon. *The Giant Jam Sandwich.* Boston: Houghton Mifflin Company, 1987.

Marshall, James. *George and Martha* Books. Houghton Mifflin Company (Sandpiper Books), 1982.

Martin, Bill Jr. *The Happy Hippopoptami.* Toronto: Holt, Rinehart and Winston, 1983.

Miles, Miska. *Small Rabbit.* New York: Scholastic Inc., 1977. (c.o.p.)

Orbach, Ruth. *Apple Pigs.* New York: Putnam Publishing Group (Philomel Books), 1981.

Piper, Watty. (retold by) *The Little Engine That Could.* New York: Scholastic Inc., 1985. (c.o.p.)

Sendak, Maurice. *Where the Wild Things Are.* New York: Scholastic Inc., 1984. (c.o.p.)

Sharmat, Marjorie Weinman. *Nate the Great* Books. New York: Dell Publishing Co., Inc., 1982.

Slepian, Jan and Ann Seidler. *The Hungry Thing.* New York: Scholastic Inc., 1980. (c.o.p.)

Stevenson, James. *Could Be Worse!* New York: Penguin Books (Puffin Books), 1983.

Viorst, Judith. *Alexander and The Terrible, Horrible, No Good, Very Bad Day.* New York: Macmillan Publishing Company (Aladdin Books), 1977.

Viorst, Judith. *My Mama Says There Aren't Any Zombies, Ghosts, Vampires, Creatures, and Demons.* New York: Atheneum, 1977. (c.o.p.)

Waber, Bernard. *Ira Sleeps Over.* Boston: Houghton Mifflin Company (Sandpiper Books), 1975 and New York: Scholastic Inc., 1984.

Zion, Gene. *No Roses for Harry.* New York: Scholastic Inc., 1978.

Zolotow, Charlotte. *The Quarreling Book.* New York: Harper & Row, Publishers, 1963.

Level 9

Aliki. *Keep Your Mouth Closed Dear.* New York: Dial Books for Young Readers, 1980.

Blegvad, Erik. (Illus.) *The Three Little Pigs.* New York: Macmillan Publishing Company (Aladdin Books), 1985.

Blume, Judy. *The One in the Middle is the Green Kangaroo.* New York: Dell Publishing Co., Inc., 1986.

Brown, Marc. *Arthur Goes to Camp.* Boston: Little, Brown and Company, 1984.

Buckley, Richard. *The Foolish Tortoise.* Natick, Massachussetts: Picture Book Studio, 1985.

de Paola, Tomie. *Bill and Pete.* New York: G. P. Putnam & Sons, 1978.

Dunn, Judy. *The Little Rabbit.* New York: Random House, 1980.

Flack, Margorie. *The Story of Ping.* New York: Scholastic Inc., 1987.

Freeman, Dan. *Corduroy.* New York: Penguin Books (Puffin Books), 1983.

Freeman, Dan. *Dandelion.* New York: Penguin Books (Puffin Books), 1982.

Gag, Wanda. *Millions of Cats.* New York: Putnam Publishing Group, 1977.

Grimm Brothers. *The Shoemaker and the Elves.* New York: Atheneum, 1981. (c.o.p.)

Handy, Libby. *Boss for a Week.* New York: Scholastic Inc., 1987.

Hazen, Barbara Shook. *Tight Times.* New York: Penguin Books (Puffin Books), 1983.

Johnson, Crocket. *Harold and the Purple Crayon* Books. New York: Harper & Row, Publishers, 1981.

Lobel, Arnold. *Ming Lo Moves the Mountain.* New York: Scholastic Inc., 1986.

Mayer, Mercer. *What Do You Do With a Kangaroo?* New York: Scholastic Inc., 1975.

Mosel, Arlene. (retold by) *The Funny Little Woman.* New York: E. P. Dutton and Co., Inc., 1977.

Mosel, Arlene. *Tikki Tikki Tembo.* New York: Scholastic Inc., 1984.

Payne, Emmy. *Katy No-Pocket.* Boston: Houghton Mifflin Company, 1973.

Pincus, Harriet. (Illus.) *Little Red Riding Hood, the Brothers Grimm.* San Diego: Harcourt Brace Jovanovich, Pubishers, 1968. (c.o.p.)

Stevens, Janet. (retold and illus. by) *The Princess and the Pea.* New York: Scholastic Inc., 1987.

Ward, Lynd. *The Biggest Bear.* Boston: Houghton Mifflin Company, 1973.

Williams, Vera. *A Chair for My Mother.* New York: Scholastic Inc., 1982.

Level 10

Allard, Harry. *Miss Nelson* Books. New York: Scholastic Inc., 1978-1986.

Bishop, Claire Hucket and Kurt Wiese. *The Five Chinese Brothers.* New York: Scholastic Inc., 1980. (c.o.p.)

Blume, Judy. *Freckle Juice.* New York: Dell Publishing Co., Inc., 1986.

Gross, Ruth Belov. (retold by) *The Emperor's New Clothes.* New York: Scholastic Inc., 1977.

Hoban, Russell. *Frances* Books. New York: Scholastic Inc., 1976-1986.

McGovern, Ann. *Little Whale.* New York: Scholastic Inc., 1979. (c.o.p.)

Moore, Lilian. *The Magic Spectacles.* New York: Bantam Books, Inc., 1985.

Parish, Peggy. *Amelia Bedelia* Books. New York: Avon Books (Camelot Books), 1981.

Peterson, John. *Mean Max.* New York: Scholastic Inc., 1970.

Rey, H. A. *Curious George Takes a Job.* Boston: Houghton Mifflin Company, 1974.

Slepian, Jan and Ann Seidler. *The Cat Who Wore a Pot on Her Head.* New York: Scholastic Inc., 1987.

Level 11

Dahl, Roald. *The Enormous Crocodile.* New York: Bantam Books, Inc., 1984.

Jeschke, Susan. *Perfect the Pig.* New York: Holt, Rinehart & Winston, Inc., 1985.

Lamorisse, Albert. *The Red Balloon.* New York: Doubleday, Inc., 1987.

McCloskey, Robert. *One Morning in Maine.* New York: Penguin Books (Puffin Books), 1976.

Moore, Lilian and Leone Adelson. *The Terrible Mr. Twitmeyer.* New York: Scholastic Inc., 1976. (c.o.p.)

Rayner, Mary. *Mr. and Mrs. Pig's Evening Out.* New York: Macmillan Publishing Company (Aladdin Books), 1979.

Rayner, Mary. *Mr. and Mrs. Pig's Bulk Buy.* New York: Macmillan Publishing Company, (Aladdin Books), 1984.

Rey, H. A. *Curious George Gets a Medal.* Boston: Houghton Mifflin Company, 1974.

Rey, H. A. *Curious George Goes to the Hospital.* Boston: Houghton Mifflin Company, 1966.

Rey, H. A. *Curious George Rides a Bike.* Boston: Houghton Mifflin Company, 1973.

Sonneborn, Ruth A. *Friday Night is Papa Night.* New York: Penguin Books (Puffin Books), 1987.

Williams, Vera. *Something Special For Me.* New York: William Morrow & Co., (Mulberry Books), 1986.

Wright, Freire and Michael Foreman. *Seven in One Blow.* New York: Random House, Inc., 1978. (c.o.p.)

Level 12

Averill, Esther. *Jenny's Moonlight Adventure.* New York: Bantam Books, Inc., 1982.

Averill, Esther. *The School for Cats.* New York: Bantam Books, Inc., 1982.

Barrett, Judith. *Cloudy With a Chance of Meatballs.* New York: Macmillan Publishing Company (Aladdin Books), 1982.

Lionni, Leo. *The Biggest House in the World.* New York: Alfred A. Knopf, 1987.

Miles, Miska. *Jenny's Cat.* New York: Bantam Books, Inc., 1982.

Peterson, John. *The Littles* series. New York: Scholastic Inc., 1971-1986.

Waber, Bernard. *Lyle, Lyle, the Crocodile.* Boston: Houghton Mifflin Company, 1973.

Appendixes

Appendix A: *A Proposal To Use Literature To Teach First Grade Reading*

First Grade Book Flood

Description of present reading program

Presently, all first-graders are being taught to read using a commercial basal series. Vocabulary is controlled, and the stories center primarily around family. While by second grade there is some attempt to include stories by well-known authors, at first grade level this occurs rarely.

Children are exposed to literature through a weekly library period where the librarian reads a book and students have the opportunity to sign out two books weekly. Also, the classroom teacher reads to the class on a regular basis introducing various forms of literature and periodically featuring one author.

Books for recreational reading in the classroom are few in number and in single copies. Those books that do exist in the classroom are mostly phonetically based and are not of high literary quality or interest. Emphasis in reading is on "how to" and development of reading skills. Very little time is spent in actual reading of books.

Population to be served

The population to be served is the 18 kindergarten children in a 306-member kindergarten through sixth grade elementary school building. The children are 85% minority and are from a broad socio-economic background. The kindergarten and first grade teachers report that many of the children have had very limited exposure to books outside of the school setting and limited prereading home experiences. In addition, they report that many appear unfamiliar with popular fairy tales, nursery rhymes, and children's literature. Many of the homes have no newspapers, magazines, or other reading materials available. In addition, in many cases, an adult role model who reads is not present. Experiences outside of the home and neighborhood are very limited, making the school environment particularly important for reading and language experiences.

Objectives of the proposed program

The goal of the proposed program is to "flood" a first grade classroom with multiple copies of highly motivating and interesting paperback books. These books would be used as the mainstay of the reading program with the goal being to go beyond teaching children *how* to read to develop readers who *want* to read and who acquire the habit of reading for pleasure. The program would have the following objectives:

1 To create a positive learning environment.
2 To motivate and foster reading development and positive reading attitudes through literature.
3 To incorporate and purchase (in paperback) works of literature that have the following readable elements:
   - rhyme or rhythmic quality
   - repetitive sentence patterns
   - natural language flow and imagery
   - predictability of story
   - fine illustrations
4 To have children hear literature daily.
5 To have children experience repeated readings of favorite books.
6 To promote and develop independent reading both at school and at home.

Appendix B: Sample Lesson Plans
B1 Organization of a Reading and Language Block (Grade 1) Oct. 6

9.15 - 11.40 READING and LANGUAGE BLOCK
(whole group sitting in the reading rug area)

- Read and discuss Big Books
  (old) *More Spaghetti I Say*
  (new) *The Gingerbread Man*
  evaluation — teacher observation

- Read and discuss Paperback Books
  Hush Little Baby   *Coco Can't Wait*
  Heather's Feathers   *Sam Who Never Forgets*
  evaluation — student response
  to teacher questions

- Read and discuss poems on large sheets
  The Fall   *October*
  Fall Rain   *Little Jack Pumpkin Face*
  evaluation — teacher observation
  of pupil participation

- Whole Group Phonics — Review present phonics skills being
  introduced with enlarged print cards.
  Introduce — *ch sound   chat, chap, etc.*
  evaluation — teacher observation

- Short recess if necessary
  have students return to their seats

- Writing Journal — Walk around and help with the development
  of stories.
  evaluation — teacher observation of each child's work

- Approximately 10:45, try to meet with each reading group while
  those students at their seats work on individual projects or free
  choice activities.

- Reading Group 1 *Introduce chapters 1 and 2 of Wagon
  Wheels by reading it aloud as students follow along. Discuss.*
  evaluation — teacher observation

- Reading Group 2 *I Was Walking Down The Road -
  Read aloud together as a group and then individually.*

- Reading Group 3 *Across The Stream - Read aloud together
  as a group and then read individually (read 2 or 3 times
  if time allows.)*

B2   Extended Lessons/Unit Guides on Specific Books (Grade 3)

THE COMEBACK DOG by Jane Resh Thomas

Objectives
- Appreciate literature and request selections from specific authors
- Find proof to answer questions
- Use phonetic skills for decoding and for invented spelling
- Use sentence structure to determine unknown words
- Associate sounds with digraphs and blends
- Discuss and understand vocabulary in the context of stories read
- Follow plot
- Recall main idea, supporting details and sequence
- See relationships; attribute qualities to different characters
- Identify possible themes for stories
- Make predictions and draw conclusions from text
- Demonstrate respect for books

Procedure
This plan may be stopped at any point and picked up at the next reading period.
- Introduce the story by asking any of these questions:
    What does comeback mean?
    Why would a dog keep coming back?
    Where would a "Comeback Dog" come from?
- Assign each chapter to be read silently after predicting what will happen next.
- Discuss each chapter.
- Read each chapter orally, taking turns.
- Repeat this procedure till the book is finished.

Evaluation
Use any of the following activities.
- Make a list of rules/laws to protect dogs/pets/animals.
- Write a similar story using a different animal.
- Finish this story by writing an ending of what happens if Lady does/does not stay.
- Give each chapter a title.

DANNY, THE CHAMPION OF THE WORLD by Roald Dahl

Objectives
- Appreciate literature and request selections from specific authors
- Listen and respond critically as stories are being read
- Listen as stories are being read aloud to notice flow, texture, rhythm, music
- Show enjoyment of literature by increasing frequency of independent reading
- Find proof to answer questions
- Use phonetic skills for decoding and for invented spelling
- Use context of sentences to learn unknown words
- Use sentence structure to determine unknown words
- Associate sounds with digraphs and blends
- Use rules of syllabication
- Discuss and understand vocabulary in the context of stories read
- Use table of contents, title page, and glossary
- Follow plot
- Recall main idea, supporting details and sequence
- See relationships; attribute qualities to different characters
- Make predictions and draw conclusions from text
- Distinguish kinds of fiction, and nonfiction
- Use appropriate pronunciation
- Use appropriate phrasing (not word-by-word)
- Use voice intonation to give meaning
- Demonstrate respect for books
- Develop self-control and take turns talking and listening
- Show respect for others' ideas and opinions
- Listen for stated details and draw conclusions and make inferences

Procedure
This plan may be stopped at any point and picked up at the next reading period.)
NOTE — Be sure to discuss and savor Roald Dahl's use of description to give mental pictures throughout this book.
Read Chapter 1 to the group. Discuss the main characters and the setting.
Daily procedure for all chapters.
- Assign a chapter to be read silently during the independent work period.
- Discuss the chapter that was read silently.
- Use questions in Teacher's Copy.
- Discuss the vocabulary in context.
- Read descriptions orally to get mental picture.
- Read to prove answers.
- Predict what might happen in the next chapter.

Evaluation

Make a booklet.

- On the first six pages, write a paragraph and draw a picture about six parts of the story that you liked the best.
- On the last two pages, write a paragraph and illustrate two things that Danny and his father might do together in the future.

THE GREAT QUILLOW by James Thurber

Objectives

- Appreciate literature and request selections from specific authors
- Listen and respond critically as stories are being read
- Listen as stories are being read aloud to notice flow, texture, rhythm, music
- Show enjoyment of literature by increasing frequency of independent reading
- Find proof to answer questions
- Use phonetic skills for decoding and for invented spelling
- Use context of sentences to learn unknown words
- Use sentence structure to determine unknown words
- Associate sounds with digraphs and blends
- Recognize and use root words, prefixes and suffixes to form new words
- Use rules of syllabication
- Discuss and understand vocabulary in the context of stories read
- Adjust reading approach to variety of subject area materials
- Follow plot
- Recall main idea, supporting details and sequence
- Distinguish between straight narrative and dialogue
- See relationships; attribute qualities to different characters
- Make predictions and draw conclusions from text
- Use appropriate pronunciation
- Use appropriate phrasing (not word-by-word)
- Use voice intonation to give meaning
- Demonstrate respect for books
- Recognize simple punctuation and typographical clues

Procedure

(This may be stopped at any point and picked up the next reading period.)

- Predict what the story might be about from the title and picture on the cover.
- Assign a section of the story to be read silently before the group meets again.

- At the next meeting, discuss the pages that were read silently.
- Read those assigned pages orally, taking turns.
- Stop to discuss questions written in the margin of the Teacher's Copy and the vocabulary.
- Predict what might happen in the next section.
- Assign that section to be read orally before the group meets again.
- On pages 11-16 and 20-30 assign each student one or two characters and read in play form.

Evaluation
Short answer essay test.

(Extended Plans/Unit Guides by Linda Cooper)

Appendix C: A Weekly Schedule for Grade 1, Incorporating a Reading and Language Block

Grade 1 class

	Monday	Tuesday	Wednesday	Thursday	Friday
	9:05–9:15 Announcements, Attendance. Individualized Reading				
	9:15–11:30	9:15–11:40	9:15–11:40	9:15–11:40	9:15–12:15
	Reading and Language Block — Read and discuss children's literature, Big Books, chart poems; collaborative writing; whole group phonics; students share own work; journal writing; literature-related art, drama, music, activities; reading groups; independent work				
	11:30–12:00 Library	11:40–12:10 Music	11:30–12:10 Art	11:40–12:10 Music	→
	12:15–1:05 Lunch				→
	1:15–1:45 Physical Education	1:05–1:45 Reading & Language storytime, book check free reading	1:15–1:45 Physical Education	1:05–1:45 Reading & Language storytime, book check free reading	1:15–1:45 →
	←	←	1:45–2:25 Math	←	↑
	←	←	2:25–3:05 Science and Social Studies →		↑
	←	←	3:05–3:25 Reading and language: storytime, free reading, book check →		↑

recess occurs, other than P.E. afternoons, 10 minutes each morning and afternoon.

Appendix D:　High Frequency Bookwords

*Final core 227 word list based on 400 storybooks for beginning readers**

the	1334	good	90	think	47	next	28
and	985	this	90	new	46	only	28
a	831	don't	89	know	46	am	27
I	757	little	89	help	46	began	27
to	746	if	87	grand	46	head	27
said	688	just	87	boy	46	keep	27
you	638	baby	86	take	45	teacher	27
he	488	way	85	eat	44	sure	27
it	345	there	83	body	43	says	27
in	311	every	83	school	43	ride	27
was	294	went	82	house	42	pet	27
she	250	father	80	morning	42	hurry	26
for	235	had	79	yes	41	hand	26
that	232	see	79	after	41	hard	26
is	230	dog	78	never	41	push	26
his	226	home	77	or	40	our	26
but	224	down	76	self	40	their	26
they	218	got	73	try	40	watch	26
my	214	would	73	has	38	because	25
of	204	time	71	always	38	door	25
on	192	love	70	over	38	us	25
me	187	walk	70	again	37	should	25
all	179	came	69	side	37	room	25
be	176	were	68	thank	37	pull	25
go	171	ask	67	why	37	great	24
can	162	back	67	who	36	gave	24
with	158	now	66	saw	36	does	24
one	157	friend	65	mom	35	car	24
her	156	cry	64	kid	35	ball	24
what	152	oh	64	give	35	sat	24
we	151	Mr.	63	around	34	stay	24
him	144	bed	63	by	34	each	23
no	143	an	62	Mrs.	34	ever	23
so	141	very	62	off	33	until	23
out	140	where	60	sister	33	shout	23
up	137	play	59	find	32	mama	22
are	133	let	59	fun	32	use	22
will	127	long	58	more	32	turn	22
look	126	here	58	while	32	thought	22
some	123	how	57	tell	32	papa	22

day	123	make	57	sleep	32	lot	21
at	122	big	56	made	31	blue	21
have	121	from	55	first	31	bath	21
your	121	put	55	say	31	mean	21
mother	119	read	55	took	31	sit	21
come	118	them	55	dad	30	together	21
not	115	as	54	found	30	best	20
like	112	Miss	53	lady	30	brother	20
then	108	any	52	soon	30	feel	20
get	103	right	52	ran	30	floor	20
when	101	nice	50	dear	29	wait	20
thing	100	other	50	man	29	tomorrow	20
do	99	well	48	better	29	surprise	20
too	91	old	48	through	29	shop	20
want	91	night	48	stop	29	run	20
did	91	may	48	still	29	own	20
could	90	about	47	fast	28		

* from "Bookwords: Using a Beginning Word List of High Frequency Words From Children's Literature K-3" by Maryann Eeds. pp.418-423. *The Reading Teacher*, January 1985. (Reproduced with permission of author and I.R.A.)

Appendix E: *Explanation for Parents of Book Sign Out*

SHAKER HEIGHTS CITY SCHOOL DISTRICT

MORELAND SCHOOL
16500 Van Aken Boulevard
Shaker Heights, Ohio 44120
(216) 921-1400

DELORES GROVES
Principal   September 17, 1985

Dear Parents,

Beginning today, your child will be signing out books from our classroom library.

It would be helpful if you - or a sister, brother, or relative - could
read the book to her/him first. That way your child can hear the flow of
the language and will be better able to predict unknown words. Your child
can also then enjoy the story without interruption.

Your child is then to practice reading the book again and again until
he/she is able to read it fluently and smoothly and is able to tell what
the story is about. If your child has difficulty reading a word, supply it.
Or, ask what makes sense there so that reading is a thinking process. Keep
the reading fun! Finally, the book is to be brought back to class so credit
can be earned for successful efforts when the title is entered in your
child's reading notebook.

Please encourage your child to read every night. The more your child
reads, the better a reader he/she will become.

Also remind your child that bringing the book back in the condition
he/she received it is his/her responsibility. Be sure that your child has
a waterproof bag for transporting the book. There will be a fine for damaged
books and a replacement charge for lost books.

Thank you for your help.

Sincerely,

Karen Shiba, First Grade Teacher
Sue Walker, First Grade Teacher
Regie Routman, Reading Specialist

Appendix F: Students' Reading Records

F1 Record of an Average Reader, Grade 1, September to November.

	DATE	TITLE OF BOOK
1.	9/23	In A Dark Dark Wood
2.	9/24	Brown Bear, Brown Bear
3.	9/25	Obadiah
4.	9/26	Dan, The Flying Man
5.	9/29	Will You Be My Mother?
6.	9/29	The Happy Egg
7	9/30	Grandpa Grandpa
8.	10/1	The Monsters' Party
9.	10/2	Three Little Ducks
c.	10/3	Sing A Song
11.	10/6	I Was Walking Down The Road
12.	10/9	The Teeny Tiny Woman
13.	10/14	Dan the Flying Man
14.	10/15	Whose Mouse Are You?
15	10/15	Buzz Buzz Buzz
16.	10/20	Fire Fire Said Mrs. McGuire
17.	10/21	1, 2, 3 To The Zoo
18.	10/22	If I Had
19.	10/23	Drummer Hoff
20	10/27	Each Peach Pear Plum
21	10/28	Mrs Wishy-washy
22	10/31	Who Will Be My Mother?
23	11/3	Why Can't I Fly?
24	11/4	Meg's Eggs
5	11/4	Rosie's Walk
	11-5	The Bus Ride
27	11-10	Henny Penny
28	11-10	The Bus Ride
29	11-12	The Red Rose
30.	11-13	Seven Little Rabbits
31	11-14	The Farm Concert
32	11-20	Odd One Out
33	11-20	The Gingerbread Man
34	11-21	Noisy Nora
15.	11-24	Nobody Listens to Andrew
16.	11-24	The Longest Journey in the World
37.	11-25	More Spaghetti I Say

F2   Record of a Very Good Reader, Grade 2, September to January.

READING RECORD
Alana c King

TITLE	AUTHOR	DATE
The Little's and The Big Storm	John Peterson	9-5-86
Miss Nelson is Back	James Marshall	9-1-86
Ramona and her Father	Beverly Cleary	10-6-86
ChurchMouse Stories	Margot Austin	10-16-86
The Twits	Roald Dahl	10-17-86
Rosie and Michael	Judith Viorst	10-21-86
Every Time Ic lumbatto	David McCord	10-23-86
Mustard	Charlotte Graeber	10-15-86
Dorrie And The Haunted House	PaTRicu cooma	10-24-86
The courage of Sarah noble	Alice Dalgliesh	10-28
The Hairy Horror Trick	Scott Corbett	10-31
The Shadow Nose	Ruth Chew	11-3
My Robot Buddy	Alfred Slote	11-7
Ramona the pest	Beverly Cleary	11-13
Ramona the brave	Beverly Cleary	12-5
How to eat fried worms	Thomas Rockwell	12-15-86
Farwell to shady Glade	Bill Peet	12-15-86
Buford The Bighorn	Bill Peet	12-18-86
Chocolate Fever	Robert Kimmel smith	1-7-87
The candy com Contest	Patricia Reilly Giff	1-7-87
Charlie and the Chocolate Factory	Ronald dahl	1-21-87
Charlotte's WEB	E.B. White	1-27-87

Appendix G: A Story Map Blank

<u>Story Map</u>_____

Title_____ Author_____

Setting (where and when does the story take place?)

Characters (who are the main characters?)

The Problem (what is the main problem in the story?)

The Goal (what steps are taken to solve the problem?)
   Event 1.
   Event 2.
   Event 3.
   (list as many events as needed.)

The resolution (how is the problem solved [or not solved]?)

Appendix H: Book Project Guide Sheets
H1   The Littles

The Littles Book Project.

Write an original Littles book. You can decide how long it will be, but it must be at least 8 pages. Use the Writing Center, and staple your book together.

Be sure your story includes:

Setting (where and when it takes place)

Characters (Lucy, Tom, Granny Little, The Biggs, Cousin Dinky, Hildy the cat, Mr and Mrs Little, Uncle Pete.)

Problem (What is the problem in your story?)

Events (What happens in trying to solve this problem?)

Ending

Also include a title, table of contents with chapter titles and illustrations.

You may do as many or as few illustrations as you like.

You may do as much or as little writing as you like.

Have fun!

H2 Mr. Men and Little Miss

Guide for Mr. Men and Little Miss books

1. Introduce your character on the first page. Tell who he/she is and what he/she does that goes with his/her name.

2. Tell your story.
   a. Give lots of examples of what your character does that goes with his/her name.
   b. Include many describing words.
   c. Use conversation.
   d. You may want to have other Mr. Men or Little Miss characters in your story.
   e. Tell the problem(s) your character is having. (The problem(s) will have much to do with how he/she is named.)
   f. Tell all the things that happen to help solve his/her problem.

3. Give an ending to your story.

4. Write neatly on the left side of each page.

5. Make a colorful illustration on the right side of each page.

Have fun with your imagination and your book!

Appendix I: An Explanation of Invented Spelling

Children don't need to be taught to read before we allow them to write. They seem to know this instinctively. If we ask them to "Write!" before they are given any writing instruction, they gravely *do something* with crayon, pen or pencil, even if it appears to be "scribble" or if it is a drawing without any attempt at words. But we should take these expressions seriously as establishing each child's readiness-point for individualized classroom writing.

In the past, many attempts have been made to devise a way to move children from the readiness-point into regular writing. The conference approach chooses "invented spelling" as the most natural possible way.

• The teacher simply asks the child to write whatever sound he or she hears in a word (or remembers having seen in a spelling).

• Children *tend* to begin their inventing of spelling by writing only the first consonant they hear in a word (e.g. L for "liked"); later they might add a prominent end consonant (LT or LK), and later still a vowel (LAKT). These earliest attempts to represent *sounds* are gradually refined as *sight* (visual/graphic) letters are increasingly remembered from reading, for much reading is also proceeding day by day. Thus the daily influences of integrated listening-writing-reading serve to move the child rapidly towards standard spelling, e.g. "liked" might develop in a single year through, say, L-LT-LKT-LAKT-LOKT-LIKT-LIKD-LIKED.

• In other words, natural classroom pressure moves *invention* towards correctness. While part of this pressure comes from the parallel reading program, it comes no less from the great amount of reading being done *while writing* — writing and reading continually reinforce each other.

• The teacher does not correct the child's first draft, but will write down a spelling if asked. (If a child's "book" is "published", the teacher will edit the spelling after explaining that this is what editors do to ensure that everyone can read books.)

• While spelling, a child often makes audible and sub-audible "phonic" sounds, for at this transition stage the writing is more a *speech event* than a writing event.

R. D. Walshe, *Every Child Can Write!*, P.E.T.A., Sydney, 1981, p. 123.

(Reproduced with permission of author.)

Appendix J: Ways in Which Parents Can Encourage Reading and Language Development

J1   Ways To Encourage Summer Reading

1   Take your children to the library weekly.

2   Register for the summer reading program. Your child can earn a certificate for reaching his reading goal.

3   Allow children to stay up 30 minutes or so after "lights out" if they are in bed reading.

4   Keep good and fun reading material in almost every room of the house.

5   Selectively discourage the use of television. Set limits for viewing time, such as one hour per day. Let your children know that you pay careful attention to the fine programs — for children and adults — on PBS.

6   Subscribe to a children's magazine that they can read by themselves. Ask your librarian for suggestions.

7   When your child has done something very nice or outstanding, reward him or her with extra reading time.

8   Read to your child daily. Reading to your child helps develop listening comprehension skills and exposes him or her to varied types of books, stories, and information. If he or she is a reluctant reader, it is a good way to get him or her interested in a book. Read to him or her and leave off at an exciting part. Encourage him or her to continue on his or her own.

9   Show an interest in reading by reading yourself and asking your children what they are reading. If you enjoy reading, you are serving as a model that your child can follow.

10   Encourage reading related activities. Have your child tell stories to you that either you or he or she writes down. A diary of daily experiences can be fun. Encourage letter writing to a relative.

11   Encourage reading besides books. Cook with your child and ask him or her to read the recipe. When travelling, ask your children to read the road signs. In a restaurant, encourage him to read the menu.

Usually, the more a child is exposed to books and pleasurable reading activities, the greater will be his or her interest in reading.

J2   *Ways of Applying an Understanding of Reading and Language Development*

Understanding Reading Levels When Helping Your Child Choose a Book

In order for your child to have fun and success with his or her summer reading, the book must not only be interesting but at the appropriate level for him or her.

The reading level mentioned in his or her progress report, and the level at which his or her school reading program is planned, is the INSTRUCTIONAL LEVEL. This is the level where the child recognizes 90 out of 100 words and comprehends at least 75% of the material.

The level at which your child should generally be reading for leisure and pleasure is his or her INDEPENDENT LEVEL. This level is always lower than the level he or she is being instructed on, and, in fact, it may be as much as one full grade level below the Instructional Level. On this level he or she recognizes 95% of all the words and comprehends 90% of the material. This is the easy reading level where he or she can read without teacher or parent help.

A child develops confidence from success in easy reading. If he or she knows almost all the words, it is possible to figure out the others and go on. Generally if the reading level is right for your child, he or she will "try out" the book.

For the young child, you can show him or her a simple way to help decide if the book is too hard. Have your child read a page or two from the middle of the book. Every time he or she comes to an unfamiliar word, have him or her put down a finger from one hand. If he or she makes a fist, the book is probably too hard.

Your child also has a FRUSTRATION LEVEL. At this level the material is too difficult. He or she recognizes less than 90% of the words, and comprehension is less than 75%. Guide your child and help him or her to avoid choosing books on this level.

In addition to the reading levels above, your child also has a LISTENING COMPREHENSION LEVEL. This is the level of material your child can listen to and understand when you read to him or her. Comprehension should be at least 75%. Keep this level in mind when you read to your child. Your child may be able to listen to and understand books on a higher grade level than he or she is reading on.

Ways To Develop Your Child's Vocabulary

Research indicates that the best way of learning new words is through direct experiences. The more experiences your child has, the richer his or her vocabulary — and life — will be.

1   Keep a dictionary next to the area where you and your children eat meals. Often a new word will come up in conversation. While your child may not be in the habit of looking words up in the dictionary, he or she will be only too delighted to have you look it up. Your child is the winner; his or her word knowledge grows.

2   Use dinner time to use new words deliberately. Explain the meaning of the word, and try to use it again later on so your child will remember it.

3   Take trips with your child, and talk to him or her about what you are seeing and doing. The park, the zoo, the library, a public building, the supermarket, the pet store, the airport, a sports event, a hike, a museum are all fine places to stimulate discussion.

4   Reading to your child helps to enlarge his or her concepts and vocabulary.

5   Do a project together; build something; plan a party. Discuss the steps involved in sequence, and do not talk down to your child.

Ways To Develop Your Child's Comprehension

Reading is much more than just being able to read words. If a child does not understand what he or she is reading, he or she is not reading with success. Thinking and understanding do not take place automatically. They are directly related to the child's language and experiences.

1   Ask questions about a story that stimulate thinking: "What do you think will happen next?", "What else could he have done?", "Can you make up a different ending?"

2   Your child should be able to briefly tell what the story is about, recall important details, give a sequence of events, draw conclusions from information given. Provide practice by asking good questions and guiding your child to give thoughtful answers.

3   Use sources such as the T.V. Guide, cookbook, comic strip, cereal box to have your child locate specific information, follow directions, make reasonable decisions.

4   Watch a television program together. Discuss the program; have your child predict the outcome, give the sequence of events, summarize, note whether a commercial advertisement is fact or opinion.

Appendix K: Explanation for Parents of the Process Approach to Writing and Spelling

Oct. 15, 1985

Dear Parents,

To help your child move from invented spelling to conventional spelling, he/she will need to purchase a <u>Spelling Reference Book</u> which alphabetically lists the most common spelling words in the middle elementary grades. This book has been ordered for your child. <u>Please send in $6.50 as soon as possible</u>. This book will be very useful for the next several years.

We are working on the writing process in second grade this year. This process involves these main steps:

1. Prewriting -- thinking, getting started

2. Rough draft -- writing ideas down

3. Revising -- making the writing words clearer and more interesting; making additions, deletions, changes

4. Editing and proof reading -- correcting spelling, grammar, punctuation

5. Publishing -- completing the finished work, final copy

Not all writing will go through all 5 steps. Some may only go through step 2 or 3. In that case a paper that comes home would be stamped "unedited" which means it was checked for content.

Sincerely,

Joan Di Dio, Regie Routman

Appendix L: A Format for Response Groups

RESPONDING TO ANIMAL REPORTS

RESPONSE GROUP FORMAT
Tell something you liked or learned!
Tell what you'd like more information about.
Tell what is unclear or confusing.

SPECIFIC QUESTIONS TO THINK ABOUT
1. Is there a good introductory sentence identifying the animal?
2. Do you get a clear picture of the animal or topic?
3. What is still unclear?
4. Is like information grouped together?
5. Can you leave out parts that repeat or don't belong?
6. Can you combine some sentences?
7. Are sentence beginnings varied?

ALWAYS STATE YOUR QUESTIONS OR COMMENTS IN A POSITIVE MANNER.

Appendix M: A Guide Sheet of Editing Marks

```
┌─────────────────────────────────────────────────────┐
│                                                       │
│  NAME _____                     │
│  Please edit using colored pencils.                   │
│                                                       │
│  EDITORIAL MARKS                                      │
│                                                       │
│  ¶       Make a new paragraph.                        │
│                                                  (B)  │
│  ═       Make this a capital letter.            (by)  │
│                                     be with           │
│  ∧       Add words.  (to∧his father)                 │
│                                                       │
│  ⊙       Add a period.  (... park⊙)                  │
│                                                       │
│  ─       Take out words. (by the ~old~ woman)         │
│                                      s                │
│  /       Make this letter small. (Several)            │
│                                                       │
│  ⌃       Add a comma.  (green∧blue)                  │
│                                                       │
│  ∿       Trade a place of some letters or words.      │
│                              (fre∿ind) (friend)       │
│                                          ⎛tried⎞     │
│  ○       Circle misspelled word         ⎝(tryed)⎠    │
│                                                       │
│                                                       │
│                                                       │
└─────────────────────────────────────────────────────┘
```

Appendix N: Syllabication Rules

Basic Syllabication Rules

- Divide between double consonants: yel / low, run / ner
- Divide between two different consonants: don / key, per / haps
- When a single consonant is between two vowels, divide after the first vowel: fi / nal, ce / ment
- Prefixes and suffixes form separate syllables: un / kind, use / ful
- Divide between word parts in a compound word: rain / bow, ear / phone
- "le" takes the consonant before it: pur / ple, sim / ple
- Do not divide blends or digraphs: pil / grim, mis / chief

It is most useful to teach students that, in most words, the syllables are either open (ending with a vowel, as in "lo" or "pa") or closed (ending with a consonant, as in "fed" or "vol"). An open syllable takes a long vowel; a closed syllable takes a short vowel. With a word such as "tulip", the student is asked to try it both ways: "tu / lip" and "tul / ip". By predicting and trying out while using meaningful context as a guide, students figure out most words that are already in their vocabulary.

Appendix O: Communication with Parents

O1   General Introduction to the Reading Program

August 25, 1983

Dear Parents,

Your child will be having a wonderful reading and writing experience this year. He will be learning to read with the very best of children's books available! Hundreds of books will be in our classroom, and we shall be working closely with the library to bring in additional books for more information on various topics.

The daily reading program will consist of:

1. Hearing good literature — one or more stories and poems each day.

2. Rereading with children joining in as they are ready.

3. Phonics and word attack skills instruction.

4. Small group reading instruction with teacher guidance. Books used are paperbacks and are proven favorites.

5. Nightly sign out of favorite books as children are ready.

It has been our experience, based on past teaching and research, that children can best develop a love of reading along with reading proficiency and vocabulary/language development through a literature approach in beginning reading instruction.

A large part of our program will involve daily writing. It has been demonstrated that first graders can write much more than once thought if they are allowed to use their own spellings and are encouraged to be creative. Good spelling will come later as the reading and writing process develops.

Parent involvement will make a difference in your child's reading success. We will be sending home stories, books, and poems for you to read with your child. We will also have a parent workshop soon to give you ways to best help your child and coordinate with our efforts at school.

Please feel free to contact us at any time if you have questions.

Sincerely,

Karen Shiba, First Grade Teacher

Regie Routman, Reading Specialist

O2 Explanation of Poetry Notebook

— Attention Parents —

This is your child's Poetry Notebook. It should be kept at home in a convenient place so that your child can read from it nightly. Each Friday your son or daughter will bring home 3 or 4 poems to add to this notebook. At the end of the school year, the notebook will contain about 200 poems that your child should be able to read. Please help your child add the poems to the notebook each week. This is an important part of his/her First Grade reading experience.

O3   *Information Sheet*

Child's Name _____   Pre _____

Birthday _____   Post _____

INFORMATION SHEET   First Grade Literacy Program

1. Parents or guardians _____

2. Other adults that play an important role in the child's life

   _____

3. Names and ages of other children _____

4. Names of pre-school, kindergarten, Head Start, &/or day care programs attended and length of time in program

   _____

5. Who works outside the home? _____

   Working hours _____ Work number _____

6. Where does your child go directly after school? _____

   Name and number of person responsible _____

7. What responsibilities does your child have around the home? _____

8. Does your child normally eat breakfast? _____

9. How many hours a day does your child watch television?

   _____

10. What time does your child go to bed? _____

11. What kinds of reading materials do you have in the home?

    _____

12. How does your child feel about reading? _____

13. Does anyone read aloud to your child? _____

    If so, for how long and how often? _____

14. Where do you get books for your child to read? _____

Do you and your child check books out of the public
library? _____

15. How does your child feel about writing? _____

16. What types of writing does your child do? _____

_____

17. Is there anything else we should know about your child to
help make his school year most successful? _____

_____

O4 Weekly Newsletters

Sept 16, 1983

Dear Parents,

Thank you so much for attending our
parent-teacher conferences. We have enjoyed
getting to know you and learning more
about your children.

This has been another exciting week
in reading. The children have read
three new Big Books. They are Yes Ma'ame,
Hairy Bear, and The Magic Fish. We
have also read two new songs and
learned two new poems. Ask your child
about New Blue Shoes or Mr. Gumpy's
Motor Car. Those are just a few of
the books that have been read aloud
to them.

We enjoy having parents come in
to visit our classroom during our
reading and language time each
morning. If you would like to join
us, to watch and help, please come
in any day between 9³⁰ and 12⁰⁰. You
are welcome to stay as little or as
long as you wish.

Enjoy your weekend
Karen Shiba
Regie Routman

O5 Notification of Testing Program

April 25, 1986

Dear Parents

On Monday, April 28th, we will begin Stanford Achievement testing of all first-graders. The SAT is divided into sections which test student growth and knowledge in reading, phonics, language, math and information about their world. We will be giving parts of the test each day and hope to have it completed on Friday. We ask that you help by seeing that your child has enough sleep each night, a good breakfast and that you provide support by realizing this is a somewhat stressful experience for the children. We have been doing "practice test-taking" these last few days in order to familiarize the children with the kinds of test questions and the procedures used. It is unrealistic to expect your child to "get everything right." Our expectation is that the children will put forth their best conscientious effort. Hopefully, children will not be absent during this testing week. If necessary, make-up testing will be done the following week.

Karen Shiba

O6 Academic Report (sent home weekly)

ACADEMIC REPORT

Name _____ Date _____

Your child's daily homework is to practice reading his/her paperback book(s).

	Yes	No	Comments
Is a quiet, attentive participant in Reading Center activities.			
Responsibly and successfully completes daily reading homework.			
Works to the best of his/her ability in daily journal writing.			
Behaves appropriately.			

Parent's signature _____ Please return next school day.

We welcome your comments. Please use the back of this paper.

Appendix P: How to Make Wallpaper Books

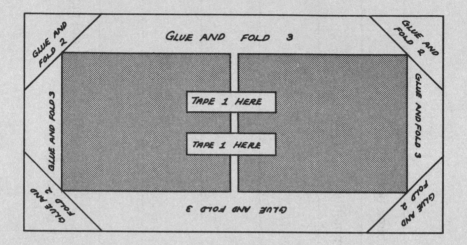

CARDBOARD: $6\frac{1}{2}'' \times 7\frac{1}{4}''$

WALLPAPER: At least $15'' \times 9''$

CONSTRUCTION PAPER: $6\frac{1}{2}'' \times 12''$

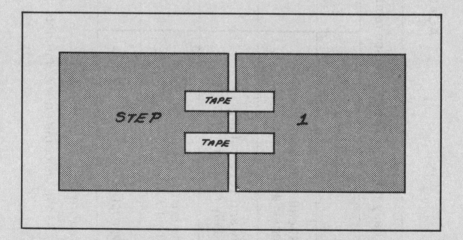

1. Tape cardboard to wrong side of wallpaper, leaving about $\frac{3}{8}''$ gap between cardboard pieces at center.

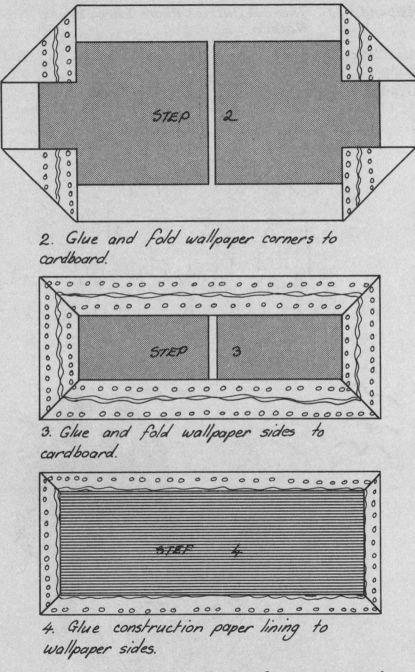

2. Glue and fold wallpaper corners to cardboard.

3. Glue and fold wallpaper sides to cardboard.

4. Glue construction paper lining to wallpaper sides.

5. Cut paper for book to fit dimensions of construction paper lining and staple to center-fold with long arm stapler.

Appendix Q: *Journal Entries From Three Years: Nathan*

A Halloween journal entry by Nathan in first, second, and third grades:

Grade 1

"I like stories about Halloween, and I like *How to Catch a Ghost*."

Grade 2
"This week I made up a poem and it goes like this:
Pumpkins may bounce and skeletons may tumble
But witches and goblins give you a scare!"

O c t. 17 1986

This weak I made

up a poum

and it gos

like this pumcyin

may bowns and

scelotins may

tumbl but wichis

and goblins give

you a scer!

Grade 3

Halloween

Skeletons dance, pumpkins glow, and monsters show.
Bats fly, and black cats roam.
Frankenstein walks lifeless,
And dead vampires walk the dimlighted streets.
Dogs will howl and witches creep.
Goblins fly, and werewolves howl.
People do not dare come out for it's Halloween!

10-30-87

Holloween Ghosts apear
scellens dance punpcuns
glow and monsters show
bats fly and black cats rome
frankinstine walks liflessand
deads vampirc walk the
dim lighted streets dogs
will howll and wiches
creep goblins fly
and werewdves howle peopd
donotdare come out
for its holloween! you're right.

Appendix R: An Editing Checklist for Use in Grades 2 and 3

TITLE _____

NAME _____ DATE _____

1. Each sentence begins with a capital letter. _____

2. Names of people and places are capitalized. _____

3. Each word in my titles and book titles are capitalized. _____

4. Each sentence ends with a period(.), question mark(?), or exclamation mark(!). _____

5. I have corrected all misspelled words to the best of my ability. _____

6. I have indented each new paragraph. _____

7. I have used speech marks (") to show where conversation begins and ends. _____

8. My writing uses descriptive words. _____

9. I have used my best handwriting. _____

10. After completing my piece and before handing it in, I have reread it and checked it for errors. _____

Appendix S: Sample Comprehension Check

Name _____

THE COMEBACK DOG   by   JANE RESH THOMAS.
    Answer in complete sentences.

1. Describe Daniel's feelings for Lady at the
beginning, middle and end of the story.
How did his feelings for the dog change?
_____
_____
_____
_____
_____
_____
_____

2. Give another title for this book.
_____

3. Why do you think this is a good title?
_____

4. How has Lady changed by the end of the book?
What does the dog do that shows this change?
_____

_____

5. What was Lady's life like before Daniel found
her? What clues does the author give to show this?
_____

_____

_____

6. On the cover, illustrate a favorite scene from
the book. Use lots of details. Why was this a
favorite part for you?
_____

_____

_____

Appendix T: Reading Report for the Primary Grades

	usually	occasionally	working on	
Reading Attitudes				Comments
enjoys books				
chooses to read				
self-selects appropriate books				
Shared Book Experience				
listens attentively				
joins in when able				
responds to questions, text, and pictures				
Reading Strategies				
understands/uses 1 to 1 matching and conventions of print				
reads for meaning uses semantic cues uses syntactic cues uses picture cues				
uses graphophonic cues initial/final consonants digraphs consonant blends vowels/vowel combinations				
makes predictions about text				
self-corrects errors				
helps self when in difficulty				
recognizes high frequency words				
reads fluently				

Comprehension				
can retell story in own words				
can figure out vocabulary from context				
understands main ideas				
can make inferences				
can analyze and think critically				

Index